Demographic Perspectives on
India's Tribes

Demographic Perspectives on India's Tribes

Arup Maharatna

OXFORD
UNIVERSITY PRESS

OXFORD

UNIVERSITY PRESS

YMCA Library Building, Jai Singh Road, New Delhi 110 001

Oxford University Press is a department of the University of Oxford. It
furthers the University's objective of excellence in research, scholarship, and
education by publishing worldwide in

Oxford New York

Auckland Cape Town Dar es Salaam Hong Kong Karachi
Kuala Lumpur Madrid Melbourne Mexico City Nairobi
New Delhi Shanghai Taipei Toronto

With offices in

Argentina Austria Brazil Chile Czech Republic France Greece
Guatemala Hungary Italy Japan Poland Portugal Singapore
South Korea Switzerland Thailand Turkey Ukraine Vietnam

Oxford is a registered trademark of Oxford University Press
in the UK and in certain other countries

Published in India by Oxford University Press, New Delhi

© Oxford University Press 2005

The moral rights of the author have been asserted
Database right Oxford University Press (maker)

First published 2005

ISBN 019 567086 8

Typeset in Galliard BT
by Innovative Processors, New Delhi 110 002
Printed by Sai Printopack Pvt. Ltd. , New Delhi 110 020
Published by Manzar Khan, Oxford University Press
YMCA Library Building, Jai Singh Road, New Delhi 110 001

To
Paramita and Anusha

Contents

ERRATA

p. 229: in the map of West Bengal, Chitrihutu (Khatra) is in Bankura district and Thupsara (Nanoor) is in Birbhum district.

p. 284, line 3: should read Miller, B. (1993) instead of Miller, Beatrice D. (ed.) (1993).

p. 284, line 7: should read Miller, Beatrice D. (ed.) (1969) instead of ——— (1969).

List of Tables

Preface

While India is a land of enormous diversities, it is frequently stated that there exists a 'magical' (or indeed, incomprehensible) binding force for her proclaimed 'unity'. However, in a practical and impassioned view, this unifying force could be the centralized power structure and administration—one of the most glorified British legacies. Indeed, the frequency and scale with which separatist movements, revolts, and rebellions have occurred across time and space in India, leave a lingering uneasiness and scepticism of the strength and sanctity of the avowed 'unity in diversity'. While tribes are generally seen as one of the ingredients of such variety, the degree and manner in which they are part of this oft-claimed 'unity' is rather vague and varied. Indeed, most of India's diversities do often get metamorphosed (rather than 'melted' as is often thought to be the situation in the USA) into a so-called 'mainstream', but tribal people continue to float like distinct patches of unmixable oil over a vast water mass. However, this prolonged and distinctive coexistence of numerous tribal communities side by side with the 'mainstream', serves as solid ground on which anthropologists build their disciplinary discourse and rich ethnography. Indeed, 'tribes' as a subject of academic inquiry, seem to have been almost a 'birthright' of Indian anthropology, though there are wide possibilities as well as the necessity for more inter-disciplinary perspectives and approaches.

Virtually everyone hearing about my ongoing research on Indian tribes immediately asked me 'Which tribe?' as if it was almost inconceivable to do research on tribes as a whole. But clearly it is not only India's tribes that embody huge diversities; the non-tribal populations present no less variety. Indeed several distinct dilemmas entailed in the existing tribal discourse appear glaring enough. First, although tribes have been intensively and extensively studied—

especially for many decades both before and after Independence, they often appear as obscure as ever. They have been highly glorified on several counts over and over again in thousands of printed pages (especially by older-generation anthropologists), but the dominant image of them in most minds is still extremely vague and indeed full of misconceptions. They are often portrayed as 'original' inhabitants and practitioners of early civilization and culture, which by many standards was 'advanced', but they now appear most marginalized and, to some, alien. Documents and narratives—official and non-official—pile up, describing vividly and most eloquently their relative plight, but their acute vulnerability seems to remain.

These persisting dilemmas reflect a resolute and real ambivalence towards tribes on the part of the state that stands, as is often the case in a democratic polity, on the electoral support of the vast non-tribal mainstream. This said, the academic discourse developed so far on tribes, their problems and remedies, cannot perhaps be exonerated of deficiencies and delusions in its understanding and policy guidance. For example, a long-standing as well as dominant perception, namely that a notion of *aggregate* tribal people is not useful, has fed into its methodological biases. This, in turn, has shaped tribal discourse as an incohesive, inconsistent statement on the country's tribal population. While not questioning the usefulness of intensive (anthropological) study of individual tribal groups at the micro-level, it should be noted that diversities in terms of a variety of features—sociocultural, environmental, and geophysical—are prominent not only among numerous tribes, but among similarly manifold non-tribal groups too. In fact it is debatable why *diversity*, rather than commonality, among the tribal population should be *more* deserving of attention, research, and publicity vis-à-vis the non-tribal population, such as lower caste groups.

Our present attempt at constructing a demographic perspective on Indian tribes is premised on the notion that the *aggregate* tribal population is valid not only in statistical and quantitative terms, but can be conceptually meaningful and functionally useful too. Its intuitive justification is simple enough: if aggregate (or rather average) patterns (e.g. demographic, sociocultural) of all tribes are distinguishably different from those of their non-tribal counterparts, this can well be a basis for treating the *total* tribal population as one entity. Unlike the anthropologists' general tendency to focus exclusively on individual tribes, our approach seeks to analyse and evaluate demographic and underlying sociocultural features of aggregate tribes by placing them in a comparative light, particularly in relation to their closest non-tribal counterparts, namely, aggregate scheduled caste (SC) people. Bypassing the anthropologists' concern with issues often of a subtle and even sterile nature, relating to identification and classification of diverse individual tribes, the present study largely relies on the census-used 'working' (or operational) definitions of tribal and non-tribal people. This is not to deny that census information on tribes entails various defects and difficulties, especially relating to enumeration and identification of specific tribes. However, considering the mine of information that the census operations over a century have made available on the aggregate tribal population, they are, on several issues, almost the single best source for arriving at systematic and coherent generalizations necessary for scientific knowledge and a clear understanding of a population. In fact, the use of official (or 'operational') definition and information (including the census) in our study—by enabling discovery of distinct demographic features of aggregate tribes—has opened up the possibility of a fresh light on the notion of 'tribe' itself.[1]

More specifically, the chief motivation behind this book has been two-fold: first, to discover, stylize, and present the core general demographic features of the *aggregate* tribal population; and to establish their broad linkage with the common sociocultural patterns and characteristics of tribal communities. While the role of sociocultural traits has often been accorded a central place in contemporary South Asian literature on demographic outcomes and behaviour, this has, so far, referred almost entirely to the mainstream (non-tribal) population. The present study attempts to extend and enrich this perspective from the standpoint of India's tribal population. Despite bountiful local-level (anthropological) literature, ethnography, and narratives on diverse sociocultural (and related) features of tribal peoples, the tasks of stylizing them and of linking them to the patterns of their

[1] For example, in consonance with large-scale initiatives and projects in development and modernization, there has been a discernible shift in the orientation of the studies on Indian tribes, from a focus on tribes as communities to a view of them as subjects or victims of modernization and development. Indeed, the contemporary discussion on so-called 'alternative development' often accords a very prominent place to tribal peoples, who are frequently seen as principal victims of such ecological degradation (Xaxa 2003).

demographic outcomes and behaviour are overdue. This is more so because demographic (and other) information on Indian tribes is not only rich and comprehensive, but uninterrupted availability of them dates as back to the 1870s (when census operations had started), offering opportunities—of course, not unlimited—for analysing both cross-sectional and temporal patterns. All this does not mean that the demographic data on the tribal population are plenty or perfect, but as our present monograph will illustrate, can indeed be utilized for systematic investigation into several prominent issues.

Chapter 1, beginning with a (short) review of key anthropological and historical concerns surrounding the notion of Indian tribes, discusses the nature, quality, and usefulness of census approaches and information relating to the tribal population. It then presents an overview of long-term demographic trends, such as, growth, regional distribution, and sex-composition of the aggregate tribal population in a comparative perspective. In Chapter 2, we compare the tribal and non-tribal population (especially their most comparable group, namely, lower caste groups or the so-called scheduled castes, hereafter SC) in terms of broad socioeconomic indicators as well as some key characteristics of the status of women, which reflect their broad sociocultural milieu, including gender relations and female autonomy. While tribes as a whole do not appear much different from their SC counterparts in terms of such socioeconomic indicators as land ownership, per capita income, or incidence of poverty, they are most deprived in education and health-care provisions. Despite these acute absolute deprivations, an overall sociocultural 'superiority' of the tribal community is manifested in some key female characteristics, consistent with more balanced gender relations and greater female autonomy than their SC counterparts (in particular). Long-standing, albeit scattered, ethnographic evidence of relative gender-equity and high female status/freedom in tribal societies could be put on much firmer ground by scrutinizing evidence such as the sex-ratio of population and the average female age at marriage for the aggregate tribal population. Indeed the implications of gender relations—as often postulated for the general population—for demographic behaviour and outcomes can be put to test in the light of evidence and the experience of the tribal population.

As a higher degree of female autonomy is often postulated as favourable to a relatively low fertility (and low infant–child mortality) regime, Chapter 3 examines tribal demographic behaviour, nuptiality, and related indicators with a bearing on female autonomy during the late-nineteenth and early-twentieth centuries. The aggregate historical data on Indian tribes evince a relatively low fertility and mortality regime, consistent with their sociocultural mooring marked by more balanced gender relations and female autonomy.

With the past patterns of the tribal demographic regime and gender relations as a background, Chapter 4 reviews contemporary evidence—both micro and large-scale data—relating to fertility, mortality, and gender biases among the tribal population. Notwithstanding inter-regional and inter-tribe variation in fertility and mortality, there emerges a baseline pattern of tribal fertility and mortality (especially infant–child mortality) that is no higher and indeed somewhat lower than those of their non-tribal counterparts. But signs of a reversal of these patterns of differential—especially in the recent past—have become distinct. Due to delayed modernization and related developments, there have been indications of rising tribal fertility in many cases, and there has also emerged a clear tribal disadvantage in mortality improvement in recent years, almost reversing the past pattern of tribal mortality advantage vis-à-vis SC groups. In Chapter 5, such tribal trends and growing vulnerabilities have come into shaper focus in the analysis of long-term trends of tribal demography in Jharkhand. Chapter 6, based on field-based primary data from two contrasting locations in West Bengal, presents illustration of how the Santhals, a major tribe of eastern India, are capable of adapting and responding by means of seasonal migration to opportunities for overcoming adversities posed by local geophysical circumstances. For example, Santhali adult men, women, and children of a relatively backward and drought-prone location migrate seasonally for work to progressive agricultural pockets, evincing not only low fertility (and low mortality), but appearing far ahead of non-migrating counterparts elsewhere, in terms of contraceptive practices and fertility control. Chapter 7 presents conclusions.

Bypassing possible controversy over the notion of the 'civilized', India's tribal people emerge (historically), in our study, as relatively civilized by the yardstick of some prominent Western sociocultural features and values, namely balanced gender relations, absence of a caste-based social hierarchy, less patriarchal dominance, marriage by love/consent, individual freedom and liberty. In fact, these admittedly admirable sociocultural features of Indian tribes have a bearing on and are largely corroborated by their demographic features and behaviour. That India's tribal people have withstood and often even overcome incessant adversities and oppositions in the course of history—often from technically superior forces—is a testimony to the inner strengths of their traditional sociocultural structure (including kinship and other organization). While this evidence abounds in voluminous local-level anthropological discourse and ethnography, we reach this conclusion chiefly from our quantitative investigation into tribal demographic features and their sociocultural underpinnings at an aggregate level. While many of these tribal features and underlying values could be seen as lessons worthy enough for emulation by much of India's non-tribal population, ironically the key questions that have haunted tribal discourse for long, have been how best they could be brought within the mainstream Hindu sociocultural milieu. It is true that many aspects of tribal culture and society have been glorified in the tribal discourse, but they are mostly in the form of emotive and reflective outbursts. The present demographic study, however, attempts to fortify these largely emotive statements and to establish statistically and systematically what have abounded as 'emotive' unsubstantiated half-truths.

Unfortunately, this relatively glorious 'portrait' of traditional tribal communities has been substantially upset, especially over recent decades, along with the increasing integration and interaction—on unfavourable and unequal terms—with the 'mainstream'. There has also been an accentuation of relative deprivation in distribution of 'benefits' of contemporary development and material advancement.

When, at the completion of my manuscript on India's tribal population, I was searching for a suitable title, my sudden encounter with *Savaging the Civilised*, a newly published biography of Verrier Elwin (Guha 1999) saddened as well as lifted my spirits up. I immediately felt dampened when I thought this title voiced exactly what I was trying to put my finger on, but after browsing through the book I felt consoled that this title was not pointing to tribe although the somewhat similar message of my book—albeit on tribes—would not go astray.

In the course of my research on tribal demography, not surprisingly, I have accumulated an immeasurably large debt by receiving assistance and help (intellectual and otherwise), encouragement, advice, and support from many individuals and organizations. The work truly took off in 1993–4 with the Career Award offered to me by the University Grants Commission (New Delhi), with which I was able to pursue research full time for three years at the University of Burdwan.

A brief visit as an Academic Visitor in the Department of Social Policy at the London School of Economics, my *alma mater*, in the summer of 1997, was highly useful for gathering material. Subsequently, the opportunity of sharpening and enriching my ongoing research on Indian tribes came with a Population Council Fellowship tenable at the Harvard Center for Population and Development Studies (Harvard University) during 1997–8, where my research benefited from efficient infrastructural facilities and sound academic environment. In 1998–9 the University of Burdwan (West Bengal) provided me with a small research grant to enable my revisit to some of the tribal villages of Bankura for more information and data. The summer of 2000 was productively spent at the Indian Institute of Advanced Study (Shimla), an institution that offers a wonderful blend of natural tranquillity and imposing colonial architectural grandeur. Finally, with a research grant from the Population Investigation Committee at the London School of Economics, the job of coalescing research and giving a final shape to this monograph was carried out at the Gokhale Institute of Politics and Economics, Pune. It was indeed a pleasant experience to have access not only to an extremely conducive, efficient atmosphere and infrastructure at Gokhale Institute but also its superbly rich Gadgil Library run by a genuinely committed and infinitely helpful staff. I am deeply grateful to each of these organizations and institutions.

The research work reported in this monograph has benefited immeasurably from the involvement of many young and inspired research assistants. Santosh Ghosh, Julfiker Alam, Biswajit Ghosh, and Mukul were involved in painstaking fieldwork in select villages of West Bengal; Debajyoti Biswas, Sugandha More, Vandana Shivnekar, Rasika Chikte, and Ketki Savant provided me with extremely efficient research assistance in innumerable ways. I thank them all with deep gratitude. Thanks are also due to K.S. James and S. Madheswaran for helping me with some computational and statistical matters. I gratefully acknowledge comments received from many participants at seminars held at the G.B. Pant Institute of Himalayan Environment and Development (Almora), Nehru Memorial Museum and Library (New Delhi), the Harvard Center for Population and Development Studies (Harvard University), and the Poverty Research Unit at the University of Sussex. For helpful comments on earlier drafts of various parts of the monograph, I would like to thank Alan Hill, Jean Drèze, Monica Dasgupta, Tim Dyson, Nahid Kamal, Sanjeevani Mulay, R. Nagarajan, Sudhir Anand, Johanne Sundby, and Elsa López. Thanks are also due to Jennifer Leaning, Amartya Sen, Ravai Marindo-Ranganai, B.B. Mohanty, Srijit Mishra, Manabi Majumdar, and Rose Frisch for useful discussions, advice, and encouragement. Finally, Paramita and Anusha, my wife and daughter respectively, deserve deep gratefulness, as they had to endure the painful 'spillover' effects of my fairly protracted engagement with this research work.

ARUP MAHARATNA
November 2004

1

Introduction
An Overview of India's Tribal Demography

Who are the Tribes of India? A Brief Historical Note

While it is perhaps not very surprising that there is no single (globally accepted) definition of tribes, they are ordinarily (or rather simplistically) viewed as those distinctively homogenous (and primitive) groups of peoples who are somewhat outside the mainstream (and modern) civilization.[1] However, defining a tribe typically constitutes, especially in the academic anthropological literature, an important, albeit complex, issue itself.[2] In fact, defining tribes in India is even more complex, partly because, unlike in most other parts of the world, the rising civilization in the Indian subcontinent neither eliminated nor quite absorbed these primitive inhabitants of the land, thereby leaving room for their continuity side by side with the 'mainstream'.[3] The complexity of the issue of tribal identity in the Indian subcontinent is quite evident in the existing large (and perhaps even expanding) academic discourse, developed by contributions

[1] Note that the Oxford Dictionary defines a tribe thus: 'a race of people; now applied especially to a primitive or barbarous condition, under a headman or chief'; quoted in Ray 1972:8.

[2] See Béteille 1986 for a succinct discussion on various approaches to a general definition of a tribe.

[3] Notwithstanding the multiplicity of perspectives and issues surrounding the notion of 'tribe' at the global (theoretical) level, we would restrict ourselves mostly to the Indian discourse, as we are directly concerned with Indian tribes in the present book.

chiefly from historians, anthropologists, and sociologists. There are, in fact, two major facets of tribal identity: one relates to their origin; and the other, perhaps more important, pertains to its evolution as shaped by long-standing processes of tribal transformation and assimilation within the mainstream—Hindu caste society. The latter aspect is summarily called the 'tribe-caste continuum'—an issue, which has been a source of protracted controversies, debates, and discussion.

The 'tribals' of India are widely known as indigenous and auto-chthonous people of the land.[4] As the mainstream tribal story goes, they had long been settled on the plains and river valleys across regions of India before the Aryan-speaking peoples came to settle down in the Indus valley and subsequently over large parts of the country (see Ray 1972: especially 11–15).[5] Compared to the newly invading Aryans, those indigenous peoples were in a lower stage of development. Many were still in a hunting–gathering economy, not knowing the use of metal; they seem to have lived in isolated settlements, spoke a variety of languages, and belonged ethnically to a variety of physical types.[6] They seem to have practised what anthropologists call 'primitive' religion, and lived in closed and well-knit, undifferentiated, and homo-genous social units, generally presided over by a headman or a chief.

The Indo-Aryan speaking peoples with a superior social organization and techno-economy are understood to have forced these indigenous peoples to move bit by bit to increasingly inaccessible regions of forests, hills, and mountain slopes. Then followed the prolonged period of the rise and spread of Hindu civilization, of which the caste-based social organization eventually became the essential feature. However, as Béteille (1986:309) writes: 'It is remarkable how close to such renowned ancient and medieval centres of civilization as Gaya, Ujjain and Maduari tribes could still be found living in their natural setting, so to say, well into the present century.' Similarly, for instance, the Konds—a dominant tribe of Orissa—'have lived within two miles of

---

[4] This question has, however, been a source of academic debates and disputes. For a concise discussion on this, see Xaxa 2003:377–9; Béteille 1998; also Guha 1999:1–9.

[5] Those indigenous peoples are generally believed to have comprised of various racial subgroups, who had come from outside. The races that had come to India before Indo-European or Aryans include Negrito, Proto-Australoid, and Dravidian (Mamoria 1958:20–1).

[6] They are Proto-Australoids, Mongolians, and to a limited extent, Nrgritos strains (Mamoria 1958:20–1).

an Orissa caste village for perhaps as many as eight centuries and have remained tribal Konds' (Mandelbaum 1970:585). Consequently, we now face two related questions: first, what was the relationship between Hindu society and tribal society? (in the so-called tribe–caste continuum issue);[7] second, why and how did the so-called tribal peoples succeed in remaining free from the dominant mainstream Hindu caste system and culture? (e.g. Ray 1972; Béteille 1986).

One may detect—at least apparently—a distinct paradox while comparing Hindu and tribal societies. On the one hand, a sharp contrast can be seen between these two: a traditional tribal society is characteristically homogenous and unstratified, while Hindu society is just the opposite. On the other hand, one often sees a certain homology between individual castes and tribes in the sense that both perpetuate collective identities in strikingly similar ways (Béteille 1986:311). To put it in Andre Béteille's words, '[i]t is no accident that observers down the ages have so persistently mistaken castes for tribes, and tribes for castes.' Individual tribes of India appear at once very similar to caste segments of Hindu society but quite different in terms of lifestyles, mode of livelihood, habitation, values, and cultural practices. This almost certainly reflects the effects of interpenetration between tribes and Hindu civilization. Indeed, as D.D. Kosambi, an eminent Indian historian argues, '[t]he entire course of Indian History shows tribal elements being fused into a general society' (quoted in Béteille 1986:312). However, since the strict rule of endogamy is not a universal feature of tribes, India's tribal endogamy reflects, it may be argued, the influence of Hindu civilization on tribal societies. Thus, what appears perhaps more important than just the 'fusion of tribal elements' is that 'collective identities outlive the conversion of tribe into caste' (Béteille 1986).

Researchers and scholars have been trying for a fairly long time to comprehend and explain the nature of this long-standing, and indeed slow, process of tribal transformation. Since many of the over 450 named Indian tribes had lived in such widely diverse conditions, a single explanation is unlikely to be equally applicable to all. One received explanation of tribal absorption—aptly called the 'Hindu method'—

---

[7] Even today Indian historians, anthropologists, and sociologists sometimes appear to only touch on the question of whether lower caste people were formerly tribes or whether tribes always have had a distinctive identity outside the Hindu caste society (see various papers in Nathan 1997, and also references cited there; see also S. Karia (1997)).

suggests that there was a symbiotic, albeit unequal, relationship between tribes and the larger society of castes (Bose 1941 and 1975).[8] As the argument goes, when the materially and technologically less advanced tribal economic base became precarious due to population expansion or for other reasons, the tribes sought economic security through closer attachment to the wider and superior Hindu society. According to this view, based on fieldwork as well as historical and classical texts, the newly attached tribe was given the lowest position in the Hindu caste society. There seem to have been several instances where the richer and more powerful sections of tribal groups had laid claim to being Kshatriyas, though they originally had started their career as tribes (Srinivas 1977:227).

While specialized occupations maintained boundaries between castes/groups, strict rules of endogamy were enforced in their absence. This Hindu method of tribal absorption affected tribes (presumably) most in interior hill and forest areas, where influences from other civilizations, whether Islamic or Chinese, were feeble or absent. These tribes—namely Bhil, Munda, Santhal, Oraon, Saora, Juang, and many others—account for the bulk of the tribal population of the country.[9] The distinctiveness of the so-called Hindu method of tribal absorption is better understood by contrasting it with the attempted complete assimilation of American Indian tribes into mainstream society in the shortest possible time, which (almost inevitably) failed, and led to continuing tribal existence as 'deviant groups'.[10] In contrast, the Hindu method never sought to efface the tribal identity fully or in the shortest time, often with the end result of tribal conversion into caste, usually of a lowest rank, but not as a deviant group.[11] Since such tribal shift

[8] The following presentation of Bose's argument draws on a useful summary available in Béteille 1986:313–15.

[9] A number of tribes that remained largely outside the influence of the Hindu caste society, include the indigenous tribes of the Andaman Islands, namely the Onge, Jarwa, and others, who in fact had remained completely isolated from the mainland until the nineteenth century. The tribes of the northeastern hill areas, namely Abor, Dafla, and a few others, because of their location on the frontiers of more than one civilization, were also better able to escape the pressure of Hindu influences for quite long, although many of them lately appear to have developed their societies on Hindu caste lines.

[10] See, for example, a case study of the Makah Indians of America, in Colson 1975.

[11] A few tribal groups in specific Indian locations perhaps did turn to

into *jati* society has almost always been gradual and undramatic, there has been an inherent permeability of the boundary between tribe and non-tribe, leaving room for borderline cases where 'there may be very little difference between a group that considers itself a tribe and one that claims to be a jati' (Mandelbaum 1970:574).[12]

We must take note of an another ongoing process of social change—the so-called Sanskritization, which has a bearing on tribal absorption into Hindu caste society. Sanskritization basically means a gradual process of emulation of higher caste lifestyles and scriptural norms by lower rung groups, including tribals.[13] While these two mechanisms of tribal absorption are by no means mutually exclusive, there are differential implications for the position of tribals in the mainstream Hindu society. For example, Sanskritization implies emulation of higher caste lifestyles and sociocultural norms by lower caste and tribal peoples, but not necessarily a recognition or identity of a higher caste.

'criminal activities', and got themselves branded as 'criminal tribes' in the British colonial period. However, the reason for their criminal predilection is often linked to their low social status and extreme vulnerability within the mainstream Hindu social fabric, apart from a general disfavour meted out to them by the British colonial administration. Indeed some recent researches have shown that a fallacious British understanding of India's caste system led to the perception that, like most major castes with a distinct professional or occupational affinity, there must be a caste that practised criminal activities as their profession (Bokil 2002). For recent discussions on some of these so-called criminal tribes of India, their predicaments, and on-the-state perceptions and responses since the British colonial rule, see Nigam 1990; Radhakrishna 1989a,b, and 2000 and references cited therein; see also Bokil 2002).

[12] As Béteille writes, '[i]t may be difficult to decide whether the Bhumij in eastern India or Dubla in western India are a tribe or a caste, but there should be no difficulty [in] deciding that the Vadama are a caste in Tanjore or the Juang a tribe in Mayurbhanj' (Béteille 1986:317).

[13] The term 'Sanskritization', popularized by M.N. Srinivas, refers to 'the process by which a "low" Hindu caste, or tribal or other group, changes its customs, ritual, ideology, and way of life in the direction of a high, and frequently, "twice-born" caste' (Srinivas 1966:6). It should be noted that 'the mobility associated with Sanskritization results only in positional changes in the system and does not lead to any structural change' (ibid:7; italics added). The Sanskritization process has already made a considerable headway in transforming several tribes such as the Bhils of western India, the Gonds and Oraons of central India, and the Pahids of the Himalayas. See Roy Burman 1992.

Consequently, Sanskritization may as well transform several socio-cultural norms and practices of a tribal group without assigning a caste status to them. For instance, the female age at marriage may decline or the child marriage practice may spread among a tribal group under the Hindu influence, with their tribal status remaining unchanged in the larger society. As Thakur and Thakur (1994:22) write, '[a]fter failing to get absorbed in Hind[u] mainstream many tribals are returning to their indigenous customs and traditions'—a process which is sometimes referred to as 'retribalization'. However, whether or not tribals have been absorbed into mainstream Hindu society, they have certainly been subject to various complex influences emanating from a developing, industrializing, urbanizing, and 'modernizing' country.

As opposed to the symbiotic nature of the relationship between tribes and mainstream caste-based society, its asymmetrical and exploitative character should not be ignored. This in fact often resulted, as mentioned already, from pushing tribes off by better organized neighbours to worse locations where the tribes could barely survive on a very precarious economic condition (Ray 1972; Roy Burman 1983). This process of pushing tribes further and further was certainly at work since the nineteenth century (for example, in the Santhal Parganas, Chotanagpur of erstwhile Bihar), and is still going on—in varying degrees and forms—in several parts of India.[14] However, the tribes—whether pushed out or pulled in—were never totally

---

[14] After Independence—when substantial development and industrialization efforts have been undertaken—the displacement of tribal peoples (especially from their remote habitat such as jungles and hills) has been continuing. This has added to an accentuation of their struggle for survival and discontent, sometimes leading to organized separatist movements in specific tribal-dominated regions (see e.g. Fürer-Haimendorf 1982, 1989; also relevant papers in Chaudhuri 1990, vol.3). The Scheduled Areas and Scheduled Tribes Commission's first report succinctly described the disruption of tribal economy and degradation of tribal society due to large-scale industrialization in the following words: 'The Tribals were dislodged from their traditional sources of livelihood and places of habitation. Not conversant with the details of acquisition proceedings they accepted whatever cash compensation was given to them and became emigrants. With cash in hand and many attractions in the nearby industrial towns, their funds were rapidly depleted and in course of time they were without money as well as without land. They joined the ranks of landless labourers but without any training, equipment or aptitude

uninfluenced by the larger currents of Hindu society.[15] Yet, India's tribal communities, at large, have continued to retain their own distinctive existence, essentially outside the purview of the mainstream Hindu caste system.[16] This persisting co-existence of 'the old and the new' and consequent phenomenon of cultural and ethnic heterogeneity may not appear surprising in the light of the sheer size of the Indian

---

for any skilled or semi-skilled job' (quoted in Fürer-Haimendorf 1989:99). Consequently, there has been, in the recent past, a lot of social activism directed against tribal displacement caused by newly initiated large-scale development projects like expansion of dams, mining, industrialization, and urbanization.

[15] David Mandelbaum, for example, cites interesting evidence of such Hindu influence even on a remote and isolated tribal group. In course of his field work in Travancore (in today's Kerala) as long ago as the 1930s, he met a tribal group of Urali, who lived in tree houses to keep out of the way of elephants and other wild animals deep in jungles, and he wrote that '[y]et these Urali, I soon discovered, would regularly pack their cooking utensils and set off for a day-long trip to market...because, they said, they would not accept food cooked by anyone but an Urali' (Mandelbaum 1970:576). For similar evidence of Hindu caste influence on other isolated tribes in central India, especially in restrictions on food sharing and eating food with other groups of people, see Jay (1968). Indeed the evidence of Hindu beliefs and practices across tribal areas has sometimes been used to advance the so-called 'nationalist' view that Indian tribes, rather than having a distinct identity different from a caste-based social structure, have been part and parcel of Hindu society throughout the history of the land (Ghurye 1959).

[16] Drawing on various examples, several scholars have recently argued that 'transformation of a tribe into a caste is not inevitable' (Nathan 1997:14; see also papers by K.S. Singh, B.K. Roy Burman, and Suguna Pathy in Nathan [1997]. Indeed there are quite a few instances of a caste group adapting itself to the tribal sociocultural milieu—sometimes being surrounded by tribal communities (e.g. the Badagas in the Nilgiris of Tamil Nadu; see Hockings 1999), and sometimes having lost political power and property rights to dominant tribes (e.g. the Bhils and the Girasia of Rajasthan; see Chauhan 1978, and Unnithan-Kumar 1997). This latter process has often been called 'tribalization', through which 'an already existing virile sociopolitical homogenous unit withdraws itself from the mainstream of the larger culture and begins leading a secluded life in an inaccessible area, thereby redefining its own world-view' (Chauhan 1978:29). However, a recent study of the Girasia of Rajasthan argues that they were 'tribalized' chiefly in the sense of their loss of political status and property to the tribals, but this was not accompanied by 'tribal' attitude and customs, as they could maintain their own customary lifestyles and social organization (Unnithan-Kumar 1997).

subcontinent and the dearth of communications. But as observed by Fürer-Haimendorf (1985:1), an authority on Indian tribes, this persisting ethnic heterogeneity is largely attributable to 'an attitude basic to Indian ideology which accepted the variety of cultural forms as natural and immutable, and did not consider their assimilation to a single pattern in any way desirable'. Consequently, it has never been anomalous to regard tribes of India as a large assortment of communities, differing widely in size, mode of livelihood, and social organization. They have all been tribes, not because they were all at exactly the same stage of evolution, but because they all stood outside Hindu civilization. This is not to ignore the continuity of the secular process of tribal absorption into mainstream Hindu society, albeit sometimes hazy and slow in some places. Recognizing the so-called tribe–caste continuum through the passage of time precludes neither the validity nor usefulness of looking at their differential states of being at a given point of time. Relatedly, despite great cultural and social differences among tribal peoples across Indian regions, there is a distinct set of core features valid for the tribal population, as a whole. David Mandelbaum (1970:576–85) for instance, classifies the broad distinctions between tribal and jati societies at an aggregate level under five heads—namely, social, political, economic, religious, and psychological. In fact, one major objective of the present monograph is to throw light on key demographic and sociocultural differences between Indian tribes as a whole and their non-tribal counterparts.

The proliferation of the 'borderline' tribal groups (i.e. in the long-standing process of tribal intermingling and eventual absorption into the Hindu caste system) and their coexistence has continued unabated—albeit slowly and sometimes even unnoticed—in the course of Indian history and civilization, especially until the establishment of British colonial rule.[17] In fact, the British administration had initiated a stir in this seemingly silent, slow, and long-standing historical process

---

[17] For example, Bailey (1961), while referring to the relationship between tribal Kond and Hindu caste Oriya people, writes: 'Long before the British came, there were colonies of Oriyas settled in the midst of the Konds... it is clear the Oriyas did not rule the Konds (p. 16)... the Oriyas were not being absorbed into the Kond tribal system; nor were the Konds being absorbed into the Oriya caste system; nor ... was there any kind of third compromise-system emerging between a caste and tribe. When the British arrived, they governed through the Oriyas and gave them power, and for a time Konds

of assimilation, and in the harmonious existence of Indian tribes within a larger caste society. There are several reasons why British rulers, unlike preceding Hindu and Muslim ones, could not afford to leave such long-standing assimilation processes unrecorded or rather undisturbed. First, in their zeal to colonize and rule Indian subcontinent, the British could not ignore patterns of tribal society and the place of India's tribal people in the context of mainstream Hindu caste society. Indeed, their interest and urge to understand these apparently peripheral ('tribal') people more thoroughly was fuelled by occasional and stiff encounters with resistance and revolts from some major tribal groups (for example, the Santhal revolts and uprisings of the nineteenth century).

Moreover, faced with the enormous complexity of tribe–caste interrelationships across India, a 'modern' state, for the requirements of law and administration, could not afford to ignore the necessity of 'a sharp definition of who is to be counted as tribesman' (Mandelbaum 1970:574). Furthermore, the British officials appeared sensitive to, and often appreciative of, the chief tribal features and customs (i.e. those which are premised on freedom and a non-hierarchical social system). A rich tradition of anthropological research and studies on the Indian tribal population had began to be established since the nineteenth century by many painstaking and detailed ethnographic works by eminent British anthropologists and administrators.[18] Indeed

---

began to be absorbed into the Oriya caste system' (p. 18). It should be noted, however, that in several regions (especially in the Dravidian south and central India) many tribals, though they came under the broad caste structure of Indo-Aryan society, had managed to retain many of their own tribal sociocultural features, including clan-tribal social organization and relatively balanced gender relations (e.g. Volchok 1964).

[18] As L.P. Vidyarthi writes, 'British scholarly administrators posted in different parts of India, for example, Risley, Delton and O'Malley in East India, Russell in Middle India, Thurston in South India, Crooks in Northern India, wrote encyclopedic inventories about tribes and castes of India, which even today, provide the basic information about the life culture of the peoples of the respective regions' (Vidyarthi 1978:9). In the course of the subsequent nationalist movement, these studies by British scholars and administrators as well as their Indian students were viewed as serving the interest of the British colonial administration through gathering of information necessary for imposing better control over its subjects. As a sequel to an anti-colonial attitude

the convention to categorize India's tribal groups was well established during the nineteenth century by British administrators (Béteille 1974:62). The process of preparing lists of tribes (apparently with the view to giving them administrative and political concessions) acquired systematic character from the 1931 census. The census operations, thus, began classifying the tribal population groups, in addition to counting them as well. Given the dominance of administrative and political concerns surrounding tribes, these lists perhaps lacked academic or logical rigour.[19] However, a political controversy seems to have emerged at the very beginning: the official anthropologists, who were mostly British members of Indian Civil Service, held that the aboriginal tribes had a distinct identity markedly different from the mainstream Hindu society. On the other hand, the nationalist anthropologists maintained that Indian tribes have always been 'part and parcel' of Hindu society (Ghurye 1943). The motivation for refuting the British stance (namely, that tribal people were essentially outside the Hindu caste system) was more nationalist and political than scientific or academic.

To the Indian leaders of the nationalist movement, the British policy of making tribal tracts 'excluded areas' under direct colonial administration was a part of the well-known British strategy of 'divide and rule'. Some historians have argued that the British policy of 'exclusion of tribals was largely responsible for relatively weak tribal participation in the national movement' (e.g. Bates 1988). In fact, the two apparently contradictory positions have both been accommodated in the constitution of independent India, which categorizes different tribal groups and castes separately but 'treats tribals, with individual exceptions, as Hindu all the same' (Béteille 1986:317). The Government of India Act of 1935 had offered some special provisions for

---

towards the British tradition of tribal studies, the political and academic climate after Independence became disproportionately favourable to the study of caste in the emerging discipline of sociology, while 'anthropology, by contrast, having been preoccupied with the study of tribes, was derided because of its colonial associations' (Unnithan-Kumar 1997:14).

[19] However, it should be noted here that '[s]everal of the earlier officials in charge of census operations were men with a passion for ethnology, and this no doubt contributed to the complexity of the categorical apparatus they created' (Béteille 1974:62–3). It is notable that since Independence, anthropologists have more or less accepted the list 'without critically examining its rationale' (ibid: 62).

tribal people, and a list of Backward Tribes was promulgated in 1936—albeit for the purpose of representation rather than protective provisions—for all the provinces except Punjab and Bengal (Kulkarni 1991).[20] Such administrative attempts at identifying and listing tribal groups—even though they might have overlooked some subtle issues, including the so-called tribe–caste continuum—have not been opposed seriously by academic sociologists and anthropologists because they were designed to distribute benefits among tribes and hence were welcome. Thus what we see, especially since the British colonial times, is a parallel development (with a certain degree of feedback between them) of two broad discourses on the identity of Indian tribes: one, 'academic' (anthropological and sociological), and the other 'administrative' or rather 'operational'. Each approach has its value.[21] Thus, with this discussion on major historical issues and perspectives on the notion of Indian tribes as a background, we now turn to the administrative/official (or rather, working) approach to resolving the issue of tribal identification and enumeration. More specifically, it is important to see how tribes have been defined and counted in successive

[20] It is worth noting that the British administration had been enacting special laws for tribal communities much earlier. For example, 'Regulation XIII of 1833 declared Chota Nagpur a non-regulated area' (Kulkarni 1991:205). The Scheduled Districts Act of 1874 (14 of 1874) provided in an appendix a detailed list of the districts declared as Scheduled, which could henceforth be excluded (by the empowered local governments, with prior permission of the Governor-General) from the purview of the enactment made for the province. Subsequently, the Governor-General was empowered (by the Government of India Act 1919) to declare any territory of British India to be a backward tract, and 'any act or a part thereof shall not apply or shall apply to such territories with specified exceptions or modifications' (ibid: 205). Notably, the British administration had offered special provisions for the areas inhabited by tribal communities (rather than for members of specified tribes), thereby linking special laws for tribal protection to specified areas rather than to specific tribes. The obvious implication of this was that the law (which was intended to protect the interest of tribes) was equally enjoyed by non-tribal peoples, if any, in those specified areas. Indeed this practice of coupling of tribal identity with areas had continued in the post-Independence period well until 1976 when the Removal of Area Restrictions (Amendment) Act was passed.

[21] As Bailey remarks, '[w]hile it might be necessary for the administration, in the process of distributing benefits and privileges, to consider a particular societies as either tribes or elements in a caste system, there is no reason why we, as sociologists, should do this.' (Bailey 1961:15). See also Nag (1968).

censuses, which have remained till today the largest source of comprehensive and consistent demographic information.

Tribes and Indian Censuses

India is one of the very few non-Western countries that has detailed and fairly rich decennial census information, available since the early 1870s, notably without a single break so far. The census reports and statistical tables have since been presenting the demographic information separately for the tribal population—and often for many individual tribes. This of course offers huge scope for research on India's tribal demography—both historical and contemporary. However the census data, like most other large-scale data sources, are not blemish-free. Indeed, considerable caution is required when drawing valid conclusions based on census data on tribal population. The difficulties are of various kinds, depending on the nature of analysis to be undertaken. For example, when the purpose is to examine long-term trends, the question of comparability of data from one census to other is of substantial importance. When a comparative demographic analysis of two population subgroups for a single census year is the chief concern, the questions of relative accuracy and coverage in a particular census are of significance. The Indian census data on tribes happen to be inflicted by both of these related defects.

In Indian censuses, religion has been a prominent criterion for classification of the population, and during almost the entire British period (except in the 1941 census) the tribal population had been presented under religious division, in the belief that tribes practised hundreds of different religions, all 'primitive' in one way or other (i.e. other than better-known religious categories like Hindu, Muslim, Sikh, Jew, Buddhist, Jain, and Christian). In fact, they used to be categorized as Animists until the 1931 census, when they were enumerated under the heading of Tribal Religion. Indeed, up to the 1941 census, by choosing the criterion of primitive religion, the censuses could avoid many complex issues—anthropological, sociological, and historical (as noted in the preceding section)—in identification and enumeration of tribes.

The British census approach to counting Indian tribes, based on religious division, has not been totally free of difficulties. The main trouble relates to the distinction between Tribal Religion and Hinduism. More specifically, there was considerable confusion over 'a line between advanced primitive religion and backward Hinduism'

(Davis 1951:188) because of the syncretistic character of Hinduism, which is so pervasive that it infiltrates nearly every group. Traces of Hindu influence on most tribal religious practices are the basis for labelling a 'primitive' tribesman as a Hindu unless he is capable of asserting himself otherwise. Another source of error was deliberate misinterpretation, especially in the wake of separate religious electorates since 1909. There was an increasing tendency among Hindu organizations to return everyone of doubtful religious status as a Hindu, and in 1931 active Hindu propaganda did succeed to a considerable extent in doing so. The net effect, obviously, was an under-enumeration of tribal people. The estimated magnitude of under-enumeration of tribals was as much as nearly 90 per cent in Bombay and 50 per cent in Madras in 1931 (see Davis 1951:189).

It was only in 1941 that the tribals were defined for the first time (by the census) not in terms of their religion or faith, but in terms of their 'origin'. The 1941 census enumerated tribals as those who had a 'tribal origin'. In fact this major shift in the criterion by which tribals were counted and classified, led to a serious difficulty of comparability of the tribal population for 1941 with the preceding census figures based on the line of religious grouping (Davis 1951, Appendix J). After Independence in 1947, there began a substantial rethinking about the tribal population. The political leaders of independent India became concerned with a deteriorating provisions for tribal and other backward (low and untouchable caste) sections, whom they wanted to be brought to a higher status gradually, through 'affection', 'friendliness', and some special protections and provisions, at par with the mainstream population. The Committee, appointed for drafting the Constitution of the Republic of India, made adequate provisions in the Constitution for their safeguards and benefits, taking account of social, cultural, political, and economic characteristics of the tribals. For the sake of effective implementation of the policy for upliftment of backward communities, the Constitution also empowered the President of India to declare any tribal community or part thereof as a 'scheduled tribe' entitled to those special provisions and benefits. With the adoption of the Constitution in 1950, the President promulgated in the same year a list of Scheduled Tribes (ST thereafter) and Scheduled Areas, which was based, in a large measure, on the list of Backward Tribes promulgated in 1936 by the British colonial administration.

At the time of the first census of independent India in 1951, the number of scheduled tribal communities or part thereof was 212. The specific areas were, however, earmarked against individual scheduled tribes. The members of any scheduled tribe were entitled to specific concessions and facilities only if they were living in the area specified for that tribe. This so-called 'area restriction' provision was used by the censuses for recording tribal status. The constitutional provisions thus 'sealed the boundaries between tribe and non-tribe' and gave to the tribal identity 'a kind of definiteness it lacked in the past' (Béteille 1986:318). As mentioned above, this administrative approach to the identification of tribes has bypassed many subtle academic issues and debates that typically abound in the anthropological discourse. While a tribe had hitherto been a part of a regional system, and tribes of different regions had little to do with each other, there emerged since the 1950s not only a definite tribal identity enjoying a legal sanction but a political interest in maintaining and strengthening that identity. Indeed the political forces released over the decades since Independence have not only disrupted the historical process of tribal absorption, but have, indeed, reversed it (see Kulkarni 1991).

While the Constitution did not lay down criteria for scheduling a tribe, the President of India was empowered to appoint a Commission, known as the Backward Classes Commission, with three major tasks: evaluating conditions of socially backward classes; recommending policy for amelioration of their hardships and deprivations; and reexamining existing lists of Scheduled Tribes for suggesting revisions, if necessary. The first such Backward Classes Commission was appointed in 1953[22], which came up with a recommendation for declaring a number of communities across India, in addition to those already declared, as scheduled. Accordingly, a modified (and enlarged) list of scheduled tribes was notified by the President in 1956, and the list was published under the Scheduled Castes and Scheduled Tribes (Modification) Order, 1956. Consequently, at the time of the 1961 census, the number of scheduled tribes rose to 427 (which was an increase by more than two times the number at the 1951 census), and then to 432 by the 1971 census.

In the face of various problems and complaints[23], the Removal of Area Restrictions (Amendment) Act of 1976 was passed to remove

[22] Under the chairmanship of Kaka Kalelkar.

[23] For example, when a particular tribe, the Warli, was notified as a Scheduled Tribe in Thane district of Maharashtra, many persons belonging to this tribe, who were living in adjacent districts, were not enumerated as members of a Scheduled Tribe. But ironically, non-tribal people of Thane district could enjoy benefits and privileges meant basically for tribals.

the area restriction on tribal identity, and henceforth the list of Scheduled Tribes was made applicable to all areas in a state. The Scheduled Tribes (ST) were then on, for official and all practical purposes, taken to constitute the tribal population of the country.[24] There are difficulties set by 'the varying definition of a tribe, by changes to the list of officially recognized tribes, by qualitative deficiencies in demographic data, administrative changes to India's regions and by the reclassification of tribes as castes' (Wiercinski 1996). But they cannot prevent scientific use of census definitions and data relating to ST and SC. The relevant census data are not beyond correction and adjustments. More importantly, these limitations of census information have usually not been strong enough to obliterate fairly distinct differences in demographic patterns between tribal and non-tribal groups, so far. Therefore, it is beyond reasonable doubt that census-based scientific, systematic, and comparative (especially at aggregate levels) investigations into the demography of tribes are not only possible and useful, but ought to be increasingly undertaken.

The scheduling of tribes had occurred simultaneously with the preparation of lists of Scheduled Castes (SC), which include communities of low social status in the traditional Hindu caste hierarchy.[25] Although there are two separate schedules for tribes and low caste peoples, these two groups are close to each other in some

[24] There might well have been some anomalous cases in the official process of recording tribal identity. A community, traditionally believed to be tribal, may have been left out, while the other, conventionally not regarded as tribal, were enlisted in the ST schedule. For example, 'all the native inhabitants of the Kinnaur district of Himachal Pradesh (who constitute an agglomeration of several Hindu castes that have been lumped together as the Kinnaura) are now classified as scheduled tribes' (Dube 1977b:4). However, despite such stray anomalies in recording of tribes, it would be difficult to argue that such distortions in the census information on ST and SC peoples are so grave as to prevent scientific and meaningful use of census data (at least) for the purpose of comparison of demographic patterns and trends. Despite such possible biases in the enumeration of ST and SC populations, a distinct contrast in respect of demographic (and related characteristics) between ST and SC people is often discernible in census data. This can be taken as an affirmation of the overall validity and usefulness of census information in comparative demographic studies on ST and SC.

[25] These communities include what were formerly labelled as 'untouchable' and 'depressed' castes, many of whom suffered a low social position, and were debarred from temples, schools, or even wells. The term 'Scheduled Castes'

(but certainly not all) respects. For example, the tribe–caste continuum and the consequent proliferation of 'borderline cases' of tribes (as discussed above) itself implies some degree of closeness between lower caste people and many tribal groups. In fact, some early attempts to prepare scheduled caste lists in several provinces of British India (e.g. Assam and Bengal) proposed to include most primitive tribes, especially the 'Primitive Hinduized' ones (see Gupta 1985:23). Yet, at an aggregate level, they are two distinct groups. Rai Bahadur Sarat Chandra Ray, known as the 'Father of Indian Ethnology', regarded the low caste (i.e. mostly SC) people as 'scattered and disorganized offshoots of the Aborigines...' and also as '...the descendants of the scattered remnants of the Aborigines who were left behind on the plains and who succumbed to Aryan domination, lost their native speech and distinctive "aboriginal" culture, and found themselves gradually degraded into landless serfs and the dregs of "Hindu" or "Hinduized" society' (quoted in Gupta 1985:22). While tribal peoples are thus often regarded (at least implicitly) as morally, socially, and culturally superior to lower caste (SC) people,[26] these two groups on the whole, as we show in the next chapter, are economically not on a very dissimilar footing (see also Gupta 1985, chapter 3). The large-scale sample survey data generally do show that SC and ST communities overall are fairly similar in terms of indicators of material well-being such as prevalence of poverty, landlessness, average income, and levels

---

was first used in the 1930s—partly to replace the terms 'untouchable' and 'depressed', which used to entail much controversy, confusion, and political overtones. The Government of India (Scheduled Castes) Order, 1936 came up with a concrete list of 'Scheduled Castes' the touchstone of which was 'untouchability', both in literal and notional senses. In this list, Christians, Muslims, and the hill and forest tribes, with tribal religion, were categorically excluded. Indeed some other conflicting claims of the aborigines were settled by the Government of India (Provincial Legislative Assembly) Order 1936, which provided a separate list of backward tribes. However, the identification of lower caste (i.e. SC) groups, which had begun as early as 1911 at an all-India level, was beset with similar insuperable difficulties as those involved in identifying tribal groups. For a helpful discussion on the origin and evolution of scheduled castes, see Gupta 1985, especially chapters 1 and 2.

[26] For example, as Sarat Chandra Ray, opposing the idea of bracketing aboriginal and low caste people for protection, wrote in 1933 about aboriginals of Bihar and Orissa: 'mostly Santhals, Mundas, Hos and Oraons have their own racial pride, and in spite of attempts often made to Hinduize them, have kept themselves a distinct community' (quoted in Gupta 1985:23).

of consumption (the details on this are provided in the following chapter).[27] Therefore it should be more illuminating to analyse tribal demographic patterns and trends in relation to those SC people who are economically similar, but are different in sociocultural characteristics.[28] Indeed, this should allow for a better understanding of the role of sociocultural influences in demographic behaviour and outcomes when economic conditions are controlled. Besides, a demographic perspective on tribes should hopefully prove helpful to a deeper understanding of the notion of Indian tribes itself and their relative position in the larger society in the past, present, and future.

Broad Demographic Patterns and Trends of Indian Tribes: An Aggregative Analysis

One important suggestion that has emerged from the foregoing discussion is that the census information on Indian tribes, although not without blemishes, can be profitably utilized for systematic investigations into several issues relating to tribal demography. No less importantly, one can even bypass—by relying on the census approaches and definitions—many intricate and subtle issues surrounding the notion and classification of tribes. Therefore, on the basis of census data, we now examine the broad features of the long-term growth of the tribal population since the late nineteenth century, especially in comparison with the general population. Table 1.1 presents census-based information on time trends of the size, growth, and sex

[27] Note that the Backward Classes Commission Report in the early 1950s distinguishes tribes (ST) from lower caste (SC) people, not on the criterion of economic conditions and related variables, but on account of their lifestyle and other sociocultural characteristics and practices. The Report writes: 'The Scheduled Tribes can also be generally ascertained by the fact that they live apart in hills, and even where they live on the plains they lead a separate, excluded existence and are not fully assimilated in the main body of the people. Scheduled Tribes may belong to any religion. They are listed as Scheduled Tribes because of the kind of life led by them' (quoted in Singh 1997) [italics added].

[28] Many sociocultural features of SC peoples belong basically to larger Hindu traditions. The SC communities, unlike tribals who typically refuse to be subservient to Hindu sociocultural traditions, are not 'completely free from the influence of the ethically loaded, partly puritanical theology and world-view of literate upper caste Hindus, whose messages they receive through verbal communication, and through cultural performances, such as dance, drama, etc.' (Sinha 1957:116).

Table 1.1 Long-term trends in population, and sex ratio for total and Tribal populations, India, 1881–1991

Year	Total Population	Tribal Population	Decadal Growth Rate (per cent)		Sex-Ratio (female per 1,000 males)	
			Total	Tribal	Total	Tribal
British India						
1881	250,155,050	6,426,511 (2.57)	–	–	954	–
1891	279,575,324	9,112,018 (3.26)	11.76	41.79	958	992
1901	283,867,584	8,184,758 (2.88)	1.54	-10.18	972	1021
1911	303,004,354	9,593,695 (3.17)	6.74	17.21	964	1016
1921	305,726,528	9,072,024 (3.00)	0.89	-7.2	955	996
1931	337,675,361	7,629,959 (2.45)	10.45	-15.9	950	1009
1941	388,997,955[a]	8,791,354[b] (2.26)	15.20	6.17	945	985
Independent India						
1951*	361,088,090	19,111,498 (5.29)	–	–	946	1021+
1961	439,234,771	30,130,184 (–)	23.10	33.84*	941	987
1971	548,159,652	38,015,162 (6.93)	24.80	26.17	930	982
1981[c]	665,287,849	51,628,638 (7.76)	24.69	30.6@	934	983
1991[d]	838,583,988	67,758,380 (8.08)	23.79	25.68	927	972
2001	1,028,610,328	84,326,240 (8.20)	22.7	24.5	933	977

[a]Includes 2,331,332 persons in North-West Frontier Province, not enumerated by religion but believed to be Muslim.
[b]In view of a change in classification in the 1941 census, this is an estimate—made for the purpose of achieving comparability with the figures of tribal population identified as Animists till 1931, or as people practising tribal religion in the 1931 census, of tribal population in 1941, derived after adjustments to the enumerated population of 'tribal origin'. See Davis (1951), Appendix J for adjustments and assumptions involved in obtaining this estimate.
[c]Excludes Assam. The decadal growth rate during 1971–81 has been calculated by excluding the population of Assam.

(d)Excludes Jammu and Kashmir. The decadal growth rate during 1981–91 has been calculated excluding the population of both Assam and Jammu and Kashmir. * See note 1 (below); + for India and Pakistan together (Visaria 1969, Table 2.9); @ This has been calculated on the basis of a revised estimate of the tribal population for 1971 (which is 39,489,232, excluding Assam) after taking account of the abolition of hitherto imposed area restrictions for most tribes by an Act of Parliament in 1976, which resulted in a larger population of several tribes in many states, according to the 1971 census, than were actually enumerated (see Sinha 1986, Tables 4.1, 4.2, and Appendix). In fact, the office of the Registrar General worked the revised population of tribals for states where the revision was necessary (see Commissioner for Scheduled Caste and Scheduled Tribes 1977; and also Sinha 1993).

Note: 1) In the 1951 census the tribal population was for the first time enumerated according to a statutory list of scheduled tribes notified by the President under Article 342 of the Constitution, which was enlarged through Modification as per order in 1956. According to the 1956 Modification order, the tribal population for the 1951 census was revised upward as being 22, 511, 584, with the revised percentage rising to 6.23. Since the tribal population in 1961 was enumerated according to the 1956 Modification list of scheduled tribes, the decadal growth rate of the tribal population during 1951–61 has been calculated on the basis of this revised tribal population for 1951. 2) Figures in parentheses are respective percentage shares of tribal population to the total population.

Source: For British India figures, Davis (1951), Table 77, p. 179; Mamoria (1958), p. 26; and Natarajan (1971), p. 9. For the post-Independence period, Census Report, Nag (1984), 15–16; and Bose (1996); Govt. of India (2004).

composition of the tribal population since 1881. It is necessary to examine population trends separately for pre-Independence and post-Independence periods, partly because of a substantial change in the geographical boundary of India following the partition in 1947, and partly due to, as was indicated earlier, recurrent changes in the criteria and classification schemes in post-Independent censuses. As can be seen from Table 1.1, except for three decades, namely 1891–1901, 1911–21, and 1921–31, the aggregate tribal population have registered an increase in other periods, although the growth rate has varied considerably. For example, during the 1881–91 decade, the enumerated total population increased by about 12 per cent, while the increase recorded for the tribal population during the period was three and half times larger. This could be related to an improvement in the later census which brought some tribal communities, who inhabited inaccessible and isolated jungles and hills, under enumeration. However, in the following decade of 1891–1901, tribes as a whole, appear to have experienced a substantial decline in their absolute number vis-à-vis a small increase in the general population. This reflected the greater mortality toll among tribals during two consecutive major famines that had occurred in 1896–7 and 1899–1900.[29] But in the following decade of 1901–11, the enumerated tribal population had increased much faster than the general population, due to less severe famines during this decade in terms of frequency, scale, and coverage,[30] and also to a quicker recovery of the tribal population who, in comparison, had suffered a greater population loss in the major famines of the preceding decade.[31]

[29] Famines might have killed tribal peoples more severely, as their mortality, though it was perhaps lower than that of general population in the normal times, was likely to have been affected 'more quickly and completely' by changes in external environment such as those in the famines (Davis 1951:191). See also Merewether (1898:156–160) for a brief narrative of the Gonds of central India who hardest hit by the major large-scale famine of 1896–97. Moreover, as Wood (1998:131) points out, '[g]eneral lack of food storage facilities' among hunter–gatherer communities could make them more vulnerable to famines.

[30] See Maharatna (1996):11–18. In this decade, a major famine had occurred in 1907–8. But its acute severity and effects were restricted to the United Provinces—a region where tribal concentration had been relatively small. A more liberal relief policy adopted during this decade, especially for vulnerable sections of the population, is also held responsible (at least partly) for a lower severity of famines (e.g. Maharatna 1996; McAlpin 1983).

[31] There are some standard demographic reasons for why a population,

The growth of the overall population during the 1911–21 decade was negligible, and this seems largely attributable to huge excess mortality during the well-known influenza pandemic of 1918. But the record of a negative growth rate for tribals in this period could be a reflection of their relative mortality disadvantage in the pandemic. Again, during 1921–31 Indian tribes appear to have experienced a decline in their aggregate enumerated size, while the general population had recorded an increase. This differential seems related to heightened activity among religious groups at the time of the 1931 census, espousing the active propaganda that 'practically everyone but Muslims, Christians, and Jews... should be counted as Hindu' (Davis 1951:188). There was, indeed, immense pressure on the 1931 census authorities to return 'everyone of doubtful status as Hindu', with a consequent under-enumeration of tribals (Davis 1951:188). Furthermore, the substitution of religious criteria by 'tribal origin' to count tribals in the 1941 census was partly responsible for the record showing a slower growth of the tribal population during 1931–41 (see Table 1.1). Except for dramatic effects of famines and epidemics, the census recorded the growth of the tribal population up to 1921 at rates no less, or even higher than the total population. However, during the three decades preceding Independence, the slow increase of the tribal population was more of a reflection of accentuated social and political turmoil on religious lines than anything else.

Another related feature of tribal population growth over the pre-Independence period—a feature which drew particular attention of Kinsley Davis—is the relative constancy of the tribal proportion to the total population since the late nineteenth century, as against a secular and steady decline in the proportion of Hindus. The proportion of tribal population ranges from 2.26 per cent to 3.26 during 1881–1941, whereas the Hindu proportion steadily declined from 75.1 per

---

which has experienced larger proportionate excess mortality (vis-à-vis other populations) in a famine, should witness a quicker recovery of the pre-famine population size. First, since a famine generally kills most of those who are in vulnerable age groups, namely infants, children, and the elderly, the adults in their reproductive span, would survive in larger numbers. Second, since an infant death shortens the mother's postpartum amenorrhoea, the more severe the famine is in terms of infant mortality, the greater the number of fecund women surviving in the immediate post-famine period, contributing to a quicker population recovery due to (relatively) larger excess fertility (see Maharatna 1996: 1–11).

cent to 69.5 during this period (see Davis 1951:178). This differential was, according to Davis, due to the higher fertility of the tribal population as compared to the Hindu population. But, as shown in the following chapter with more detailed data, this was possibly more due to relatively low mortality and fertility levels of tribal communities compared to those of the mainstream Hindu population.

In the 1951 census, the first after Independence, the enumerated size of the tribal population, unlike the total population, became twice larger than that in the preceding census, a striking trend, especially as India's partition in 1947 had truncated her geographical boundaries. In fact, the proportion of tribal population had jumped from around 3.0 per cent in the pre-Independence period to more than 5 per cent in 1951. This might have been partly because the regions (e.g. north-western parts and eastern Bengal) which were carved out from the Indian subcontinent are historically characterized by low tribal concentration. However, this can hardly be a full explanation of a recorded increase of tribal population by more than 10 per cent per annum during the 1941–51 decade, when the total population of the country reduced by about 7 per cent. In fact, this bursting increase of the tribal population was (at least partly) caused by their enumeration for the first time in 1951 on the basis of a detailed list of 'scheduled' tribes prepared by the government, without taking their religious category or their 'origin' into account as was done previously.[32] Many tribes, who had been left out from tribal category in earlier censuses on account of their religious affiliation or otherwise, got identified and enumerated as 'tribal' in the 1951 census. Interestingly, there has been a steady rising trend of tribal proportion to the total population in the post-Independence period. The proportion of tribal people rose from around 5 per cent in 1951 to more than eight per cent in 1991. Indeed the enumerated size of the tribal population—an Indian minority group—is nearly 70 million according to the 1991 census, which is almost equal to (in some cases even more than) the population of many western countries. Furthermore, and somewhat relatedly, there

---

[32] Just after the declaration of Independence and the partition in August 1947, the newly formed Government of India published, in September of that year, a handbook on the population of communities and states, according to the 1941 census. Notably, this official publication reported that the total tribal population of independent (i.e. divided) India was twice as large as the enumerated tribal population for undivided India (Government of India 1947). This assertion was largely based on the much-expanded list of scheduled tribes that was prepared by the Indian government immediately after Independence.

has always been a higher decadal rate of growth of the tribal population than of the general population in the post-Independence period (see Table 1.1). Note however that the gap in growth rates between the tribal and general population was highest during the 1951–61 decade, and it seems to have narrowed down over the following decades (perhaps with the exception of the 1971–81 period).

There are several plausible explanations—some more readily obvious than others—for higher rates of tribal growth and concomitant rises in the tribal share in post-Independence censuses. First, a substantial enlargement of the list of scheduled tribes especially up to the late 1970s, as well as the removal of area restrictions in 1976, certainly contributed to a relative swelling of the enumerated tribal population.[33] This tendency seems to have been fuelled by a mounting demand for recognition of tribal identity among several hitherto unidentified tribal communities, especially in some regions where local-level activism and state support was relatively more pronounced in assuring tribal rights and privileges.[34] However, this is far from complete as an explanation for the rising share of tribal population. In fact, fairly strong evidence suggests a higher real natural growth of the tribal population as compared to that of the total population. For example, the decadal growth rate of the aggregate tribal population between 1961 and 1971, estimated on matched populations of scheduled tribes, turns out to be only about one per cent point lower (25.3 per cent) than that (26.2 per cent) based on unadjusted tribal populations in these censuses (Sinha 1979). Moreover, the estimated growth rate of even matched tribal population appears higher by about one per cent than that for the total population (24.8 per cent), suggesting a higher natural rate of growth among tribes vis-à-vis the general population.[35] Thus, apart

---

[33] As Béteille (1986) observes, '[p]aradoxically, the number of communities deemed to be tribes has increased with the modernization of the India between 1950 and 1976.' Note that according to the 1991 census there are now as many as 573 tribes and 1,091 caste groups that have been scheduled (Unnithan-Kumar 1997:17).

[34] For example, the Vidarbha and Marathawada regions of Maharashtra witnessed an abnormally high growth of newly enumerated tribes (see e.g. Gaikwad 1986; Guha 1999). Note that this trend can hardly be taken as a reflection of so-called 'retribalization', since the categories involved are often very different (in form and orientation) from those of the past.

[35] Although a higher growth of matched populations of scheduled tribes in two censuses is conceivably consistent with over-returns in the enumeration of even those specific tribes, this does not seem very likely.

from inclusion of new tribes in the schedule, a genuinely larger natural increase of the tribal population than of the non-tribal population must have contributed to a rising tribal share in the total population in the post-Independence period.

A high growth of tribal population may not be very surprising in view of various large-scale development and modernization initiatives of the newly independent state. The modernization process should have brought some changes in lifestyles, customs, and values, and some material improvements. Indeed many of these changes, especially at an early stage, was characterized by the negligible prevalence of modern contraception (as was certainly the case with many tribal communities during first several decades after Independence) often conducive to rising fertility, and hence the growth rate of population. There are four standard changes in the early phase of the modernization process, which are commonly thought to contribute to the 'pre-transition rise of fertility'—a rise of fertility before it begins to decline. They are: a reduction in breastfeeding intensity and duration, a reduction in postpartum abstinence, a reduction in widowhood, and reduction in sterility due to improvement of public health services (see Nag 1980; and Dyson and Murphy 1985 for details).[36] While some of these factors seem relevant, both to tribal and non-tribal (particularly SC) communities, there are reasons why the phenomenon of pre-transition fertility rise should have been relativity prolonged, and perhaps more pronounced among the tribes. First, as many ST communities typically lag behind the SC people in the modernization process (for reasons discussed earlier), the pre-transition fertility rise for the former should occur relatively late. Second, while tribal females traditionally marry relatively late (more on this is in the following chapters), the Sanskritization process in which tribals tend to adopt traditional Hindu practices, including early marriage (for example, the 'child marriage') norm, could exert a downward pressure on the age of tribal females at marriage. This, in turn, may contribute to rises in tribal fertility. And such increases in the fertility of tribes could well occur even at a time when higher caste and SC peoples—already ahead of the tribal group in the modernization process—have started delaying

[36] With modernization and integration, an erosion of traditional and indigenous methods of fertility control among tribal communities is reported as a contributory factor of their temporary 'fertility rise' at an early stage, when modern contraceptive methods are yet to be in practice (e.g. Sennyonga 1993).

the female age at marriage.[37] Furthermore, since the 'pre-transition fertility rise' is contingent upon an absence of modern contraception, one could perhaps hypothesize its relatively late and protracted occurrence among Indian tribes or it could be manifested in a comparatively slow fertility decline if it is already underway. This hypothesis is premised largely on the fact that the tribal population as a whole is relatively isolated and backward, and therefore more likely to remain relatively unaffected by family planning programmes and campaigns later than others.[38]

A remarkably higher growth rate of the tribal population during 1971–81 was largely fuelled by the inclusion of new communities under the ST category (and by removal of 'area restriction' following the 1976 Act), although 'pre-transition' rises of fertility in many lately modernized tribal groups played a role too. What emerges on the whole (ignoring periods of dramatic losses of population due to famines, epidemics, and the like) is a picture of the tribal population growing, much like total population, at a very moderate rate during pre-Independence decades, but at much higher rates (with concomitant rises in its population share) thereafter. A relative inflation of tribal growth rate in the post-Independence period seems to have resulted both by a wider recognition of tribal identities and by delayed tribal modernization and consequently, a late 'pre-transition rise of fertility'. However, like the total population, an indication of the onset of a declining trend in the growth of the tribal population in recent decades is discernible.

What appears quite glaring is the substantial difference in the sex ratio (female–male ratio) between the tribal and general population (see Table 1.1). While the sex ratio has been historically unfavourable

[37] There is a considerable evidence and literature on the possible negative impact on fertility of a rising female age at marriage in the context of the Indian mainstream population and society. To illustrate, an estimated reduction in birth rate (ranging from 16 to 50 per cent) could occur if the average marriage age of females rises from 15 to 19–20 years, other things (e.g. contraceptive use, age-pattern of fertility) remaining the same (see Goyal 1964; Agarwala 1966; Mandelbaum 1974:35–41 among others). Conversely a fertility-raising impact can be hypothesized when female age at marriage declines, as can be expected among ST groups in the initial phase of emulation (by them) of conservative Hindu practices of early female marriage.

[38] This is, however, not true for all tribal groups in India. Indeed, there is evidence of a rapid fertility transition and high degree of contraceptive prevalence among certain tribal people in specific locations.

to the females of India's total general population, it has been always more balanced among tribal communities. Indeed, the females outnumber males in entire Western world and in most other developing countries outside Asia and North Africa. This is consistent with the biological edge of female (given the absence of any discrimination in care and treatment) over males in survival, and also with relative male-bias in vulnerability to wars, accidents, and unhealthy lifestyle (e.g. smoking). The relative female deficiency as reflected in low female–male ratios in India's aggregate population is thus striking, and indicates the influence of social factors adverse to females, which seems to offset their (biological and somewhat intrinsic) favourable effects.[39] Indeed, there have been several attempts at estimating what Amartya Sen in the early 1990s called 'missing women' in a country with a very low female–male ratio (i.e. for a comparable country where an anti-female social environment is known to be absent). The figure of missing women (e.g. about 37 million in India with the sub-Saharan female–male ratio of 1.022 being used as a benchmark) gives us a broad sense of how many more females could be alive if an anti-female social environment did not exist.[40]

Perhaps more importantly, a long-term trend of a deteriorating female–male ratio among India's general population since the early twentieth century (as seen in Table 1.1) has been found, and is a matter of concern in academic and official circles. After several decades of academic discussions and research, some stark, unquestionable facts have emerged in the Indian context: (a) that the low overall female–male ratio in the total general population is largely related to a female mortality disadvantage (vis-à-vis males), especially in infancy and young childhood; (b) that this relative female disadvantage, in turn, is a manifestation of familial discrimination and neglect, mostly against

[39] The imbalance of the sex ratio in India's total population (which seems bizarre in the light of expected patterns) drew the attention of Census Commissioners since the early days of census operations. In fact, lengthy and thoughtful analyses of this female deficiency abound in the pages of early census reports. After several decades of systematic analyses by several scholars, it is clear that a relative deficiency of females in India's total population is real and not any artefact of data biases or sex-selective migration.

[40] See Sen 1999:105–6. In the recent past, there has been a considerable discussion relating to various issues (including methods of estimation) and implications surrounding the notion of missing women in the wider Asian context (e.g. Klasen 1994; Coale and Banister 1994; Griffiths et al. 2000).

girls in respect of distribution of resources, especially medical attention and health care; (c) that a secular decline in the female–male ratio—especially in the post-Independence period—implies not only a worsening of the relative 'deal' for females in the context of improving health and medical facilities, but, more importantly, strongly indicate an intensification, along with development and ongoing shift towards a smaller family, of these gender biases, often more selectively against, for example, higher parity daughters born already or abortion of high parity female foetus after prenatal sex determination.[41] All this is seen as being essentially linked with a pervasive culture of 'son preference' (i.e. preference for sons over daughters).[42] It must be stressed that such strong son preference is often found to be one prominent expression of a more fundamental cultural framework of patriarchy in which female status and autonomy is generally low.[43]

[41] See Bhat 2002; Kynch and Sen 1983; Sen 1989, 1999:104–7; Drèze and Sen 1989, 1995, 2002; Croll 2002; Agnihotri 2000; and the literature cited therein.

[42] To invite more focused attention to mounting evidence of familial neglect and discrimination against female infants and young girls, perhaps to death (including sex selective abortion) in much of Asia, some scholars have recently suggested replacing such terms as 'missing women' and 'son preference' by 'missing girls' and 'daughter discrimination' (Croll 2002: 7–12).

[43] A relatively low female–male ratio in India's aggregate population, which serves as an index of pervasive gender biases, however, hides a 'north–south divide' within India (e.g. Miller 1982; Dyson and Moore 1983; Sopher 1980). More specifically, many states in the north and north-western regions that have lower female–male ratios, are broadly characterized by a pronounced patriarchal structure, with low status and autonomy of women and related anti-female familial biases. In contrast, the 'south' encompassing states lying south of the Satpura hills historically evince a relatively more balanced sex ratio, with much less patriarchal domination and more balanced gender relations. Perhaps more balanced gender relations, with a higher position and autonomy of women in south India, is related to the specific history of the region, where the Dravidian civilization and culture seems to have been more directly akin to a tribal origin, influence, and social features. It is somewhat striking that most south Indian tribes speak ancient Dravidian languages and dialects. Perhaps more interestingly, the south Indian mainstream people historically (and even now) evince several sociocultural features (e.g. marriage patterns and payments including cross-cousin marriage and bride price) that have traditionally characterized tribal societies in much of India too. In any case, this 'north–south' sociocultural divide (in terms of such indicators as

Against this disquieting growing imbalance in the sex ratio for India's general population, the tribal record of a far more balanced sex ratio is of considerable interest. Indeed, tribal sex ratios contrast

female status and autonomy, marriage patterns and payments) appears to play a key role in explaining differential demographic regimes between these two regions (e.g. Dyson and Moore 1983; Das Gupta 1987; Basu 1992; Kishor 1993, among others). While relatively lower fertility, infant- and child-mortality levels, less gender biases and discrimination are broadly the characteristics of the less patriarchal south, a somewhat opposite demographic regime holds in the strong patriarchal 'north'. Some scholars have attempted to explain this regional divide in female status and autonomy in terms of a differential 'economic worth' of women between these two different geophysical settings, with corresponding differences in crop composition and female labour requirements. For example, a greater scope for women's participation in wet-rice cultivation in the south and east has, according to this line of argument, ensured a higher worth (hence greater status and autonomy) of women than that of their counterparts in the north and north-west regions with a much less scope for productive role in dry-crop cultivation (e.g. Bardhan 1974; Miller 1981; see also Krishnaji 2000). But received research, so far, on balance, reaffirms that India's 'north-south' regional divide is overwhelmingly the expression of two intrinsically different sociocultural moorings in these regions, rather than of other differences (e.g. in economic, technological, or geophysical). However, it is of much interest that anti-female discrimination and neglect of a daughter (at least as reflected in the female–male ratio of child population) seem to get intensified with higher income and property levels of households—a phenomenon which is often called 'prosperity effect' (Agnihotri 2003). Somewhat relatedly, there is a growing body of literature reporting an ongoing erosion of traditional balance in gender relations and kinship (e.g. rise of dowry, decline of cross-cousin marriage) across contemporary south India. More importantly, the prominent manifestations of gender biases (e.g. imbalance in sex ratio, sex differentials in mortality, and other indicators) also seem to be increasingly surfacing (at least) in some of these southern states (Tamil Nadu in particular) (Basu 1999; Rajan et al. 2000; Agnihotri 2003). While some of these recent tendencies of south Indian society towards an anti-female pattern seem to have resulted from specific demographic developments (e.g. 'marriage squeeze' and rise of dowry as discussed by Bhat and Halli 1999; the tension between the small-family norm and son preference, as analysed in Das Gupta and Bhat 1995; Basu 1999), they are essentially sociocultural changes. It appears almost certain now that a pervasive spread of patriarchal (anti-female) sociocultural norms and practices has been well underway over the recent past even in regions where gender relations have traditionally (and historically) been more balanced and equitable. Scholars are currently grappling to explain these unhealthy, unwelcome social trends across Indian regions. (e.g. Block et al. 2004; Rao 1993, 1997.)

consistently and sharply with much lower ratios observed for the general population as well as the SC group (see Table 1.1). Following our foregoing discussion for the general population, a higher female–male ratio in the ST population could well be taken as reflection of a much less, or possibly negligible, anti-female discrimination and gender biases among tribal communities. The view that tribal female children and infants, unlike their non-tribal counterparts, do not suffer (or suffer to a much-lesser extent) deliberate neglect and discrimination, finds support in the fact of much higher juvenile female–male ratios in the tribal population (e.g. Agnihotri 2000:153). Indeed, as we would analyse in greater detail in later chapters, there is substantial anthropological evidence suggesting that relatively little (or even absence of) gender biases and relatively balanced gender relations have traditionally been prominent features of overall tribal society and culture.[44]

However, what is disturbing is a distinct trend for the tribal sex ratio, especially over the last few decades, to conform to the mainstream secular pattern of increasing imbalance in sex ratio against females. A ten-point drop of the tribal female–male ratio from 983 to 972 during the 1981–91 decade is particularly noteworthy. This may well be a reflection of increasing tribal transformation towards India's mainstream anti-female patterns, both at sociocultural and economic fronts.[45] As will be discussed in considerable detail later, Indian tribes, of late, appear increasingly dispossessed of their traditional sociocultural and economic moorings characterized by relatively balanced gender relations and the high status of women. And this has been happening largely in the wake of ongoing processes of cultural assimilation and integration with the mainstream (e.g. Sanskritization, Hinduization,

---

[44] It is important to stress that the overall female–male ratio is far more balanced (indeed generally showing excess females over males) in sub-Saharan Africa's population, who traditionally have many similar sociocultural and lifestyle features of Indian tribes. Indeed, a relatively balanced sex ratio in sub-Saharan Africa has also been found consistent with the findings showing a relative advantage of females (girls in particular) over male counterparts in terms of nutritional and mortality indicators (e.g. Svedberg 1990), which clearly points to relatively little or even an absence of anti-female gender biases.

[45] A recent study, noting this 'sharp' drop in the tribal female–male ratio, remarks, '[t]he patriarchal norms of the higher castes, and Sanskritization and detribalization are similarly assimilating tribal peoples into a national culture of discrimination against girls and women' (Atkins *et al.* 2000:199).

industrialization, and urbanization).[46] It would be useful to quote Berreman's remarks summarizing the effects of Sanskritization as being:

> especially damaging to females because it encourages and enforces patriliny (in both descent and inheritance), patrilocality, early marriage and widow celibacy, limitation of divorce to male initiative, dowry marriage, preference for and favouring of male children, male ownership of virtually all property (especially productive property), low priority to female education, literacy and even health, earning power restricted to males, isolation of social and physical mobility largely to males, and total economic, political and social dependence of females on males (Berreman 1993:388).

Regional Distribution of Tribal Population

Having analysed the broad patterns of the growth of the tribal population and a few related features at the all-India level, we now address the question of regional dimensions and diversities of tribal population. Table 1.2 provides census-based information on the state-wise shares of ST population for 1961 and 1991.[47] Since the physical size of each state varies widely, the state level shares of tribal population should be analysed, both in relation to the total state population as well as to the total tribal population of the country. Notwithstanding the possibility of regional variation in the nature and extent of biases in the census enumeration of tribes, the census data are fairly reliable for the purpose of gleaning chief patterns of spatial distribution of the tribal population. As can be seen, the tribes, though dispersed across

---

[46] See e.g. Maharatna 2000a and literature cited there; Roy Burman 1987; Thakur and Thakur 1994, especially chapters 1 and 2.

[47] Taking into account historical, ethnic, and sociocultural differences, anthropologists have sometimes constructed a somewhat different geographical classification for Indian tribes. For example, one such regional classification is as follows (Roy Burman 1972:39–50; see also Vidyarthi 1972): (a) Northeast India comprising Assam, Arunachal Pradesh, Nagaland, Manipur, Mizoram, and Meghalaya; (b) the sub-Himalayan region of north and northwest, comprising north and northwest Uttar Pradesh, Bengal, and Bihar; (c) Western India comprising Rajasthan, Gujarat, and Maharashtra; (d) Central and east India covering West Bengal, Orissa, Madhya Pradesh, and Andhra Pradesh; (e) South India comprising Tamil Nadu, Karnataka, Kerala, and the different Union Territories, including all the islands of the region. This regional classification is often used as a proxy for a broad classification of major Indian tribes (Agarwal 1977 and Mehra 1977).

Table 1.2 Regional patterns of growth and distribution of India's tribal population, 1961–91

State / UT	Proportion of ST Population to:				Average Annual Growth Rates					
	Total Population		Total Tribal Population		1961–71		1971–81		1981–91	
	1961	1991	1961	1991	Total	Tribal	Total	Tribal	Total	Tribal
INDIA	**6.90**	**8.08**	**100**	**100**	**2.2**	**2.2**	**2.2**	**2.7**	**2.1**	**2.3**
STATES										
Northeastern:	**22.9**	**25.8**	**11.0**	**12.0**	–	–	–	–	–	–
Assam	10.74	12.82	3.86	4.24	3	3.2	–	–	–	–
Manipur	31.92	34.41	0.82	0.93	3.2	2.9	2.8	1.5	2.6	4.9
Meghalaya	83.07	85.53	2.11	2.24	2.7	2.1	2.8	2.8	2.8	3.4
Nagaland	93.92	87.7	1.13	1.57	3.4	2.8	4.1	3.5	4.5	4.7
Tripura	31.52	30.95	1.19	1.26	3.1	2.2	2.8	2.6	2.9	3.8
Arunachal Pradesh	88.59	63.61	0.98	0.81	3.3	2.1	3	1.8	3.1	2.2
Mizoram	98.1	94.75	0.86	0.96	2.2	1.8	4	4	3.3	3.3
Eastern:	**10.6**	**9.4**	**34.7**	**25.9**	–	–	–	–	–	–
Bihar	9.05	7.66	13.93	9.76	1.9	1.6	2.2	1.7	2.1	1.3
Orissa	24.06	22.21	13.99	10.38	2.2	1.8	1.8	1.5	1.8	1.7
West Bengal	5.88	5.6	6.8	5.62	2.4	2.1	2.1	1.7	2.2	2.2
Sikkim	–	22.36	–	0.13	–	–	–	–	2.5	2.1
Central:	**20.6**	**23.3**	–	–	–	–	–	–	–	–
Madhya Pradesh	20.62	23.37	22.13	22.73	2.5	2.3	2.3	2	2.4	2.5

(*Contd.*)

Table 1.2 (contd.)

| State / UT | Proportion of ST Population to: | | | | Average Annual Growth Rates | | | | | |
| | Total Population | | Total Tribal Population | | 1961–71 | | 1971–81 | | 1981–91 | |
	1961	1991	1961	1991	Total	Tribal	Total	Tribal	Total	Tribal
Western:	**9.4**	**11.6**	**25.0**	**28.2**	–	–	–	–	–	–
Gujarat	13.34	14.92	9.12	9.09	2.6	3	2.4	2.6	1.9	2.4
Maharashtra	6.06	9.27	7.94	10.8	2.4	2.1	2.2	4.1	2.3	2.4
Rajasthan	11.66	12.44	7.79	8.08	2.4	2.8	2.8	2.9	2.5	2.7
D. & N. Haveli	88.43	78.99	0.16	0.16	2.5	2.3	3.3	2.2	2.9	2.9
Goa, Daman & Diu	–	11.54	–	0.02	–	–	2.4	3.4	1.6	1.2
Northern:	**0.16**	**0.35**	–	**0.74**	–	–	–	–	–	–
Uttar Pradesh	–	0.21	–	0.42	–	–	2.3	1.6	2.3	2.1
Himachal Pradesh	4.34	4.22	0.4	0.32	2.1	1.5	2.1	3.3	1.9	1
Southern:	**1.8**	**3.6**	**6.5**	**10.3**	–	–	–	–	–	–
Andhra Pradesh	3.68	6.31	4.38	6.2	1.9	2.2	2.1	3.6	2.2	2.8
Karnataka	0.81	4.26	0.63	2.83	2.2	1.8	2.4	19.4	1.9	0.5
Kerala	1.25	1.1	0.7	0.47	2.3	2.3	1.8	3.1	1.3	2.1
Tamil Nadu	0.74	1.03	0.83	0.85	2	2.1	1.6	1.5	1.4	1
Islands:	**5.3**	–	**5.4**	**0.10**	–	–	–	–	–	–
Andaman & Nicobar Islands	22.22	9.54	0.04	0.04	5.9	2.5	4.9	2.1	4	1.8
Lakshadweep	97.02	93.15	0.07	0.07	2.8	2.3	2.4	2.5	2.5	2.4

Source: Sinha (1994), Tables 5.1, 5.12

almost the entire country, are mostly found in the eastern, western, and central regions, which together (including the far-eastern states) is home to nearly 90 per cent of India's tribal population. By contrast, the shares of northern and southern states in the total tribal population is quite small. The largest number of the ST population enumerated in the 1991 census was in Madhya Pradesh (15.1 million), followed by Maharashtra (7.3 million), Orissa (7.0 million), Bihar (6.6 million), and Gujarat (6.2 million) in that order. Indeed, the recent regional pattern of distribution of the tribal population does not appear substantially different from the pattern recorded three/four decades earlier (see Table 1.2). For example, there is hardly any correlation between the state's share to the country's total tribal population and the proportion of tribals in the state's total population. While this is not surprising in view of the wide variation in the size of states, the specific regional patterns in terms of these state-level tribal shares have continued largely unaltered.

There are several small states in the far-eastern region, where tribals are the overwhelming majority, but they constitute a relatively meagre proportion of the total tribal population of the country. On the other hand, the share of Madhya Pradesh alone in the total tribal population is nearly 23 per cent, although the tribal proportion to the total population of the state is far smaller than that for most of the far-eastern states (see Table 1.2). Indeed, the total tribal population of Madhya Pradesh is about three times as large as that of the eastern states put together. The three western states, namely Maharashtra, Gujarat, and Rajasthan, constitute more than one-fourth of the total tribal population of the country.

However, there have been some notable changes in the regional distribution of the census-enumerated ST population, especially in terms of the states' relative shares to the aggregate tribal population. First, except for the eastern region, the rest of the country has had a record of enhanced tribal proportion. In some regions, the magnitude of increase of the tribal proportion has been enormous, for example, in the southern region where the share in the aggregate tribal population of the country has nearly doubled over the period 1961–91. However, the increase in tribal share has not been uniform across individual states within the region. For instance, the increase has been negligible in Tamil Nadu and even negative in Kerala, while Karnataka and Andhra Pradesh have experienced a big jump in their shares of tribal population, both within the state population as well as within the country's enumerated tribal population. The tribal share of the western region, as a whole, has got larger within the country as well as the region—although quantum of increase is somewhat greater in terms of the country-level share. Among the three major states of western India (Gujarat, Rajasthan, and Maharashtra), which have gained in terms of tribal share, especially within the state population, Maharashtra seems to have gained the largest tribal share in terms of per cent-point increase within the state as well as the country. At least, a part of this has been contributed by what is often described as 'infiltration' of people into the ST-fold, especially before 1971. For example, Maharashtra, being a region of relatively strong (pre-legislation), tribal movements for land distribution has witnessed comparatively effective implementation of legislative measures of distributing ownership titles of communal and common property resources to the tribals (Guha 1999; Mohanty 2001).

In contrast, Madhya Pradesh (MP), the region with the highest tribal concentration (both absolutely and relatively), has witnessed nearly a three per cent increase in the share of ST within the state total population, virtually without experiencing any increase in its share in the country's total ST population. The pattern recorded for the northeastern region on the whole, is similar and is a reflection of the relatively high tribal population growth. Note also that Rajasthan and Maharashtra of the western region, the majority of the small northeastern states, Andhra Pradesh, and Karnataka of the south have experienced a somewhat higher population growth than the national average, both for the tribal and general population in most of the period between 1961 and 1991. Putting aside enumeration biases relating to tribals, which is perhaps relevant to a few states (e.g. Karnataka and Maharashtra), the inter-state differential in the growth of the tribal population should be shaped by regional variations in death and birth rates (i.e. in natural rate of growth), and migration flows and patterns. For example, a higher growth rate of tribes in a state tends to increase the tribal share in the total state population, but whether the state's share in the country's tribal population would be higher or not depends on their respective relative rates of growth. Apart from the differential natural rates of growth (depending on differentials in birth and death rates), the nature and direction of inter-state tribal mobility and movement can also contribute to the outcome of regional patterns of tribal population. For example, tribal migration from Bihar to neighbouring or even to distant states is fairly well-known (more on these issues has been discussed in Chapter 5).

However, changes in the inter-state tribal composition of the population can get even more complicated if perceptible differentials in enumeration biases relating to tribes exist across states. Such biases in tribal enumeration in a state occur not just randomly, but depend on the character and intensity of politics centred on tribes and ethnic minorities in the state. Indeed, over-returns of tribals in the census enumeration is likely to have occurred in some states. For example, the record of an abnormally high growth of the ST population in Karnataka during 1971–81 (namely 19.4 per cent per annum as against 2.4 per cent for the general population of the state, and also against 2.7 per cent for country's ST population) is a clear pointer to an upward bias in tribal growth rate (Sinha 1994:300).[48] In fact, a similar pattern of a surge in the growth rate of the enumerated ST population during the 1971–81 decade—albeit to a lesser extent than in Karnataka—was also recorded for Maharashtra, Andhra Pradesh, Himachal Pradesh, and Kerala. In the case of a few tribal groups, the sociopolitical factors such as movement for inclusion of new tribal groups in the schedule (for example, the Lambada in Andhra Pradesh before the elections of 1977) must have been important in accounting for a recorded inflation of tribal population growth in these regions.[49] However, one should not ignore the influence of possible changes in demographic behaviour, namely a pre-transition rise of tribal fertility along with mortality improvements.

In contrast to this scenario, in many southern and western states, a distinct drop in the growth rate of the ST population during 1971–81 in West Bengal, Arunachal Pradesh, and Madhya Pradesh is of interest. While it is possible to conjecture some enumeration biases (e.g. conversion of tribes into non-tribal categories), they cannot constitute a major explanation.[50] The explanation could well lie in relatively high or even enhanced mortality levels (related to accentuated mass material deprivation during the 1970s when these states were passing through

---

[48] This apparently anomalous situation has largely been created by the removal in 1976 of 'area restriction' in identifying scheduled tribe populations, as was discussed earlier.

[49] It may be noted that the infiltration of people officially into the tribal fold is relatively easy in southern and western India where names of tribes and castes are often similar, and indeed in many cases almost indistinguishable, unlike in much of eastern and central India.

[50] The criteria for tribal enumeration generally takes account of their conversions and makes sure that they are enumerated as ST.

a phase of economic stagnation), and/or in tribal out-migration to relatively fast advancing states of western and southern regions since the mid-1970s. In fact, these factors were to a large extent true for the general population too, as is reflected in its slow down of growth rates, although by a smaller magnitude.

It is noteworthy that Bihar and Orissa—which are historically regions of tribal concentration—have experienced a perceptible decline in tribal shares between 1961 and 1991, not only within state population but even more prominently within the country's total tribal population. The rates of growth of the tribal population in these two eastern states have been remarkably low, especially in comparison with high rates of growth in many other regions, such as central and western India. Tribal growth rates have indeed been noticeably lower than national averages throughout the period since 1961. This differential in tribal population growth between eastern, central and western states, particularly during the 1971–81 decade has been attributed to a weaker execution of 'removal of area restrictions' during the 1970s in the western states (Roy Burman 1993:200). It is worth noting that the rates of growth of the general population have also been comparatively low in these states—in Bihar particularly during 1961–71 and in Orissa during the entire period since 1971. Putting aside the possibility of worsening quality and coverage of census enumeration in these states or other enumeration biases,[51] the reasons for this record of low rates of population increase includes relatively high mortality levels, low birth rates, and the occurrence of a large exodus. As for Orissa's lower than average growth rates, both of the tribal and the general population, comparatively high mortality and low fertility rates have been held at least partly responsible (e.g. Padhi and Mishra 2000: Table 3.1, 3.2).[52]

While low population growth in Orissa (particularly of tribals) has often been viewed as a 'puzzle' by scholars, this has remained largely unexplored, except for sporadic and inadequately substantiated remarks regarding fertility, mortality, and migration. In fact, the higher mortality

[51] While the record of the slower growth of the tribal population in these states could possibly be due to a weaker tendency towards infiltration into the ST category, as compared to the scale in which it had occurred in some western and southern states, this cannot be a complete explanation.

[52] For example, while the estimated crude birth rate for the whole of Orissa in 1971 (34.6 per thousand population) was found to be lower than the national average of 36.9, the crude death rate (CDR) of 15.4 was indeed higher by about one person per thousand than the all-India figure.

level in Orissa (or in the eastern region, for that matter) is not surprising, but plausible reasons for Orissa's (comparatively) low fertility levels in the 1960s and 1970s has often been a subject of speculation. For example, one received hypothesis links the low birth rates of Orissa in this period to a relatively large proportion of tribals, who, because of their greater vulnerability and lesser political clout, easily succumbed to the mass sterilization zeal of India's family-planning programme (Bose 1983).[53] Interestingly, observing not only the comparatively low fertility but also its considerable decline in Orissa, especially in the face of a sluggish decline in mortality, some scholars have described the scenario as a 'premature fertility transition' (Padhi and Mishra 2000:25–6). Indeed, it is possible to imagine a few mechanisms by which in the relatively large tribal concentration areas such as Orissa a (comparatively) low overall population growth in the region was shaped. First, as will be shown in the following chapters (especially Chapters 3 and 4), the fertility of tribes has historically (and till recently) been, partly for their distinctive sociocultural and other settings, somewhat lower than their non-tribal counterparts. Furthermore, what is often additionally relevant to the tribes of Orissa and eastern region at large, is that their acute food deprivation and undernutrition did not only contribute to high mortality, but also dampened fecundity and fertility. Anyway, this question has remained an open area deserving painstaking research and serious attention.

In Bihar, the relatively high mortality (combined with low fertility) could be one major contributory factor for a slower growth rate of the population during 1961–71, while subsequent increases in the birth rate may have raised growth rates to the level of the national average. The information on demographic rates for Bihar is notoriously sparse for the period before 1981. During the subsequent periods, both birth and death rates have been clearly higher than the all-India figures. The estimates for 1997 show that the gap in birth rate (about 4 per thousand) between Bihar and India as a whole, is wider than for death rate (about 1 per thousand), with a much larger natural rate of population increase in Bihar in recent times. This said, the long-standing phenomenon of tribal out-migration is also a contributory factor for a record of relatively slow population increase in these two eastern states, particularly in Bihar during the first several decades

[53] That India's family-planning programme has till recently been characterized by an overwhelming predilection to mass sterilization is well-known. See Maharatna (2002) for a critique and literature cited therein.

after Independence.[54] (An analysis of demographic trends in Bihar and Jharkhand follows in greater detail in Chapter 5).

To summarize: a broad regional pattern of India's tribal population, with tribes concentrated (in descending order) in central, eastern (including northeastern), and western regions (these together constituting about 90 per cent of total tribal population), has remained largely unshaken since the early 1950s. However, there have been some recent changes in the tribal share of a few states. A distinct decline of the tribal share of eastern states (particularly Bihar and Orissa) over the post-Independence period is notable. The issue of enumeration biases (for example, over-return of tribals) has, of course, been of some significance in southern and western regions, especially up to 1981. But the explanation for the changes in the regional composition of the tribal population seems to lie in large part in inter-state differences in real demographic parameters (e.g. birth and death rates) and their trends, as well as in the pattern of spatial mobility and movement of tribal people.

It is important to note, however, that despite the number of scheduled tribes having recently exceeded 500, it is only a few major tribal groups that constitute a large bulk of the aggregate tribal population of the country. For example, as Table 1.3a shows, about nine major tribal groups constitute about half of the country's total tribal population, and they are concentrated mostly in the central, western, and eastern parts. They are: 1) Bhil, concentrated mostly in central and western regions (Gujarat, Madhya Pradesh, Rajasthan); 2) Gond, mostly concentrated in the central, western and eastern neighbourhood regions (Madhya Pradesh, Orissa, Andhra Pradesh, Maharashtra); 3) Santhal, concentrated in eastern states (Bihar, Orissa, Tripura, West Bengal); 4) Oraon, concentrated in eastern and central parts (Bihar, Madhya Pradesh, Orissa, West Bengal); 5) Mina, concentrated mostly in Rajasthan; 6) Munda, mostly in eastern parts (Bihar, Orissa, West Bengal, Madhya Pradesh); 7) Khond, concentrated mostly in central and southeastern regions (Andhra Pradesh, Orissa). It is of interest that the tribe-specific composition has remained broadly unaltered over the post-Independence period, despite a process of proliferation and formal recognition of many new tribal sub-groups. For example, the shares of Bhil and Gond populations have risen, admittedly marginally, with a similarly meagre reduction in the share of the Munda population.

[54] See, for example, Sharma 1994.

Table 1.3a Growth of population of numerically large tribes, 1941–91, India

Tribe	Regions of Habitation	Population				Average Annual Growth Rate (%)		
		1941#	1961	1971	1981**	1941–61	1961–71	1971–81
Bhil	Gujarat, MP, and Rajasthan	23,30,270 (9.2)	38,36,308 (12.8)	51,82,625 (13.6)	73,92,983 (14.3)	3.23	3.51	4.26
Gond	MP, Orissa, AP, and Maharashtra	32,01,004 (12.6)	39,91,767 (13.4)	48,09,165 (12.7)	73,87,376 (14.3)	1.24	2.05	5.36
Santhal	Bihar, Orissa, WB, and Tripura	27,32,266 (10.7)	31,54,107 (10.5)	36,33,459 (9.6)	42,60,842 (8.3)	0.77	1.52	1.73
Oraon	Bihar, MP, Orissa, and WB	11,22,926 (4.4)	14,47,429 (4.8)	17,06,091 (4.5)	18,65,779 (3.6)	1.44	1.80	0.94
Mina 3.61	Rajasthan		–	11,55,916 (4.0)	15,33,513 (4.0)	20,86,692	–	3.27
Munda	Bihar, Orissa, WB, MP	7,06,869 (2.8)	10,19,098 (3.4)	11,63,338 (4.0)	14,22,830 (2.8)	2.21	1.42	2.23
Khond	AP, Orissa	7,44,904 (2.9)	8,45,981 (2.8)	9,11,835 (2.4)	–	0.68	0.78	–
Boro@	Assam, WB, Tripura	5,94,979 (2.3)	3,51,583	–	–	-2.05	–	–
Varli		–	3,74,184	–	–	–	–	–

** (Roy Burman 1993:199); the percentage shares have been calculated by the present author on the total tribal population of India (exclusive of Assam).

AP – Andhra Pradesh; MP – Madhya Pradesh; WB – West Bengal.

Figures in parentheses are respective per cent shares to the total tribal population.

@ Borokacharis

These are the 1941 census enumerations of specific tribes on the criterion of 'tribal origin' (rather than tribal religion used in 1931 and before). Therefore, the respective shares of tribal groups have been calculated on the total enumerated tribal population of 25, 441,548, which is much larger than adjusted figure of 8,791,354 as presented in Table 1.1.

Source: Roy Burman 1993:199; Government of India (1961), Sinha (1986), Table 4.3, p. 47.

There are quite a few tribal groups that constitute slightly more than 1 per cent of the total tribal population, namely Ho (1.42) in eastern India and Naga (1.23) in the northeastern states.[55] Apart from them, there are numerous smaller tribal groups dispersed across the country. In fact, there are some 'small' so-called primitive tribes of which enumerated populations range from as low as 20. Table 1.3b presents a list of such small tribal communities for 1961, 1971, and 1981. Ignoring possible biases, both in enumeration and compilation of enumerated data from three censuses, it is clear that many such tribes are indeed on their way towards extinction. This often leads to an alarmist note on so-called 'vanishing' tribes, articulated mostly by anthropologists, whose professional and academic affinity chiefly lies in micro-level studies of small tribal communities. It should be noted, however, that such a phenomenon of shrinking population is often localized and specific to a very small group of tribal people who are situated in very special circumstances. These most vulnerable tribal groups, who are often branded as 'primitive tribes', currently number around 75, and constitute nearly 2 per cent of the total tribal population which include Onges, Shompens, the Greater Andamanese, Rajjis Didayis, Hill Korwas, and Bondas. To arrest the phenomenon of declining population size among these small tribal groups and to rehabilitate them is a challenging task, but little more than a mere recognition of this problem has so far been forthcoming. For example, the shrinking tribes (especially Onge and Jarawa) of the Andaman and Nicobor Islands have often been attributed to specific genetic factors that have been nurtured by complex and long-standing interactions between geophysical features, tribal seclusion, and forces of modernization.[56] Acute deprivation and extreme vulnerability to death and disease are held responsible for the declining numbers of small tribal groups of people in specific locations (e.g. Bhagwan 1997).

While this 'vanishing tribes' phenomenon deserves attention and effective public action in its own right, it is important not to be alarmist about the aggregate scenario of India's tribal population.[57] In fact,

---

[55] These figures are for 1971, and they are taken from Sinha (1986), Table 3.4, p. 35.

[56] See also Naidu 1998.

[57] One may well find some specific non-tribal groups (e.g. informal sector workers living in city slums or workers in mining and/or hazardous industries), who, because of extreme poverty and health vulnerability, also have an extraordinarily high mortality level, and hence low or even negative population

the major tribal groups (other than those small so-called 'vanishing' ones) are not experiencing a uniform positive rate of population growth. Table 1.3a presents information on the differential pattern of population growth between major Indian tribes (see Table 1.3a). While Bhil and Gond, dominant central and western tribes, have had an accelerating population growth since the early 1960s, Santhals, Mina, and Munda—mostly eastern tribes—have had far less population increase. The differential growth rates between major tribes broadly correspond to the regional differentials in tribal growth as presented in Table 1.2. This is, perhaps, a reaffirmation that the pattern of growth of the major Indian tribes shapes not only the pattern of growth of the aggregate tribal population, but its regional dimensions too. However, there are instances of a few tribes, which have experienced a vastly different pattern of population change vis-à-vis the general population of the same region or state. For example, the population of Katkari, an originally nomadic tribe of the Konkan region of

Table 1.3b Population of numerically small tribes

Community	1961	1971	1981
Arandan	44	5	95
Kochu-velans	47	8	–
Rona/Shova	23	12	–
Andamanesae	19	24	42
Sentinese	50	82	–
Shompen	71	92	223
Onge	129	112	97
Makkurun	248	275	–
Jarawa	500	275	31
Toda	716	945	–

Source: Roy Burman (1993), p. 199.

growth. For example, survival chances among black men in Harlem district of New York city—of course, vastly inferior to those of other districts of the city or of US as a whole—are even worse than in some of the poorest countries (e.g. Sen 1999:23 and references cited therein). But the alarmist attention that this fact invokes about the excessive death rate of black men of Harlem is not equally relevant to the entire black male population of America. Likewise, the 'vanishing tribes' phenomenon, being restricted to some specific subgroups under particular circumstances, should not necessarily make us alarmist about India's overall tribal population.

Maharashtra, has, according to census counts, been almost stationary during 1961–71, as compared to the nearly 2.3 per cent average annual growth rate of the aggregate tribal population in the state (Kulkarni 2002). While this could well be related to a relatively acute (absolute) material deprivation, other possibilities (for example, the effect of removal of area restriction) cannot be ruled out. Notably, in the following decade of 1971–81, the rate of growth of the Katkari population went up to about 2 per cent per annum, but remained far less than that of many other tribal communities and the total ST population of Maharashtra (about 10 per cent).

For example, among the major tribes of central and western states (e.g. Bhil, Gond, and Mina), the growth rates of population have been above the national average for the total population; and perhaps, more importantly they even accelerated in the post-Independence period, at least up to the 1980s. As noted before, this rapid growth of the tribal population, especially over several decades since Independence, seems to have been contributed by a relatively late occurrence of mortality improvement in the tribal population, and (somewhat relatedly) by 'pre-transition fertility rises' following a late beginning of modernization in several tribal communities.[58] In contrast, the major tribes of eastern India (e.g. Santhal, Oraon, Munda, and Khond) have experienced much lower rates of population increase in comparison with both the general population in this region and the tribes of western and central India. As was mentioned earlier, a relatively higher degree of under-enumeration of tribal people in this region, especially during the late 1970s, could be a factor, since recognition of tribal status continued here for longer on the basis of area restrictions after its official repeal in 1976 (see Roy Burman 1993:200). But this cannot be a full explanation for the comparatively slow population growth of eastern Indian major tribes. A relative mortality disadvantage among these tribes (vis-à-vis those of central and western India) is a likely contributor, especially over recent past, although the empirical base of this hypothesis is often not very strong.[59] A comparatively

[58] Note that the scope for additional improvement of mortality should be larger, if the initial level of mortality is higher. On this reasoning, a relatively late occurrence of mortality decline (as has happened among India's tribal population) should be associated with a (proportionately) larger pace of decline vis-à-vis non-tribal groups, thus contributing to a higher tribal population growth.

[59] Much of the literature portraying a picture of excessive mortality in many tribal areas is based on anecdotal/journalistic evidence, or is often deduced

low tribal fertility has also been a contributory factor. Furthermore, the migration propensity and flow of eastern tribes (both short- and long-term) can hardly be ignored, as there are some broad historical and sociocultural factors which have made the major east Indian tribes relatively more prone to long-distance migration and movement (e.g. Roy Burman 1993:201–2).

In sum, three major tribal groups, namely Bhil, Santhal, and Gond constitute nearly 40 per cent of the country's total tribal population, and this numeric dominance of just a few major tribes amidst hundreds of tiny groups and sub-groups across India has been continuing for a long time. This certainly adds substantially to the credibility and meaningfulness of an aggregative analysis of India's total population, despite the criticism often voiced by anthropologists.

Concluding Remarks

The study of Indian tribes for a long time, particularly since the early twentieth century, has remained the almost exclusive jurisdiction of anthropology.[60] Indeed, there has been a remarkable lack of inter-disciplinary ventures and feedback in understanding India's tribes. Indian tribal studies, mostly done by anthropologists, have remained largely closed to potentially useful influences from other disciplines such as economics and demography, resulting in the predilections, orientations, and methodology adopted by the Indian anthropological discourse on tribes. As the micro-level intensive participatory survey is the prime feature of the anthropological approach, a meticulous classification of individual tribes has been a major chunk of its output (e.g. Fuchs 1973 and the references cited).

---

indirectly from information on such indicators such as starvation, under-nutrition, and distress migration. However, mortality data even for the general population in eastern India often appears inferior, thereby contributing to the haziness of this entire issue of relative tribal mortality (we will return to this later). Tribal migration can complicate any explanation for slow population growth too.

[60] By the time of India's Independence, there emerged, to use T.N. Madan's words, 'a tripartite division in the study of culture in India. While Indology was regarded as the study of Pali and Sanskrit texts, sociology was seen as the study of Hindu society and anthropology as the study of Indian tribes' (Madan 1982:12).

The protracted debates and discussions on the notion or definition of 'tribe' is widely agreed to have been 'unproductive' and 'sterile' (Agrawal 1977; Misra 1977). The census (operational) approach to the definition and enumeration of Indian tribes—though it has, of course, drawn greatly on anthropological discourse—has been pretty handy for undertaking tribal research. Despite such issues as the tribe–caste continuum and/or nature of their interaction and co-existence and related debates, there are indeed, as will be clear in course of the present book, distinct overall tribal features that differentiate them from the aggregate caste population.[61] It is important to recognize (perhaps more explicitly than it has been so far) that it is not only valid, but also useful and necessary to identify the core common features (e.g. geophysical, sociocultural, and demographic) of India's aggregate tribal people.[62] For example, despite numerous named tribes classified meticulously, there have been just a handful of major tribes that constitute the bulk of the total tribal population of the country, with a similarly limited geographical concentration of their habitation. Indeed, analyses of tribal characteristics at an aggregate level should be no less viable, acceptable, and useful than those for the aggregate SC population, who have as many diversities across regions.

In fact, the pattern of the long-term trend of population growth has not been remarkably different between the tribal and general population since the 1880s, except for periods of historically contingent events (e.g. famines and epidemics) and for the effects of the lag in 'modernization' that percolated among tribes in contemporary times. This, of course, does not negate entirely the phenomenon of a shrinking population (and of some facing impending extinction), which one often comes across in the ethnographic-anthropological literature. But such evidence on highly select and small groups should not be used as a basis for spreading any alarmist message regarding the whole tribal population. Indeed, there has been a clear rising share of tribal population over several decades since independence at all-India level

---

[61] These, according to one author, include, for example 'cohesiveness, habitat, stress on clan structures, ethnicity bonds, higher position of women, strong sense of identity' (see Nathan 1997:23). However, there are other distinguishing features of tribal people, especially demographic and sociocultural (which will be illustrated throughout this book).

[62] This is not to question the usefulness or validity of anthropological methodology centred on micro-level intensive studies on individual tribal communities. This approach has, of course, its own value and usefulness.

and in many states, except a few in the eastern region, namely Orissa and Bihar. This was, initially, due to the emergent enthusiasm in many regions for a wider recognition and enumeration of tribes, largely because of declarations of discriminating protection and promises for several special benefits for ST people in the early decades after Independence. Thus such rises in the tribal share (e.g. due to the expansion of the ST list) in the first few decades were a result of redistribution of people in census enumerations. But sooner or later, there emerged more substantive and real (demographic) reasons for this trend of the rising tribal share to continue into the future. A much delayed occurrence of mortality and fertility declines and even an ongoing 'pre-transition fertility rise' following modernization and integration have held tribal growth rate at a higher level, thereby slowing down their demographic transition. However, tribal transition to a slower population growth has evidently been underway recently, although at a slower pace than that of non-tribal population.

What distinguishes the aggregate tribal population rather sharply from their mainstream counterpart is a more balanced sex composition and, by implication, less gender bias and discrimination in tribal societies, on the whole. However, recent declines in tribal female–male ratios seem to provide indications of a process of erosion of the tribal tradition of gender equity. Such tribal trends, their underlying forces and implications are indeed among the major concerns of the present book. The ongoing and long-standing assimilation and absorption processes (e.g. Sanskritization and Hinduization), along with overall development and integration of the economy, are making overall tribal gender relations conform increasingly to mainstream anti-female patterns. This and related issues, including implications for their demographic behaviour and outcomes, will recur throughout this monograph. The following chapter examines the relative position of the aggregate tribal vis-à-vis non-tribal (SC in particular) populations, in terms of broad socioeconomic indicators as well as some key female characteristics, which generally have some bearing on the nature of gender relations (e.g. women's status and autonomy), and on its cultural underpinnings.

2

Material Levels of Living and Sociocultural Moorings of Indian Tribes
A Comparative Perspective

From the foregoing overview of key historical (and anthropological) issues surrounding the notion of Indian tribes and their broad demographic trends, composition, and distribution, it appears that, notwithstanding substantial diversities and dispersion across the Indian subcontinent, the notion of India's aggregate tribal people (like other aggregate social categories) is useful. This is particularly because of the overall distinctiveness of aggregate tribes on various counts from their non-tribal counterparts. As will be clearer in the course of the book, the demographic analyses of India's aggregate tribal vis-à-vis other non-tribal groups like the scheduled castes (SC) can be highly illuminating, and indeed useful from the standpoint of framing policy.

The present chapter examines both the absolute and relative position of the aggregate tribal people (vis-à-vis non-tribal groups, especially SC) in terms of broad indicators of material well-being and of the sociocultural milieu. The economic and sociocultural features, though sometimes seem to have mutual interactions, are generally treated as two broad independent sources of influence on many facets of human attributes, including demographic behaviour. After presenting a comparative assessment of socioeconomic conditions between tribal and non-tribal groups (in the following section), this chapter (then) focuses on some key demographic and other characteristics of tribal and non-tribal women, with the aim of ascertaining differential patterns of gender relations and female status in these communities.[1] Despite acute material deprivation, the tribal sociocultural milieu as reflected in various characteristics of women appears superior, as they imply more balanced gender relations and greater female status and autonomy, as compared to their non-tribal counterparts.

Socioeconomic Conditions of the Tribal Population: Aggregative and Comparative Perspectives

Table 2.1 presents various socioeconomic indicators for the aggregate ST populations vis-à-vis non-tribal social groups, namely SC and others (i.e. non-ST/SC) in rural areas.[2] The country-wide information on several aspects of material well-being separately for these groups are periodically collected by large-scale sample surveys undertaken by the National Sample Survey Organisation (NSSO), and occasionally by the National Council of Applied Economic Research (NCAER). As can be seen, the proportionate shares of population and land areas are fairly balanced for the tribal people as a whole, while for the SC population, the proportionate share of land is far less in relation to their share in total population. Despite a larger increase in the SC share in total owned land areas over two decades since the early 1970s, the average land owned per household among the ST population (1.06 hector) in the 1990s is more than twice the average land size owned by an SC household (0.5 hector). Although the percentage of landless households was higher among the tribal population in the early 1980s,

---

[1] The status and position of women and gender relations in a given society are often thought to be an outcome, shaped by economic as well as intrinsic or independent sociocultural influences. But, since these two sets of influence sometimes appear to interact with each other, it remains difficult to settle which one is more foundational than the other. For example, women's greater 'economic worth' in terms of their participation in productive activities may well have some influence in shaping their higher status and autonomy, but specific sociocultural milieus could well circumscribe women's work participation outside the home, in the first place (more on this later).

[2] There are two major reasons why we focus on rural areas. First, an overwhelming majority of ST and SC people live in rural areas, with respective percentages of about 93 and 82. Second and somewhat relatedly, the rural (rather than urban) level of living would better capture the tribals' relative position (vis-à-vis SC groups) in terms of overall economic standing, since occupations, environment, and living conditions should be relatively more uniform across these social groups in urban areas than they are in rural areas.

it has declined to become close to the figure for the SC group by the 1990s. A relatively larger average ownership of land per ST household (compared with their SC counterparts) is of interest. Since tribal communities have been historically pushed to hills, mountains, forests, and other semi-arid areas, much of which were under common property resources; it was perhaps easier for the state to distribute ownership titles or informal/formal rights/leases on the ground of their long-standing habitation and livelihood. The need for state action to protect tribal people became increasingly pressing in the face of shrinking areas under forest and hills (the areas of predominantly tribal habitations), along with expansion of roads and various development projects in the post-Independence period.[3] Besides, various special protective and supportive measures taken by the government to uplift tribal communities should also have helped them—of course, in varying degrees across regions—get land ownership, though mostly in relatively harsh and infertile/arid locations. Indeed, this relatively greater tribal share of recorded land ownership seems consistent with a much higher proportion of 'cultivators' (farm labourers) to total 'main workers' among the tribal population as compared to that for the SC group (see Table 2.1).[4]

[3] See, in particular, Agarwal (1990, 1994) for a discussion on the nature of state actions in hastening the process of distributing land/property rights to tribals, especially after Independence, and also for a critical analysis of 'official' perceptions and predilections. As Agarwal has argued, by favouring the mainstream pattern of individual property rights, the state missed opportunities to introduce other modes of ownership (e.g. cooperative and/or collective) with greater potential gender-equity than what actually had happened. As for instance, shifts from *jhum* (shifting) cultivation (in which tribal women traditionally have a substantial role) to settled agriculture in such Indian regions as the northeastern states, 'could be accomplished through a more egalitarian and co-operative form of cultivation in a context where land was not traditionally private property, as among Garos' (Agarwal 1990:55).

[4] In fairly large parts of India (e.g. in western and southern India), the tribals did gain land ownership in the post-Independence period. They, as Guha concludes (in the context of tribal districts of Maharashtra), 'moved from being mainly landless to acquiring shares of land not much below their share of population', although a part of this land gain was offset by increased 'infiltration of the Scheduled Tribes by other groups' (Guha 1999:189, 193). In contrast, the tribals, for example, of Bihar and Orissa did not receive similarly effective protection, particularly against long-standing in-migration of non-tribals into the tribal belts and related adverse economic consequences for them, such as, exploitation, bondage etc.

Table 2.1 Socioeconomic indicators for tribal population: a comparative profile, all-India, 1970s to 1990s

	Scheduled Tribes		Scheduled Castes		Other	
	Early 1970s	Early 1990s	Early 1970s	Early 1990s	Early 1970s	Early 1990s
Land-ownership etc.						
Share in population (NSS data)	9.2 (1982)	10.0	16.8 (1982)	17.9	74.8 (1982)	72.1
Share in land (NSS data)	10.1 (1982)	11.7	7.9 (1982)	10.3	82.0 (1982)	78.0
Area owned per household (ha) (NSS)	–	1.06	–	0.5	–	1.01
% of 'Tribal Majority Villages' where majority do not practise settled cultivation	–	11.2 (1988–89)	–	–	–	–
% of landless households	17.1 (1982)	11.5	12.6 (1982)	13.3	10.2 (1982)	10.5
Inequality in distribution of land-holdings (Gini coefficient)	0.65 (1982)	0.64	0.65 (1982)	0.76	0.70 (1982)	0.70
Occupational Distribution						
% of cultivators to total main workers	57.6	54.5	27.9	25.4	45.1	39.7
% of farm labourers to total main workers	33.0	32.7	51.8	49.1	20.2	20.0
% of workers in household industry to total main workers	2.43^	1.42##	6.42^	3.31##	6.38^	3.46##

(Contd.)

Table 2.1 (contd.)

	Scheduled Tribes		Scheduled Castes		Other	
	Early 1970s	Early 1990s	Early 1970s	Early 1990s	Early 1970s	Early 1990s
% of other workers to total main workers	8.33^	11.48##	15.97^	20.29##	24.11^	30.0##
Access to Basic Amenities						
% of households having (NSS)						
safe drinking water	–	43.2	–	63.6	–	64.1
electricity	–	22.8	–	28.1	–	48.1
toilet facilities	–	7.2	–	11.2	–	28.6
% of villages having protected water source (NCAER)	–	22.5	–	45.5	–	48.0
Literacy/Educational Participation						
Literacy rate (all) (%)@	11.4	23.6 [29.6]	14.7	30.1 [37.4]	33.8	47.7 [52.2]
Male	17.6	32.5 [40.6]	22.4	40.2 [49.9]	44.5	57.6 [64.1]
Female	4.9	14.5 [18.2]	6.4	19.0 [23.8]	22.3	37.0 [39.3]
Enrolment ratio (%) (I–V)$	69.5	85.1	82.2	87.6	84.6 (all)	92.1 (all)
Male	–	96.9	–	96.6	–	100.8
Female	45.5	73.2	57.8	78.0	69.9	82.9
Dropout Rate (primary) (%)	74 (1981–82)	62.5	59.2	49.4	–	–
Male	–	61.9	–	45.9	–	–
Female	–	67.0	–	53.7	–	–

Income/Consumption etc.

% of population living in urban areas	3.41	7.4	11.9	18.7	22.8	29.2
Monthly per head consumer expenditure (rural) (Rs)	87.2 (1983) –	123.0 (1987–8) 234.3 (1993–4)	94.3 (1983) –	133.1 (1987–8) 238.9 (1993–4)	129.0 (1983) –	169.2 (1987–8) 302.1 (1993–4)
Mean annual (rural) income (Rs) (NCAER, 1994)	–	3643	–	3298	–	5088
Average daily earnings (Rs) (Rural labour households)	–	18.5 (Men) 14.9 (Women)	–	21.7 (Men) 15.7 (Women)	–	21.3 (Men) 15.2 (Women)
Average no. of earners per household (Rural labour households)	–	2.23	–	1.9	–	2.0
Poverty and Under-nutrition						
% of population below poverty line (NSS data)	68.1 (1977–8)	49.9 (1987–8)	56.3 (1977–8)	41.5 (1987–8)	–	–
Rural population (Total)	67.2 (1983)	62.7 (1987–8) 51.9 (1993–4)	61.6 (1983)	56.1 (1987–8) 48.1 (1993–4)	43.1 (1983)	39.4 (1987–8) 38.2 (1993–4)
Agricultural labour household	–	62.8 (1993–4)	–	59.2 (1993–4)	–	57.7 (1993–4)

(Contd.)

Table 2.1 (contd.)

	Scheduled Tribes		Scheduled Castes		Other	
	Early 1970s	Early 1990s	Early 1970s	Early 1990s	Early 1970s	Early 1990s
% of population below poverty line (NCAER data) (rural)	–	50.0 (1994)	–	50.0 (1994)	–	33.2 (1994)
% of children (under 4 years) severely malnourished (NFHS)	–	25.3 26.0 (1998–9)	–	23.7 21.2 (1998–9)	–	19.5 13.8 (1998–9)

* % of population literate aged 5 years and above ; ** % of population literate aged 7 years and above; # The category 'other' (i.e. non-ST/SC group) is exclusive of 'Neo-Buddhist' group, and that is why per cent shares across three social groups do not add up to 100; $ these data are respectively for early 1980s and the late 1990s; participation ratio in primary stage is number of students on rolls in classes I–IV divided by population aged 6–11 years; @ literacy rate calculated here (and up to the 1981 census) refers to the proportion aged 5 years and above. The figures within [] brackets are the respective literacy rates for 7 years and above age group, and this 7+ age literacy rate under non-SC/ST group refers to the total population; ^ refers to 1961 (% being out of main and marginal workers); ## refers to 1981.

Source: Thangaraj (1995); Chakrabarty and Ghosh (2000); Govt. of India, National Commission For Scheduled Castes and Scheduled Tribes (1996–97 and 1997–98, vol. 1); Tendulkar et al. (1993); Govt. of India (2000), Govt. of India (1995), Jabbi and Rajyalakshmi (1997), Govt. of India (1989); Govt. of India (1985), Table 1, p. 55; Suryanarayana (2001); Sarvekshana 17.2, 1993; Sarvekshana 21.3, January–March 1998; Singh, G. (2001).

However, a comparatively large size of landholdings per tribal household does not necessarily reflect their better economic standing and material well-being as compared to the SC people. There are several reasons for this. First, a relatively larger part of the land under tribal ownership is often in rocky, unirrigated, hilly terrain, which is far too difficult to put into productive use. Second, the average size of land-ownership does not say anything about the pattern of its distribution among the households. The estimated degree of inequality of landholding distribution (in terms of the Gini coefficient) was found very similar among ST and SC groups during the early 1970s, although it increased considerably among the SC group by the 1990s. However, as reflected in the proportionate shares of 'other' occupational categories, tribals appear to have been least involved in secondary- and tertiary-sector employments as compared to non-tribal groups.

Indeed, the tribals do not fare any better than other non-tribal communities in terms of basic indicators of human living (see Table 2.1). For example, tribals have the least accessibility to safe drinking water, electricity, and toilet facilities. This seems consistent with the fact that a comparatively large number of tribal households is located in remote and inaccessible areas (like hills and jungles). However, the relative inaccessibility of tribes to such civic amenities does not necessarily leave them vastly worse off than their SC counterparts, in terms of broad, economic, and livelihood patterns. Indeed, on the commonly used criteria of average monthly expenditure, income/ earnings, and headcount ratio of poverty, the position of Indian tribes, on the whole, appears similar to the levels of SC people. Although tribal figures on most of these indicators often appear worse than the respective SC levels, the differences have always been marginal, with even some indications, of late, of a narrowing tendency. Moreover, the differences in real levels of living between ST and SC groups may be even smaller than these marginal differences in numeric estimates of some economic indicators. For example, although consumption expenditure per head as estimated by NSS is reported to be lower for tribal people as compared to the SC group, especially in the earlier periods (see Table 2.1), this may not be so in terms of real consumption levels. This is because of the tribals' greater dependence on forest, food gathering, and common property resources with less degrees of monetary transactions and valuations.[5] Likewise, a slightly lower

[5] For an elaborate discussion on the reasons why real consumption in the past might have been underestimated by NSS data, as well as why current

average per capita earnings of tribal people may be (at least partly) compensated for, by their higher so-called 'earning strength' (i.e. the average number of earners per household). In a recent NCAER survey (1994), the poverty level among ST groups at the all-India level is found lower than that for the SC group, and mean incomes for the poor and non-poor alike under the ST category appear somewhat larger than the respective levels for the SC group (Chakrabarty and Ghosh 2000). Thus tribal people, as a whole, do not appear worse off than their SC counterparts on such economic criteria as average income and consumption, incidence of poverty, or even ownership of land, but this does not seem to have guaranteed them a similar quality of life.[6] As will be shown below, India's aggregate tribal people have fared distinctively worse than the SC group, especially over the recent past, in terms of two prime indicators of human development, namely, education and health.

Tribal Deprivation in Education

In terms of expansion of literacy and basic education—over the post-Independence period—the aggregate ST people appear clearly behind the SC group, although the goal of universal primary education is still quite distant, even for the latter group (see Table 2.1). In fact, the lack of educational progress is most glaring among females. Even as late as the 1990s, about four-fifth of the total female population aged above 5 years have remained illiterate among the SC/ST communities clubbed together, a fact which, while it deserves urgent attention and public action, often remains overlooked. Apart from the fact of tribal literacy being the least among the three groups compared in Table 2.1, the gap between tribal and non-tribal literacy rates widened during the 1970s and 1980s, especially for females. Researchers and official circles alike, have been adducing (rather casually and routinely) some

---

consumption data could be overestimates of real levels for India's general population, see Suryanarayana (2000).

[6] Although the recently implemented practice of official identifications of below-poverty-line households often portrays an overwhelming majority of tribal households (in poverty) in specific locations, they do not necessarily contradict our above point. First, these household-level poverty estimations by local level officials are often subject to various deficiencies, inaccuracies, and biases. Second, they refer to specific micro-level situations, not to overall levels relevant to our discussion.

proximate reasons for a slothful development of tribal education. They include language barriers, dearth of tribal teachers, the non-tribal teachers' unwillingness to work in tribal areas, unsuitability of course content and curriculum for tribal students, inappropriate and inflexible school calendars and hours, and so on (see e.g. Mohanty 2002; Mohana 1997; Srivastava 1997; Shah and Patel 1985, among others). While some of these immediate problems do deserve redress, systematic analyses of why they persist for so long, and of how can they be remedied, have rarely been attempted. Indeed there is substantial scope and need for systematic, comprehensive, and insightful studies to analyse and explain the deplorably slow pace of progress in the sphere of tribal education.

It is notable that official enrolment rates for tribal children in primary schools, though they were indeed much lower during the early 1970s than those for their non-tribal counterparts, are no longer very different from those of other groups nowadays (see Table 2.1).[7] Not only are the overall enrolment rates fairly similar among these three groups, but the female enrolment ratio has remained typically lower than that for males by about 20 per cent point during the 1990s. For the tribal group, this gender gap in enrolment in primary schools was largest during the 1990s, despite substantial increase in the overall enrolment ratio over last two decades. While the enrolment ratio is often a rather weak (perhaps even misleading) indicator of literacy achievement, the fact that the female enrolment ratio is found consistently smaller than that of their male counterparts certainly reflects a distinct gender bias in education.

[7] While the enrolment-ratio is simply the percentage of children in the relevant age group whose names are entered in school registers, these figures are very likely to be of limited reliability so far as the actual number of children attending school is concerned. This is because of the huge dropout and non-attendance rates, which we shall discuss in a little while. An in-built upward bias in school enrolment figures is a reflection of typical bureaucratic emphasis on records and numbers. For instance, if student strength is measured merely by the number of students enrolled as per register, it is likely to be lower than the number of students who are actually attending the school (not to mention far fewer who are effectively receiving education and being truly literate). In fact, this in-built tendency of the school management to exaggerate educational participation levels by using enrolment figures is often in congruence with parents' interest (not necessarily pecuniary) in getting children's names at least enrolled in school.

However, the achieved level of literacy, even when majority children are (officially) enrolled, depends substantially on the rate at which the enrolled students drop out of schools. It is clear that the incidence of dropouts is considerably larger among ST children than among their SC counterparts, although there has been a noticeable reduction in the dropout rate across both the groups over the 1970s and 1980s (see Table 2.1). While the relatively high dropout, non-attendance, or discontinuation rates for the ST group do seem to be major proximate reasons for their disturbingly low literacy outcome, there are exceptions. For instance tribals, particularly Santhals, in parts of Bihar appear to have fared better than the SC people in terms of enrolment and literacy rates (Jabbi and Rajyalakshmi 1997). Early and sustained missionary activities among specific tribes in particular locations, for example, might well have been instrumental in achieving more literacy (proportionately) among tribal children than among their SC counterparts. But what emerges overall, chiefly from recent large-scale surveys, for India as a whole, is a substantially higher dropout or discontinuation rate among ST children vis-à-vis SC and other non-tribal counterparts.

The NSSO 42nd Round (1986–87) collected detailed information relating to the major reasons for non-participation in education (see Table 2.2). As can be seen 'the other economic reason' (which perhaps subsumes the cost of education),[8] appears as one rather prominent reason cited for non-enrolment, and this is indeed the most commonly cited reason for males across all social groups. 'Not interested in education' as a reason for non-participation in education, though not very clear, is another frequently cited reason for non-participation in education; this, in fact, appears as the single most important reason cited for females of all social categories. Adducing 'not interested in education' for non-enrolment is a catch-all (and perhaps somewhat evasive) response, reflecting parents' attitude of low priority and perceived value of children's education, or sometimes a concealed expression of dissatisfaction with extremely inadequate and inconvenient schooling facilities. The participation in household economic/other useful activities, though frequently cited as a reason for non-enrolment, does not emerge as the most important reason.[9]

[8] The relevant NSSO report does not specify what exactly is included under 'other economic reason'.

[9] In fact, the number against 'participation in household economic activity' as a reason for non-enrolment may be somewhat inflated here in Table 2.2a,

This is noteworthy particularly in view of the long-standing and pervasive belief, especially among Indian official circles, that a substantial majority of children of poor households cannot attend schools chiefly because of their productive and useful role within the household economy. However, it is notable that non-availability of school facilities appears doubly important as a reason among ST groups as it is for non-tribal categories. This clearly indicates a relative lack of schooling facilities in the tribal-dominated areas. Also noteworthy is the largest gender gap found for the ST group, in terms of lack of interest in education as one reported reason for non-enrolment in schools, with the smallest (proportionate) number of tribal males falling under this category. This comparatively larger female lack of interest reported as a reason for non-enrolment, is particularly noteworthy. This is partly because this, being a rather vague response itself, is very likely to subsume familial/parental pressure and priority on basic education. For example, this particular sex differential in adducing this as reason for non-education does reflect at least partly a lower familial priority regarding girls' basic education. This is also of interest, since such anti-female differential is not readily in line with overall better gender relations among the tribal population.

It is often thought that children of school-going ages in poor households, who are compelled by necessity to spend a large part of their time on useful domestic activities and on productive activities within the household economy and organization, can barely have time to attend schools. Their relatively disadvantaged habitation, with extremely limited civic provisions (e.g. scarcity of drinking water), as well as low productivity and incomes are reasons for staying away from school.[10] A derivative of this line of argument would be the

---

as many of never enrolled persons, who are adults, generally do participate in economic activities. But if the enquiry were restricted only to children of school-going ages, this reason would have perhaps been cited even less frequently.

[10] The question of how important is children's net value in household economic and domestic activities has been debated and discussed over the preceding three decades, especially in the context of poor parents' fertility decisions and preferences (see Maharatna 1997 for a review of the issues and findings on this area). See also Dasgupta (1993) for a recent discussion (and evidence) on the economic role that children are often observed to play in poor households, which according to his argument, makes sense—from individual family standpoint—for a relatively high fertility (or slower pace of

hypothesis of the even higher economic utility of tribal children than their non-tribal counterparts, as many tribes inhabit a relatively harsh and more degraded environment.[11] But this has, so far, remained a hypothesis, which for the sake of confirmation (or rejection) calls for detailed and comparative studies. In fact, the long-standing argument or perhaps perception that children's (necessary) participation in household economic/useful activities is a big hurdle in spreading basic education, has recently come under serious doubt and scrutiny. Several recent studies have shown that a large majority of out-of-school children do not spend a significant number of productive hours in household activities (e.g. Maharatna 1997; Lieten 2000; Drèze and Sen 2002:154–59, and relevant references cited therein). The major factors that account for the high incidence of non-enrolment and dropouts include poor parents' lack of means to bear incidental expenses of schooling, limited accessibility (e.g. long distance to travel to school), and poor quality and value of teaching as perceived by the parents (PROBE Team 1999). A host of these factors together generate what has been summed up as the 'discouragement effect' on poor parents where sending children to schools is concerned (Drèze and Sen 2002:158). However, the recent introduction of mid-day meals at schools seems to have met with considerable success in improving school attendance (e.g. Drèze and Kingdon 2001), pointing to the huge potential of such innovative and committed state actions for quick expansion of basic education. The deepest educational deprivation in tribal communities has often been explained, echoing what Drèze and Sen (1995) attribute as a reason for India's failure in basic education, by a chronic government apathy and indifference, which seems consistent with the relatively little political clout of tribal minorities in the hierarchical (elitist) mainstream social structure. (e.g. Mohanty 2002; Choudhury 2001).

Many researchers often cite non-enrolment and dropout rates as indicators of low parental demand for children's basic education. But

---

fertility reduction), and lower literacy and school attendance among children in many developing countries.

[11] An illustration of how widely the actual time use on household activities like fetching fuel and firewood varies with diverse geophysical circumstances is that women in the plains of Uttar Pradesh spend about 50 minutes per day in gathering cow dung and agricultural waste for meeting fuel needs, while their counterparts in the hills need to spend nearly five hours a day for fulfilling firewood requirements (see Desai 1994:28 and references cited therein).

ironically, an acute dearth of school facilities and infrastructure, as well as poor quality of teaching (most of which can be taken care of by expanded fund allocation and/or political will and commitment) are among the major reasons adduced by parents for children's non-attendance and discontinuation in school.[12] For instance, according to the NCERT country-wide educational survey in 1993, about 46 per cent of government-run primary schools of the country do not have usable blackboards, about 50 per cent do not have adequate supply of dusters, and about 40 per cent do not even provide an adequate supply of chalk (NCERT 1999:127–8). The school facilities for tribal children are, on the whole, substantially worse than those for the general population. To illustrate differential (infrastructural) facilities for school education between tribal majority villages (TMV) and other villages at the all-India level during the late 1980s: while 36.6 per cent of all hamlets within TMV had reported having a primary school within the hamlet, this was about 52 per cent for other villages; while for 34.2 per cent of 'tribal hamlets' reported as having electricity, the corresponding figure for 'non-tribal hamlets' was about 60 per cent; the per cent of villages that reported any development of school building during the five years preceding the survey, was about 35 within TMV, while it was 51 per cent for other villages; and finally, the index of various infrastructural facilities available in TMV worked out to be 2.7, which was about half the index obtained for non-tribal majority villages.[13] As one recent study (based on the NCERT sixth educational survey data) has shown, on the criterion of school facilities existing within one's habitation, 'the scheduled tribes are a more disadvantaged population than the scheduled caste population' (Rao and Kulkarni 1999:179). In sum, therefore, the tribals on the whole, have had the greatest educational deprivation among all social groups considered here, and this can largely be attributed to a relative dearth of educational

---

[12] See, for example, PROBE Team 1999, Verma 2000, and also National Council of Educational Research and Training (1999) for information relating to the dearth of facilities available for the population group and its role in dampening parents' enthusiasm for sending children to schools.

[13] This information is based on NSSO 44th Round (July 1988–June 1989) survey as reported in Govt. of India (1994), NSSO, *Sarvekshana*, 18(1), 60th Issue. A 'tribal village' is defined as one that has more than 50 per cent ST population of the total; a 'tribal hamlet' is also one with more than 50 per cent of ST population.

facilities in tribal-concentrated areas.[14] The extremely slow progress of female education among tribal communities is not only distressing, but it is somewhat bizarre in light of the widely known notion of greater gender equities in tribal societies (we will elaborate on this later). We, therefore, turn our attention below to this aspect of female deprivation in school education among tribal communities.

Tribal Girls and School Education

Perhaps more disturbing than the slow expansion of tribal education is the fact that tribal females remain far behind their male counterparts in literacy and basic education. Indeed, tribal females have been almost always the least literate.[15] Since the male–female gap (in terms of percentage point) in tribal literacy is not much larger than those observed for SC and other groups, it may be tempting to take all this as a reflection of India's deep-rooted and pervasive gender inequality and anti-female cultural value system.[16] From another angle, however, this anti-female gender gap in tribal literacy sounds puzzling because, as was pointed out earlier, tribal communities traditionally seem to have much less anti-female discrimination and far more balanced gender relations than those found among the non-tribal mainstream population (including SC). While authors of several studies on tribal education have found and noted such distinct female disadvantage in tribal literacy as being surprising, the explanations are often casual and lack systematic rigour and depth of analysis. For example, 'economic [e.g. poverty, care of siblings, lack of parental motivation] and school related factors' [e.g. distance of schools, unsuitable timings, lack of physical facilities

---

[14] It is worth noting that this basic fact of relative neglect of educational provisions for tribes often remains camouflaged in various casual explanations made by official and non-official circles alike: for example, that tribals are not interested in the mainstream educational system; that their children have high economic value, which means they cannot afford to send their children to schools.

[15] For example, in a recent econometric analysis of primary household survey data collected from four villages and two urban wards in West Bengal, the estimated chance of dropping out from school for ST girls between 7 and 18 years has been found to be five times as large as that for general caste Hindu girls, and is two times larger than that of its SC counterparts (Sengupta and Guha 2002).

[16] An insightful discussion on the ways by which a low value attached to female education in a large part of the Indian subcontinent is linked to deep-seated features of gender inequality is available in Drèze and Sen 2002:161–62.

in schools] (e.g. Srivastava 1997) are mentioned almost routinely to explain female disadvantage in tribal education. But these problems seem pretty common for most children, male or female, tribal or non-tribal. There is hardly any systematic attempt to identify the specific tribal circumstances in which female children suffer relative educational deprivation compared to boys—about as much as their non-tribal counterparts suffer in the context of deep-rooted gender inequalities and a broadly patriarchal milieu.

The observed gender gap in tribal literacy is like an 'echo', or a reflection of the 'demonstration effect' or the 'convergence effect'[17] emanating from non-tribal mainstream culture and practices characterized by pervasive gender inequalities. Tribes may get, gradually and even perhaps unknowingly, influenced by what is happening around, by observing that non-tribal communities do not attach as much value to a girl's schooling as they do for a boy. In fact, a large chunk of India's rural tribal population live in village hamlets side by side with the mainstream non-tribal communities, and send their children to the same schools as their non-tribal counterparts, making a channel for tribal emulation of non-tribal cultural traits and inhibitions. However, this cannot be a complete explanation of the tribal gender gap in literacy. In fact, the question that remains is why tribals follow non-tribal cultural norms of gender inequality so closely only in the sphere of schooling and basic education, while the overall tribal socio-cultural milieu still appears much more balanced and much less discriminatory against females in most other aspects of life (say, in female work participation, female autonomy, intra-familial distribution of basic necessities of life, marriage norms and payments) as compared to non-tribal mainstream societies in much of India. There could be some female-specific factors (cultural or otherwise, which are not necessarily akin to standard mainstream anti-female features, and which lean towards 'balanced' gender relations) among tribal communities that might have been holding girls away from schools, as compared to boys.

One plausible hypothesis on this issue is that tribal girls generally bear a large brunt of domestic chores to enable grown-up members of both sexes of the family to do directly productive activities. The girls' greater involvement in domestic chores is also true among SC and, to

---

[17] This term has been introduced by Drèze and Sen (2002:244). Although they have used this in the context of trends of sex ratio, it refers to a broader issue of gender inequality and relations.

some extent, for other non-tribal communities too. But the much larger adult work participation rate among tribal females should perhaps make the supportive role of tribal girls at home more compulsive (and demanding) than that for their non-tribal counterparts. For example, the adult female work participation rate in Jhabua district of Madhya Pradesh—where 86 per cent of the population is tribal—is as high as nearly 80 per cent, and female school attendance rate is one of the lowest at 15.2 per cent in the age group 5–14 years (Jayachandran 2001:14–15). If this is to serve as an explanation of gender bias in tribal literacy, then it must imply that tribal girls are generally engaged more than boys to play such a supplementary role at home in order to release adult members for productive work. There is indeed fairly sound evidence that this is so. Across all social groups in India, it is generally the case that girls, as compared to boys, perform a disproportionately large part of household chores. According to the NSSO 42nd Round data, for example, among the total out-of-school children aged between 6 and 14 years in rural India, as many as 40 per cent of girls report 'domestic duties' as their usual activity status, while the corresponding figure for boys is only about 9 per cent.[18]

While the greater role played by girls in household chores is amply distinct across all social groups (see Tables 2.2a and b, and also Table 2.3), there are reasons why this role is even more pronounced and crucial in tribal households. Indeed, the responsibilities and work intensities in performing domestic chores is much larger in a typical tribal household scenario, in which adult members (including adult females) are busy with farming or similar directly productive activities. In contrast, non-tribal mothers and other adult females generally take part to a much smaller extent in agricultural or other directly productive work, especially outside the home. The non-tribal girls, therefore, often only supplement (rather than take on the full burden as tribal girls generally do) their mothers' and other adults' activities in managing domestic chores. For example, as shown in Table 2.4(a), the (proportionately) large number of tribal girls between 5 and 14 years, especially within the 'never attended school' category, help in household chores. It is notable that among female children (5–9 years) who were reported as 'not working', about 53 per cent have dropped out of schools in the ST group, while the corresponding figure for SC and other categories are respectively about 46 and 34 per cent (Table 2.4b).

[18] See Govt. of India (1989), Table 18 (p. A-II-79–80).

Table 2.2a Percentage distribution of persons never enrolled as students by reason, ST, SC, and others, rural India 1986–7

Reason for non-enrolment	ST		SC		Others*	
	Male	Female	Male	Female	Male	Female
Too young for school	4.4	3.7	4.7	3.6	6.4	3.9
Non-availability of school facilities	14.7	15.1	7.9	7.7	9.6	10.1
Not interested in education	19.8	30.9	23.1	31.1	26.0	33.0
For participating in the household economy	19.8	12.1	18.9	8.6	18.6	8.7
For other economic reasons	27.5	22.5	38.0	30.3	29.4	21.6
Busy attending domestic chores	1.6	7.1	0.9	9.2	1.3	10.6
Waiting for admission	0.9	0.3	0.8	0.5	1.0	0.6
Others	11.4	8.4	5.7	8.9	7.6	11.2
All	100	100	100	100	100	100

Table 2.2b Percentage distribution of dropouts by reason, ST, SC, and others, rural India 1986–7

Reason for dropout	ST		SC		Others*	
	Male	Female	Male	Female	Male	Female
Not interested in education or further education	26.0	36.3	29.6	32.6	26.0	33.3
For participation in household economic activity	29.8	12.0	22.2	8.5	27.5	9.4
For other economic reasons	20.4	14.0	25.6	18.3	19.6	14.5
Busy in attending domestic chores	3.24	15.8	1.4	13.7	2.1	14.2
Failure	13.4	13.7	15.8	16.4	19.4	16.9
Others	7.3	8.3	5.4	10.6	5.5	11.8
All	100		100	100	100	100

*exclusive of neo-Buddhists
Source: Govt. of India (1989).

Table 2.3   Percentage distribution of persons not currently enrolled as students by usual activity status by sex and age, rural India 1986–7

Usual activity status	6–11 years		12–14 years		15–17 years	
	Male	Female	Male	Female	Male	Female
Self-employed in agriculture	6.83	3.52	23.10	9.19	35.32	11.92
Self-employed in non-agriculture	1.47	0.76	3.88	1.62	7.13	1.80
Regular wage employment	1.28	0.32	5.21	1.08	6.06	1.42
Casual wage labour	4.72	2.88	20.46	12.19	30.78	16.10
Did not work but seeking and/or available for work	0.89	0.35	4.77	0.84	6.19	1.30
Attended educational institution	0.64	1.07	0.95	1.17	0.69	1.63
Attended domestic duties	8.07	23.36	9.72	53.22	4.75	60.07
Retired/pensioners	0.22	0.15	0.51	0.04	0.03	0.02
Others	75.88	67.59	31.39	20.66	0.05	5.66
All	100	100	100	100	100	100

Source: Govt of India (1989).

Table 2.4a   Per cent of children who 'help in household chores', by age (years), sex, and social group, rural India 1993–4

	Scheduled Tribes		Scheduled Castes		Others	
	5–9	10–14	5–9	10–14	5–9	10–14
Dropped out:						
Male	19.6	58.9	13.4	51.9	11.1	50.2
Female	24.3	67.6	18.3	66.6	18.2	64.8
Never Attended:						
Male	12.9	26.5	10.0	20.4	10.4	17.5
Female	9.1	39.1	10.9	30.7	17.0	28.7
Currently Attending:						
Male	19.0	37.5	17.5	37.1	16.1	34.3
Female	22.3	43.2	21.2	42.5	18.2	41.0
All Children:						
Male	–	44.8	–	40.8	–	36.8
Female	–	56.7	–	54.4	–	49.2

Source: Govt. of India (1997).

Since household chores are not included in classifying those who are 'working', it is highly presumable that a large number of those recorded as 'not working' are actually involved substantially in household activities. On this logic, the finding that only about 40 per cent of non-working tribal females aged 5–14 years are found currently attending schools, with the corresponding male figure being 56 per cent, indicates that girls bear much a larger share of household responsibilities and chores than boys do in tribal societies. While this is true for SC and other groups too, the implied relative share of girls in the burden of domestic chores appears largest for the ST category (Table 2.4b). Note that the gaps between tribal and non-tribal groups in terms of the proportion of non-working children attending schools, are larger for girls than that for boys.

Table 2.4b   Per cent distribution of children who are not working, by status of school attendance, age (years), sex, and social group, rural India 1993–4

	Scheduled Tribes		Scheduled Castes		Others	
	5–9	10–14	5–9	10–14	5–9	10–14
Dropped out:						
Male	40.0	16.4	35.0	16.2	25.9	10.0
Female	52.6	31.8	46.3	36.4	34.3	25.8
N\ever Attended:						
Male	3.1	3.0	3.9	2.8	3.7	2.6
Female	4.0	2.9	4.3	3.8	3.9	3.2
Currently Attending:						
Male	53.9	58.1	59.5	66.1	69.2	76.6
Female	39.6	38.2	47.0	43.3	60.3	58.6

Source: Govt. of India (1997).

It is of interest to examine why girls, even more so among tribal societies, are generally made to bear greater responsibilities than boys of taking care of household chores. It is worth noting that even in matrilineal tribal communities with land rights vested in females and with their attendant high status, authority and freedom, the overall pattern of gender division of labour typically assigns to women the responsibilities for domestic work and child care (Agarwal 1994:146–51). Domestic chores such as fetching water and fuel wood, cooking, looking after younger kids are considered more suitable to females (at least in a broad sociocultural sense). Thus, the observed gender bias in tribal education may not necessarily reflect a socioculturally low female status and deeply unequal gender relations, as is often the case for mainstream (non-tribal) people, of which one concomitant is lower perceived value of female education (e.g. Drèze and Sen 2002, and references cited). Let us re-quote here from Boserup (1970:16) what Margret Mead wrote on this subtle issue: 'The home ... into which men bring the food and women prepare it, is the basic common picture the world over. But this picture can be modified, and the modifications provide proof that the pattern itself is not something deeply biological.' However, Boserup, who has portrayed women as being no less (sometimes even more) productive than men in provisions of food (for example, in large parts of Africa and elsewhere), could not help branding 'the preparation of food as a monopoly for women in nearly all communities' (Boserup 1970:16).[19]

The greater educational deprivation of tribal females (vis-à-vis male counterpart) could possibly arise from a culturally and perhaps even partly biologically shaped gender division of activities, rather than a deep unequal (anti-female) valuations of gender roles, as is generally the case with the mainstream non-tribal population.[20] By sharing the larger burden of domestic chores (but not necessarily by spending overall longer hours of work per day than the boys), the tribal female children are more disadvantaged when it comes to attending school, since household chores, unlike directly productive activities, are hardly season or weather specific, and thus can hardly offer any respite or any favourable seasons and timings.[21] To illustrate the female child's larger

[19] Indeed this specific pattern of gender division is often viewed as one distinct illustration of persistent gender inequity in family oriented institutions—even in Western and other developed societies (McDonald 2000).

[20] In this context one can hardly deny the possibility—even in tribal communities—of what Amartya Sen (1985) calls 'adapted perception' beneath which some degree of 'conflict in the interest between sexes' exists.

[21] For example, a local micro-level field survey among 200 tribal girls aged 7 to 15 years in five tribal villages of Nanded district of Maharashtra shows that they spend nearly four and half hours per day on average on household chores, and this was the principal work activity for as many as 91 per cent of girls (Rodge et al. 2001). It is presumably very difficult to reshuffle these four to five hours across the day so that these girls can attend school. Furthermore, there is extremely limited leverage for adjusting to the calendar of school days and timings over the year to allow these girls to attend schools for specific months. This is because the time needed for domestic chores has relatively

role in the domestic front (vis-à-vis male counterparts), a large-scale household survey in Madagascar in the 1990s shows that while out-of-school girls spend on an average as much as 21.1 hours per week on all households tasks, the corresponding figure for boys who do not attend schools is only about 9 hours (Bredie and Beeharry 1998:Table 5c). This amply confirms that girls, unlike their brothers, do perform a lot of household chores, which restrict their participation in education.[22] Indeed, female literacy and school attendance (even at primary level) rates are remarkably lower than those for males in much of sub-Saharan Africa too, where gender relations (proxied by sex-ratio of population) are far more balanced, and female work participation rates are also quite high.[23] And higher female work participation rates among tribal communities of India—and among people of sub-Saharan Africa too, who are fairly akin to Indian tribal people and culture as well—could be seen as a source of their higher status and advantage (more on this later).

While tribal girls suffer a relative disadvantage in school education (vis-à-vis non-tribal girls) because of their specific, culturally ordained, role of performing household chores, especially when adult females are busy with directly productive work, there are other gender-specific obstacles to tribal girls' schooling. Although many gender-specific obstacles, such as, risk of sexual abuse are common across communities (e.g. Desai 1994:32), they may get even more pronounced in typical

---

little seasonal variation compared to what is as for many agricultural activities. Nor can the time schedule for various domestic chores be flexible enough for girls to attend both school and do domestic chores. This is why the girls, who perform more domestic chores, have a greater disadvantage where attending school is concerned, as compared to those who participate more in directly productive activities.

[22] Even when boys work, the work performed by them, unlike girls' household activities, is often compatible with schoolwork. One field-based study on school education in Ethiopia writes: 'For example, they [boys] can study while they are working in the fields looking after cattle, whereas girls are unable to do so while performing their household chores, which do not give them a breathing space' (Rose and Tembon 1999:96).

[23] For example, the female rate (percentage of age group) of enrolment at primary level was found to have been only 60 per cent for sub-Saharan Africa as a whole, while the corresponding figures were 82, 89 and 105 respectively for South Asia, Middle East, North Africa, Latin America and the Caribbean (World Bank 1995: Table 28). See also papers in Heward and Bunwaree (1999).

tribal circumstances. For example, since schools in the tribal areas are generally few in number, and hence relatively less accessible than they are in non-tribal areas, tribal girls are faced with greater disadvantage in attending schools, since their parents become more apathetic about their daughters' schooling.[24] However, there are examples such as Himachal Pradesh where inherent gender-specific obstacles to female education, both sociocultural and biological, have been largely overcome by relatively committed state action and spontaneous cooperation and participation of people (e.g. Chakrabarti and Banerjea 2000; also Drèze and Sen 2002:177–84). To summarize: the persisting wide gap between tribal male and female educational level and participation seems to be largely an outcome of the tribal girls' crucial role of performing household chores in an overall context of very sparse provisions for schooling. This gender differential in tribal education should, perhaps, not be equated with that of the non-tribal population, though it is marked by a pervasive gender inequity, a low social position and status of females, and a high degree of patriarchy. This said, the tribal peoples' ongoing internalization of such mainstream anti-female sociocultural attitudes and practices should not be ignored.

Tribal Deprivation in Health

After discussing the dimensions of tribal deprivation (in comparative terms) in elementary education at an aggregate level, we now examine the relative position of Indian tribes in the sphere of another important aspect of human well-being, namely health and mortality. Health and mortality are being increasingly accorded importance as a major goal of economic development and progress.[25] Table 2.5 presents information on mortality and morbidity as well as on health care provisions and their utilization pattern for ST, SC, and other groups. In fact, the large-scale sample surveys of NSSO and NCAER during the 1980s and 1990s amply reflect the relatively disadvantaged position of ST people in terms of health infrastructure and provisions (see Chakrabarty 1998; Singh 2001). For example, about 43 per cent of

[24] For parents in many African countries, one prominent reason for not sending daughters to school (apart from the opportunity cost related to their role in domestic front), is the risk of their unwanted pregnancy, which may result in lowering of the daughter's value in the marriage market, and hence reduce the bride-price (see Odaga and Heneveld 1995).

[25] See Sen (1998) for an insightful discussion on the importance of mortality as an indicator of development.

Table 2.5 Morbidity, and health facilities: A comparative
profile at all-India level

	Scheduled Tribe (ST)	Scheduled Caste (SC)	Others (Non-ST/SC)
Per cent distribution of untreated spells of sickness (1986–87) across social group by reason[#]:			
non-availability of medical facilities	28.9	15.6	55.3
financial reasons	12.6	27.8	59.2
lack of faith in medical system	8.8	18.3	72.8
all	11.4	20.7	67.4
Per 1000 distribution of tribal and non-tribal villages by distance from nearest Primary Health Centre/ Sub-centre (Hospital), 1988–89:			
5–10 km	107 (66)	230 (193)[*]	
above 10 km	426 (816)	129 (275)[*]	
Per cent of 'SC and ST villages' for which no subcentre/hospital within 5 km, 1994	75.0	65.2	58.1[**]
Per cent of ante-natal immunization, 1994 (rural)	42.2	57.6	57.5
Average total expenditure (rural) per hospitalized case over last one year by type of hospital (Rs) (1995–96):			
Public Hospital	1262	1778	2534
PHC	851	540	801
Public Dispensary	2015	1693	1960
Private Hospital	2711	8362	3684
Any Hospital	1636	3942	3133
Per cent distribution of hospitalized cases across social groups by type of hospital (1986–87)[#]:			

(Contd.)

Table 2.5 (*contd.*)

	Scheduled Tribe (ST)	Scheduled Caste (SC)	Other (Non-ST/SC)
Public Hospital	5.5 [8.4]	20.2 [24.3]	73.8 [67.2]
PHC	10.2 [15.0]	20.6 [25.2]	68.7 [59.4]
Private Hospital	3.4 [4.0]	12.3 [16.0]	83.8 [80.0]
Nursing Home	1.0 [1.9]	7.9 [20.5]	90.7 [77.5]
Charitable Inst.	4.9 [6.3]	19.9 [25.9]	75.2 [67.7]
Others	3.6 [5.4]	21.5 [14.7]	74.6 [79.8]
All	4.8 [6.3]	17.1 [20.3]	77.6 [73.3]

*Includes all non-tribal villages.
**All villages.
#The category 'other' (i.e. non-ST/SC group) is exclusive of 'Neo-Buddhist' groups, and that is why per cent shares across three social groups do not add up to 100. The figures within [ ] brackets are respective figures obtained from the NSS 52nd Round during 1995–96.

Source: Thangaraj (1995); Chakrabarty and Ghosh (2000); Govt. of India, *National Commission For Scheduled Caste and Scheduled Tribes* (1996–7 and 1997–8, vol. 1); Govt. of India (1989), Govt. of India (1998), NSSO, 52nd Round (July 1995–June 1996), Report No. 441, Tables 19, 12.

'tribal villages' were located beyond 10 km of the nearest primary health centre/subcentre, as compared to only around 13 per cent being similarly distant from the nearest health facility among the 'non-tribal' villages. Even around the mid-1990s, as many as 75 per cent of 'ST villages' are reported to have had no access to any health centre/ subcentre within 5 km distance, and the corresponding figure for 'SC villages' is 65 per cent. The differential in health care accessibility between tribal and non-tribal peoples, more realistically, should be even larger than what the information on average distance from health centres by itself suggests. This is because traversing and reaching a health centre is substantially more difficult and hazardous from tribal villages, as they are situated in relatively more remote, inaccessible areas with fewer road and communication facilities.[26]

---

[26] In the absence of readily available information on the existing differential in road facilities between tribal and non-tribal villages, let us report the differential in the development of link roads over five years preceding the survey year of 1988–9 as an indication of greater relative vulnerability of tribal areas in terms of transport and communication: while about 30 per cent 'tribal majority villages' reported some development of link roads, the corresponding

The comparative inaccessibility to health care facilities for tribals also manifested in the extent and pattern of utilization of health care provisions: out of 100 reported cases of hospitalization in rural India, the ST share in 1986–7 was less than 5 per cent, about half the percentage share that they constitute in the total rural population (according to the 1991 census). For the SC group, the share in hospitalization cases is almost coequal with their share in total population. In fact, the tribals' relative position in utilization of hospital services is even in sharper contrast with the non-ST/SC group, of which the share in total hospitalized cases (at nearly 78 per cent) was larger than their share in the total population by about 6 per cent point. And an overwhelming majority of hospitalization cases in private hospital and nursing home are constituted by the non-ST/SC group, with an almost negligible proportion for ST group. It was only in the primary health centre that the tribal share in total hospitalized cases was commensurated with their share in the total population.

The finding of proportionately fewer hospitalization cases among the ST group may appear a priori as a reflection of a relative health advantage, but this could be an indication of a relative tribal disadvantage in utilization of health facilities and infrastructure. Although there has been some amelioration of this tribal disadvantage in utilization of health care in the 1990s, the extent of improvement has been rather meagre (see Table 2.5). Moreover, while both SC and other non-tribal groups seem to have augmented their utilization of private health care provisions, it is only the ST group whose share in government health centres has increased over the period. This seems to confirm the relative (and perhaps increasing) tribal disadvantage in the utilization of health care services, since the quality of care in government health centres and hospitals in many Indian states and even at all-India level has worsened, especially in the recent past.[27]

---

figure for other villages was nearly 45 per cent (Govt. of India, NSSO, *Sarveskshana*, 18(60), 1994, p. S-194–5).

[27] Although it is extremely rare to find a systematic comparative analysis of the quality of health services and its trend between public and private sectors, there are some broad indicators by which a direction of trends in hospitals and health centres can be judged, especially in the public sector. For example, a discernible declining trend in the share of government expenditure on public health, combined with stagnant level of per capita expenditure, since the early 1980s (e.g. Narayana 2001) has adversely affected the quality of health care in

The average expenditure incurred per hospitalized case turns out to be the largest in the private sector and strikingly enough, the expenditure incurred per case in private hospitals is not only largest for the SC group, but is about three times larger than the amount spent on average by ST and non-ST/SC groups. This seems consistent with a substantial rise in the SC share in the proportionate utilization of private hospitals, signalling a greater incidence of sickness deserving hospitalization among SC communities as well as a larger rise in affordability of private health care as compared to the ST group.

A decline in the share of non-SC/ST groups in hospitalization cases (in all types of hospitals, except charitable institutes) from the 1980s to the 1990s, along with corresponding rises in the respective shares of ST and SC, is of interest. The changes in group-composition of hospitalization cases as well as the changes in their public–private mix among ST, SC, and other categories should be the outcomes of (at least) three sets of forces, namely a) the change in the group composition of the population; b) differential change in the health profile (or more specifically in the disease and illness pattern) of these groups; and c) inter-group differential changes in the incidence of hospitalization as well as in its private–public hospital composition. For example, the increased shares of ST and SC groups in hospitalization cases in rural India between 1986–7 and 1995–6, as are shown in Table 2.5, could just be a reflection of enhanced shares of these two groups in the total rural population (as was noted earlier), all other things remaining the same. But the increased proportions of hospitalization cases for ST and SC groups could well be due to their enhanced accessibility to hospitalization facilities and/or due to a change in their disease profile, comparatively tilted towards hospitalization. To identify the precise effects of these various influences on the net differential changes in the shares of hospitalization cases is difficult, particularly due to the limited information available on the overall pattern and differentials in health/disease profiles of these three groups.

It is notable that about 55 per cent of reported spells of sickness that is untreated due to non-availability of medical facilities belong to the non-ST/SC category, whereas about 29 and 16 per cent of such cases were reported by ST and SC groups respectively. The fact that ST and SC groups attribute cases of untreated sickness far less frequently

---

public hospital and health centres at an all-India level. On a distinct deterioration of quality of services in public health centres and related aspects, see Drèze and Sen 2002:201–07 and literature cited there.

to non-availability of health facilities than non-ST/SC groups does, is surprising, especially in the light of far lesser accessibility to health provisions for ST and SC groups. This anomalous revelation is similar to the well-known 'puzzle' in Kerala where a record of low mortality rate coexists with a high (reported) morbidity level. The similarity between these responses seems to lie in a greater awareness of the non-SC/ST group about the extent and reach of health provisions as well as about their deficiencies. This group, therefore, tends to attribute untreated sicknesses to non-availability of facilities, despite much better provisions/accessibility for them, compared to ST and SC groups. Thus a greater health and morbidity awareness among the non-ST/SC people who are far more educated and articulate than the ST and SC groups, could well be the clue to their greater reporting of non-availability of health facilities.

More important is the finding that as many as 73 out of 100 spells of sickness untreated owing to 'lack of faith in the medical system' came from non-ST/SC groups, and only about 8 and 19 cases were shared by ST and SC categories respectively. This does not support the commonly held notion that tribal communities have a general disbelief and apathy towards the modern medical system of treatment. While there could well be some specific tribal groups in particular locations, who still may appear quite averse to modern modes of treatment, this is not a general scenario of tribal life of India. The casually (and commonly) alleged tribal disbelief in the modern allopathic medical system is increasingly proved to be a myth or artefact of 'over-generalizations'. As a recent study on health status and health care facilities in Orissa highlights, a great majority of the tribal population (e.g. about 80 per cent of treated cases), according to the NSSO special survey on individual tribes during 1988–89, go in for the allopathic system of treatment (Padhi and Mishra 2000:10). Indeed, of late, the tribal research literature is increasingly recognizing and exposing the long-standing myths about tribal health (see relevant papers in Basu 1994b).

What emerges clearly from our foregoing discussion is that in the overall context of large-scale human deprivation in India, the tribal population is even worse off than their SC counterparts, particularly in terms of health care and basic education. In fact, tribals, who generally inhabit relatively harsh and less accessible areas, are the most deprived section so far as the distribution of infrastructural facilities and provisions of basic amenities (particularly those for education and health) is concerned. However, the overall economic standing (based on landlessness, per capita income, occupational pattern, and incidence of poverty) of the aggregate tribal population is not remarkably different from that of the SC group. Indeed, researchers often club SC and ST people together as the most economically deprived social groups. However, as was indicated in the preceding chapter, despite their similar economic position, these two groups differ substantially in terms of sociocultural features, especially in gender relations. A careful comparison of these two communities can give us a deeper understanding of the link between cultural features and demographic behaviour. Consequently, the following section examines differentials in some key demographic features, which presumably have differential sociocultural underpinnings (especially pertaining to status and autonomy of women) between ST and SC communities.

Some Key Demographic and Other Characteristics of Tribal Women: A Comparative Perspective

It is well established now that the link between demographic behaviour and sociocultural characteristics in a society is often mediated, to a considerable extent, by patterns of gender relations (particularly, the role, status, and autonomy of women). With this perspective, we analyse some important demographic and related features of tribal women. The reason for focusing on female characteristics is twofold. First, the relatively high status and autonomy of tribal women stands out among sociocultural and related features that distinguish the tribal population from the aggregate non-tribal community (including the SC group) (for example, Nathan 1997a,b; Maharatna 2000, 1998). Notwithstanding the forces eroding the traditional gender equities within tribal communities, a relatively higher position and comparative freedom of tribal women vis-à-vis their non-tribal counterparts seems unquestionable, although there has been some scepticism (especially from a feminist angle) about these notions (for example Unnithan-Kumar 1997; Kelkar and Nathan 1991). While higher female labour force participation is generally seen as conducive to higher female status and autonomy (Dreze and Sen 2002), tribal women, as we will show a little later, participate substantially in directly productive activities. However, a high female labour participation is seen as a concomitant of their habitat and the material base of tribal economy (for example, dependence on forests, shifting cultivation, food-gathering, horticulture, labour shortage, which are are associated with relatively high women's labour contribution [Boserup 1970]). But as will be clearer later, more balanced gender relations and greater gender equities in tribal societies as compared to the non-tribal mainstream is a foundational sociocultural mooring in which the tribal women's large productive role and economic worth is warranted and logical. Sharp differences in the extent of labour participation between tribal and non-tribal females exist even when both share the same geophysical context and similar material base of the economy. Furthermore, an extensive emulation of high caste Hindu social norms by lower caste and tribal people (as visualized in the so-called Sanskritization process), is generally believed to have been responsible for a considerable withdrawal of womenfolk from directly productive work (for example, cultivation) in specific Indian regions. Thus, household decisions on whether women can participate in directly productive and 'gainful' activities outside home falls under the purview of the sociocultural domain.[28]

Second, gender relations (including female status and autonomy) have, of late, been accorded a key significance in shaping demographic outcomes (for example, fertility, mortality, and infant mortality rates) and its transition.[29] It is the women's agency that is often found to play a crucial role in achieving some broad indicators of human development, especially in contemporary developing countries (e.g. higher life expectancy, lower fertility, lower infant mortality, and better nutrition). While this literature and discussion has mostly referred to the mainstream population and society, these findings and insights could indeed be sharpened and enriched by linking them to differential gender relations between tribal and non-tribal population groups. For example, the so-called women's agency (e.g. through female autonomy and decision-making power) is often found stronger when the levels of literacy and basic education are high, especially among females.[30] But as will be illustrated below, tribal women, though the least literate,

[28] There is considerable anthropological literature on the connection between women's relative work contribution and their status (see, for example, Ember 1983 and literature cited). While a host of issues are involved in explaining the positive association between women's labour participation and their autonomy and status, the balance of evidence posits this connection as often mediated by other factors, such as where females work.

[29] See, for example, Desai 1994; Sen 1999: chap.8 and the literature cited therein; Dyson and Moore 1983; Basu 1992 among others.

[30] See, for example, Sen 1999; Drèze and Sen 1995; Drèze and Murthi 2000; Murthi et al. 1995 among others.

possess a considerable agency potential with their culturally ordained larger female autonomy and involvement in decision-making.[31] This is, of course, not to undermine the importance of female education in enhancing the agency role; it rather reinforces its importance by drawing on hitherto neglected and less publicized tribal society and culture. Given these above points as a background, see Table 2.6, which has relevant census-based information on females of three groups, namely ST, SC, and general.

Female Age at Marriage: Trends and Implications

Information on age at marriage is not always accurate, as the majority do not keep an exact record of age. However, since the age of female marriage has some cultural underpinnings, the reported mean age at marriage, though largely based on guesses and memories, can be expected to approximate closely to the culturally ordained norm.[32] As can be seen from Table 2.5, the mean age at which tribal females get married, is almost always higher than that of their non-tribal counterpart, especially as recorded in the 1971 and 1981 censuses. The age at which females generally get married in much of the Indian subcontinent has historically been shaped by the sociocultural ethos under broad Hindu religious traditions. As is well-known, the practice

[31] This does not undermine the role of female education in enhancing female status and autonomy. In fact, the expansion of female education can augment the women's agency role through promotion of more scientific attitudes and information. Again, whether and how far the alleged greater autonomy and freedom of tribal women is real and effective, has been put into question by researchers, especially those with a feminist bent.

[32] There is an alternative (somewhat indirect albeit fairly reliable) method of estimating the mean age of marriage, the so-called singulate mean age at marriage, which is based on data on the age distribution of women by marital status. Although this estimate is entirely based on census age distribution, it is hardly possible to estimate the singulate mean age at marriage for tribal and lower caste women for the post-Independence censuses, in which, though information on female age at first marriage is available, the information on age distribution by marital status is mostly unavailable. In contrast, this method is perhaps the only option for calculating mean female age at marriage in the pre-Independence period as age distribution data for women by marital status is provided, but not direct information on age at first marriage. Consequently, we base our analysis for the post-Independence period on directly calculated mean age at first marriage, though later we will undertake an analysis based on the singulate mean age at marriage for tribal and other social groups.

(Contd.)

Table 2.6 Some demographic and other characteristics of Tribal women: A comparison with Scheduled Castes (SC) and general populations, major states, India, 1961–91

State	Social Group	Female Mean Age at Marriage#				Female Literacy Rate*		Female Work-Participation Rate@		Sex-Ratios (Females per 1000 Males)			
		1971	1981	1991	1998–99**	1961	1991	1961 (f/m)	1991 (f/m)	1961	1971	1981	1991
India	SC	14.9	16.1	16.1	16.23^	2.45	19.03	34.4 (0.58)	25.9 (0.51)	957	935	932	922
	ST	16.4	17.1	17.1	16.15^	2.43	14.49	52.0 (0.85)	43.7 (0.8)	987	981	983	972
	ALL	15.4	16.5	17.4	17.35^	12.95	32.16	28.0 (0.49)	22.3 (0.43)	941	930	934	927
Andhra Pradesh	SC	14.2	15.5	–	14.76	2.24	17.11	56.5 (0.75)	46.7 (0.84)	980	972	971	969
	ST	16.4	16.7	–	14.73	1.14	6.87	56.7 (0.86)	50.6 (0.88)	987	981	962	960
	ALL	14.5	15.8	16.6	16.55	12.03	27.31	41.3 (0.66)	34.3 (0.62)	981	977	975	972
Assam	SC	15.5	–	17.1	–	12.42	34.3	26.0 (0.47)	18.1 (0.37)	882	768	–	919
	ST	18.2	–	18.5	–	13.52	30.93	48.6 (0.90)	33.8 (0.7)	956	970	–	967
	ALL	16.4	–	18.2	–	15.98	34.29	30.9 (0.57)	21.6 (0.44)	869	896	910	923
Bihar	SC	13.7	15.5	15.5	15.77	0.82	5.43	40.3 (0.70)	23.5 (0.47)	1033	981	966	914
	ST	16.5	17.3	17.2	16.41	2.28	11.75	56.0 (0.90)	37.7 (0.71)	1014	1003	993	971
	ALL	14.5	15.9	16.9	16.99	6.89	18.05	27.1 (0.49)	10.0 (0.31)	994	954	946	911
Gujarat	SC	16.5	18	18.2	16.97	4.51	37.71	33.6 (0.66)	25.9 (0.54)	971	950	942	925
	ST	18	18.7	–	16.78	1.28	19.64	49.1 (0.84)	46.9 (0.83)	970	968	976	967
	ALL	16.9	18.2	18.9	18.58	19	40.62	27.9 (0.52)	26.0 (0.48)	940	934	942	934
Haryana	SC	14.9	16.3	16.9	17.27	–	18.86	–	11.6 (0.24)	–	871	864	860

Table 2.6 (contd.)

State	Social Group	Female Mean Age at Marriage#				Female Literacy Rate*		Female Work-Participation Rate@		Sex-Ratios+ (Females per 1000 Males)			
		1971	1981	1991	1998–99**	1961	1991	1961 (f/m)	1991 (f/m)	1961	1971	1981	1991
	ST	–	–	–	–	–	–	–	–	–	–	–	–
	ALL	15.2	16.5	17.6	18.04	–	32.72	–	10.8 (0.22)	868	867	870	865
Himachal Pradesh	SC	15.6	16.4	16.9	–	1.5	33.73	57.6 (0.88)	35.6 (0.70)	932	950	959	967
	ST	18.1	18.3	18.3	–	1.45	25.69	60.9 (0.93)	45.6 (0.86)	977	1000	978	981
	ALL	16.1	16.9	18	–	6.24	43.76	55.8 (0.88)	34.8 (0.69)	938	958	973	976
Karnataka	SC	15.4	16.4	16.9	15.77	2.47	20.92	41.8 (0.68)	36.6 (0.70)	965	957	968	962
	ST	16.4	16.4	17.1	15.4	2.55	19.09	46.3 (0.77)	39.6 (0.71)	953	957	971	961
	ALL	15.9	16.6	17.8	17.48	14.18	36.96	32.0 (0.55)	29.4 (0.54)	959	957	963	960
Kerala	SC	18.5	18.9	19	–	13.4	65.02	43.0 (0.81)	31.7 (0.62)	1084	1012	1022	1029
	ST	18.2	18.7	18.8	–	9.1	43.53	40.2 (0.75)	36.9 (0.68)	1006	995	992	996
	ALL	18.6	19	19.7	–	38.9	75.24	19.7 (0.42)	15.6 (0.33)	1022	1016	1032	1036
Madhya Pradesh	SC	13	14.6	14.9	15.2	1.12	14.26	50.5 (0.82)	35.2 (0.69)	973	941	932	915
	ST	13.7	16.3	16.5	15.39	0.81	8.4	58.0 (0.91)	48.3 (0.85)	1003	998	997	985
	ALL	15.1	15.5	16.4	17.2	6.73	23.07	44.0 (0.73)	32.7 (0.63)	953	941	941	931
Maharashtra	SC	14.9	15.8	16.4	16.38	3.86	33.78	44.4 (0.78)	36.5 (0.74)	962	947	948	944
	ST	16	16.7	16.9	15.75	1.42	19.18	55.8 (0.88)	49.7 (0.85)	978	973	974	968
	ALL	15.2	16.3	17.5	16.72	16.75	43.3	38.1 (0.67)	33.1 (0.63)	936	930	937	934

State	Category												
Manipur	SC	17.9	18	18.3		10.6	39.45	39.0 (0.65)	31.0 (0.66)	942	913	956	973
	ST	19.9	20	19.4		15.49	37.08	52.1 (1.08)	46.0 (0.97)	1022	1003	975	959
	ALL	19.8	19.1	19.4		15.93	39.58	44.5 (0.94)	39.0 (0.86)	1015	980	971	958
Meghalaya	SC	16.8	16.4	16.6		–	24.37	–	13.9 (0.26)	–	–	790	821
	ST	19.1	19.2	18.8		–	33.62	–	37.8 (0.78)	–	996	1002	997
	ALL	19.1	18.9	19.2		–	34.74	–	34.9 (0.70)	937	942	954	955
Nagaland	SC	–	–	–		19.56	–	–	–	–	–	–	–
	ST	21.3	20.6	19.7		9.92	44.73	59.7 (1.03)	40.2 (0.92)	1007	973	955	946
	ALL	21.2	20.4	20.3		11.33	44.78	58.2 (0.96)	38.0 (0.81)	933	871	863	886
Orissa	SC	16.8	17	17.2	16.82	3.2	17.02	32.1 (0.43)	23.4 (0.43)	1016	993	988	975
	ST	17.2	17.7	17.7	16.36	1.57	8.28	44.1 (0.69)	39.8 (0.68)	1015	1007	1012	1002
	ALL	17	17.2	17.9	18.13	8.64	28.83	26.6 (0.44)	20.8 (0.38)	1001	988	981	971
Rajasthan	SC	13.9	15.3	15.3	15.92	0.71	6.48	39.4 (0.67)	28.9 (0.59)	923	914	913	899
	ST	14.7	16	16.1	16.17	0.25	3.46	50.9 (0.82)	40.6 (0.78)	927	930	945	930
	ALL	14.2	15.5	16.5	16.61	5.84	16.31	35.9 (0.62)	27.4 (0.56)	908	911	919	910
Tamil Nadu	SC	18.1	18.1	18.3	17.28	4.32	29.5	44.4 (0.71)	40.9 (0.73)	993	981	980	978
	ST	17.5	17.9	18	16.59	2.09	16.94	49.0 (0.76)	44.5 (0.75)	950	951	968	960
	ALL	18.2	18.3	19	21.65	18.17	44.57	31.3 (0.52)	29.9 (0.53)	992	978	977	974
Tripura	SC	14.8	15.8	16.2		2.97	36.42	9.2 (0.15)	8.9 (0.19)	929	940	942	949
	ST	17.5	18	17.9		1.64	21.78	48.3 (0.88)	25.3 (0.55)	955	954	962	965
	ALL	16	16.8	17.7		10.19	40.58	20.9 (0.38)	13.8 (0.29)	932	943	946	945
Uttar Pradesh	SC	14.1	15.6	15.9	15.46	0.91	8.31	27.8 (0.46)	17.6 (0.35)	941	896	892	877
	ST	14.5	16.4	16.6	15.42	–	15.66	–	32.9 (0.62)	–	880	915	914
	ALL	14.6	16	17.1	16.82	7.02	20.02	18.1 (0.31)	12.3 (0.25)	909	879	885	879

(Contd.)

Table 2.6 (*contd.*)

State	Social Group	Female Mean Age at Marriage#				Female Literacy Rate*		Female Work-Participation Rate@		Sex-Ratios (Females per 1000 Males)			
		1971	1981	1991	1998–99**	1961	1991	1961 (f/m)	1991 (f/m)	1961	1971	1981	1991
West Bengal	SC	14.9	15.8	16.1	16.22	3.51	23.35	10.84 (0.2)	13.2 (0.25)	916	927	926	931
	ST	15.7	16.8	16.8	16.32	1.37	12.03	41.6 (0.71)	41.0 (0.76)	969	955	969	964
	ALL	15.2	16	16.8	17.06	16.97	38.43	9.43 (0.17)	11.3 (0.22)	878	891	911	917
Andaman Nicobar	SC	–	–	–	–	–	–	–	–	–	–	–	–
	ST	20	20.2	20.2	–	–	40.7	51.6	27.4 (0.55)	930	942	930	947
	ALL	16.8	17.6	18.5	–	19.37	53.61	18.8 (0.27)	13.1 (0.25)	617	644	760	818
Arunachal Pradesh	SC	16.1	17.4	17.1	–	–	31.39	–	12.4 (0.19)	–	904	592	627
	ST	18.8	18.8	–	–	–	19.51	–	44.1 (0.93)	–	1006	1005	998
	ALL	18.6	18.7	18.5	–	–	22.96	–	37.5 (0.7)	894	861	862	859

Note: * Female Literacy Rate is calculated by taking total female population (all ages) as the denominator.
@For 1991; the per cent of total female workers (main and marginal) to the total female population, where 'main workers' are those who worked for the major part of the year preceding the date of enumeration i.e., those who were engaged in any economically productive activity for 183 days or six months or more during the year, and 'marginal workers' are those who worked for less than 183 days or 6 months. In 1961, a person was classified as a 'worker' if he had worked regularly during the last season or if he had worked at least for one day in regular (non-seasonal) work during the preceding fortnight. 'Total workers' (main workers and marginal workers) of 1991, would correspond to the 'Workers' for 1961.
#Unweighted average of mean age at first marriage, calculated from NFHS II data.
**'All' refers to 'Other'.
^ Here India refers to 14 major states. F/m=ratio of female to male work participation rate.

Source: Agarwala, (1972); RG (1966a, 1966b, 1966c, 1975, 1976a, 1977, 1988, 1993, 1994a, 1994b, 1998); IIPS (1995), (2000); quoted in Bhattacharjee and Shastri, (1976), Table 24, p. 35, Sinha (1994).

of early marriage, popularly known as 'child marriage', has historically been a part of Hindu sociocultural norms, perceived justification of which rests on an overriding concern for female 'purity' and chastity. As a strategy to minimize the risk of familial stigma due to virginity loss (especially after puberty) of an unmarried daughter, marrying the daughter off early had emerged as a widespread social norm among Hindus. In contrast, being devoid of such Hindu notions of 'purity', tribal females traditionally marry much later, and generally not before puberty.

Note that except for the southern and northeastern states, tribal females of almost all other regions (where the ST population is enumerated in censuses) appear to marry later by at least a year (and often by two years) than their non-tribal counterparts do, especially during the 1970s (see Table 2.6). It is worth noting, however, that in northeastern states there has been little difference in the marriage age between tribal and general populations, but the difference between ST and SC groups was fairly large, especially in the earlier decades (see Table 2.6). Since tribal people are an overwhelming majority in these states, the tribal feature of relatively late marriage seems to dominate over the state average figures of female age at marriage. In southern states, however, the female age at marriage is not only relatively high but is so across all social groups. This is consistent with the fact of a higher overall level of women status and female autonomy in this region. In fact, there are several states (for example, Andhra Pradesh, Assam, Bihar, Himachal Pradesh, Madhya Pradesh, Manipur, Tripura, and Arunachal Pradesh) where the mean female age at marriage for the ST category is higher by more than two years than those of non-tribal counterparts, especially those belonging to the SC group.

There are quite a few important implications of a higher age at marriage among tribal females. First, it shows that tribal females enjoy greater freedom in such important matters as marriage, since they generally marry after attaining puberty and mental maturity, unlike their non-tribal counterparts.[33] Second, perhaps more importantly from

---

[33] A recent study of a young generation of *bidi* workers in a village of Tamil Nadu observes a constancy of female age at marriage, and even a tendency for early marriage along with an enhanced incidence of 'love marriage' (Dharmalingam 1994:569). These new trends have been largely attributed to 'economic independence and personal autonomy' that resulted from increased female employment and incomes. Although this local-level finding seems

the demographic point of view, a relatively late marriage should be, or indeed often has been, a reason for relatively low tribal fertility rates as compared to those of non-tribal groups, especially the SC group (see more on this later). This causality between them arises chiefly from the fact that a late marriage curtails the effective span of the reproductive career of a woman, assuming that children are born only within marriage, and that the negative effect on fertility of a shortened reproductive span is not neutralized by more child bearing.[34] As discussed later, tribal fertility in late-nineteenth and early-twentieth

inconsistent with our argument that relatively late marriage practice of tribal females reflects their greater independence and autonomy, there are reasons why this micro-level study (of non-tribal females) does not undermine our point. First, the female age at marriage in the study area was already fairly high (around 19 years), which is even higher than the average marriage age of tribal females in several regions and, of course, that of the general population in many other states. A relatively high female age at marriage is by now (after the pioneering paper by Dyson and Moore in 1983) a well-known feature that historically distinguishes much of south India's society, characterized by a higher female autonomy and less patriarchal social structure. Thus, if female age at marriage ceases to rise any further in this region, this should not be construed as a departure from the overall rising trend of marriage age at an all-India level. However, it should also be noted that this high female age at marriage within the mainstream (non-tribal) population of Tamil Nadu has not been, unlike tribal communities, due to the widespread practice of 'love marriage', and/or greater social permissiveness that allows females to choose their own partners.

[34] There is a considerable body of literature on fertility effects of changes in the overall nuptiality level, including changes in female age at marriage. The raising of the female age at marriage has a considerable fertility-reducing impact (Goyal 1964; Agarwala 1966). However, opinion has varied over the extent to which fertility can actually get influenced by the changes in female age at marriage, especially in the Indian context (where age at marriage does not necessarily signify the beginning of effective biological cohabitation). But there is evidence that it is not only the mean age at marriage but also the mean age at consummation (that is, when biological cohabitation begins) is often higher among tribal females (Sinha 1994). Moreover, the expansion of female education, generally held as an effective means to fertility reduction, often contributes—directly and indirectly—to postponing female marriages. It has sometimes been argued that merely raising of age at female marriage (through enforcing a marriage law) cannot achieve a considerable fertility decline, if it is not accompanied by expansion of female education and women's employment opportunities (Karkal 1968).

century India seems to have been distinctively lower than that for the mainstream Hindu population, partly because of the relatively late marriage practice among tribal females. Finally, the Hindu custom of child marriage or very early marriage, with concomitant early conceptions and maternity, often entails an enhanced risk of biological (maternal) complications and even death, both for the mother and the baby. Thus, the traditional norm of relatively late marriage among tribes on the whole, as compared to mainstream Hindu population groups should have wider demographic significance and implications, especially for fertility as well as maternal and child mortality.

However, long-standing processes of assimilation and interactions with the Hindu mainstream society and culture seem to have influenced many tribal communities in several regions towards lowering the female age of marriage. As can be seen from Table 2.6, the gap in terms of mean age at marriage between tribal and non-tribal groups seems to have narrowed over time, especially up to this 1991 census. This has happened mostly along with overall rising (declining) trend of non-tribal (tribal) female age at marriage during the 1970s and 1980s. In the 1990s, there seems to have been a slow down in the increase in age at marriage, together with an indication of a decline for tribal group at the aggregate all-India level. One may doubt the comparability between the mean age at marriage based on NFHS and those based on census information for earlier years on two points. First, the former is based on a much smaller number of responses, and second, they refer to ever married women (instead of currently married as in the census). One possible upward bias in the mean age figure based on currently married women (as in the census) might have occurred because of a possible under-representation of older women, who, on the whole, used to marry earlier than their younger counterparts. And this could perhaps be a reason why a slow down in increases of mean marriage age as shown by NFHS-2 data is more apparent than real. However, this possible upward bias in census data vis-à-vis NFHS-2 data may partly be neutralized by a much larger sample size in the census. There are thus reasons why NFHS data can well be used for the purpose of ascertaining broad recent trends. Interestingly, there is an indication of decline in female age at marriage for the ST category during the 1990s. The observed tapering off of increases in female age at marriage for general population during the 1990s could stabilize at some overall point, possibly around the statutory minimum set by the government.[35] However, the NFHS-2 finding of the recent decline in the mean age at marriage among tribal females in the 1990s is of interest, and is a reflection of lately intensified tribal integration with, and their emulation of, traditional Hindu norms of early marriage.[36]

In fact, the tribal trends towards early female marriage had begun as early as the 1930s or even much before in some regions,[37] and they seem to have continued at least till the early 1970s in the case of several tribes.[38] In many cases, the declining trend of tribal female age of marriage has continued well into the 1990s, and in some cases, is even continuing. For example, a recent study of one tribal group of Manipur (Gangte) has observed a decline in mean age at female marriage from 19.3 years among women aged 40 years and above to 15.5 years for

[35] According to one persuasive line of argument, an overall rising trend of female age of marriage over the last several decades across India has been not so much because of 'rising levels of education or legislative measures against child marriage', but mainly due to the so-called 'marriage squeeze' in the form of a relative excess supply of eligible brides over the available number of prospective grooms. This imbalance is, as the argument runs, chiefly an outcome of interactions between sociocultural norms of marriage (for example, spousal age-gap at marriage, degree of toleration of widow remarriage) and age-sex patterns of mortality decline (Mari Bhat and Halli 1999). Since sustained decline of mortality over a long period has initiated the marriage squeeze phenomenon, more recent tapering off of mortality decline has slowed down increases in female age at marriage. Somewhat relatedly, recent evidence also suggests that a rising age at female marriage has generally been accompanied by shortening of the average duration between marriage and first birth (Sivakumar 2001b).

[36] Apart from traditional Hindu influences, early marriage practice in some contemporary tribes has sometimes been interpreted as being a strategy for augmenting the number of working hands within the farm household economy (for example, among Chenchus of Andhra Pradesh, see Gangadharam 1999:144).

[37] For instance, W.V. Grigson, an eminent British administrator, who became an authority on the Maria Gonds of Bastar (in the state of Madhya Pradesh), wrote in his classic study in 1938:

'Pre-puberty marriage never occurs among the Hill Marias, who look upon it as an utterly abhorrent custom of the Kasor or Hindus. Unfortunately, a few Bison-horn Marias are beginning to ape their Hindu neighbours in this as in other matters; but even now presumably only three in a hundred Bison-horn marriages are child marriages' (Grigson 1938:250).

[38] See Roy Burman 1987; Thakur and Thakur 1994, chapter 1; Mann 1985; Sachchidananda 1964; Sinha 1986:77; also Bhagat and Unisa 1991.

the cohort, who are younger by ten years (Hemam and Reddy 1998: Table 5). It is ironic that early female marriage, nowadays, is frequently held as a reason for higher fertility reported among contemporary tribal communities in various regions (for south Indian tribes in the 1960s, see Nag 1973; for some tribes in Rajasthan during the mid-1980s, see Das and Shah 1991), while the late marriage norm seems to have contributed to lower tribal fertility until the recent past (more on this later). Interestingly, some tribes, who came under the Hindu fold relatively early and had begun lowering female age at marriage much earlier (for example, Bhils in Rajasthan, and Gonds in Madhya Pradesh) than others, have evinced a reversal of attitude, with 'a growing preference for post-puberty marriage' (Shashi 1995:41).[39]

Such an apparent reversal of tribal marriage customs and practices to their past traditions has been viewed as an indication of what is called 'retribalization' (Thakur and Thakur 1994:19–22).[40] But this is certainly a manifestation of the ongoing tribal integration with mainstream society, and hence of their sharing in the general rising trend of female age at marriage across the whole of India over the last several decades (see Table 2.6). Note that in some states the tribal age of female marriage seems to have increased or remained unchanged from the level of the preceding census (for example, Orissa, Rajasthan, Kerala, and West Bengal). However, the record of a decline in the marriage age of tribal (and SC) females in the late 1990s, especially in some southern states (Tamil Nadu, Andhra Pradesh) might be a reflection of broader changes in marriage patterns, practices, and payments that have been taking place in these regions (for example, rising dowry, and/or tendency towards early marriage, reduction of cross-cousin marriages (see Dharmalingam 1994). In other states (Uttar Pradesh, Madhya Pradesh, Maharashtra), the reported decline of the marriage age among tribes could be a reflection of an ongoing emulation of the traditional Hindu ritual of early marriage.

[39] For instance, a recent demographic study of Dudh Kharia in Sundargarh district (Orissa)—the tribe who had adopted settled cultivation, and also have a fair degree of interaction with mainstream culture and society—has found a mean age at female marriage of 21.4 years, which is even higher than the statutory minimum age of 18 years (Basu and Kshatriya 1997:124).

[40] With the aim of maintaining tribal (cultural) identity in the face of ever-increasing influences of dominant and mainstream patterns and trends, some anthropologists advocate what they call the 'revitalization movement' among the tribal community (which includes 'going back to their roots', 'discovering the "lost script" of their language' and 'cultural revival') (see Miller 1969).

To conclude thus far: there is clearly much scope and need for systematic studies on recent trends in nuptiality (for example, female age at marriage, in particular) among the tribal population of India, and also on the major underlying forces that shape them. For example, while about 17 per cent of SC females aged 0–14 years were reported as 'married' in the 1961 census in Bihar, the corresponding figure for ST females was only about 6 per cent. Furthermore, about 13 per cent of ST women in the age group 15–44 years were enumerated as unmarried, while it was only about 3 per cent among SC counterparts in 1961. At the all-India level, the proportion of unmarried ST females between 15 and 44 years was nearly double the corresponding figure for SC community in 1961. These nuptiality differentials between ST and SC groups (which have continued to be evident in 1981 too, despite a general rising trend of women in an unmarried state for more years) appear consistent with a higher female autonomy of tribal females and better gender relations, which generally have favourable implications for demographic behaviour too (this issue will be discussed in greater detail in the following chapter).

It is notable that this relatively late marriage practice among tribal females, with its implied female status and autonomy, seems largely sociocultural. This assertion is reinforced by the fact that these features of tribal women have combined with a pitifully low level of elementary education, are often found to relate to higher levels of women's status and female autonomy. Table 2.6 provides information on regional patterns of differential female literacy rates and its expansion between ST, SC, and total populations during the three decades between 1961 and 1991. The literacy rate for 1961, given for the population of all age groups including those aged 0–4 years, has been made comparable with the rates for 1991 by taking the population of all ages as a denominator (instead of the population aged 7 years and above). As was discussed above, what is appalling is the extremely low level of female literacy, especially among SC and ST groups even as late as 1991 in many states, after more than four decades since Independence. However, several northeastern states, namely Assam, Manipur, Meghalaya, Tripura, and a few others like Kerala and Himachal Pradesh, have fared relatively better in terms of the spread of female literacy. However, the pitiably slow progress in tribal female literacy has been made in some of the states where the tribal population is relatively numerous (Madhya Pradesh, Maharashtra, Rajasthan, Bihar, Orissa, West Bengal). As late as 1991, the record of about 4 (as in Rajasthan) or less than 10 literates out of 100 tribal females (as in Madhya Pradesh, Andhra Pradesh, or even at the all-India level) is truly shameful. This is in contrast with the faster progress of female literacy for their closest counterpart, the SC group. As was noted above, at an aggregative level, the expansion of education of tribal females is the least, and in most states seems to be fundamentally related to relative inaction and neglect on the part of state governments. One can only conjecture how much longer it would take for the persisting relative disadvantage of tribal females in education to place their non-tribal counterparts at par with them in terms of their larger (intrinsic) freedom and high status!

Differentials in Female Labour Participation

As was noted earlier, the nature and extent of females' direct participation in productive activities (popularly known as 'female labour force participation rate', FLPR for short) is of much significance from the standpoint of gender relations. We examine here, chiefly on the basis of census information, the differentials on this count between tribal and non-tribal women (see Table 2.6). It is not only that the FLPR is determined by complex interactions among various economic and non-economic factors, but an adequate understanding of these mechanisms requires a rich data base.[41] A strict comparability of

[41] Substantial literature has developed on various issues relating to the magnitude of female labour force participation, its trends and explanations, mostly from the standpoint of general population. This literature is, however, fraught with difficulties arising from data limitations as well as complexities due to diverse forces and influences (Jose 1989; Agarwal 1985; Sen and Sen 1985; Dreze and Sen 2002; Visaria 1996; Jain and Banerjee 1985 among others). The decennial censuses and NSS are two major sources of time series information on labour force participation and employment. Apart from data difficulties (for example, changing census definition and persistent fuzziness of notions of productive work/labour, and a lack of comparability between census and NSS), there seem to be several ongoing processes, sometimes with opposite effects, relating to the nature and trends of female work participation. For example, a trend of increasing female displacement from rural employment has often been discerned, of course in varying pace across regions, along with structural and technological changes (e.g. farm mechanization) with a male bias. On the other hand, detailed micro-level studies on gender division of economic activities often detect a so-called 'feminization' of subsistence (farm) activities with a corresponding fall in male

information on labour force participation between censuses (especially up to 1981) is lacking because of changes of criteria by which 'worker' has been identified from one census to other. For example, the 1961 census employed both 'usual status' (if worked regularly in the last season), and 'current status' (if worked at least for a day in the preceding fortnight) criteria for classifying workers, while the 1991 census focused on usual status (at least 183 days in the year) for classifying main workers, and on current status (less than 183 days) for marginal workers. However, the changes in questionnaires were made with an eye to the need for comparability; the census authorities for 1981 expected 'total workers' (including main and marginal) to broadly correspond to the 'workers' for 1961 (Census of India 1981, Primary Census Abstract, Part IIB(i): p.xiv). As there was no major change in the criteria, this statement should hold true for 1991 census too. Thus, it is hard to feel fully confident about time trends of work-participation levels based on 1961 and 1991 censuses. Indeed, the judgement about cross-sectional differentials in the work-participation rate between the social groups at a given point of time is also not free of difficulties. One relates to the possibility of differential under-reporting of women's actual participation in economic activity. For example, a larger part of women's work may remain unreported in non-tribal communities in which women's involvement in work outside home is usually associated with low social status, as compared to tribal communities which traditionally attach no negative connotation to women doing field-related work (see Agarwal 1994:322–23). Notwithstanding such possible response errors, it seems both possible and useful to glean the broad indications of differential patterns of female work-participation rate and their changes.

Regarding cross-section differences between the ST, SC, and total population, the general picture that emerges is fairly clear, namely, that the work-participation rate has been the highest among tribal females, followed by the SC and general population groups. This applies both to the 1961 and 1991 censuses, although there appears

---

farm work-participation rate. In the case of tribal women, deepening deforestation and shrinking entitlements to common property resources have been dispossessing them of their traditional economic role and productive value, often producing an adverse impact on their well-being and social position (for some lucid but penetrative accounts see Fernandes and Menon 1987; Shiva 1988).

to have been an across-the-board decline in the participation rate. In view of the recent evidence showing the enhancement of female work participation and opportunities as a route to achieving demographic goals of gender equity, fertility reduction, child health and nutrition (see Bennett 1992), tribal females can thus be said to be at least potentially ahead of their non-tribal counterparts. That females take part in directly productive activities such as farming, roughly as much as or even more than their male counterparts, is a well-known characteristic among tribal communities of India and elsewhere (see Boserup 1970, especially chapter 1). The ratios of female–male work participation rates in Table 2.6 clearly show much greater gender equality in the tribal workforce, as compared to those for non-tribal groups. In fact, in a few states (Manipur and Himachal Pradesh) the tribal females appear to take part in productive activities nearly equally (in proportionate terms) as their male counterparts.

It is of interest that aggregate SC people, who, as we have shown above, are not much different in terms of overall material levels of living and livelihood from their ST counterparts, appear much closer to the general population so far as female work-participation is concerned. This is consistent with the relatively greater effect on SC people of the process of Sanskritization, in which productive female labour-participation outside home is socially frowned upon, resulting in women being gradually withdrawn from the formal 'labour force'. Interestingly however, in a few states, namely Himachal Pradesh, Manipur, Madhya Pradesh, and Tamil Nadu, the extent of female work-participation differs relatively little between ST and SC groups. These regional variations may be related to the differentials in the timing, intensity, and pace, with which broad historic processes of the tribe–caste continuum (as discussed in the preceding chapter) as well as Sanskritization have been taking place.

Assuming a reasonable degree of comparability of census information on the female work-participation rate between 1961 and 1991 (see Table 2.6), there seems to have been a general decline at all-India level—by about 10 per cent point each for ST/SC groups, and by 6 point for total population. Note that these falls in FLPR have been accompanied at an all-India level by falls in the respective ratios of female to male labour-participation rates, which reflect larger (per cent point) declines in FLPR vis-à-vis those of males for all the groups. These declines in female work-participation, if real, could be an outcome of a temporal (relative) shrinkage of female employment opportunities, and also of a gradual withdrawal of females from the workforce due to deepening influences of Sanskritization, and/or due to rising incomes and expanding female education.[42] A systematic examination of these alternative hypotheses, though important on their own right, are beyond the scope of the present monograph. For example, the declines in FLPR both for SC and ST groups in Andhra Pradesh have been accompanied by rises in the female–male ratio of work-participation rates, signifying a larger decline in male-labour participation. Conversely, for SC and ST communities in a few states (e.g. Bihar and Tripura), there have been very large declines both in FLPR and female–male ratios. In any case, there can hardly be any doubt that a very high female share to the total tribal workforce (more than 80 per cent in 1961) has remained to be largely true at an aggregate level. But non-tribal groups with an initially much lower relative female share in the total workforce, even in the early 1960s seem to have experienced a further decline over the following three decades (see Table 2.6). In some states, the relative female share in the workforce among SC group has declined quite strikingly (for example, in Bihar, Kerala, Madhya Pradesh, and Himachal Pradesh). In these states, the ST group too has witnessed a worsening of the female share in workforce, albeit to a lesser extent.

In sum, a distinctively greater productive role of tribal females vis-à-vis their non-tribal counterparts is amply clear, although the differential is less pronounced in a few states, especially where gender composition of the aggregate workforce seems to have been relatively balanced historically (Himachal Pradesh, Madhya Pradesh). This relatively higher female labour-force participation for the general population in these regions, possibly is itself a reflection of greater and deeper 'tribal' influences, an hypothesis which deserves a persuasive investigation. This said, the material base of the tribal economy such as jungles, hills, and shortage of labour, is sometimes such that the female labour-force participation is more of an imperative need than anything else.

Following our earlier discussion, however, one major implication of greater female work-participation in tribal communities should be less gender inequities (as well as more female autonomy), as compared

[42] Berreman (1993:385), for example, describes Sanskritization 'as subordination of women, especially through restriction of their interactions and activities outside the home, including avoidance of employment, if the family can afford these "luxuries"'.

to non-tribal societies. This link presumably arises (at least partly) because of a comparatively high 'economic worth' (that is, a larger productive role) of tribal females (Boserup 1970). Consistent with this is the fact (as noted already) that gender relations are relatively balanced in large parts of sub-Saharan Africa, where female labour-force participation (and hence economic 'worth' of women) is also fairly high.[43] Notably, a few Indian studies based on district-level data (Rosenzweig and Schultz 1982, and Kishor 1993) have shown a significant inverse relationship between female labour-force participation and female disadvantage in childhood mortality. However, the precise mechanism underlying this relationship is not readily clear. While there are several distinct possibilities on this association, there is little evidence to distinguish between the alternative hypotheses (for a useful discussion on this, see Murthi et al. 1995:754). However, as discussed earlier, a (relative) female mortality disadvantage in infancy and childhood in the general population results proximately from a pervasive (familial) discrimination against girls (often selectively), but it seems to be fundamentally related to the relatively low social 'status' or 'position' of females and imbalances in gender relations. In this context, the estimated negative regression coefficient of the district-level female disadvantage in child mortality on the proportion of tribal population is noteworthy (Murthi et al. 1995). More interestingly, this negative relationship holds even after the district-level female labour-force participation rate is controlled, a fact which suggests that tribal people have other features (than just a greater 'economic worth' of women) that contribute to enhancing relative survival chances of female children.

Indeed the anthropological literature does not always provide a clear and uniform picture of the reasons why a greater productive role of females is associated with a higher position and autonomy.[44] In

[43] See for example, Drèze and Sen 1989; Svedberg 1996; Klasen 1996.

[44] A few recent Indian studies have reported that a greater female work participation per se cannot always guarantee greater female status and autonomy, especially in tribal societies (see Harriss and Pryer 1990; and Rana 1996). For non-tribal population too (in parts of South Asia and even elsewhere), 'women's domestic power is not necessarily related to their productive labour' (Malhotra et al. 1995:283 and references cited). However, women's wage work participation, distinct from non-wage (unpaid) work, is generally found to be favourable to women's bargaining power within households (for example, Agnihotri 2003:4359).

fact, female productive contribution is hardly sufficient, though often necessary, for ensuring a high status and power of women (Sanday 1973; Ember 1983). One can often observe a mediating role played by such factors as ecological circumstances of production, market structure for the produce, or even religious and magical taboos relating to female control and power. Indeed, there is anthropological evidence of several societies where a high degree of female productive contribution coexists with extremely low female status and power (see Sanday 1973:1695 for such references). That the link between female subsistence contribution and women's status/power is hardly automatic is suggestive of the foundational and mediating role of broad sociocultural patterns, practices, and values in a society, especially the pattern of gender relations and kinship systems.[45] Thus, there could well be (an intrinsic) tribal sociocultural pattern, which allows for a greater productive role of females and thereby, a higher female status and autonomy. For example, the reason why SC women, despite often being in similar economic circumstances, do not take part in productive activities as much as their ST counterparts, is at least partly because of sociocultural barriers to women's work participation outside the household.[46] Furthermore, recent researches show that while female education is often found to enhance female autonomy, this effect turns out to be distinctively much less in those societies that are characterized by a higher degree of patriarchy and gender stratification (Jejeebhoy 2000). This reaffirms the (somewhat independent) role of basic sociocultural structure in shaping gender relations in general, and the nature of female status and autonomy in particular, notwithstanding

[45] However, it is not always easy to be sure whether female work-participation is a cause or effect of female status, especially among lower caste and tribal communities.

[46] Of course, because of the proximity of forests and a natural environment (where 'village commons' and/or other common property resources are comparatively large), tribal women seem to have greater scope for productive activities (for example, gathering of forest products) than SC women can have in villages in a different environment. But this fact alone cannot explain the aggregate picture of the higher workforce participation rate of tribal females vis-à-vis their SC counterparts. First, a substantial proportion of India's total tribal population share almost the same geophysical setting with SC people. Indeed, a much greater tribal female work participation rate (than that of SC women) is also often observed, even when both groups not only co-inhabit the same village, but they are at par with each other in terms of economic circumstances (we will present similar evidence in Chapter 6).

the effects of greater female labour involvement and the spread of female education. This said, it is quite plausible (and indeed consistent with the existence of a cultural structure with balanced gender relations) that greater gender equality in the tribal workforce often reinforces and sustains greater economic independence and autonomy of tribal females as compared to their non-tribal counterparts.

As already noted for the whole of India, a much higher female–male ratio in the tribal population in most of the states (where the ST population are enumerated) testifies broadly to their more balanced gender relations and less anti-female discrimination. However, in the southernmost states (Kerala, Tamil Nadu, and more lately, in Karnataka and Andhra Pradesh) the tribal female–male ratio appears somewhat lower than that of non-tribal groups (see Table 2.6). This is particularly interesting because, the overall sex ratio in southern India is distinctively more balanced than in the rest of India (except a few states like Himachal Pradesh). It is hard to attribute this apparently anomalous finding to specific enumeration biases in the south Indian tribes, although many of them inhabit inaccessible terrain like hills and jungles. It is worth wondering if the explanation at least partially lies in the history and evolution of 'tribes' vis-à-vis 'non-tribes' in this region. While pre-existing tribal domination and influences in large parts of northern India were supplanted by the overpowering Aryan (and subsequently Brahmanical) society, the ancient Dravidian (or even pre-Dravidian) civilization, which was overwhelmingly 'tribal' (see, Roy 1912:iii–x; Kosambi 1956:230; Inden 1990:178), retained its distinctiveness longer, even within the caste-based Brahmanical social structure. For example, E. Thurston wrote in the Introduction to his seven-volume classic treatise on south Indian tribes and castes:

> Whether the jungle tribe are, as I believe, the microscopic remnant of a pre-Dravidian people, or, as some hold, of Dravidians driven by conquering race to the seclusion of the jungles, it is to the lasting influence of some such broad-nosed ancestor that the high nasal index of many of the inhabitants of Southern India must, it seems to me, be attributed (1901:lv; italics added).

The lasting elements of pre-Aryan (and hence Dravidian) society and culture are often evident in contemporary mainstream caste society in large southern states of India. As Enthoven (1920:x–xi) writes for the southern parts of the Bombay Presidency, 'the castes are clearly organized on primitive lines', and he also noted 'strong evidence of the primitive origin of some important elements in the castes'. While describing the Dravidian south India as predominantly 'tribal' is not infrequent (for example, Kosambi 1956:230; Inden 1990:178), the basis of this assertion is drawn from several distinct similarities between 'tribes' and the Dravidian mainstream, say in language, marriage, and other sociocultural patterns, and even in physical features. For example, a contemporary study of marriage and kinship among the Raj Gonds of Andhra Pradesh concludes, '...the Gonds have a marriage system that fits into the wider south Indian Dravidian kinship system...' (Yorke 1979:113). That a very small proportion of population is classified as tribes in the entire south India could be a reflection of the relatively blurred social division between tribes and castes in the history of the region. Greater female autonomy and status along with little difference in such sociocultural characteristics between SC, ST, and other populations in south Indian states, as seen in Table 2.6, further illustrates the lasting and overriding imprint of 'tribal' culture and society in south Indian history. Thus, it may not be too cavalier to posit the lasting influence of pre-Aryan (and hence chiefly tribal) social systems (including gender relations) as being a clue to the sociocultural distinctiveness of contemporary south India in evincing features of greater female status and autonomy.

But a lower tribal female–male ratio than for non-tribal groups in parts of southern India deserves a systematic investigation beyond the scope of the present monograph. One may wonder, for instance, if social movements of lower caste people against higher caste (Brahmanical) domination (the so-called Dravidian movements since the early twentieth century) in the mainland south have left fringe tribal groups largely untouched and unreformed, and hence relatively more patriarchal than the mainstream population. Indeed, while describing the so-called Dravidian tribes of the south as 'forgotten sons of the soil', Subbarayan (not dated: 18) states that they 'have nothing but Hindu customs and traditions. Indeed, some very Aryan customs [i.e. perhaps generally more patriarchal]—so-called—prevail amongst them, more so than among the plainsmen'. A lot of serious research is called for before this historical hypothesis can be made conclusive.

Apart from historical specifics, the higher maternal mortality found among contemporary tribal societies across India (Bhat 2002) could be a contributory factor for a lower female–male ratio in the tribal population in south India, where overall mortality levels are low, compared to northern regions. This explanation, of course, calls for systematic and detailed investigations for a convincing confirmation.

Concluding Remarks

It is amply evident that India's tribal people suffer massive deprivation and vulnerability. The social group, which happens to be closest to tribes in terms of material levels of living, are the lower caste people (SC). Our scrutiny of available evidence posits India's aggregate SC population as being little better than their tribal counterpart, in terms of key indicators of material deprivations and levels of living. But tribes presently appear most disadvantaged in the spheres of health and education facilities, especially females. This is, at least, partly linked to the fact that SC population is mostly dispersed across the mainstream villages, while a large section of tribal people live in relatively isolated, remote locations. For example, the village-level data shows a strong negative association between 'tribal concentration' (i.e. proportion of ST people) and levels of infrastructural/developmental indices (see Gupta 2003).

Despite chronic vulnerabilities and material deprivations, what clearly stands out for India's overall tribal population almost everywhere (especially in comparison with their closest comparable group, namely SC people) is their greater gender equality in labour force participation, higher female age at marriage, and more balanced sex composition in population. Such differentials in gender relations in the context of broadly similar material levels of living between ST and SC people attests to the predominance of sociocultural (rather than economic) influences on the gender situation of a society. The sociocultural underpinnings of the distinctive features of tribal females are analogous to what are widely known to be the hallmarks of the Western sociocultural milieu, namely, balanced gender relations and less patriarchal kinship, hierarchy and domination. Indeed, the roots of south Indian gender-equality and greater female autonomy could be linked to the greater lasting imprint and influence of pre-Dravidian (tribal) society and culture on the mainstream. In fact, the promotion within the mainstream population of more balanced gender relations, traditionally a major trait of tribal societies, is currently being seen as a route to achieving avowed demographic goals, such as elimination of anti-female gender biases, reduction of fertility, and child/infant mortality. In the following chapter, we will examine whether and how far the above-mentioned tribal (sociocultural) features shaped their past demographic regime, thereby putting into test the hypothesis that greater gender equities and female autonomy are conducive to maintaining relatively low fertility and infant/child mortality.

3

Tribal Fertility and Mortality in Late Ninteenth- and Early Twentieth-Century India

One distinct suggestion that has emerged from the foregoing analyses is that the aggregate tribal population, though seemingly diverse among themselves, evince an overall distinctive sociocultural structure from that of their non-tribal counterparts, even when both share broadly the same geophysical setting. This, of course, opens up opportunities for a deeper understanding of the broad issue of interrelationship between sociocultural characteristics (for example, gender relations and biases in particular) and demographic outcomes. However, as noted earlier, within the massive ethnographical and anthropological literature on Indian tribes, there is relatively little systematic analysis of tribal patterns of demographic behaviour such as fertility and mortality, especially in a historical perspective. But historical studies of demographic behaviour can provide important insights into contemporary debates and discussions on the relative importance of different sociocultural and economic factors that are generally thought to shape the nature and pace of demographic transition. Indeed, India offers a rare opportunity among developing countries for undertaking serious historical demographic studies, as it has a long and fairly rich tradition of census and civil registration, beginning as early as the 1870s (see Dyson 1989). While India's 'historical demography' is a relatively new academic field (perhaps still not beyond its 'infancy'), the body of demographic studies on tribes in the historical past is yet to be formed. In the present chapter, we will examine tribal fertility and mortality in the context of late nineteenth- and early twentieth-century India, in a comparative perspective. Hopefully, such studies of past demographic behaviour would help form a better understanding of more recent demographic differentials between tribal and non-tribal societies.

Kingsley Davis' View

In the context of the sparse historical literature on tribal fertility and mortality, even for the periods after census-taking had started, the celebrated pioneering historical study by Kingsley Davis of India's population, based on a meticulous scrutiny of census information prior to Independence, deserves a special mention. With relatively little available evidence, Davis attempted a comparison of fertility between religious groups (including tribal people) during 1911–31 (Davis 1951: chapter 10). In fact, there was hardly any direct, reliable evidence on reproductive behaviour and performance (for example, birth rate and total fertility rate) by religious groups during this period or earlier. In this context, the child–woman ratio (for example, the number of children aged 0–4 per 1000 women and/or married women aged 15–39, as was employed by Davis) seemed to be the only measure, which could be used to infer differential fertility behaviour in the past. This is possible because Indian censuses starting from 1881 provide distribution of enumerated population by age, sex, and religion. However, as noted earlier (in Chapter 1), there have been recurrent changes in census definition/criteria for classification of tribal and other religious groups, and consequently, one needs to be careful about the comparability of data on the tribal population from one census to another during this period. The census data at an aggregate all-India level posits a comparatively high average child–woman ratio (CWR for short hereafter) for the tribal category during 1911–31; indeed, the tribal figure was found to be the highest among all groups when ratios were taken to married women. Thus, Davis' conclusion that overall tribal fertility has had a marked 'superiority', especially as compared to the Hindus (and also to most other minor religious groups except Muslims), has served as the conventional wisdom so far. Davis, while explaining—as an informed guess rather than a systematically established thesis[1]—India's relatively high tribal fertility, refers to two

[1] It should be noted that a detailed and systematic explanation of differential fertility and mortality was beyond the scope and purpose of Davis' monograph,

facts: one, '[t]he Tribals are primitives, with presumably the reproductive behaviour of most aboriginal groups,' (pp. 79–80); and second, '...their greater toleration of widow remarriage' [especially as compared to Hindus] (p. 82). However, two respective queries can be raised: first, the statement that most aboriginal groups have had a relatively high reproductive performance does not appear to be entirely true, and may turn out wrong in various cases after a careful scrutiny of relevant information across time and space. Indeed, there is a long-standing debate in the global (and historical) context among demographers over the question of whether fertility levels of 'tribal and primitive societies' were generally low or high (see Carr-Saunders 1922; Krzwicki 1934; Lorimer 1954; and Nag 1962). Second, while 'greater toleration of widow remarriage' as a possible factor favourable to a relatively high tribal fertility is almost unquestionable, there may well be other aspects of tribal marriage patterns and practices which could exert just the opposite or negative influence on their fertility. A prominent pattern was their relatively high female age at marriage as compared to most other religious groups. Tribal societies also seem to tolerate a greater extent of celibacy among both males and females, a fact that should influence their fertility negatively. Thus, one can argue that the finding of a relatively large tribal CWR could be a net outcome of positive influences outweighing the negative ones on tribal fertility of their opposing nuptial forces. But unless one does quantify the negative and positive nuptiality influences on fertility, this argument would remain far from established. In fact, as we would argue later, this whole explanation of higher tribal fertility solely (or even largely), in terms of a greater tribal toleration of widow remarriage, is at best incomplete, and involves several assumptions, some being quite doubtful.

---

in which he set upon himself a much broader canvas to be drawn. As Davis himself made it clear, the basic motivation behind his analysis of differential fertility was the need to offer an explanation for a steady decline of the relative share of the Hindu population vis-à-vis a corresponding rise for Muslims and a constancy of tribal proportion in the total Indian population during 1881–1941. And he had no choice but to rely heavily on census-based child–woman ratios in an effort to offer an explanation of the above trends, which he happened to find in the (CWR-based) 'superiority' of Muslim and tribal fertility over the Hindus, at an aggregate level.

In fact, there are a host of issues involved in judging differential fertility based only on CWRs of two groups. First, the differential age–sex pattern of mortality may well vitiate a fertility comparison based on only respective CWRs. If, for example, adult and elderly survival chances relative to those for infants and young children in a tribal society are lower, as compared to those for the Hindu population, a higher tribal CWR would not necessarily mean a higher tribal fertility. It is worth quoting the report on the Bengal census of 1901, explaining a higher tribal ratio of children per 10,000 population:

> The aboriginal tribes are believed to be comparatively short-lived....[T]he greater number of their children... may also be due in part to the fact that there are fewer old people amongst them (see *Census of India 1901*, vol. 6, part I, p. 218).

Again, if maternal mortality is sufficiently higher for tribals, a higher CWR may fail as proof of their higher fertility. For instance, the report on the census of Central Provinces/Berar in 1911 attributed a relatively great deficiency of tribal females in their reproductive period in Chota Nagpur states to a 'more than proportionate death-rate of women in child-birth' (*Census of India 1911*, vol. 10, part I, p. 118).[2] Furthermore, this problem of incomparability of CWRs for evaluating differential fertility can get even more complex if age patterns of child-bearing differ markedly between the groups. Several of these issues may not appear 'major' while evaluating time trends of fertility differentials (Guilmoto and Rajan 2001:717), but they may matter in an evaluation of fertility differentials between social groups at a given point of time.

Notwithstanding these possible sources of pitfalls in comparing CWRs, it should be noted that no better measure of fertility in the context of India's historical past could be employed, especially at a time when Davis' study was undertaken. But this does not preclude

---

[2] There is further evidence suggesting a higher relative mortality among adults and elderly people vis-à-vis children in tribal communities as compared to (non-tribal) general population. As one author writes about Indian tribes during the first several decades of last century, '...investigations in specified areas have shown the phenomenal absence of aged people among the tribal people' (Mamoria 1958:111). Referring to the 1931 census figures, he writes:

> while the proportion of aged people is comparatively small among the tribal people, that of children 0–5 years is decidedly higher than it is among the higher castes; among Hindus it is 15 per cent but among the tribal it is 19 per cent (ibid: 111).

the possibilities for subsequent improvement. In fact, it seems possible to extend and improve upon Davis' analysis based on C–W ratios on several lines. First, it may be worthwhile to attempt a more disaggregative picture of tribal fertility across regions (at least at the province-level) than Davis' analysis. It is obvious that various tribes, dispersed across different Indian regions, would not evince a uniform pattern of reproductive performance and behaviour, even though fertility levels of most tribes must have been close to their respective natural limits, particularly in the early twentieth century. Such inter-regional variation in tribal fertility is expected not only because of socioeconomic and sociocultural diversities, but may also be partly due to inter-tribe variation in biological aspects of fecundity.

The available individual surveys (including those conducted as part of census operations)[3] of various tribes across Indian regions do not posit tribal fertility as always higher than that for non-tribal population groups (see Nag 1973). For example, an anthropological study of one hill-tribe (Kanikkar) of Travancore in the early 1950s has indicated a much lower tribal fertility as compared to the general population (Nag 1954). In fact, more recent large-scale surveys (including those by census organizations and NFHS) have shown that tribal fertility not only varies across states, but is higher in some and lower in others as compared to respective levels of fertility of the mainstream population (more on this in the following chapter).

Given all this as a background, let us evaluate tribal fertility in comparison with the most numerous group, namely, the Hindus during the late-nineteenth and early-twentieth centuries. More than 70 per cent of India's population were recorded as Hindu in the censuses prior to 1941. Despite considerable heterogeneity within the Hindu population, the aggregate Hindu population is a reasonable choice for a comparative assessment of tribal fertility, especially because of the distinct sociocultural contrast.[4]

Our present analysis of tribal fertility in the historical past is primarily based on census data and reports (available since the early 1880s) up to 1931. (Unfortunately, the civil registration system does not provide

[3] These surveys and studies are of limited scope and coverage, and of varying reliability. We undertake a critical review of post-Independence literature on many of these issues in the following chapter.

[4] Of course, tribal fertility could be compared with other religious groups as well. But the Hindu population represents India's mainstream patterns because of its overwhelming proportion.

separate information for tribal populations.) As we indicated in the first chapter, the term 'tribal' is far from well-defined, and several complexities (mostly historical and anthropological) surround the notion and identification of a tribe. However, as we have discussed already, despite defects in census information on tribes, they can be profitably used for a comparison with other religious groups. Thus, the census definition of 'tribe' will be followed, relying on census-based information on the tribal population. As mentioned earlier, the 'tribal' population in census reports (at least until 1931) is shown under a routine classification of population by religion; tribal people were classified as 'animists' alongside other religious groups (e.g. Hindu, Muslim, Christian, Jain, Parsis, Sikh, Buddhist, Jewish, and others) until 1931. There may well be biases in census enumeration of populations by religion, and the issue of comparability of population by religion between different censuses is certainly relevant. In this context, the distinction between Hindus and tribals was particularly troublesome, an issue discussed by Kingsley Davis with his characteristic precision and meticulousness (see Davis 1951: chapter 19). However, as Davis wrote, '[e]xcept the case of Hindus and tribals in 1941, the census definition of religious groups is thought to be reasonably consistent and accurate' (Ibid:178, footnote 5). Moreover, we are not concerned here with the size of the tribal population as such (or other religious groups), and need not be distracted by definitional comparability of a religious group between censuses. Instead, we need to be concerned if a significant number of non-tribal people were recorded as 'tribal'—which, however, seems unlikely, especially in censuses up to 1931. Rather, the converse, namely counting some tribal peoples as Hindus seems likely at least up to 1931 due to various reasons, both social and political (see Davis 1951:188–91 for a useful discussion on this). To illustrate, 24 per cent of the total Oraon population in Ranchi district of Bihar were found to have been returned as Hindus or Christians, and the rest were returned as Animists (i.e. tribals) in the 1911 census. The corresponding figure for Bihar and Orissa was about 11 per cent (Ray 1915:Appendix IV). This bias seems to have subsided subsequently, and was possibly reversed in some regions in the post-Independence period (as was discussed earlier). Although tribes were dispersed across India during the late-nineteenth and early-twentieth centuries (i.e. the time period of our present study), their geographical concentration was highest in the Central Provinces/Berar and Bihar/Orissa, followed by Bombay/Gujarat, Bengal, and Assam, followed by both southern and northern India. Also, despite the anthropologists' meticulous classification of numerous tribes, the most dominant ones were Bhil and Gond of central and western India, and Santhal and Oraon of eastern and central India (for details of numerical and geographical distributions of various tribes during this period, see census reports).

Child–Woman Ratios of Tribal and Hindu Populations: A Re-examination

We now examine and compare CWRs between tribals and Hindus in greater detail. We begin by recapitulating Davis' main conclusion relating to the fertility differential between tribals and Hindus (see Table 3.1). Apart from a much higher tribal C–W ratio, what is striking is the larger gap in the ratio of children to married women between tribals and Hindus than the ratio of children to all women. Although this fact, by itself, does not lend any additional doubt about the inference of higher tribal fertility, it seems to run counter to Davis' own argument that higher tribal fertility is in 'a good part' due to 'their greater toleration of widow remarriage'. If that were indeed the case, one would have expected a smaller difference in the ratio of children to married women, as compared to the gap in the ratio of children to all women.[5] In fact, Davis, while comparing child–woman ratios of all religious groups, summed up as follows: '...the ratio of children to married women shows smaller differences between religions than does the ratio of children to all women of specified ages' (p. 80). But he did not pay particular attention to the fact that his above statement does not apply to the comparison between tribals and Hindus (see Table 3.1).[6] However, as we argue below, this could precisely be seen as a clue to the puzzle of differential fertility and its explanation.

[5] Moni Nag, as back as 1973, noted and commented upon this inconsistency in Davis' analysis. In fact, Nag posited CWR for Madras in 1961 to be consistent with a greater tribal rate of widow remarriage as a possible factor behind their higher CWR. But interestingly, the record of higher tribal CWR could not be explained by the differentials in female age at marriage and/or in divorce/separation rates between these groups (Nag 1973:116–17).

[6] See Davis (1951), Table 28, chapter 10 for child–woman ratios of all religious groups.

Table 3.1   Child–woman ratios for Tribals and Hindus, all-India, averages during 1911–31

	Tribals (1)	Hindus (2)	Difference (3)=(1)–(2)
Children 0–4 years per 1000 women 15–39 years	808	678	130
Children 0–4 years per 1000 married women 15–39 years	1023	817	206

Source: Davis (1951) Table 28, chapter 10. Based on census enumerated population by age and religion.

In Table 3.2, we present child–woman ratios for the whole of India, and also for select provinces during 1891–1931.[7] It shows a higher ratio of children to women for the tribal population, as compared to Hindus (except in Madras in 1921). However, in some regions (for example, Madras and the Central Provinces/Berar) the differential in the child–woman ratio between tribals and Hindus was much smaller than Davis' all-India figure of 130 per 1000 women (see Table 3.1), while it was vastly larger in Bihar/Orissa.[8] Since the child–woman ratio is subject to opposing influences of fertility and mortality patterns, it is important to be cautious, especially if there are reasons for a considerable differential in the age–sex pattern of mortality between the compared social groups.[9] For example, the ratio of children aged 0–4 years to women 15–49 is found substantially lower (349 per 1000 women) for the tribal population than that for Hindus (537) in 1911. Thus, although the census-based higher CWR for aggregate tribes seems consistent with an overall constancy of tribal proportion in face of both a rising Muslim share and a declining proportion of Hindus in total population during 1881–1931, one should hardly jump to a judgement about tribal fertility relative to that for the Hindus.

[7] The selection of provinces and time periods was partly circumscribed by the degree of ready availability/accessibility of old census materials.

[8] Note that for both Madras and Bihar/Orissa, the age group of children is wider (0–9) than in other regions.

[9] See Guilmoto and Rajan (2001:716–17) for a discussion on the possible difficulties of CWR as an index of fertility. They have come up with district-level estimates of what they call the child–woman index, which is CWR adjusted for (i.e. divided by an appropriately chosen model life table) survival rate ($_nL_x/5$) from birth up to the children's age in question for each district, expressed in standardized form with reference to a grand average of mortality-adjusted CWRs of all districts.

Table 3.2   Child–woman ratio (number of children 0–4 per 1000 women 15–44 years) for Hindu and Tribal populations in several Indian locations, 1881–1931

		1881	1891	1901	1911	1921	1931
India	Tribal	1774*	732	597	730	626	–
	Hindu	1357*	510	536	576	538	–
	Difference	417	222	61	154	88	–
Bengal	Tribal	NA	731	719	NA	464^	–
	Hindu	NA	568	555	NA	489^	–
	Difference	–	163	164	–	–25	–
CP/Berar	Tribal	NA	NA	610@	732	455^	753
	Hindu	NA	NA	620@	677	456^	686
	Difference	–	–	–10	55	–1	67
Madras	Tribal	NA	1410#	1680#	1770#	1610#	1620#
	Hindu	NA	1320#	1620#	1750#	1760#	1610#
	Difference	–	90	60	20	–150	10
Bihar	Tribal	NA	918	–	2200#	2120#	803
	Hindu	NA	581	1590#	1650#	1630#	630
	Difference	–	337	–	550	490	173

*children (0–9 years) per 1,000 women aged 14–39 years
#children (0–9 years) per 1,000 married women aged 14–39 years
@children (0–5 years) per 1,000 women aged 15–40 years
^children (0–4 years) per 1,000 women aged 15–45 years

Source: Relevant census reports

In fact, there are several complexities involved in explaining the observed differential in CWRs. Table 3.3 presents information (based on sample surveys of married women during census operations in 1921 and 1931) on the average number of children ever born and the proportion surviving per family by caste and tribe in the Central Provinces/Berar.[10] It seems that a higher CWR among tribals may have been partly due to lower infant and child mortality compared to

[10] The selection of sample households was not made randomly. Rather, questions on, among others, the numbers of children born alive and still living were asked of those couples who: (i) could give their exact age; and (ii) were still alive. While this sample procedure is likely to invite selection biases, it seems reasonably safe to draw a comparative assessment between tribes and Hindus on the basis of this evidence, of course, under the assumption of a negligible differential in possible selection biases between the groups.

Table 3.3   Average number of children born and proportion surviving to families (with Completed Fertility), Central Provinces/Berar 1921–31

	Average No. of Children born per Family with Completed Fertility		Proportion Surviving per 1,000 Children Born to Families with Completed Fertility		Average No. of Children born to Couples Married for 33 Years and Above	
	1921	1931	1921	1931	1921	1931
Hindus	6.11		612		6.59	
Brahmins		6.8(3.9)		591.8(688.5)		6.6
Higher cultivators		6.4(3.8)		539.5(711.5)		7.3
Higher artisans		6.6(4.3)		623.8(637.1)		7.6
Serving castes		6.7(4.3)		582.6(658.1)		7.2
Lower class artisans and tribes		7.1(3.9)		606.8(711.1)		6.9
Primitive tribes		6.2(3.8)		625.5(746.4)		6.6
Gonds	5.64		790		6.11	

Notes: (1) Family with completed fertility is one where the wife has crossed the age of 40 years.

(2) The figures in parentheses are the respective average numbers for all families with and without completed fertility.

Source: Census of India 1931, vol. 12, part-1: Central Provinces and Berar, pp. 172–3,168–9; and Census of India 1921, vol. 12, part-1: Central Provinces and Berar, pp. 98–101.

the Hindu population. As can be seen, the proportion of surviving children per 1000 born was highest for primitive tribes in the Central Provinces/Berar, and it was indeed considerably higher than most of the Hindu caste groups. Note too that even more direct evidence on fertility levels than CWR, namely the average number of children born to families with completed fertility, indicates the lowest fertility for primitive tribes among all groups considered in Table 3.3. Even three decades later, a similar survey in Nagpur, geographically within same region of central India, confirms broadly this historical pattern of lower fertility and mortality among Gonds vis-à-vis other lower caste groups (Driver 1963:Table 96:108). While a marked mortality advantage of tribal infants and children (compared to Hindu counterparts) may appear somewhat counter-intuitive, several reasons can be adduced in support of its plausibility. First, as tribal women may have had a longer birth interval (and possibly lower fertility for reasons discussed below), this exerts a favourable influence on relative health and survival chances of their infants and children. Indeed, tribal lifestyles (for example, less crowded and closer contact with nature) and child-rearing practices (including prolonged breastfeeding combined with early food supplementation) are often thought to promote health. Second, relatively little neglect and discrimination against female children in tribal communities contribute to relatively improved survival chances of overall tribal children as compared to non-tribal counterparts of the Hindu mainstream.[11] In fact, it has often been reported, albeit mostly for non-tribal populations, that the higher the status and autonomy of women in a society, the more superior are the chances of survival of infants and children (see Bajkhaif and Mahadevan 1993:10–12).

The foregoing discussion tends to cast doubts on the conclusion of a higher tribal fertility if drawn merely on the basis of their higher child–woman ratio. In an earlier sample enquiry (in the 1911 census)

[11] See below for further discussion on this, and see also Murthi *et al.* 1995 for contemporary evidence on less anti-female bias in childhood mortality in tribal societies (vis-à-vis the total population). A comparatively small differential in CWR between tribal and Hindu populations in Madras Presidency (as seen in Table 3.2) attracts attention. This may partly be a reflection of a similar fertility level between tribal and non-tribal populations. In fact, Nag, noting the distinctiveness of Madras, provided evidence to show a higher age at female marriage in the mainstream (non-tribal) population of Madras Presidency than that for the rest of India, and this could well be a reason for a smaller difference in C–W ratios between tribal and non-tribal communities. Note that there is hardly any difference in age at female marriage between these two groups in Madras, unlike other regions of India (Nag 1973:115–16). Second, relatively higher levels of miscarriages, child and infant mortality among tribal communities of Madras vis-à-vis other regions could be another contributory factor behind a relatively smaller CWR. For example, the report to the Madras census of 1911, while discussing Todas, a major tribe in southern India, observes:

'[t]he race as a whole is so rotten with syphilis that miscarriages are extremely frequent; while children actually born are in many cases horribly diseased, and die off like flies'; see *Census of India 1911*, vol. 12, part I, Madras, 1912, p. 169. In case of another tribe, Khond, in the plains of Madras presidency, the report, while describing the intercensal population change, puts much emphasis on their antenuptial promiscuity and drunkenness, 'which leads... to a low natality of children, frequent abortion, female sterility, and the spread of venereal diseases'; ibid, p. 62.

on fertility in the Central Provinces/Berar, a somewhat smaller average number of children ever born per family was reported for Gonds (4.6), the prominent tribe in those regions, than those for Rajput (4.8), Chamar (5.3), and even for the total population (4.8).[12] Notwithstanding several limitations and selection biases in these survey data, it is plausible that the tribal population had lower fertility as compared (particularly) to that of the lower caste non-tribal population in Central Provinces/Berar during the early decades of the last century. In fact, some best-known anthropologists of British India took special note of a relatively low fertility and indigenous methods of birth control (including abortion) among tribal communities, often in the context of individual tribes in specific regions. For example, Verrier Elwin observed a distinctively low fertility among Baiga, a tribal group of central India. Although he could not come up with strong evidence on their contraceptive behaviour, he did hint at several indigenous methods of birth control and abortion (Elwin 1939:218–22). While describing Gonds, another major tribe of central India, C. Fürer-Haimendorf mentioned an indigenous medicine, prepared of certain leaves and herbs, 'which is said to prevent conception' (Fürer-Haimendorf 1979:287–88). Note too that even more recent fertility surveys among currently married women as late as the 1980s in a district of Madhya Pradesh (which was a part of the pre-Independence Central Provinces/Berar) shows the lower fertility of Gonds as compared to non-tribal people (Pandey 1989). However, with such micro-level evidence for one location, it is difficult to generalize about the overall fertility of India's tribal population (as a whole) vis-à-vis aggregate Hindu population.[13] However, it is possible to apply indirect demographic techniques (as developed under the sponsorship and support of the United Nations Population Division during 1960s and 1970s and subsequently modified) appropriate to our present situation, where usable vital registration data are extremely limited and

---

[12] See Census of India 1911, vol. 10, part-1, Central Provinces and Berar.
[13] The all-India figures of the average number of children born alive to couples married for 33 years and more, based on sample surveys as a part of the 1931 census operations, show a slight (and perhaps almost negligible) difference between tribals (4.1) and Hindus (3.9); see *Census of India 1931*, vol. I, part-1 (India). It is worth mentioning, however, that recent large-scale fertility surveys (e.g. the National Family Health Survey, 1992–93 and 1998–99) does evince, at all-India level, a lower fertility of tribal vis-à-vis (non-tribal) lower caste population (i.e. SC group). [The following chapter discusses these findings in detail relating to more contemporary periods.]

incomplete, but census-based age–sex distribution exists. Consequently, in the following section, we undertake an exploratory exercise in fertility and mortality differentials based on indirect techniques of demographic estimation.

Differential Demographic Rates Between Tribes and Hindus, 1901–1911: Indirect Estimates

Here we report results of some of our exercises in indirect techniques of demographic estimation to census-based age distribution and child–woman ratio data for tribal and Hindu population groups during 1901–11 (see Table A3.1 in Appendix for age–sex distribution of tribal and Hindu populations during 1891–1911). It is of interest to see whether the developments in demographic techniques subsequent to Davis' 1951 study support his conclusion of a higher tribal fertility (based only on CWRs) or an opposite hypothesis (e.g. lower tribal fertility and mortality) that our foregoing analysis tends to suggest. The 1901–11 decade has been chosen partly because, unlike preceding decades, there were relatively few major mortality crises (related to famines and epidemics), resulting in a positive growth rate of population at the all-India level for both groups being compared here. However, as was shown in Chapter 1, the tribal population experienced a much larger population growth during this decade than the general population did (see Table 1.1). For example, the Hindu population grew at an average annual rate of only 0.43 per cent during this intercensal period, while the corresponding rate for the tribal population, as a whole, was much higher (1.56 per cent; see Davis 1951:179). Although it is tempting to take this higher growth of tribal population as an indication of higher fertility, there are other possibilities. In this context, it would be of interest to attempt at (at least) some indirect demographic estimates (based on Model Life Tables). For example, we have estimated mortality levels of these two groups by matching the proportions of population below 15 years of age i.e. C(15) in 1911 and the respective annual growth rates during 1901–11 with the South Model (Females) Life Tables by means of interpolation.[14] The results are as follows:

	e_0	CDR
Tribals	28.55	38.55
Hindus	20.64	44.48

[14] For the details of indirect methods for estimating demographic measures from census (age distribution and growth rate) data by using model stable

The indirect estimates of death rate as well as life expectation at birth, based on census information on proportions of children and population growth rates, indicate a distinctively better mortality situation for the tribal population as compared to Hindus during the first decade of the twentieth century. As is well-known, however, such indirect estimates are not only based on assumptions relating to the construction of model life tables, but are sensitive to biases in age distribution data.[15] We used the proportion of children below 15 years on the ground that biases due to age misreporting should be at a minimum for the aggregate population below 15 years. In any case, once we have determined respective mortality levels, albeit on the basis of unsmoothed population distributions by age, we may now apply the method suggested by J.R. Rele (1967, 1987) for estimating fertility rates on the basis of child–woman ratios for these two groups. This method of fertility estimation essentially hinges on an observed close linear relationship between CWR and gross reproduction rate. Following this method,[16] we have come up with the estimated total fertility rates (making adjustments for usual patterns of differential age misreporting between children of 0–4 and 5–9 years) of 6.4 and 6.1 respectively for tribals and Hindus. While these indirect fertility estimates posit tribal fertility as being only about 5 per cent higher than that of Hindus early last century, the average differential in terms of enumerated CWRs was as much as 16 per cent during this period (see Table 3.1). (Note that the CWR turned out to be as much as 30 per cent higher for tribals, although the difference was reduced to about only 10 per cent in the following decade of 1891–1901—a decade which had witnessed two successive severe famines with huge excess mortality.) Thus, the above indirect technique, even based on CWRs, does not necessarily end up showing a much higher tribal

---

population parameters, see United Nations 1967, especially chapter 1; 1983: chapter 7). South Model Life Tables (for females) are relatively appropriate for Indian overall mortality conditions in the early twentieth century.

[15] For a useful discussion on possible implications of defective and biased age data (owing to, for example, age heaping) for determination of mortality and fertility levels on the basis of model life tables and stable populations, see United Nations 1967, 1983. As Indian census data on age distribution of population, especially in the past, was far from perfect, one has to be cautious while using them for demographic estimation and its interpretation; see for example, Rele 1987.

[16] For details see Rele 1987:516–18.

Table A3.1 Distribution of census-enumerated population by age and sex for Hindus and Tribals, India 1891–1911

	HINDUS					
	1891		1901		1911	
Age	M	F	M	F	M	F
0–5	14,462,558	15,095,052	12,685,642	13,102,732	14,317,322	14,805,956
5–10	14,808,850	13,955,475	14,309,201	13,720,154	14,804,500	14,202,167
10–15	16,680,438	13,265,378	13,335,714	11,028,381	12,753,469	10,491,997
15–20	12,229,892	11,376,709	9,159,144	8,300,783	9,429,880	8,587,783
20–25	11,743,796	12,577,424	8,360,264	9,074,216	9,262,382	9,967,043
25–30	12,828,365	12,680,985	9,326,528	9,151,835	10,061,045	9,760,412
30–35	9,126,561	8,865,148	9,654,163	8,860,106	9,334,164	9,118,170
35–40	6,487,309	5,702,220	6,461,239	5,830,561	6,967,340	6,089,890
40–45	7,054,177	6,688,045	7,027,622	6,906,912	7,259,106	7,002,991
45–50	3,869,997	3,308,424	3,992,882	3,585,045	4,318,517	3,742,245
50–55	4,552,439	4,569,566	4,737,031	4,805,140	4,946,388	4,948,948
55–60	1,817,200	1,679,533	1,912,023	1,783,329	2,008,462	1,815,800
60+	4,913,806	6,039,721	4,784,837	5,776,433	5,311,108	6,114,310
Total	120,575,388	115,803,680	105,746,290	101,925,627	110,773,683	106,647,712

TRIBALS

Age	1891 M	1891 F	1901 M	1901 F	1911 M	1911 F
0–5	699,384	757,343	582,482	625,857	834,391	884,321
5–10	778,352	737,075	665,365	654,642	805,461	780,318
10–15	565,734	472,950	652,473	497,139	559,448	492,420
15–20	336,986	342,603	370,773	387,883	382,924	411,107
20–25	307,274	370,410	328,948	397,819	366,467	467,881
25–30	357,925	387,434	363,653	381,708	446,099	484,000
30–35	387,241	385,500	364,227	363,712	439,200	431,232
35–40	256,918	233,714	252,791	237,426	315,191	275,560
40–45	304,529	268,053	275,347	256,105	320,665	284,198
45–50	127,015	108,761	128,042	122,506	162,289	140,473
50–55	174,527	159,908	158,050	157,180	190,761	182,664
55–60	51,032	52,327	56,228	61,241	66,656	65,625
60+	183,594	212,374	143,130	176,429	195,689	229,504
Total	4,530,511	4,488,452	4,341,509	4,319,647	5,085,241	5,129,303

fertility as compared to that for the Hindus. It is arguable that a relatively lower level of estimated mortality for the tribal population could be, at least partially, a clue to why the differential in estimated fertility rates between these two groups is negligible as compared to much wider differences between their respective CWRs. This presumed link rests on the hypothesis that the relatively lower level of tribal (overall) mortality is largely due to comparatively lower levels of infant and early childhood mortality among tribal vis-à-vis the Hindu population. If this is true, then higher tribal CWR may not necessarily be an indicator of, as was thought by Davis, a higher tribal fertility. It may be noted that our application of Palmore's equation for 'Class 4 countries' (where IMR data is not available) gives an estimate of tribal fertility rate (5.36), which appears lower than that for the Hindus (5.96) in 1911 (see Palmore 1978; and Rao et al. 1987).[17]

The question of differential age-patterns of mortality is an important consideration in using a model stable population. For example, the above estimation of mortality levels for two groups has been based on our selection of the South Model Life Tables. However, if the North Model were selected for the tribal population on our presumption (deduced above on their high CWRs) of low infant and childhood mortality levels relative to those for adult and other age groups, one may end up having a lower (estimated) tribal fertility (or CBR) than Hindus.[18] If we take, for illustrative purposes, the tribal mortality level determined (as above) by using South Model Tables and then match it for tribal fertility in the North Model, the tribal CBR estimate would be about 40, while it is around 50 for the Hindus based on South Model Tables.

[17] Our argument seems to be consistent with what was observed by the celebrated Mysore study in Karnataka in the 1950s, namely, that increases in the proportion of children were chiefly related to a relatively rapid decline of child mortality, rather than fertility increases. In fact, a rise in the proportion of children had occurred even in the presence of declining fertility (as quoted in Mutharayappa 2000:17).

[18] Careful indirect estimates of India's past mortality often suggest an age pattern being characterized by relatively heavy adult mortality vis-à-vis that of children in the late-nineteenth and early-twentieth centuries, which calls for downward revision of fertility and mortality estimates (Bhat 1989). This past age pattern of mortality is, perhaps, related to the occurrence of several major famines in this period, which, as recent research shows, had generally a more adverse mortality impact (in proportionate terms) on adults vis-à-vis young ages (Dyson 1991; and Maharatna 1996).

Table 3.4   Distribution of females by marital status and age for Hindu and Tribal populations in select locations of India
(Per thousand)

Location/ Age	Marital Status	Hindus			Tribes		
		10–14	15–19	20–24	10–14	15–19	20–24
India	UM	427	102	25	763	282	71
(1881)	M	532	848	893	227	698	894
	W	21	50	82	5	20	35
CP/Berar	UM	408	82	–	916	692	–
(1891)	M	578	894	–	82	299	–
	W	14	24	–	2	9	–
Madras	UM	679	219	–	847	405	–
(1891)	M	310	750	–	148	568	–
	W	11	31	–	5	27	–
Bengal	UM	–	75	20	–	376	133
(1901)	M	–	859	880	–	593	813
	W	–	66	100	–	31	54
CP/Berar	UM	484	139	–	780	303	–
(1901)	M	494	812	–	208	641	–
	W	22	49	–	12	56	–
India	UM	495	122	–	815	376	–
(1911)	M	488	836	–	179	601	–
	W	17	42	–	6	23	–
Bihar/Orissa	UM	434	104	–	808	398	–
(1911)	M	539	851	–	185	580	–
	W	27	45	–	7	27	–
Madras	UM	756	265	–	904	489	–
(1921)	M	234	699	–	86	486	–
	W	10	36	–	10	25	–
Bihar/Orissa	UM	504	91	–	772	313	–
(1931)	M	481	873	–	220	660	–
	W	15	36	–	8	27	–
Madras	UM	756	208	–	853	307	–
(1931)	M	237	754	–	142	669	–
	W	7	38	–	5	24	–

Note: UM = unmarried, M = married, and W = widowed.
Source: Census report.

However, the usefulness of indirect techniques of demographic estimation (and hence the reliability of the results) in a particular context is often circumscribed by the level of relevance (and appropriateness) of some key assumptions involved.[19] Thus, the foregoing analysis so far does not necessarily lead us to a conclusive statement that tribal fertility was lower than that for the Hindus (or for that matter, the whole mainstream population). But what has emerged is a strong indication that India's aggregate tribal population during the early-twentieth century had a lower fertility rate than the mainstream Hindu population, and at least some specific tribal groups inhabiting particular locations must have had a comparatively low fertility in the period considered here. As will be shown in the next chapter, the available evidence (both micro-level and large-scale) for the contemporary period until very recently testifies to a distinctively low tribal fertility as compared to that of their non-tribal counterparts (especially SC) in the majority of Indian locations and, of course, at all-India level.

Having said this, it seems reasonable to wonder about plausible explanations for a relatively low fertility and mortality regime of India's tribal people in the past. Since modern methods of contraception and health care were almost non-existent in the late-nineteenth and early-twentieth century India, the explanations should mainly lie in differential sociocultural norms, values, and practices, which have bearing on reproductive behaviour and performance, and perhaps on infant and child mortality. Indeed biological determinants of fertility variations, such as in postpartum sterility and breastfeeding between social groups are often found on sociocultural characteristics. As was indicated in the preceding chapter, a major plausible explanatory candidate for the differential fertility, especially in the natural fertility context of the past, is differential nuptiality levels and patterns, including marriage patterns and practices between tribals and the Hindus, which we will analyse below.

Marriage Patterns and Fertility: Tribal and Hindu Populations

One feature that distinguishes tribal women from their Hindu counterparts, albeit with a tapering prominence, especially in the recent times, is a relatively late entry into marital union. That this has been clearly so in history is amply borne out in Table 3.5, which presents

[19] For a useful discussion of these assumptions involved and their applicability in various contexts, see Coale and Demeny 1983: chapters 1–3; and also see United Nations 1967, 1983.

(census-based) distribution of 1,000 females by both marital status and age for both tribal and Hindu groups in select provinces during the late-nineteenth and early-twentieth centuries. Putting aside the possibility of differential age-reporting biases between these two groups of women, while more than 50 per cent Hindu females aged 10–14 years were (except in Madras presidency) recorded as married, as many as nearly eighty per cent of tribal females had remained unmarried at this age. Note too that the tribal proportion of unmarried females between 15 to 19 years seems to have been around three times the figure for Hindu counterparts at the all-India level. [About 70 and 40 per cent of tribal females were enumerated as unmarried respectively in CP/Berar (1891) and Bihar/Orissa (1911), whereas the respective Hindu figures were about 8 and 10 per cent.] Furthermore, at the all-India level, the proportion of unmarried tribal females aged 20–4 years appears nearly thrice the figure for the Hindus. Note that more than 13 per cent tribal females were reported unmarried in the Bengal census of 1901, whereas the corresponding figure for the Hindus was only 2 per cent. All this is clearly suggestive not only of a relatively late female marriage norm but of a greater incidence of celibacy (and hence of a lower level of overall nuptiality) among tribal population in the historical past. This past historical differential in marriage patterns is still being echoed (as we have seen in the preceding chapter) through the present times, although on a more subdued note.

Table 3.5   Coale's index of proportion married (I_m), India and selected provinces, 1901–21

	India 1901–21	CP/Berar 1901–21	Bihar/Orissa 1911–21
Hindus	0.80	0.85	0.82
Tribals	0.77	0.81	0.74

    H.H. Risley, India's Census Commissioner during the early-twentieth century, while discussing the Santhals, the dominant tribe of eastern India, wrote in the Ethnographic Appendices to the 1901 census report: 'Girls are married as adults mostly to men of their own choice... [while] high-caste Hindus ...marry their daughters between the ages eight and twelve' (*Census of India 1901*, vol. I, Ethnographic Appendices, Calcutta 1903:145). This same statement, we believe, would hold more or less true for many other Indian tribes across various regions. In the 1901 census, for instance, the average female age at marriage in Mysore was reported to be 14 years among Hindus and 18.1 years among tribal people (Mandelbaum 1954:6). Unlike post-Independence censuses, detailed information on age–sex distribution of population by marital status for all religious groups, including tribals, are available in Indian censuses during the late-nineteenth and early-twentieth centuries. This makes possible the calculation of singulate mean age at marriage (SMAM) for both sexes for tribals and Hindus (see Appendix Table A3.2).[20] The female SMAM appears to have been almost always higher than that of their Hindu counterparts, although the difference in male SMAM is clearly less striking (except for a few cases, for example, the Central Provinces). Note that the positive gap in the singulate age at marriage between tribal and Hindu females in many regions was often of four years, and was of three and half years at all-India level. Note too that the spousal age-gap at marriage is generally smaller in tribal populations than for the Hindus. In the case of tribes like the Bondos, 'the girls prefer to marry younger boys' (Garg 1960:195). This (relatively) late female marriage practice among tribal communities seems consistent with the larger incidence of female celibacy than observed among the Hindus. Indeed, past census data show clearly that the proportion of unmarried (i.e. never married) tribal women in their forties, though perhaps smaller than the European standard, is often much larger than that of the Hindu counterparts (see Appendix Table A3.3). For instance, while the number of unmarried women per 1,000 aged 40–45 years was about 11 for aggregate Hindus in 1911 and 1921, the corresponding figures for tribals is more than twice this number. In fact, in some provinces (Bihar/Orissa in 1911 and 1921, Bombay in 1921), the proportion of tribal women who had remained unmarried is as much as 3–4 times the corresponding Hindu figure. A systematic investigation into possible reasons (e.g. demographic and sociocultural) for a greater incidence of tribal celibacy, while interesting and important, is beyond the scope of our present study. But all this should certainly have exerted

---

[20] SMAM for females (males) is basically an estimate of the average years of life lived in the single (unmarried) state by women (men) in a population, based on proportions of single women (men) for each age group between 15 and 49 years. This index of nuptiality, originally developed by John Hajnal, is widely used as an average age at marriage, especially when information on individual age at marriage is unavailable or highly defective.

Table A3.2   Singulate mean age at marriage (years), Hindu and Tribal
population, various regions of the Indian subcontinent, 1901–41

	Females				Males			
	1901	1911	1921	1931	1901	1911	1921	1931
Assam								
Hindu	14.8	14.7	15.4	14.3	23.9	24.0	24.2	22.9
Tribal	17.8	17.9	18.2	18.0	22.5	22.8	23.0	22.2
Baroda States								
Hindu	12.8	12.5	12.8	–	17.2	18.3	18.4	–
Tribal	15.1	16.7	18.1	–	18.9	20.4	21.8	–
Bengal								
Hindu	11.9	11.7	12.2	10.7	18.9	21.1	22.0	20.5
Tribal	16.7	15.5	15.9	14.8	21.1	21.2	21.7	19.7
Bihar and Orissa								
Hindu	–	12.5	13.1	11.2	–	17.3	17.9	16.9
Tribal	–	16.8	17.3	16.2	–	20.6	20.8	19.5
Bombay								
Hindu	–	12.4	12.6	13.2	–	19.3	19.8	18.9
Tribal	–	15.1	16.8	16.5	–	19.6	20.6	20.1
Central India Agency								
Hindu	14.7	12.7	–	13.1	18.5	18.7	–	16.9
Tribal	15.9	15.2	–	14.7	19.3	20.0	–	18.6
Central Provinces/Berar								
Hindu	11.5	12.1	12.5	10.7	17.0	17.5	17.3	16.2
Tribal	15.6	15.3	16.2	14.5	22.0	17.3	21.0	18.6
Madras								
Hindu	15.4	15.2	15.4	14.9	23.9	22.9	23.4	22.2
Tribal	17.9	–	17.8	15.3	23.4	–	23.2	17.9
Rajputana								
Hindu	13.9	–	13.3	12.4	19.9	20.6	20.6	18.7
Tribal	16.5	–	15.2	15.5	20.5	20.2	20.2	19.3
India								
Hindu	13.4	13.2	13.6	13.5	–	19.9	20.3	19.1
Tribal	16.7	16.6	17.1	15.8	–	21.6	21.8	19.7

*For all religions

Note: The appropriate modifications in the original Hajnal formula for calculation of SMAM have been made both in the face of the early (or even child) marriage practice in the Indian subcontinent and variation in age grouping for census reports. For example, we have taken 10–14 years as the starting age group for proportion of the unmarried for calculating SMAM, instead of taking 15–19 years as was originally suggested by Hajnal in the European context. In calculating the number of years lived in the single state we have taken care about different age-groupings in some census reports, for example, 20–9, 40–59 years.

Source: Present author's own calculations; Agarwala (1972) quoted in Bhattacharjee and Shastri (1976), Table 24, p. 35.

Table A3.3   Number of women enumerated as 'unmarried'
per 1000 aged 40–45.

State	1901		1911		1921	
	Hindus	Tribals	Hindus	Tribals	Hindus	Tribals
India	–	–	**10.6**	**20.6**	**11.5**	**26.1**
Assam	–	–	5.1	10.3	–	–
Baroda	3.4	5.7	–	–	1.7	16.4
Bihar/Orissa	–	–	8.8	29.8	8.7	39.3
Bengal	7.6	28.1	–	–	–	–
Berar	6.7	13.0	–	–	–	–
Bombay Presidency	–	–	14.1	12.4	15.4	23.0
Central Provinces	4.5*	6.2*	–	–	13.7	16.0
Madras	12.3	18.9	–	–	11.0	19.4
Mysore	17.6	10.4	–	–	–	–
Rajputana	5.3	11.4	–	–	5.9	11.8
Travancore	21.2	26.7	–	–	–	–

*Refers to women aged 40–60 years.
Source: Relevant census reports.

a negative influence on the fertility of tribals vis-à-vis Hindu women.[21] On the other hand, however, the Hindu proportions of women widowed are generally much higher (indeed much more than twice at all-India level) than the corresponding tribal figures, a fact which put some restraint on the overall reproductive performance of mainstream Hindu women.

Therefore, there seem to have been two opposite influences of tribal marriage practices (e.g. relatively late marriage together with greater celibacy on the one hand and greater widow remarriage on the other)

[21] There is reason why SMAMs for tribes could be even higher than those presented in Table A3.2. This is because of a modification made by us to original formula, namely, incorporating information on proportion of single in the age 10–14 years while arriving at number of years lived single. This was done in order to make it more suited to the child marriage practice mostly in the mainstream, which however was not (or much less) relevant to tribes. Therefore, if calculation of tribal SMAM would have been based, more realistically, on the (original) assumption that all tribal persons lived single years before age 15, it would have been even higher and the gap in SMAM between tribal and Hindus would have been larger than shown in our calculations in Table A3.2.

on their fertility.[22] It is not really easy to estimate these separate nuptial influences on total fertility, especially when detailed information on natality for different religious groups is unavailable. However, in an effort to gauge the net differential impact on the fertility of these two different nuptiality and marriage patterns, we have applied an indirect method, namely Coale's Index of Proportion Married (I_m) given by[23]

$$I_m = \frac{\sum m(i)f(i)}{\sum w(i)f(i)}$$

where, $m(i)$ = number of married women at age group i
   $w(i)$ = total number of women at age group i
   $f(i)$ = age-specific marital fertility rate at age group i for the Hutterites.

This index (I_m) basically is a measure of the contribution that marital status would make towards the attainment of maximum fertility,[24] 'if married women experienced fertility not subject to parity-related restriction, and non-married women bore no children at all' (Coale and Treadway 1986:34). In other words, it gives, ceteris paribus, an idea about the proportion of births that would be generally lost in a community due to its specific patterns of celibacy, age at marriage, and the state of widowhood or divorce/separation. Thus, this index seems useful for our present purpose of comparing the net effects on fertility of differential nuptiality and other marriage practices (e.g. age at marriage, incidence of widow remarriage, or divorce/separation). Table 3.6 presents I_m during the first two decades of this century for tribals and Hindus, both at the all-India level and also for the Central Provinces/Berar and Bihar/Orissa. (Note that both these provinces are historically characterized by a relatively large tribal proportion in the total population.) It shows that the net negative nuptiality effect on marital fertility is consistently larger for tribals than that for the

[22] For more recent evidence on a greater proportion of 'never married' women among tribal groups in northeastern regions, see Dey 1969:10.

[23] See Coale 1969, and also Coale and Treadway 1986.

[24] The Hutterites, an Anabaptist sect, who live in the north-central area of the United States and in the southern part of central Canada, have kept accurate statistics of births. The married Hutterites experienced the maximum rates of child-bearing by age of the mother during 1921–30 as far as all reliable records of child-bearing rates all over the globe are concerned, because they 'scrupulously adhere to a religious proscription of contraception and abortion, and because of early weaning of their infants' (Coale and Treadway 1986:33).

Table 3.6   Sex ratio (females per 1, 000 males) among Tribal and Hindu populations, selected Indian locations, 1881–1931

Location		1881	1891	1901	1911	1921	1931
India	Tribal	1009	991	1016	1008	996	1009
	Hindu	1002	962	969	963	954	953
Bengal	Tribal	997	999	990	967	973	964
	Hindu	999	969	951	931	916	908
Bihar/Orissa	Tribal	–	1004	–	1040	1032	1027
	Hindu	–	1045	–	1040	1027	1005
CP/Berar	Tribal	1010	1015	1049	1042	1037	1028
	Hindu	982	996	1017	1008	1002	1000
Madras	Tribal	–	–	969	989	996	1006
	Hindu	–	–	1029	1033	1029	1026

Source: Census reports.

Hindus. A relatively small gap in I_m for the Central Provinces/Berar is noteworthy and is consistent with the fact that major tribes (e.g. Gonds and Bhils) of Central Provinces/Berar were already more deeply assimilated within the mainstream Hindu culture and religion, a point which was noted earlier.[25] However, at the all-India level in the early decades of the last century, the negative fertility effect of relatively late female marriages and a larger incidence of female celibacy among tribal communities seem to have outweighed the positive fertility effect of their greater toleration of widow remarriage. While there is, thus, an implied possibility of a lower tribal fertility than that for Hindus, the direct fertility evidence for this period is, unfortunately, lacking. However, considering the nature of variation in nuptiality (including

[25] See also Mamoria 1958:51; *Census of India 1911*, vol. 10, part-1:130. While talking about the Gonds of Central Provinces, the report to the 1911 census, for example, observes: '...tribal system is breaking down and ...are coquetting to a varying extent with Hindu gods' (*Census of India 1911*, vol. 1, part-1:130). While discussing tribal transformation four or five decades later, Mamoria too mentioned Gonds and Bhils of Central India as being those who left their 'tribal moorings and have settled in the neighbourhood of higher cultural groups they serve' (Mamoria 1958:51). In contrast, shortly after the rebellion of 1855 'the more wealthy Santhals', the major tribe of eastern India, started as a fashion to 'imitate the usages of high-caste Hindus and marry their daughters between the ages of eight and twelve. This fashion has, however, since been abandoned...' (*Census of India 1901*, vol. 1, Ethnographic Appendices:145).

marriage age) between the tribal and Hindu population in the past, one may not expect a higher tribal fertility in the early-twentieth century, other things being the same. In fact, our foregoing discussion strongly indicates that it could indeed be lower due to delayed marriage and celibacy among females. For example, the finding of lower fertility among hill tribes of Assam during the early 1960s was, in fact, attributed to their somewhat 'European pattern' of marriage (i.e. relatively delayed marriage and high proportion of people who never married) (Dey 1969).[26]

It is important to note that these tribal nuptiality features (for example, relatively delayed marriage and considerable celibacy) are in large part a reflection of a greater female autonomy and freedom in tribal societies. For example, the report of the Census of India for 1901 (written by H.H. Risley) while discussing Santhals, noted that Santhali girls generally married men of their own choice and '[s]exual intercourse before marriage is tacitly recognized...'; (*Census of India 1901*, vol. 1, Ethnographic Appendices, Calcutta 1903:145). Although this is merely one aspect of female autonomy and for only one tribal group, evidence of a greater female status/autonomy even in other aspects of life such as decision-making and freedom of movement abounds in anthropological literature encompassing many other tribes across India. Therefore, apart from fertility-suppressing effects of tribal features of nuptiality, the implied indications of greater female autonomy and gender equities could provide an additional largely behavioural ground for relatively lower tribal fertility in the historical past.

Patriarchy, Gender Relations and Tribal Fertility: A Comparative Perspective

Contemporary demographic literature suggests the crucial role that differentials in female status and autonomy and the degree of patriarchy play in shaping differential demographic outcomes (in particular,

---

[26] There have been several attempts to estimate the possible magnitude of reduction of fertility or birth rates due to a given increase in the average age at female marriage (Agarwala 1966; Malakar 1972; Cassen 1978; and Premi 1982). These estimates vary according to assumptions employed by individual scholars. There are estimates that clearly show a higher marital fertility rate for women married below 18 years of age than for women who had married later (that is between 21 and 23 years) (see Premi 1982, Table 23; author's own calculation based on SRS and census data for 1971 and 1978).

fertility) between groups and regions.[27] More specifically, a distinct inverse connection between female status/autonomy/patriarchy and fertility is now established beyond reasonable doubt. There are several standard (suggested) mechanisms, not necessarily mutually exclusive, by which a more patriarchal society encourages higher fertility.[28] For example, patriarchy and male domination, which is basically a system of hierarchical relationships within a family, often places control of fertility decisions in the hands of older male and female members, who, in turn, are mostly interested in deriving disproportionately large material benefits of high fertility. Second, the woman's sense of insecurity, which arises from her almost complete economic and social dependence on men, breeds a strong desire 'to produce sons, as many and as soon as possible' as an insurance against the risk of events which threaten her well-being (such as loss of her husband's support). This heavy economic dependence of women on men typically arises because of the limited control women have over familial resources as well as fairly strong restrictions on their movements and income-earning activities. Furthermore, a typical lack of female autonomy and decision-making power suppresses the innovative behaviour of women and decisions favourable to fertility limitation. Since a large part of the cost of child-bearing/rearing is disproportionately borne by women due to captivity during pregnancy, risk of maternal complications, and death, the major disincentives against frequent childbirth arise from women but remains suppressed under stark patriarchy. Indeed, a number of empirical studies over the recent past that have examined this hypothesized inverse relationship between female autonomy and fertility have generally confirmed this, albeit mostly with reference to the mainstream population of South Asia.[29] Comparative studies of minority communities (including tribes) from this perspective are remarkably rare, but such studies could be of much interest, particularly because of the opportunity they offer to evaluate the wider significance and robustness of these hypotheses.[30]

[27] See Caldwell 1978; Cain 1982; Dyson and Moore 1983; Basu 1992; Morgan and Niraula 1995; Malhotra and Kishor 1995; Desai 1994 among others.

[28] For a review of the major perspectives on relationships between patriarchy and other gender inequalities on the one hand and fertility on the other, see Koenig and Foo 1992; also Desai 1994.

[29] See Dharmalingam and Morgan 1996, Morgan and Niraula 1995, Malhotra and Kishor 1995, and Basu 1992 among others.

[30] Harbison *et al.* 1989 is perhaps only one such study.

Given these current perspectives on gender inequality and fertility, one could well presume that a marked differential in female autonomy (and more broadly in gender relations) between tribal and Hindu communities in the past must have contributed to producing a fertility differential between them. In the absence of modern methods of fertility control during the historical period considered here, any effect of female status and autonomy on fertility should have worked by means of sociocultural behaviour and practices such as marriage age, female labour participation, and spousal separation and abstinence. Although issues of gender relations and status of women in tribal societies have been drawing the attention of researchers (mostly anthropologists) for long, systematic investigations of their implications for tribal demographic behaviour are extremely rare. What appears consistently from ethnographic and anthropological literature is a relatively high female status, autonomy, and freedom among most Indian tribes (see Maharatna 1996).

Following our discussion in the preceding chapter as well as contemporary literature, sex ratio (females per 1,000 males) and female work participation rate can be taken as broad, though indirect, indicators of female status and autonomy, especially for a comparison between tribal and Hindu societies in the past. The past censuses (especially those before 1951) do not provide detailed information on work participation simultaneously by sex and social/religious group. But the relatively large role of tribal women in productive work activities is well-known. Indeed, as was discussed in the preceding chapter, the censuses in post-Independence India amply and consistently bring out this fact, and there are few reasons why this might not have been the case early last century or even before.[31] In fact, past ethnographic literature on tribal people provides scattered evidence on substantial work participation by tribal females. Therefore, on this count of the productive role of women and their economic worth and independence, tribal women should have fared much better than their Hindu counterparts in the past. At an aggregate level, this should have exerted an influence towards making tribal fertility relatively lower than that of the Hindu population. Indeed as noted

[31] Just for a quick illustration, according to the 1961 census, about 52 per cent of India's tribal women were reported to have participated in economically 'gainful' activity, whereas the corresponding proportion was slightly less than 12 per cent for the non-tribal population (Raza and Ahmad 1990:370).

earlier, some recent statistical analyses of district-level data do provide a strong indication that female labour-force participation influences fertility negatively (Murthi *et al*. 1995). Thus, a higher labour-force participation of tribal females could well have been instrumental for their lower fertility in historical past periods too, presumably by enhancing female autonomy and its fertility-suppressing agency role.

Our foregoing argument that tribal gender relations have historically been more balanced than for the general mainstream population is also consistent with a higher aggregate female–male ratio for the tribals during the historical period considered here (see Table 1.1 in Chapter 1). Table 3.6 presents sex ratios for tribals and Hindus for the whole of India and select provinces between 1881 and 1931. As can be seen, tribals have had a consistently more favourable sex ratio towards females than that for Hindus in the historical past, with perhaps the exception of Madras. A distinctively lower tribal female–male ratio vis-à-vis that of the Hindus in Madras during the early twentieth century was more pronounced in patterns of contemporary differential between tribal and general sex ratios in much of south India (as was discussed in the preceding chapter). It is also noteworthy that *Hindu* sex-ratios in Bihar/Orissa and the Central Provinces/Berar, both the homeland of a large chunk of India's tribal population, seems to have comparatively been more balanced than the overall Hindu sex-ratio for India (as a whole) during this period. A relatively greater presence of tribal people and male-selective out-migration are plausible factors for a relatively balanced Hindu sex ratio in these regions.

While a tribal proneness for migration (often perhaps male-selective) for work is sometimes taken as a reason for their relatively high female–male ratios in specific regions/provinces, this can hardly be valid at all-India level. As the report on the 1931 census of India writes, '[t]he general conclusion as to the sex ratios of India proper is therefore that in the aboriginal tribes the numbers of two sexes are approximately equal, whereas in the rest of the community males exceed females' (Govt. of India 1931:200). If the relatively more balanced tribal sex ratio does imply greater women's status and female autonomy as compared to the aggregate Hindu community, this would add plausibility to our hypothesis of a lower overall tribal fertility in the late nineteenth- and early-twentieth century India. This said, one should not be oblivious to the possibility of considerable inter-regional and inter-tribal variations and diversities too.

Discussion and Concluding Remarks

The purpose of the present chapter was two-fold: one, creating a historical background of tribal demographic behaviour, against which contemporary evidence can be better placed and evaluated; second, making more explicit the need, potential scope, and reward for systematic historical research on differential demographic behaviour and its sociocultural underpinnings (rather than providing the best possible demographic estimates). Although much research is currently being undertaken on the role of differential sociocultural and organizational features, family systems, gender relations in explaining differential demographic outcomes in developing countries, the attempts to verify and enrich such dominant perspectives by drawing on past reality and historical materials is extremely rare in India.[32] For example, the differential fertility behaviour between groups must be an essential element of a larger story of fertility transition.[33] Indeed, our foregoing analysis has clearly pointed to the necessity of being cautious about the use of child–woman ratios in inferring on fertility, and hence about Davis' conclusion that Indian tribes, on the whole, have had a higher fertility (and perhaps higher mortality too) than that of the Hindus early last century.[34] But our illustrations in this historical period, based on indirect techniques of demographic estimation, seem suggestive of an opposite scenario, namely that tribal

[32] This is in sharp contrast with the existence of voluminous literature on European fertility in the historical past (that is, the well-known Princeton European Fertility Project, and long tradition of using parish records in European demographic research). While this contrast can largely be attributed to a (relative) scarcity of historical demographic materials in the majority of developing countries, the present-day countries of the Indian subcontinent have a distinct advantage on this score, as they have had an uninterrupted record of census operations since the early 1870s.

[33] As the European Fertility Project and subsequent studies bring out, a remarkably diverse fertility behaviour was found across European countries before the onset of 'fertility transition'. In fact, a sound knowledge of these differentials has been helpful for explaining observed variations in magnitude, timing, and speed of subsequent fertility transitions in these regions.

[34] Davis (1986), more than three decades later, proclaimed in his equally illuminating study in an evolutionary perspective a lower fertility among primitive tribes and hunter-gatherers. This was largely as a conscious demographic response, tailored largely via sociocultural features to their physical circumstances of livelihood.

fertility and mortality levels (on the whole) could well have been lower than those of the mainstream Hindu population.

A relatively better overall tribal mortality level was perhaps in large part due to their relatively lower infant and childhood mortality as compared to Hindus. Indeed, the contemporary evidence from large-scale country-wide surveys (for example, National Family Health Survey the 1990s, NSS, NCAER 1994 survey) generally report that, until very recently, tribal infant mortality rate (and even child mortality) to be lower than that of their non-tribal counterparts (SC) (details in the following chapter). In fact, our suggested relative mortality advantage of tribal children in the past could be thought to have left its echo in more recent periods.

Plausible reasons for a (relative) tribal mortality advantage, especially in infancy and early childhood years as early as 1901, are not very difficult to find in fragmentary ethnographic evidence. These explanations, to be relevant to the times we are considering, have something to do with differential lifestyles, environment, as well as sociocultural traditions and practices. For example, relatively prolonged breastfeeding and early start of food supplements for infants among tribes has often been mentioned as the possible sources of such differential.[35] Other good features of infant and child-care practices among tribes include their holding infants and children vertically during most of their waking time and a greater physical contact with mothers (Konner 1976). In contrast, many mainstream (non-tribal) customs and practices during childbirth and afterwards are often reported to be inimical to survival chances of the infant. In this context, let us quote an illuminating passage from the report of the Bengal census

[35] A study of Santhal and (non-tribal) SC women in a particular location of West Bengal in a more recent period has brought out the fact of a remarkably prolonged breastfeeding and concomitantly lower risk of conception for tribal women (vis-à-vis their non-tribal counterparts) (Pakrasi and Manna 1989). As authors note: '[t]he tribal mothers give solid food to their infants after 6 months post-partum and most of them continue with breastfeeding' (ibid: 46). See also Chandrasekhar 1972:228–38 for a useful discussion of the role of supplementary food in lowering the risk of infant/childhood mortality and also for evidence to testify that the Hindus (vis-à-vis tribes) are generally late in giving solid food to older infants. It is also noteworthy in this context that a recent finding of (relatively) low levels of infant and childhood mortality (and even of overall mortality to a smaller extent) among one tribal group in Kenya has been largely attributed to a milk-based diet and long periods of breastfeeding (Ssennyonga 1993).

1881 on mortality advantage of tribal children vis-à-vis Hindus (Govt. of India 1883:120):

> For the years of infant life from the beginning of the first to the end of the fourth complete year the percentage of living children to the whole population is higher among the aboriginal tribes [18.20] than among the followers of any other religion [14.03 for Hindus; 15.77 for Muslims].
> ...and the fact affords a fresh illustration of the well-known law that the productive powers of man are in inverse proportion to the standard of luxury which has reached; and that given a sufficient quantity of food without excessive hardships of climate, the off-spring of the primitive tribes is more numerous and more healthy than that of their more civilized neighbours. More particularly is this case in India, for it is impossible to conceive customs more prejudicial to the chances of survival than those which prevail both among Hindus and Mohamedans at the birth of a child [e.g. suffocating atmosphere created by closed windows, smoke and overcrowd].

Furthermore, almost total absence (or insignificance) of child marriage practice among tribes in the past might have been a reason for tribal comparative mortality advantage in infancy, as the risk of death is generally higher among the infants of very young mothers. Understandably enough, a comparatively low tribal fertility itself (as a result longer duration of birth spacing as well as breastfeeding) could be a reason for a lower infant and childhood mortality. Relatedly, relatively better nutritional levels of tribal children could also follow, in line with several empirical studies among poorer households, from comparatively greater female autonomy and command over intra-household resources in tribal communities (see Agarwal 1994:29–30).

Moreover, there are fairly strong indications, especially prior to mass use of antibodies and vaccinations (and a wide network of contact), that communities such as tribes who lived in less-crowded settlements and in great intimacy with a natural environment (for example, forests and hills), generally fared better in mortality terms (see Wirsing 1985). And this might well have been true for India's tribal people too in the past, when their main settlements were not only in mountainous and hilly tracts but also in circumstances with less chance of exposure to contamination and disease transmission. There is also a possibility of relatively effective indigenous methods and medicines for medical treatment among tribes vis-à-vis Hindus in the pre-modern period of epidemiology and medical science. Due to the relative closeness to nature and forests, tribals have generally been better at using herbs and leaves for many purposes, including health care. Besides, tribal people, partly because of these healthy aspects of their habitation, and partly due to their isolation from the mainstream population, were relatively less inflicted by epidemics. Although evidence in support of this hypothesis seemed hard to gather in the Indian context, it may be noted that the mortality effect of the great Influenza Pandemic of 1918 was found relatively less pronounced among pygmies and bushmen compared to other populations of the Kalahari desert (Dornan 1975:141). Indeed, spread and transmission of disease and associated mortality elevation among tribes is often seen as a major negative aspect of their increasing contact and integration with the mainstream population and culture (Mamoria 1958:48).

In fact, several other hypotheses can be adduced to explain relatively better mortality for India's tribal population in the past. For example, malaria, which was almost the largest killer during the period considered here, might have been less deadly in tribal habitations in high altitudes with greater dryness. Furthermore, the incidence of diarrhoeal and respiratory diseases might have been relatively less among the tribal population, presumably because of their greater consumption of spring water and less density and crowding in their habitation. There is indeed evidence that 'foraging societies experience relatively low levels of infant and child mortality due to synergistic effects of nutritional patterns yielding adequate growing and maintenance requirements and a relatively low incidence of infectious disease' (Handwerker 1983:15).

Thus, a relatively low mortality of infants and young children vis-à-vis adults in the tribal population could have been a reason not only for a higher tribal CWR, but also for the relative stability of tribal proportion in the total population vis-à-vis the declining Hindu proportion in the late-nineteenth and early-twentieth centuries. Our estimated lower tribal mortality level [based on C(15)] not only rejects the thesis (proposed by Davis) of a higher tribal fertility as the cause of constancy of their proportion, but strongly suggests a lower fertility (and mortality) for India's aggregate tribal population than those for the Hindus early last century. Indeed, it is worth quoting what Fürer-Haimendorf, a leading authority on Indian tribes for more than half a century, remarked in 1985:

...only one or two generations ago many tribal communities enjoyed the advantages of a well balanced ecology fully in tune with the natural resources of their environment and boast an overall quality of life superior in many ways to that of large sections of the Indian rural population. Adequate food supplies, non-exploitative social structure, freedom from indebtedness and other forms of dependence on non-tribal outsiders, equality of the sexes, and a remarkable tolerance in all interpersonal relations were outstanding characteristics of such tribal societies. Moreover, there seems to be no reason to assume that their way of life could not have continued for the foreseeable future without requiring any aid from outside sources, particularly as in most tribal areas there was no excessive population growth threatening the ecological balance... (Fürer-Haimendorf 1985:170).

Apart from well-known fertility-reducing effects, both biological and motivational, of lower infant mortality/childhood mortality (Preston 1978), there are some other good reasons, particularly relating to patterns of marriage, gender relations, and social organization, to expect tribal fertility to have been lower than that for Hindus in the historical past.[36] In terms of Coale's classification (Coale 1965), India's tribal population seems to have had both 'Malthusian' (that is, delayed marriage) and 'neo-Malthusian' elements (that is, higher status and work participation rate for women) of low fertility.[37] Indeed relatively delayed marriage among tribal females seems to resemble the European historical pattern as a tribal man had to postpone his marriage until he had accumulated enough money to pay the bride-price and to set up his own household (Majumdar 1947:81). For instance, it was not really rare among the Hos of Chota-Nagpur for a tribal girl to wait till her mid-thirties before her boyfriend could accumulate enough money

[36] Note that a lower fertility of two nomadic pastoral populations as compared to that of a sedentary cultivating group in Central Mali has been found to be related to differential marriage patterns, with the former being dominated by monogamy, which maintains a comparatively large number of currently unmarried women (Randall 1996). For a similar patterns of differential fertility arising from differences in marriage patterns, breastfeeding practices and social organization between diverse ethnic groups in Africa, see Hill 1985. As Hill concludes, '...the very different lifestyle of the different ethnic groups comprising the national population of any Sahelian country are likely to have characteristic patterns of mortality and fertility even though the physical environment may be roughly comparable between the groups' (ibid:62–3).

[37] Indeed there has been a long-standing debate in the global (historical) context over the question of whether fertility levels of 'tribal and primitive societies' were generally low or high (Carr-Saunders 1922; Krzwicki 1934; Lorimer 1954; Nag 1962; also Caldwell and Caldwell 2003).

by working to pay for the bride-price (Roy Burman 1987; and Majumdar 1950).[38] Thus, like a large part of historical Europe, where fertility was relatively low largely due to delayed marriage practices (and greater incidence of spinsterhood) (Coale 1986:8), Indian tribes, too, historically had practised late marriage norms, resulting in their relatively low fertility.[39] Also, tribal people were familiar and perhaps fairly efficient in using indigenous medicines and methods of prevention of conception (including abortion) (see Elwin 1943; Mamoria 1958:112–15).[40] Relatively prolonged breastfeeding and larger birth intervals (Puri 1992) and perhaps a greater incidence of sterility and infertility, both primary and secondary, among tribal communities might have been other contributors to relatively low tribal fertility.[41] As will be seen in the following chapter, the suggested regime of relatively low fertility and mortality for India's tribes in the past has

[38] There is evidence, in the African context, of delayed female marriage among nomadic tribes, thereby contributing to their relatively low fertility as compared to that for women of settled tribes, who marry earlier than the former (Henin 1969).

[39] Referring to historical Europe, Hajnal writes that 'men marry late because they cannot "afford" to marry young' (Hajnal 1965:133). Likewise '[m]arriage is usually late in tribal society' because young men cannot afford to pay bride-price 'till late in life' (Mazumdar 1947:81). Mazumdar, while referring to some major Indian tribes as late as 1947, also wrote: 'Girls seldom marry before 18 and 20, and men seldom below 25 or even 30' (ibid:81). Indeed, there is also scattered evidence of a much higher proportion of never married tribal females as compared to their non-tribal counterparts (Dey 1969).

[40] For more contemporary evidence, see Mutharayappa 1998:123.

[41] See Howell 1976, 1979 and White 1959 among others, for evidence on these factors in Africa and elsewhere. Indeed a relatively low fertility of Kung women has sometimes been attributed to their relatively smaller weight responsible for making them take longer to ovulate, and partly to the incidence of venereal diseases (Howell 1979:chapters 7–10). Indeed nutritional deficiency, excessive physical work activity, and relatively harsh livelihood patterns might have made some contribution relatively low female fertility among some Indian tribes. But separating out such nutritional and other biological effects on fertility from those of sociocultural influences, including mobility patterns of Indian tribes, is extremely difficult. For example, the question of how different the energy expenditure patterns are between tribal and lower caste women—taking into account their differential patterns of work—has hardly been addressed systematically yet. For a useful discussion of the role of nutrition and physical work in fertility performance in natural fertility populations, see Frisch 1997, and Garenne and Frisch 1994 and the literature cited therein; see also Krishnaji 1992, especially chapter 7.

continued to be echoed, albeit with varying intensity across regions, in more contemporary periods.[42] While the current scenario would understandably be more complex, the historical patterns of demographic differentials between social groups should serve as a useful guide to analysing contemporary evidence and patterns. For example, what Szreter (1996:533) calls in the British context a 'socially divisive' nature of fertility in the historical past could provide useful insights for a better understanding of India's current fertility transition. As 'distinct fertility regimes changing alongside each other' characterized the British history of fertility transition, the Indian fertility differential between tribal and non-tribal societies and its evolution might also be fruitfully analysed in such a broad general perspective. Furthermore, such an historical differential in demographic regimes appears consistent with an even broader homeostatic perspective in which diverse human societies are seen to adopt varied regulatory mechanisms that keep the long-term overall pattern of low growth (see Wilson and Airey 1999).

The foregoing analysis has also shown that demographic analysis of historical information can profitably be reframed in the light of both newly discovered methods and knowledge as well as of contemporary debates and concerns. For example, the strength and ramifications of contemporary perspectives on the role of female status and autonomy (more broadly, the women's agency) in demographic behaviour and transition can be examined with such historical analyses. Conversely, more historical research on tribal demographic behaviour and its sociocultural underpinnings can enrich the understanding of contemporary demographic phenomena and of the theories and explanations being currently offered. Thus, with the foregoing historical patterns of demographic regime for Indian tribes (vis-à-vis the mainstream) as a broad background, we will analyse (in the following chapter) the contemporary evidence on tribal demographic phenomena and trends, and their wider significance—mostly in a comparative perspective.

[42] This seems consistent with global anthroplogical literature suggesting that nomadic, hunting, and forest-based lifestyles and social organizations are generally akin to comparatively low fertility (and perhaps mortality too) levels as compared to settled and sedentary groups (see Howell 1976, 1979; Dyson 1977; Lee and DeVore 1976; and Henin 1968, 1969; Davis 1986; Handwerker 1983). This view, however, has been questioned by several researchers (on a debate on this, see Caldwell and Caldwell 2003).

4

Fertility, Mortality, and Gender Bias among Indian Tribes
The Contemporary Scenario

Introduction and Background

Over the last several decades, demographic concerns have come to occupy a central place in the development discourse.[1] In this fast growing literature, the role of 'culture', including kinship patterns, gender relations, and female autonomy often appears, as noted earlier, as a key explanatory candidate in demographic behaviour across the Indian subcontinent. As is well established now, sociocultural traits of a society play an important (and somewhat independent) role in shaping demographic outcomes (for example, fertility, mortality and

[1] Even a browsing of World Development Reports and Human Development Reports for the last several years, and also a hurried reading of the deliberations in the past few Population Conferences (for example, Cairo, Delhi, and Beijing) and also in the Social Development Summit (in Copenhagen), all testify to a heightened global concern about the demography of the Third World. Issues like rapid population growth across the Third World, continuing high fertility in various parts, high infant and child mortality, low status of women and their reproductive health, sex-discrimination and sex differential in mortality appear to be the overriding items on the global agenda for immediate attention and research. See, in particular, Drèze and Sen (1995) and Sen (1999) for a feel of how much importance is currently being accorded to demographic issues (that is, to fertility, women's status, infant and child mortality and its sex differentials, literacy) in discussions on development experiences of developing countries; and see also Sen 1989, 1994.

its gender bias), although often indirectly via their crucial influences on female status and autonomy.[2] In the last chapter, such a broad connection between sociocultural features and demographic outcomes has been elucidated in the historical (and comparative) context of tribal and Hindu populations of India. Tribes, as a whole, seem to have experienced different demographic processes in the past from those of non-tribal populations, and it is therefore of interest to see whether and how far these historical patterns of tribal demographic differentials have persisted through contemporary times. This chapter seeks to address this question by critically reviewing the existing literature on contemporary features of tribal demographic behaviour and their trends in a comparative perspective.

Hypotheses

Although there is a large and growing literature on lifestyle patterns and sociocultural characteristics of contemporary Indian tribes, it is not easy to form a general a priori hypothesis about relative fertility levels of tribal vis-à-vis non-tribal populations. For example, as tribals (including nomadic and primitive groups) are generally less 'modernized', they can be expected to have a relatively high fertility. Relatedly, as indicated earlier, tribal communities, especially in the early phase of modernization, can be hypothesized to experience a rising fertility owing to the disappearance of age-old fertility-inhibiting practices and customs (that is, prolonged breast-feeding and postpartum abstinence). Moreover, such a 'pre-transition fertility rise', though relevant to the non-tribal population too, should occur later among tribals, as they are behind the 'mainstream' in being modernized. Also, with a traditional practice of relatively late marriage among tribal females, its possible (and continuing) declines in the contemporary period because of the ongoing Sanskritization and/or similar

[2] What ordinarily appear as cultural traits of a society could sometimes be outcomes of a symbiosis between culture and economics. Women's status and autonomy, for example, though it does appear as a cultural parameter of a society, is sometimes amenable to manoeuvre via economic and social policy changes (namely, spread of female work opportunities and work participation, and increased female literacy and education). For discussions on the role of socio-economic changes in enhancing women's status/autonomy, and hence its 'agency role' in demographic transition (that is, lower fertility and infant and child mortality rates), see Drèze and Sen 1995:140–78; Drèze and Murthi 2001; Murthi *et al.* 1995; Sen 1999; Drèze and Sen 2002; also Kishor 1993; Rahman and Rao (2004).

assimilation processes could also be a reason for a somewhat late occurrence of a pre-transition increase of tribal fertility.

On the other hand, tribal culture and social organization, including gender relations and kinship patterns (which are usually more egalitarian and community-oriented as well as less discriminatory and hierarchical) may well make one expect—as noted earlier—a relatively low tribal fertility. Their nomadic or even certain features of a settled lifestyle, such as, greater female autonomy and female work participation, and mobility patterns, seem to be inimical to raising and rearing a large number of children. Conversely, a relatively harsh tribal habitat may be thought consistent with their greater need for children as productive assets. But, following Howell's study of Kung! women showing longer birth intervals (hence lower fertility), due to relatively less body fat and hence delayed resumption of ovulation, low fertility can also be visualized for India's tribal women, who may subsist on a deficient diet but who undertake excessive physical activity (see Krishnaji 1983). Thus, given these conflicting forces, one can hardly settle down to a single unambiguous judgement on the expected relative fertility level (and its trend) for tribal in contemporary times.

A similar ambiguity could vitiate one's a priori judgement on the relative mortality level of tribals vis-à-vis the non-tribal SC group in the contemporary period. For instance, as tribes are generally less modernized and have less exposure to modern health provisions, they can be hypothesized to experience a higher mortality as compared to the mainstream. However, because of greater intimacy with the natural environment in a primitive habitat with less crowding and pollution, as well as because of healthy lifestyle patterns and practices, such as child care and use of indigenous herbal/natural medicines, tribes could be expected to experience a (relative) mortality advantage. But the task of formulating hypotheses on their comparative demographic outcomes can get even more difficult due to a host of diverse influences, namely, diet, drinking habits, nutritional status, tribal health taboos, and so on. However, as already indicated in the preceding chapters, notwithstanding tribal diversities, what emerges (with a few dubious exceptions) as one of the commonest traits is relatively greater female autonomy and less anti-female discrimination. As noted earlier, anti-female discrimination and its manifestations in the sex-differential of mortality and in the sex-ratio are much less among tribal communities. However, long-standing assimilation and transformation processes, like acculturation, modernization and Sanskritization) in varying pace and degree across regions and tribal groups should have made tribal societies increasingly internalize mainstream anti-female sociocultural features. Indeed, as will be detailed later, a distinct tendency towards an anti-female bias and discrimination is emerging among some contemporary tribal groups in specific locations.

Some General Points relating to Existing Studies

Despite a substantial body of anthropological literature on tribal societies and on their present predicament, careful studies focusing on patterns of their demographic behaviour are relatively few. S. Chandrasekhar, an eminent Indian demographer, while welcoming a newly published book on tribal demography in the 1950s, remarked:

> [f]or some strange reason, all the studies on Indian demography have hitherto ignored the question of India's aboriginal population... In fact, we do not have a single demographic study of any one of the tribes based on the intensive field work (Mamoria 1958:vii; italics added).

This relative academic neglect of tribal demographic phenomena has continued.[3] Understandably, much fewer are the studies which systematically address possible linkages between tribal sociocultural features and demographic outcomes, such as fertility and mortality. Indeed, the study of tribal demographic behaviour by professional and academic demographers has so far been disturbingly minimal. The few field-based demographic investigations of tribal groups undertaken are by anthropologists whose interest in tribal demographic patterns often appears routinized and peripheral in terms of depth of analysis.[4] Even where demographic behaviour is the prime concern of a tribal study

---

[3] To take a simple example, recently published multi-volume compilations of articles on Indian tribes present nearly 300 papers by individual scholars, but virtually none focuses on the features of tribal demographic behaviour as such (Chaudhuri 1992; and Pfeffer and Behera 1997). By citing these books, we, of course, do not intend to comment on their orientation and design. Indeed as we discuss below, a few demographic aspects constitute a fairly common theme of anthropologists' enquiry into tribal populations. However, a few books of collected papers devoted explicitly to aspects of tribal demography, have appeared of late (see Bose et al. 1990).

[4] However, there are broadly two categories of secondary sources that we analyse below, namely, local micro-level (field-based) studies, and large-scale sample survey data.

by an anthropologist, the results often appear unsound from the standpoint of demographic and statistical methods. Many demographic studies by anthropologists lack a proper understanding of demographic concepts and measures.[5] So far, most anthropological Indian research on tribal demographic behaviour has offered unreliable and sometimes even misleading findings.[6] Systematic and scientific studies on tribal demographic behaviour, both by professional demographers and by anthropologists equipped with a proper grasp of demographic techniques, are distressingly rare.[7]

Furthermore, the existing studies very rarely undertake a comparative analysis. When tribal demographic features are examined they are usually presented as such, without placing them against those for non-tribal people. And even when a few studies have brought out a contrast of demographic outcomes between tribal and non-tribal groups, a systematic explanation of the observed differential is inadequately attempted (see below for details). However, despite the above difficulties and limitations it is both possible and important to utilize

[5] The unsoundness of fertility estimates in such studies takes various forms, like presenting relevant information in ways that are not in line with standard demographic measures (for example, using average number of living children per woman aged 15–49 years as a measure of fertility without expressing any reservations [Dubey and Bardhan 1978]), misinterpreting information (for example, using CBR estimates uncritically for fertility levels (Sinha 1990), unclear procedure of fertility calculation (for example, Verma 1977; Pandey 1994), ignoring the possibility of selection biases (owing to sampling procedure and sample size), etc. Similar defects can be detected in some studies on estimations of tribal mortality and death rate too.

[6] For example, some studies provide information on the average number of children ever born to women who are, in some cases, 'currently married', and in other cases 'ever married', and who are either about to complete their reproductive career or are already past that age; again, some studies give the average number of children surviving to such women, and some concentrate only on the child–woman ratio, while some other studies calculate the average live births or average pregnancies per couple and sometimes per mother (see Padmanabham 1985). There is even an instance where the conclusion about fertility has been based on information only on the proportions of females who have given birth one, two, three,... times (see Tripathi 1992), an example of whimsical and utterly unscientific fertility estimation!

[7] The few studies with sophisticated and rigourous applications of demographic techniques and concepts to anthropological data on specific Indian tribes include Ray and Roth 1984, 1991; Ray *et al.* 1984a, b; Roth and Ray 1985; and Nag 1954, 1976.

existing secondary literature, and hence we attempt below to extract
and put together discernible facts and issues about major aspects of
demographic behaviour of Indian tribes. To do this, the main findings
of micro-level (field-based) studies relating to fertility, mortality, and
the sex ratio for various individual tribes in different locations have
been summarized and presented in a comparative format in Table 4.1.
The major facts that emerge from these micro-level studies are then
judged in the light of findings from large-scale sample surveys (as
presented in Tables 4.2 and 4.3, respectively, for fertility and mortality).
Apart from defects pertaining to the quality of care in collecting and
handling large data sets, one problem with large-scale survey data,
especially in which both majority and minority social classes are covered
on a proportional random principle, relates to a very small number of
sample cases that get selected for minority groups like ST. However,
this is not much of a problem in those large-scale surveys that are
specifically designed and undertaken for investigating the minority
communities, as done by well-known agencies like the Registrar
General's Office (RGO), National Sample Survey Organization
(NSSO), and the National Council of Applied Economic Research
(NCAER).

Tribal Fertility

The geophysical and sociocultural diversities of Indian tribes constitute
a stumbling block when generalizing the level and trend of 'tribal
fertility'. In fact, most tribal studies refer to specific context, tribe, and
region, and their coverage both in terms of area and number of tribes
is limited (see Table 4.1). Drawing on such micro-level studies, an
attempt to discern regional (and temporal) patterns of tribal fertility
is obviously fraught with difficulties. First, while fertility may vary
between different tribes inhabiting the same region, one individual
tribe (say, Santhals) may evince different demographic behaviour in
two regions (that is, in Bihar and Orissa), corresponding to broad
spatial variations in economic, sociocultural, or ecological
circumstances. However, this difficulty is somewhat eased by the fact
that a broad pattern of spatial distribution of major tribal groups exists
across Indian regions. Besides, geophysical, environmental, economic,
and infrastructural specificities of a region are likely to even out intrinsic
inter-tribal differences in demographic patterns.

Table 4.1 Summary of demographic estimates from micro-level studies across various regions and tribes of contemporary India

Author/Source (1)	Year of Survey (2)	Area/Region (3)	Tribal and Non-tribal Groups (4)	Fertility (5)	Measure used (6)	H/L/ND (7)	Mortality (8)	Measure used (9)	H/L/ND (10)	Sex Ratio (11)
Nag (1954)	1952	Trivandrum and Quilon districts, Travancore	Kanikkar Travancore (1931)	4.74(a)	ANCEB	L	185.5@	IMR	–	920
				6.49(a)	ANCEB	–	–	–	–	–
Ray and Roth (1991)	1954	Orissa	Juang	5.79	TFR	L	–	–	–	–
			Koya Dora	6.55	TFR	H	–	–	–	–
			Orissa (1961–66)	6.1	TFR	–	–	–	–	–
Roth and Ray (1985); Ray and Roth (1984)	1954	Orissa	Juang sedentary	5.14	ANCEB	L	33.4+	CDR	L	–
			nomadic	6.93	ANCEB	–	–	–	–	–
				5.35	ANCEB	–	37.8+	CDR	–	–
			India (1952)	5.90(b)	ANCEB	–	–	–	–	–
Sen (1956)	1955	Dehra Dun hills, Uttar Pradesh	Jaunsaris	3.1	ANCEB	–	L	–	–	–
			Uttar Pradesh (1961–66)	6.3	TFR	–	–	–	–	–
Basu (1967)	1961	Nilgiri district, Madras	Irula	6.5	ANCEB	–	–	–	–	962
Basu (1978)	1961	Nilgiri hills, Madras	Kota	4.1	ANCEB	–	–	–	–	–

Source	Year	Region	Group	Value	Measure	Level	Value	Measure	Value
Das and Banerjee (1964)	1962	West Bengal	*Zone II* Relatively tribal zone (Bankura, Midnapore and Purulia)	3.2	ANCEB	L	–	–	–
			Zone I (Darjeeling/Jalpaiguri)	5.8	ANCEB	L	–	–	–
			Zone III (24-Parganas, Nadia and Murshidabad)	5.5	ANCEB	L	–	–	–
			West Bengal (1961–66)	6.7	TFR	–	–	–	–
Agarwal (1967)	1963–4	Little Andaman	Onges	1.68	ANCEB	–	–	–	–
Rakshit (1972)	–	Bastar district, MP	Dorla	4.9	ANCEB	–	–	–	–
			Dhurwa	5.1	ANCEB	–	–	–	–
Nag (unpublished) in Nag (1976)	1964–5	Ranchi district, Bihar	Oraon	4.0	ANCEB	L	–	–	–
			Bihar (1966–71)	6.3	TFR	–	–	–	–
Verma (1977)	1965–6	Hazaribagh district, Bihar	Santhal	6.9	ANCEB	H	16.7	CDR	940
				(7.1)	(TFR)	–	(192.6)	(IMR)	{0.90}
			Birhor	6.3	ANCEB	ND	39.5	CDR	977
				(6.2)	(TFR)	–	(218.8)	(IMR)	{0.83}
			Bihar (1966–71)	6.3	(TFR)	–	16.4	CDR	–
				(6.3)	(TFR)	–	(138)	(IMR)	–

(Contd.)

Table 4.1 (contd.)

Author/Source (1)	Year of Survey (2)	Area/Region (3)	Tribal and Non-tribal Groups (4)	Fertility (5)	Measure used (6)	H/L/ND (7)	Mortality (8)	Measure used (9)	H/L/ND (10)	Sex Ratio (11)
Nag (unpublished) in Nag (1976)	1965–6	Koraput district, Orissa	Kondh Orissa (1966–71)	3.7	ANCEB	L	–	–	–	–
				5.9	TFR	–	–	–	–	–
Kumar et al. (1967)	1966–7	Ranchi district, Bihar	Munda Bihar (1966–71)	6.7	ANCEB	H	–	–	–	–
				6.3	TFR	–	–	–	–	–
Ghosh (1976)	1966–8	Nilgiri hills, Karnataka	Kota Karnataka (1966–71)	3.7	ANCEB	L	–	–	–	–
				5.6	TFR	–	–	–	–	–
Chakraborty and Malakar (1969)	late 1960s	Totopara, West Bengal	Toto West Bengal	6.9	ANCEB	H	–	–	–	–
				6.1	TFR	–	–	–	–	–
De (1970)	1969	Little Andaman	Onges	2.1[c]	ANCEB	–	–	–	–	–
Sharma (1978)	1971	Kalahandi district, Orissa	Khonds Orissa (1971–76)	5.4	ANCEB	ND	38.2	CDR	–	–
				5.6	ANCEB	–	–	–	–	–
Das (1979)	1974	Keonjhargarh, Orissa	Juang	3.19	TFR	–	–	–	–	–
Sarkar (1989)	1976	Udaipur district, Rajasthan	Bhills	7.14	ANCEB	H	–	–	–	–
			Garasia	5.23	ANCEB	ND	–	–	–	–
			Rajasthan	5.1	TFR	–	–	–	–	–

Source	Year	Location	Group							
Kumar (1986)	1978	Santhal Parganas, Bihar	Mal Paharias	5.0	ANCEB	L	330.1	IMR	L	–
			Total population	–	–	–	397.1	IMR	–	–
			Bihar (rural) 1981	5.8	TFR	–	–	–	–	–
Saha (1993)	1978–80	Bastar, MP	Muria	5.1	ANCEB	L	–	–	–	–
			MP (rural), 1981	5.5	TFR	–	–	–	–	–
Rizvi (1987)	1979	Udaipur district, Rajasthan	Mina	6.13	ANCEB	L	40.7	CDR	L	–
							(137.0)	(IMR)		
			Rajasthan (rural) 1984	6.4	TMFR	–	(141)	–	–	–
Deka (1989)	not clear	Jaintia Hills, Meghalaya	Jaintias	8.1	ANCEB	L	–	–	–	–
			Meghalaya 1981	8.5	TMFR	–	–	–	–	–
Saxena (1990)	1981	Nainital district, UP	Tharus	8.0	ANCEB	H	–	–	–	–
			Buksas	6.8	ANCEB	H	–	–	–	–
			UP (rural) 1981	6.1	TFR	–	–	–	–	–
Reddy and Reddy (1986)	early 1980s	Chittor, Andhra Pradesh	Sugali	6.5	TMFR	H	–	–	–	–
			AP (rural) 1981	4.8	TMFR	–	–	–	–	–
Choudhury (1988)	1980s	Rajmahal hills, Sahebgaunje, Bihar	Santhals	5.2	ANCEB	L	184$$	–	–	{0.88}&
			Pahariyas	4.6	ANCEB	L	291$$	–	–	–
			Bihar(rural) 1984	6.3	TMFR	–	–	–	–	{0.95}&
Pande (1991)	1982	Kumaon (UP)	Tharu	42.4	CBR	H	138	IMR	L	–
			Boksa	38.7	CBR	L	128	IMR	L	–
			Bhotia	36.2	CBR	L	119	IMR	L	–

(Contd.)

Table 4.1 (contd.)

Author/Source (1)	Year of Survey (2)	Area/Region (3)	Tribal and Non-tribal Groups (4)	Fertility (5)	Measure used (6)	H/L ND (7)	Mortality (8)	Measure used (9)	H/L ND (10)	Sex Ratio (11)
			Raji	37.4	CBR	L	146	IMR	L	–
			Jaunsari	38.1	CBR	L	139	IMR	L	–
			UP (rural) 1982	40.0	CBR	–	166	IMR	–	–
Bagchi (1994)	1984	Midnapore district, West Bengal	Lodha	–	–	–	129	IMR	H	972
			Mahali	–	–	–	117	IMR	H	983
			Kora	–	–	–	88	IMR	ND	990
			Santhal	–	–	–	83	IMR	L	896
			Munda	–	–	–	82	IMR	L	884
			W.B. (rural) 1984	–	–	–	88	IMR	–	935
Padmanabham (1985)	1984	Valsad district, Gujarat	Naika	6.0	ANCEB	L	9.2	CDR	L	–
			Gujarat (rural) 1984	8.4	TMFR	–	(95.2)	(IMR)	–	–
							12.3	CDR	–	–
Gangadharan V (1999)	1984–5	Prakasam and Kurnool districts, AP	Chenchus	4.5	TFR	ND	–	–	–	–
			A.P. (1981)	4.8	TFR	–	–	–	–	–
Gandotra (1989)	1985–6	Dangs district, Gujarat	Bhils	5.5	TFR	H	10.1	CDR	L	–
			Gujarat (rural) (1986)	4.0	TFR	–	(87.0)	(IMR)	–	–
							11.7	CDR	–	–
							(124)	(IMR)	–	–

Reference	Year	Location	Group							
Pandey (1989, 1994); Pandey and Tiwary (1993)	1986	Jabalpur district, MP	Gonds	5.3[a]	ANCEB	L	9.1	–	L	987
			Non-tribal group	5.9[a]	ANCEB	–	(106.1)^	CDR	–	–
							9.8	(IMR)	–	933
							(111.8)^		–	–
Das and Shah (1991)	1986	Dangs district, Gujarat	Kukanas, Bhils, Varlis	5.5	TFR	H	10.1	CDR	L	1005
			Gujarat (rural) (1986)	4.0	–	–	(87.0)	(IMR)	–	–
							(98.0)		–	–
Basu and Kshatriya (1989); Basu (1994a)	(not clear) early 1980's	Bastar district, MP	Muria	5.64	TFR	ND	123.3	IMR	L	{0.94}
			Mariya	6.00	TFR	H	85.4	IMR	L	{0.98}
			Bhatra	5.95	TFR	H	148.6	IMR	L	{0.96}
			Halba	5.89	TFR	H	92.8	IMR	L	{0.93}
			MP (rural) 1981	5.5	TFR	–	152.0	IMR	–	–
Sharma and Khan (1990)	not clear	Surguja district, MP	Khairwar	10.5	ANCEB	H	145	IMR	L	–
			MP (all)	6.4	TMFR	–	152	–	–	–
Basu and Kshatriya (1997)	Early 1990?	Borgaon and blocks of Sundargarh district, Orissa	Dudh	5.34	TFR	H	11.8	CDR	H	–
			Kharia	(6.70)	(TMFR)	–	(52.0)	(c_0)	–	–
			Orissa (rural), 1984–86	4.3	TFR	–	13.5	CDR	–	–
				(5.2)	(TMFR)	–	(52.4)	(c_0) (1984–85)	–	–
Heman and Reddy (1998)	Not clear early 1990?	South district, Manipur	Gangte (shifting)	6.45	ANCEB	H	74	Q5	H	–
			Gante (settled)	7.11	ANCEB	H	49.4	Q5	H	–
			Manipur 1990–92	4.9	ANCEB	–	39	Q5	–	–

(*Contd.*)

Table 4.1 (contd.)

Author/Source (1)	Year of Survey (2)	Area /Region (3)	Tribal and Non-tribal Groups (4)	Fertility (5)	Measure used (6)	H/L/ ND (7)	Mortality (8)	Measure used (9)	H/L/ ND (10)	Sex Ratio (11)
Mutharayappa (2000)	1989	Mysore district, Karnataka	Jenu Kuruba	3.8	ANCEB	L	22.5	CDR	H	908
			Kadu Kuruba	4.5	ANCEB	L	(105)	(IMR)	–	884
			Karnataka (rural) 1990	5.1	TMFR	–	20.9	CDR	H	–
							(102)	(IMR)	–	–
							9.0	CDR#~	–	–
							(89)	(IMR#~)	–	–
Koshal (1996)	1991	Madhya Pradesh	ST	4.1	TFR	L	–	–	–	–
		Five villages	SC	4.8	TFR	–	–	–	–	–
			MP Rural	4.9	TFR	–	–	–	–	–
Kapoor and Kshatriya (2000)	1992	Midnapur district, WB	Munda	5.23	ANCEB	ND	86	$_0q_4$	L	–
			Santhal	3.97	ANCEB	L	51	$_0q_4$	L	–
			Lodha	4.19	ANCEB	L	87	$_0q_4$	L	–
			West Bengal (rural) 1991–3	5.28	ANCEB	–	94	$_0q_4$	–	–
Pandey et al. (2000)	1992–3	34 villages, Jabalpur district, MP	Gond (1992)	4.7	ANCEB	L	–	–	–	–
			MP (1992)	5.5	ANCEB	–	–	–	–	–
Kapoor and Kshatriya	1994–5	Baran district, Rajasthan	Sahariya	4.28	ANCEB	L	84	Q/5	L	–
			Rajasthan (1996)	5.52	TMFR	–	140	Q/5	–	–

(2000)	1997	Udaipur district, Rajasthan 1991	Mina	5.2	ANCEB			67	Q/5	L	–
			Bhil	5.3	ANCEB	ND		71	Q/5	L	–
			Rajasthan (1998–9) RCH	5.2	ANCEB	ND		129	Q/5	–	–

Notes: ANCEB = Average number of children ever born to women aged 45–49 years
    TFR = Total fertility rate
    TMFR = Total marital fertility rate
    CBR = Crude birth rate
    CDR = Crude death rate
    IMR = Infant mortality rate
    ST = scheduled tribe
    SC = scheduled caste
    H = higher, L = lower, ND = not different

(a) Based on currently married (not ever married) women;
(b) Average number of children born to rural women married for 22 years and over in 1952 (based on NSS fourth round data); quoted from Das Gupta et al. (1955);
(c) Based on women aged 35 years and above;
~ SRS data 1986;
** represents judgement based on only *TFR* figures;
^ for 1983–85;
@ Number of children dead at age 3 years and below per 1000 live births;
+ represents life expectancy at birth;
& ratio of female to male child mortality rates; and
$$ Number of children dead between 0–5 years per 1000 live births.

Table 4.2 Fertility differentials among social groups, India and major states: Large-scale survey results, 1978–99

State	Social Group	1978 TFR Rural	1984 # TFR Rural	1984 # TFR Total	1992–3 TFR Total	1994 TFR Rural	1998–9 TFR Total
India	SC	4.78	5.4 (4.7)	5.2 (4.7)	3.9 (5.4)	4.7	3.15 (4.85)
	ST	4.07	5.3 (4.5)	5.2 (4.5)	3.6 (4.8)	4.4	3.06 (4.74)
	OTHER	4.48	4.8 (4.6)	4.4 (4.6)	3.3 (4.8)	4.3	2.66 (4.20)
Andhra Pradesh	SC	3.94	4.6 (3.4)	4.4 (3.5)	2.6	2.9	2.51 (4.33)
	ST	4.57	5.0 (3.9)	4.8 (3.9)	3.7	2.3	2.75 (4.95)
	OTHER	4.05	4.0 (3.6)	3.9 (3.7)	2.5	3.1	2 (3.62)
Assam	SC	4.73	4.2 (4.6)	4.1 (4.6)	2.8	–	2.6 (4.6)
	ST	4.38	5.3 (5.6)	5.1 (5.5)	3.7 (6.3)	–	2.1 (4.3)
	OTHER	3.97	4.5 (5.0)	4.3 (4.9)	3.5 (5.6)	–	2.4 (4.4)
Bihar	SC	4.34	7.0 (4.0)	6.9 (4.1)	4.0 (5.5)	5.7	3.91 (5.44)
	ST	3.21	6.4 (3.7)	6.3 (3.7)	3.4 (4.8)	5.1	2.45 (4.6)
	OTHER	4.34	5.9 (4.1)	5.7 (4.1)	4.1 (5.3)	5.3	3.13 (4.81)
Gujarat	SC	4.61	5.5 (4.8)	5.1 (5.0)	2.98 (5.21)	3.7	3.02 (4.52)
	ST	4.56	4.6 (4.6)	4.3 (4.6)	3.34 (4.27)	4.2	2.95 (4.63)
	OTHER	4.6	4.2 (4.7)	4.0 (4.7)	2.93 (4.40)	3.7	2.45 (3.50)
Himachal Pradesh	SC	3.33	3.9 (4.8)	3.9 (4.8)	3.1 (4.4)	2.6	2.15 (3.98)
	ST	NA	5.0 (5.5)	4.9 (5.4)	4.2 (4.8)	–	NA
	OTHER	3.37	3.9 (4.6)	3.8 (4.6)	2.9 (4.4)	2.7	2.05 (3.71)
Karnataka	SC	3.59	4.7 (4.1)	4.7 (4.2)	3.2 (4.8)	3.1	2.49 (5.12)

	ST	NA	4.7 (4.2)	4.6 (4.3)	2.2 (5.4)	–	2.38 (4.98)
	OTHER	3.71	4.1 (4.5)	3.8 (4.5)	2.9 (4.6)	2.4	2.24 (3.92)
Kerala	SC	2.74	2.2 (4.3)	2.3 (4.3)	1.4	2.5	1.52 (2.77)
	ST	NA	3.6 (4.9)	3.7 (4.9)	1.3	–	NA
	OTHER	2.86	2.5 (4.4)	2.6 (4.3)	2	2.2	1.85 (2.97)
Madhya Pradesh	SC	5.95	6.0 (5.2)	5.8 (5.3)	4.71 (5.69)	4.5	3.87 (5.8)
	ST	4.51	5.2 (4.7)	5.1 (4.7)	4.05 (5.02)	4.5	3.69 (4.99)
	OTHER	5.61	5.4 (5.1)	5.1 (5.1)	3.76 (5.24)	4.3	2.49 (4.68)
Maharashtra	SC	3.38	4.1 (4.9)	3.9 (4.9)	3 (4.3)	4.6	2.42 (4.16)
	ST	3.68	4.6 (4.8)	4.5 (4.8)	3.2 (4.8)	4.6	2.93 (4.15)
	OTHER	3.6	4.2 (4.8)	3.8 (4.6)	2.8 (4.2)	3.7	2.59 (3.62)
Northeastern Region	SC	5.02	4.3 (4.7)	4.0 (4.6)	NA	3.7	NA
	ST	4.14	5.1 (4.3)	5.0 (4.3)	NA	5.0	NA
	OTHER	3.77	3.7 (4.7)	3.5 (4.6)	NA	3.9	NA
Orissa	SC	3.93	4.8 (4.7)	4.7 (4.6)	3.7 (5.0)	4.3	2.85 (4.04)
	ST	3.63	4.1 (4.2)	4.0 (4.2)	2.9 (4.0)	4.1	2.66 (4.23)
	OTHER	4.76	4.4 (4.9)	4.3 (4.9)	2.8 (5.1)	3.7	2.07 (4.17)
Rajasthan	SC	5.58	6.9 (5.5)	6.6 (5.5)	4.26 (5.36)	8.2	4.34 (5.83)
	ST	5.35	6.4 (5.1)	6.4 (5.2)	3.87 (5.01)	–	4.31 (5.72)
	OTHER	5.48	5.7 (5.2)	5.4 (5.1)	3.38 (4.88)	6.8	3.44 (5.05)
Sikkim	SC	NA	NA	NA	NA	–	3.42
	ST	NA	NA	NA	NA	–	2.66 (4.38)
	OTHER	NA	NA	NA	NA	–	2.69 (4.68)

(Contd.)

Table 4.2 (*contd.*)

StateSocial	Group	1978 TFR Rural	1984 # TFR Rural	TFR Total	1992–3 TFR Total	1994 TFR Rural	1998–9 TFR Total
Tamil Nadu	SC	3.70	4.1 (3.8)	4.0 (3.9)	2.79 (4.99)	3.1	2.25 (4)
	ST	NA	4.4 (3.4)	3.5 (3.7)	NA	–	2.39
	OTHER	3.39	3.3 (3.6)	3.2 (3.7)	2.39 (4.04)	3.0	1.69 (2.21)
Uttar Pradesh	SC	5.98	6.5 (5.3)	6.4 (5.3)	5.56 (6.51)	6.1	4.44 (5.9)
	ST	NA	NA	–	5.89 (7.40)	6.2	4.83 (6.2)
	OTHER	5.85	6.0 (5.2)	5.9 (5.2)	4.66 (5.86)	5.9	3.77 (5.44)
West Bengal	SC	3.98	4.8 (4.8)	4.4 (4.7)	3.5 (4.7)	3.8	2.34 (4.67)
	ST	2.96	4.6 (4.4)	4.6 (4.4)	3.0 (4.5)	2.5	2.31 (4.25)
	OTHER	3.43	4.5 (5.0)	3.7 (4.6)	2.9	4.3	2.21 (4.11)

Note: Figures in the parentheses are respective average numbers of children ever born to women in the age group 40–49.
Other = Non-SC/ST

Figures for number of children ever born to women aged 40–49 years in the parentheses are respective unweighted averages of figures for women aged 40–44 and 45–49 years.

Source: Registrar General (1982; 1989a); NCAER/HDI (1994); IIPS (1995); IIPS (2000).

Table 4.3 Mortality differentials between ST, SC, and others, India and major states: Large-scale surveys, 1978–99

State	Social Group	1978		1984			1981–91(NFHS-I)		1991@		1994	1988–98 (NFHS-II)	
		IMR#	0–4M#	CDR	IMR	0–4M	IMR*	UNDER-5M*	IMR	UNDER-5	CDR#	IMR*	UNDER-5M*
India	SC	152	NA	16.2	126.5	51.6	107.3	149.1	84	118	13.0	83.0	119.3
	ST	120	NA	14.7	101.1	45.0	90.5	135.2	88	121	9.0	84.2	126.6
	Others	NA	NA	11.7	99.2	36.0	82.2	111.5	74	96	11.0	61.8	82.6
Andhra Pradesh	SC	132	51.1	14.8	96.6	36.4	94.4	114.8	68	93	17.0	95.4	122.4
	ST	144	43.9	15.7	—	36.1	85.4	134.4	72	96	6.0	103.6	115.9
	Others	NA	NA	8.3	75.1	23.9	68.0	89.1	49	68	16.0	47.1	64.7
Assam	SC	120	54.5	18.6	150	58.6	N.A	N.A	92	126	—	44.8	56.3
	ST	83	22.5	13.4	—	37.9	89.6	150.3	70	98	—	59.3	73.5
	Others	NA	NA	12.5	91.2	35.8	95.3	144.5	85	117	—	68.2	86.9
Bihar	SC	120	47.6	17.5	101.3	57.0	120.4	171.0	82	111	11.0	86.3	133.8
	ST	74	21.9	17.0	74	46.4	97.2	135.6	81	103	9.0	81.9	116.6
	Others	NA	NA	13.6	96.1	40.6	94.0	132.3	70	89	10.0	61.2	89.3
Maharashtra	SC	87	24.4	12.7	107.1	37.4	85.2	124.0	66	93	18.0	52.6	66.1
	ST	98	32.0	14.9	118.5	47.2	66.4	98.8	87	122	11.0	73.6	92.3
	Others	NA	NA	8.6	68.9	24.5	52.2	69.2	58	72	11.0	48.9	65.9
Orissa	SC	148	42.3	15.8	136.6	47.2	160.8	175.8	114	136	13.0	83.9	122.7
	ST	107	45.5	15.7	101.1	43.8	113.4	148.8	109	165	14.0	98.7	138.4
	Others	NA	NA	13.5	141.4	46.9	115.3	128.1	108	160	13.0	79.1	92.9

(Contd.)

Table 4.3 (*contd.*)

State	Social Group	1978		1984			1981–91(NFHS-I)		1991@		1994	1988–98 (NFHS-II)	
		IMR#	0–4M#	CDR	IMR	0–4M	IMR*	UNDER-5M*	IMR	UNDER-5	CDR#	IMR*	UNDER-5M*
Rajasthan	SC	188	90.3	17.3	136.6	58.8	90.5	121.7	91	151	12.0	98.9	140.7
	ST	125	54.7	17.7	149.9	59.6	75.4	123.8	106	149	–	94.7	155.0
	Others	NA	NA	13.1	113.6	43.7	71.1	96.9	81	109	12.0	81.6	109.3
West Bengal	SC	78	28.2	13.0	98.1	36.2	96.8	136.7	72	–	20.0	55.4	81.5
	ST	67	26.7	15.6	86.8	39.7	107.1	133.0	77	98	11.0	85.1	100.1
	Others	NA	NA	9.9	75.7	27.9	77.3	101.9	67	88	21.0	45.0	63.4
Northeastern Region	SC	86	12.3	10.2	112.5	31.8	–	–	–	–	13	–	–
	ST	59	30.6	11.7	79.6	31.0	–	–	–	–	–	5	–
	Others	NA	NA	7.4	65.1	19.8	–	–	–	–	7	–	–
Uttar Pradesh	SC	180	73.3	21.8	181.9	76.5	138.1	202.1	100	84	11	110	158.1
	ST	168	65.6	16.0	144.7	59.0	167.5	222.9	95	131	9	83.3	124.5
	Others	NA	NA	16.9	147.3	56.9	110.2	151.3	89	120	11	82.3	112.1
Gujarat	SC	149	53.0	15.1	114.6	46.3	69.9	119.3	79	65	5	80.1	123
	ST	145	46.3	12.0	116.5	45.4	91.5	126.7	77	106	8	60.3	94.6
	Others	NA	NA	10.3	101.6	35.5	69.9	97.7	69	85	8	53.7	70.3
Karnataka	SC	76	32.0	12.7	87.7	36.1	98.4	126.0	74	155	3	69.9	104.6
	ST	82	28.2	14.1	121.6	50.0	85.6	120.3	82	112	–	85	120.6
	Others	NA	NA	9.0	69.2	24.2	70.6	97.1	60	81	5	56.4	69.8

Kerala	SC	85	28.5	6.3	39.7	15.9	–	–	52	61	4	–	–
	ST	36	11.2	8.2	21.8	1.2	–	–	72	92	–	–	–
	Others	NA	NA	6.4	28.0	8.7	–	–	37	46	5	20.5	23.9
Madhya Pradesh	SC	155	76.3	19.1	120.4	57.9	124.1	167.8	112	134	11	101.5	156
	ST	140	49.5	14.5	98.4	42.6	103.1	166.6	112	159	9	101	179.6
	Others	NA	NA	13.0	127.3	45.2	90.1	129.8	107	159	9	72.4	94.8
Tamil Nadu	SC	121	69.4	15.0	98.5	42.4	90.0	127.3	65	79	16	22.5	63.3
	ST	119	37.8	5.0	–	4.1	–	–	62	78	–	–	–
	Others	NA	NA	11.2	73.5	24.8	64.8	84.7	53	69	12	–	–

CDR = Crude Death Rate; IMR = Infant Mortality Rate; 0–4 M = Estimated death rate for age group 0–4; # For rural area; IMR*Probability of dying before 1st birthday; UNDER5M*Probability of dying before 5th birthday; NA = Not available; @other = all.

Source: Registrar General (1981, 1989b); NCAER/HDI (1994); IIPS (1995); IIPS (2000); Rajan and Mohanachandran (1998).

Second, conceptual issues surrounding standard measures of fertility aside, a typical lack of uniformity in fertility measures used in the literature compounds difficulties in tracing regional and temporal features. For example, while the average number of children ever born to women at the end of their reproductive period (that is around their mid/late forties) appears to be a popular measure of fertility, the findings are not strictly comparable.[8] This is because, the women (whose number is used as a denominator in calculating the average number of children per woman) are 'ever married' in some cases, 'currently married' in other cases, and 'all women' in yet other studies. Likewise, the age groups are not exactly the same (for example, 45–9 years in some cases, past reproductive period beginning at 50 and above in other cases, and even age groups beginning much earlier than the end of the reproductive period, say 35 and above, in other cases). Its implications for comparability of fertility estimates are fairly obvious. For instance, ever married women aged 50 years include women both who have and have not completed their reproductive career, while currently married women of that age include, exclusively, those who have completed their reproductive span. Similar difficulties of comparability arise in connection with age differences of women whose average number of children is calculated. However, despite such difficulties with the existing studies, it is useful to draw some broad conclusions about India's tribal fertility (see Table 4.1).

The non-uniformity of fertility measures used by various scholars should not be a problem while comparing fertility between two groups. Thus it is possible, even on the basis of studies using different fertility measures, to indicate regional patterns of fertility differential between tribal and non-tribal groups. However, as mentioned before, very few studies of tribal fertility concern themselves with a comparative assessment. Many do not take a comparative perspective at all or focus on tribal fertility alone, while others provide at least some indication of relative tribal fertility as compared with either a non-tribal group or with the aggregate societal level. In the former category of studies, we have added, in order to gain a comparative insight, the closest

[8] While the ease with which this measure of fertility can be calculated (especially in terms of information required) is perhaps the main reason behind its popularity among empirical researchers, this measure has some obvious limitations, namely that it is not a good index of current fertility, and also that its focus on a particular cohort of women (that is, those aged 45 years and above at the time of survey) is likely to show selection biases in findings.

comparable fertility (and mortality) measure for the corresponding state (or district) level either for the same year as the survey or for the nearest available period. These state-level fertility and mortality measures are mostly official estimates provided either by the Registrar General office or by large-scale sample surveys like NFHS or NCAER.

As can be seen from Table 4.1, a considerable fertility variation across different tribes (even in the same region) is discernible. This is clearly brought out in a few individual studies, which estimate and compare fertility for more than one tribe.[9] As we will see shortly, a considerable fertility variation across major Indian states becomes fairly prominent from large-scale sample survey data too.

The fact that the tribal fertility level is distinctly different in most parts is worth noting (see Table 4.1). In several places, and for some tribes, the fertility estimate is found higher than that for the non-tribal counterpart,[10] while it is lower for other tribes.[11] In some studies, they are almost the same. Among all these micro-demographic studies, tribal fertility is reported lower in nearly 60 per cent cases, higher in less than 30 per cent cases, with no significant differences in the remaining cases. In a number of studies, where only the tribal fertility has been reported, it appears quite low.[12] While such fragmentary micro-studies give us a mixed picture of relative tribal fertility in the context of various small locations and tribal groups, the balance of evidence seems to be tilted towards lower tribal fertility. However, detailed attempts to explain observed fertility differentials between tribal and non-tribal groups are almost non-existent. Almost all of the studies reporting a comparative assessment of tribal fertility seemingly stop there, without undertaking a detailed investigation into causes for the differential. For example, the survey design of a study in Madhya Pradesh enables the author to demonstrate the observed lower fertility of tribal women as a direct consequence of their lower level of fecundibility, but the underlying reason behind such differential fecundibility itself is left unexplored (Pandey 1989).[13] Similarly, after

[9] See, for example, Verma 1977; Sarkar 1989; Das and Banerjee 1964; and Ray and Roth 1991.

[10] See, for example, Gandotra 1989; Sinha 1990; Nag 1990; Mahapatra 1970; and Chaudhuri 1988; and Kumar 1986.

[11] See, for example, Pandey 1989, 1994; Nag 1954; Padmanabham 1985.

[12] Sen 1956; Das 1979; De 1970 in Table 4.1.

[13] In this connection, we may mention one study where the observed lower fertility among Lepchas (as compared with Sherpas) has been attributed to

demonstrating the differential age composition of fertility between tribal and non-tribal women with survey data from one district of Gujarat, Gandotra (1989) makes no attempt to explain such proximate differentials in terms of differences in sociocultural and/or other foundational characteristics. In fact, anyone looking for a systematically established explanation of observed distinctive features of tribal fertility would be disappointed with the existing literature on India's tribal demography.[14] Almost none of the studies sets out with an explicit theoretical background discussion containing plausible and testable hypotheses about differential demographic behaviour between tribal and non-tribal groups.

While scattered local-level studies do not reach any single generalized conclusion about relative tribal fertility, there are a few large-scale surveys that present an aggregate picture of relative fertility for tribes (as a whole) vis-à-vis the non-tribal population both at state and all-India levels (see Table 4.2). Period fertility measures like TFR and TFMR as well as cohort fertility measures (for example, the average of children ever born to women at the end of their reproductive age) are presented for a better understanding of differential fertility changes. Since these surveys are not wholly uniform in procedure and coverage, the results are, perhaps, not strictly comparable, but there is no reason why they should not provide reasonably genuine indications about overall time trends in differential fertility levels across the groups. However, the census-based figures for 1981 should be viewed differently from others, particularly because they are based only on currently married women. In any case, such biases should not vitiate the judgement about cross-sectional differentials based on an individual survey data.

Concentrating on cross-sectional differentials between the three groups at an all-India level, a lower fertility rate of the aggregate tribal population is discernible, as compared to non-tribal counterparts, especially the SC group. This is evident during about three decades

___

their food habit dominated by a type of tuber (diascoria), which is known to have a fecundity-inhibiting function (Basu 1990:137).

[14] Establishing a fertility differential between tribal and non-tribal women, most researchers hint at 'relatively low adolescent sterility' and 'a greater premarital sex' (Gandotra 1989:270) or 'lower fecundity' as possible reasons for a relatively high or low tribal fertility, without attempting to provide concrete evidence on these possibilities. All these are, at best, in lieu of proper explanations of fertility differentials.

since the 1970s, although fertility gaps between them seem, of late, to have narrowed down. For example, in the late 1970s, India's overall tribal fertility rate was lower than those of both SC (by 0.71 children per woman) and other groups (by 0.41 children). By the early 1990s, tribal fertility has still remained lower than that of the SC, albeit by a smaller magnitude (that is, by about 0.30 children per woman) than before, but the fertility rate of the non-ST/SC group became lower than the tribal level even by the early 1980s. This reflects that the pace of fertility decline has been slowest among the aggregate ST population over the entire post-Independence period. In Bihar, however, the ST fertility seems to have declined more sharply than that of the SC population during the 1990s, leading to a wider fertility gap between these two groups than that during the 1970s and 1980s. On the other hand, in a few states, tribal fertility has almost never been lower than that of the SC people, the most prominent being Kerala, Andhra Pradesh, and Himachal Pradesh.

Thus, like the variation of tribal fertility in diverse local-level micro-studies, the nationally comparable large-scale surveys also show a wide variation of tribal fertility between major Indian states (see Table 4.2). Although this is certainly a variation in 'regional–tribal fertility' rather than inter-tribe variation in fertility within a region, it partly reflects the fertility differential between different tribes in accordance with the distribution of dominant tribal groups that have distinct regional patterns.[15] However, the regional pattern of fertility variation for Scheduled Tribes (ST) corresponds largely with those for Scheduled Castes (SC) and others, simple correlation coefficients being in the range between 0.74 and 0.94 in the surveys starting from 1984 (while they were found to be around 0.60 for the earlier surveys). This suggests that tribal fertility, much like non-tribal fertility, is partly shaped by broader regional circumstances and specificities (e.g. geophysical, sociocultural, infrustructural, etc.), especially in the later periods when family planning is more widespread. This said, rank correlation coefficients of state-level ST fertility with that for SC and others, being within the range of 0.39 and 0.65, are clearly weaker than what simple product-moment coefficients imply. This signifies a certain degree of distinctiveness and the immunity of 'tribal fertility behaviour' from influences of a broader regional (socioeconomic) context. In fact, a

[15] The coefficients of variation of TFR (with NFHS-1 data) across 14 major Indian states are found to be 0.31, 0.29, and 0.25 respectively for ST, SC, and others.

degree of dissociation between states' ranks in tribal and non-tribal fertility partly reflects inter-state differences in the extent of tribal assimilation and integration with mainstream society and economy.

Also evident from large-scale survey results is a considerable decline in tribal fertility, especially in more recent decades. While temporal declines in TFR do indicate fertility transition, another fairly consistent, albeit indirect way of detecting fertility change over time is to compare period fertility (i.e. TFR) with completed cohort fertility (i.e. the mean number of children ever born to women who are at the end of their reproductive span at the time of the survey, ANCEB for short). For example, when the latter, a fertility measure which focuses on reproductive performance of only older cohorts of women, is found higher than the TFR, which is based on current age-specific fertility rates of younger and older cohorts of women, it implies a secular decline of fertility. On this count, however, there seems to have been a rise in current (period) fertility in the 1984 survey, as the TFRs for all social groups surpassed respective completed (cohort) fertility levels in most states, and of course at the all-India level (with exceptions of Kerala, Maharashtra, and Himachal Pradesh). Indeed, for most states the record of current (period) fertility exceeding the completed (cohort) fertility seems particularly prominent among ST and SC groups. Ignoring the possibility of data biases, this implies a rise in the period fertility rate during the late 1970s and early 1980s. This surge in period fertility rates in the early 1980s could be due to a major setback suffered by the family planning programme following the excesses of the Emergency of 1976–7.

However, a distinct (and substantial) fertility decline has been registered for all social classes, including tribes by the early 1990s. As shown by NFHS data, the mean number of children ever born to women aged 40–9 is found almost everywhere larger than the total fertility rates, suggesting a considerable fertility decline in the recent past. This fertility decline (gauged in terms of the gap between TFR and ANCEB) has been pervasive, but it seems to have happened more sharply in the mainstream population. In fact, the majority of states seem to have experienced a smaller decline of fertility for the ST population than that for the mainstream populations. Such a relatively slow decline of tribal fertility seems consistent with our hypothesized late occurrence of a 'pre-transition rise' of tribal fertility, as this could have partly neutralized the tribal pace of fertility transition along with the overall development and spread of the family planning programme. A slower decline of tribal fertility could also be a reflection of a less effective implementation of family planning programmes in tribal areas, presumably because of communication barriers (in transport or in language and other cultural difficulties). Additionally, there might be a lack of felt political pressure on the administration to act effectively implement family planning programmes in tribal areas where the relative size of the tribal population is small, and tribal cultural identity is considered worth preserving.[16]

Thus, tribal and non-tribal fertility estimates, both from micro-level studies and large-scale surveys, show a considerable regional variations and a declining temporal trend (albeit slower for tribals). But it is important to note that the fertility estimates for tribes (as a whole) vis-à-vis non-tribal population at the all-India level (and, of course, in the majority of states, especially where the proportion of tribal population is not small) have been lower than those of their closest counterpart, the SC population. Indeed, there are a few major states, especially in eastern India (Bihar and West Bengal), where the ST fertility level is found lower than that of the upper caste general population as late as the end of 1990s (Table 4.2). According to the NFHS data, generally considered relatively reliable in terms of data quality and coverage, the ST fertility level is found lower than that for the SC group in about eight out of fourteen major states (for which data was available), while about four states (Assam, Himachal Pradesh, the northeastern region, and Maharashtra) show the reverse (see Table 4.2). A recent statistical analysis of district-level census data pertaining to the whole of India for 1981 has strongly indicated that tribal fertility is generally low, relative to the level for the mainstream population (Murthi *et al.* 1995). As the regression results of this study show, the fertility level is significantly lower in districts with a higher proportion of the ST population. Therefore, the overall fertility level for Indian tribes, on the whole, appears lower than that for the non-tribal mainstream population. Keeping in mind the historical perspective presented in the preceding chapter, this finding of relatively low overall tribal fertility in the contemporary period can well be seen as a legacy of the past. However, it is worth emphasizing that this differential has

[16] Ironically, however, the acceptance rate of family planning has often been relatively larger in tribal areas of some states (e.g. Rajasthan, Gujarat, Madhya Pradesh, and Maharashtra) [see Jolly 1990]. In some regions, tribal people have been easy to bring into sterilization camps thereby allowing family planning personnel to fulfil the targets that used to be imposed on them (see Bose 1988 for Orissa's experience).

been getting narrowed, and has disappeared and even been reversed in many places, especially in relation to non-SC/ST groups. Note that the SC–ST gap in fertility at the all-India level has dropped from 0.3 births per woman in NFHS-1 to 0.1 births in NFHS-2. Contemporary literature on tribal demography, it must be noted, has hardly noticed this differential pattern of fertility at an aggregate level and its evolution. It is ironic that this existing literature generally takes high tribal fertility for granted, without caring to attempt a systematic explanation, thus being oblivious to a different reality.

As we have already indicated in the preceding chapter, there were not only good reasons for a lower tribal fertility in the historical past, but they seem to fall mostly in the purview of sociocultural features, practices, and lifestyles.[17] In this context, it is an important question whether, and how far, broad development trends and integration processes have tended to contribute to gradual erosion of those traditional tribal features, favourable to a comparatively low fertility (and also low infant/child mortality), and thus to the recent reversal of the past pattern of fertility differential.

For example, the census reports as far back as 1931, or even earlier, routinely mentioned the Hinduization of tribes, particularly in the form of an increasing acceptance of child marriage. As one author writes, 'For the tribes trying to get accepted as Hindu castes the temptation of child marriage has always been great' (Saxena 1964:65). Fürer-Haimendorf also commented on the Chenchus tribe of the Deccan as far back as the early 1940s as follows: '...the growing contact with Hindu ideas is generally modifying old principles and ...the custom of marrying girls before they are mature is steadily gaining ground' (Fürer-Haimendorf 1943:140). Thus, it is ironic that while there is clear evidence on the late marriage practice of tribal women in not a very distant past, recent researches often point to early marriage (and a decline of breastfeeding duration) as being contributory factors for their currently observed high fertility (and infant/child mortality rates) (see Choudhury 1988; Ram 1999; and Pakrasi and Manna 1989). The finding of the mean age at marriage of about 14 years for a group of Gond females during 1992–93 in Jabalpur of Madhya Pradesh (Pandey *et al.* 2000) contrasts, indeed shockingly, with the early

---

[17] To recapitulate, they include delayed female marriage, prolonged breastfeeding and longer birth intervals, greater gender equity and female autonomy, lower infant/childhood mortality, and use of indigenous means of birth control and abortion.

twentieth-century scenario of tribal marriages rarely taking place before attainment of maturity (or at least puberty) (see, for example, Grigson 1938: 244–50 on Maria Gonds of Bastar district in Madhya Pradesh). Such declines of female age at marriage might well have contributed to a fertility rise or a stalling of fertility transition among Indian tribes. While this change of nuptial pattern (that is, declining female age at marriage) results from tribal emulation of mainstream society mores and culture, it can occur even when the latter have started delaying their female marriages under modernizing and related influences. This is why these lagged changes in tribal culture and customs are often more aptly described as 'Hinduization' or 'Sanskritization', rather than 'modernization', since these contemporary changes make them appear less 'modern' or 'advanced' in the common sense of the term. For instance, a relatively high fertility recorded for Santhal, Birhor, and Munda in a tribal district of Bihar during the mid-sixties (Verma 1977 and Kumar 1967 in Table 4.1) could well be a reflection of such as pre-transitional rise of fertility, as tribal fertility levels in this region were presumably lower than those of the non-tribal population groups in the early decades of the last century. Similarly, another example of a fertility-enhancing effect among tribal communities, as a result of an expanding mainstream (Hindu) influence could be a growing gender imbalance and anti-female discrimination. While contemporary literature shows that tribal gender relations are, in line with our observations in the historical past, more balanced than is seen among non-tribal communities (including SC people), there is mounting evidence of tribal communities taking, in varying degrees, to broad mainstream anti-female sociocultural patterns and features (more on this later). This tribal trend can be thought to be a contributing factor in their recent fertility rises or the relatively slow pace of fertility decline.

Tribal Mortality

Compared to fertility, mortality is a less researched area in the whole demographic discourse. This is confirmed by the existing demographic literature on Indian tribes. However, unlike fertility, measures of mortality that have generally been used in the literature, like CDR and IMR, are relatively straightforward and simple, and thus the mortality estimates in various local level micro-studies (as presented in Table 4.1) are conceptually more easily comparable. However, the question of reliability of estimates still assumes importance here, particularly due to possibilities of sampling and non-sampling errors.

In addition to likely defects in respondents' information (both owing to poor record-keeping and recall lapses), the possibility of selection biases in various ways (especially in small-scale anthropological data) should be borne in mind while interpreting results.

First, as can be seen from Table 4.1, tribal mortality, like fertility, varies quite widely across various tribes and regions, betraying a single generalized conclusion about tribal mortality levels. For example, apart from a large inter-state differential in tribal mortality (Sinha 1990; Parasuraman and Rajan 1990 in Table 4.1), there is also evidence of a wide intra-state variation in death rates between different tribal groups (for details see Parasuraman and Rajan 1990). Interestingly, as the study by Verma (1977) shows, even in the same district of Hazaribagh of Bihar, the Birhor tribal group experiences about 2.5 times the mortality level recorded for the Santhal group. A considerable inter-tribe variation of mortality in the same locality is also confirmed in terms of IMR variation.[18] Such an inter-tribe mortality differential, especially in the same location reflects differences in sociocultural features, lifestyles, attitudinal, and ideational factors, as there is barely any significant economic differential between them. This said, a considerable gap that is often found between mortality levels of the tribal and non-tribal population (particularly SC people) within a state is of much interest. The differential is not unidirectional. Some studies, in the context of specific tribes and locations, report a higher tribal mortality (particularly in terms of higher IMR) as compared to non-tribal groups, while others show a distinct mortality advantage for tribal people (Table 4.1). Putting aside the issue of reliability and generalizability of the micro-level findings, these mortality differentials should largely correspond to specific local circumstances, relating to relative vulnerabilities of tribal and non-tribal communities.

A wide regional variation of tribal mortality reflects, to a considerable extent, the regional pattern of overall mortality. For example, in one application of indirect techniques, the estimated death rate for the Bhil tribal group has been found to be widely divergent among states (being 23.1, 20.1, 16.1 and 13.5 respectively in Gujarat, Maharashtra, Rajasthan, and Madhya Pradesh) [Parasuraman and Rajan 1990:136]. The aggregate state-level results from various large-scale surveys on mortality are summarized in Table 4.3. As can be seen, both tribal and non-tribal mortality levels (mainly in terms of IMR) generally appear

[18] See, for example, Basu and Kshatriya 1989; Basu 1994a; Bagchi 1994.

to have been, and even presently are, much higher in some states (Bihar, Orissa, Uttar Pradesh, and Madhya Pradesh) than in others (Maharashtra, Kerala, and Himachal Pradesh). For example, as the NFHS-1 data show, in Gujarat the IMR for ST groups is found higher than that for SC people by as much as 22 infant deaths per 1000 live births, whereas it is lower by about the same order in Madhya Pradesh. While such regional variation partly reflects inter-state differential in tribal development and assimilation, inter-tribe differences in sociocultural features (including lifestyles and food habits) should also constitute a part of the explanation.[19] However, there is a clear indication that tribal mortality has been declining almost everywhere, although at a varying pace across regions.

Despite mixed results reported by various local level small-scale surveys on relative levels of tribal mortality, Indian tribes (particularly tribal infants and children) as a whole, as revealed by country-wide large-scale sample surveys, seem to have had (until very recently) a mortality advantage over non-tribal counterparts, especially the SC group. It is remarkable, indeed, that child mortality and IMR, in particular, for the ST groups at the all-India level have been distinctively lower than the corresponding levels for SC (at least) up to the early 1990s (see Table 4.3). For example, according to the data of the 1978 special survey on differential infant and child mortality across Indian states by the Registrar General office, all the states (for which data is presented in Table 4.3) show a unidirectional superiority of the tribal population over the SC group in terms of infant and child mortality, except that Andhra Pradesh reports a marginally higher IMR (but not the child mortality) for ST. Such tribal relative superiority over SC groups continued to be evident in a subsequent special survey by the Registrar General's office in 1984. About a decade later, the NFHS-1 data for the early 1990s show that estimates of IMR in 8 out of 11 states (for which relevant information was available) were found lower among the ST group than those of their closest comparable group, namely the SC people, and it was indeed lower for the aggregate tribal population of India (see Table 4.3). [It was, however, almost always (except very few cases) found higher than that of the non-ST/SC

---

[19] A substantial literature—mainly by anthropologists—has developed on tribal health, its sociocultural dimensions, their health-seeking behaviour, their own perceptions and practices relating to health problems in the context of various tribes in different locations; see Basu 1994, Chaudhuri 1985, and references cited therein.

group]. In Orissa, the neonatal and infant mortality rates among the ST population were found lower than not only those of the SC but also of the non-SC/ST group during 1988–9 to 1992–3, as revealed by NFHS-1 data (see Padhi 2001, Table 15).

Civil registration information for 1978 and 1984 for the whole of India, together with NFHS-1 data show a relatively low tribal IMR and 0–4 age group mortality as compared to those for the SC population. In terms of the 1984 nation-wide survey on differential mortality by the Registrar General, the overall death rate (CDR) of India's aggregate tribal population was found lower than that of the SC group by one and a half deaths per thousand population. Indeed, a decade later, in 1994, the large-scale survey undertaken by the National Council of Applied Economic Research has also confirmed, at all-India level, not only much lower IMR for the ST group than that of the SC group in rural areas, but also the lowest (rural) death rate for tribes (9 per thousand) in comparison with the levels for SC (13) and the total general population (11). It is true that these large-scale survey results are not sacrosanct, and are often subject to various biases arising from sampling and non-sampling sources. However, cross-section (not temporal) comparisons are often relatively free of data distortions so long as there is no reason strong enough for suspecting differential response deficiencies across the social groups being compared. For example, one could perhaps wonder whether tribals would be more prone to suppressing death as a demographic event over the preceding twelve months as compared to other groups considered here. But several points can arise about this hypothesis.

First, we have not come across any direct evidence or reasons in support of this specific conjecture, although this, by itself, is not firm ground to reject the hypothesis. In fact, there is clear evidence of 'more complete' reporting of child deaths in specific tribal locations (see Bang et al. 2002). Second, even if we accept as valid the speculation that there is a greater tribal propensity for under-reporting of deaths over one year preceding the survey date, this should hardly affect the infant and under-five mortality rates, as unreported deaths remain uncounted, both in numerator and denominator. Similarly, the comparability of death rates between groups may not be hampered greatly by differential under-reporting of deaths, if respective denominators (that is, mid-year population at risk) for calculating the rates are based on registered numbers of deaths. Since CDRs for 1984 are calculated on the basis of the mid-year population estimated by using registered births and deaths, the argument of underestimation of tribal death rates on the ground of a greater under-reporting of tribal deaths becomes weak. However, the NCAER 1994 survey result of a substantially lower aggregate (rural) mortality level among ST than that of the general population seems a bit odd and even difficult to accept in the light of evidence from other macro-level surveys as well as individual studies. But considering all the large-scale survey data (as presented in Table 4.3), a tribal mortality advantage (especially for infants and children) over the SC counterparts at the all-India level seems genuine enough, at least until recently.

A fairly rigorous econometric exercise using district-level census and registration data for the whole of India (for 1981) has shown a statistically significant inverse relationship between district-level child mortality (that is, under-five mortality rate) and the proportion of the ST population, even after controlling for poverty and literacy (Murthi *et al.* 1995). This finding not only supports the hypothesis of tribal superiority in infant and childhood mortality at an aggregate level as revealed by the countrywide surveys (at least vis-à-vis SC people until the early 1990s), but is also consistent, as the authors suggest, with the notion that 'tribal lifestyles have some healthy aspects, for example relatively low levels of crowding and pollution' (ibid:765).[20] As was suggested earlier in the context of the historical past, relatively prolonged breastfeeding and longer birth interval practices, common among Indian tribes, may well continue to be a reason for their superior position of infant/child mortality in more recent periods. In fact, some contemporary evidence clearly endorses this hypothesis (Mudgal *et al.* 1979; Puri 1992). As one author concludes about the tribes of Orissa, '[a]mong tribals, there are strong traditions and powerful health considerations favouring child spacing in comparison with Scheduled Caste and General Caste communities' (Pati 1991:229). Indeed, ethnographic narratives for several tribal communities, especially prior to very recent periods, often suggest their relatively healthy patterns and quality of child care (Naik 1956:105–21; Quilici 1972; Wirsing 1985). Furthermore, the evidence of a substantially higher intake of

---

[20] While the authors admit that an adequate explanation for this statistical association requires further detailed investigation, tribal literature (as noted earlier, particularly in Chapter 3) provides scattered indications of how tribes could have enjoyed a mortality advantage, especially until recently. For example, so-called ethno-medicine could also provide a partial clue as to how tribal and primitive communities have been traditionally taking care of their morbidity, health, and illnesses (see Boban 1998).

certain key nutrients among the children whose mothers work as wage labourers vis-à-vis those whose mothers do not (Walker and Ryan 1988; quoted in Bennett 1992:17), could perhaps be seen as an added mechanism for a (relative) mortality advantage of tribal infants and children. This suggestion derives support from two contingent propositions, namely, that the nutritional level is one of the major determinants of infant and childhood mortality, and secondly, that a proportionately greater number of tribal women participate in directly productive (or income-earning) activities. Linking our analysis of the late nineteenth- and early twentieth-century evidence (as presented in the preceding chapter), this contemporary record of relative mortality advantage of tribal infants and children vis-à-vis those of the mainstream (especially scheduled and other backward castes) can well be seen as a legacy from the past. However, the question of whether such traditional tribal mortality advantage, especially for children and infants, has been eroded in the course of tribal integration with mainstream development, and culture is of greater contemporary relevance and importance.

Note that the aggregate all-India scenario of tribal mortality advantage (especially vis-à-vis the SC group), as has been revealed by large-scale surveys up to the early 1990s, seems to have disappeared in the late 1990s (see Table 4.3). In line with the findings of some micro-level studies (see Table 4.1), some Indian states show indications of tribal mortality (infant and child mortality in particular) levels surpassing those of SC and others since the early 1980s (Himachal Pradesh, Rajasthan, Maharashtra, and Andhra Pradesh) (see Table 4.3). In many of these regions, the proportion of lower caste population is comparatively large and/or have witnessed relatively strong lower caste and *dalit* movements, which probably culminated in a somewhat better deal for SC people (relative to ST) in matter of resource distribution.[21]

[21] Note that the pair-wise correlation coefficients between state-level mortality levels (that is IMR or childhood mortality, or CDR) of three social groups (ST, SC, other/all) always appear positive, signifying the influences of a region's overall mortality situation on all the social groups. However, interestingly, the state-level non-ST/SC (or total population) mortality indices appear correlated more strongly and more significantly with the corresponding variation for the SC group than they are for the ST group. This is a reflection of some degree of independence of tribal mortality (especially in infancy and childhood years) from the aggregate mortality situation prevailing in a region.

Thus, as can be seen from Table 4.3, although there has been a secular decline in mortality (including those of infants and children) across all social groups (as revealed by the large-scale surveys at different points of time), the pace of decline has been noticeably less among tribal people. For example, the extent of mortality advantage of ST over SC (as measured by positive differences in IMR or 0–4 mortality between SC and ST groups) has declined over time at an aggregate level. The positive difference in IMR at the all-India level between SC and ST (32 infant deaths per thousand births) was larger in 1978 than was found in the 1984 survey (25.4 infant deaths per thousand births), and it declined further (16.8 infant deaths) in the NFHS-1 in the early 1990s. Indeed the gap, according to census-based indirect estimates of IMR for 1991, was found to be negative—with marginally higher IMR for the ST group. The NFHS-2 data (see Table 4.3) for 1998–99 show more clearly a complete reversal of the long-standing tribal mortality advantage over the SC group, particularly in infancy and childhood years. In fact, the reversal of the tribal advantage in infant and child mortality manifested itself even earlier according to some estimates. For example, a study on (indirect) estimation based on the 1991 census has shown higher, although marginally, infant- and child-mortality levels among the ST population than those for the SC group at the all-India level (Rajan and Mohachandran 2001). In any case, the narrowing of the gap between SC and ST infant mortality rates over 1980s and 1990s clearly suggests a relative worsening of the tribal mortality situation during the period.

Although there are some states (Bihar, Madhya Pradesh, West Bengal, Orissa, and Uttar Pradesh) with tribal-mortality rates lower than those of SC groups, the fact that long-standing tribal mortality advantage has been disappearing rather fast across India is beyond doubt. For example, a significant inverse association between the district-level childhood mortality and proportion of tribal population that had emerged from the analysis of the 1981 census data (Murthi *et al.* 1995), no longer shows up in the similar analysis with 1991 data

---

However, the suggestion emerging from the temporal trend in the values of these coefficients is that the strength of (state-level) positive association between mortality indices (especially IMR) of these social groups has somewhat waned in the 1990s. This, in turn, implies that over the recent past, there have emerged greater social differentials in the achievements of recent mortality improvements and in the accessibility and affordability of health-care provisions.

(Drèze and Murthi 2001). Comparatively high tribal mortality levels found for some tribes in specific regions (as shown in Table 4.1) corroborate with the overall picture of a reverse tendency towards a relative mortality disadvantage for tribal people in general, and for tribal infants and children in particular. The implied message from this is clear, namely, that in the overall process of development and mortality improvements, the tribal people of India have been lagging behind even their closest social group, the SC population. A recent review of contemporary evidence on tribal mortality and health concludes, 'the low health status of the tribal population is not because of their ethnicity or tribalness but because of their ruralness, illiteracy and poverty' (Singh *et al*. 1993:179).

Quite a few states, namely, Bihar, Orissa, Assam, and Karnataka seem to have experienced even increases in infant mortality during the 1980s, especially among the tribal population. Strikingly enough, the IMR for tribals of Bihar and Karnataka (as revealed by the NFHS-2) during the late 1990s appears higher than what was reported even two decades earlier, and for the tribals of Uttar Pradesh, it has stayed almost the same over this long period (see Table 4.3). Similarly, recent careful (indirect) estimates of maternal mortality, based on data from the NCAER Human Development Survey 1994, show the greatest vulnerability of tribal women (652 maternal deaths per 10,000 ST births, followed by 584 and 516, respectively, for SC and others) (Bhat 2002a). While this differential has to do mostly with differential accessibility (and affordability too) of health care (that is, safe delivery) facilities, this relative deprivation of the tribal population seems to have been growing over the recent past.[22] This reaffirms the indication (in Chapter 2) that India's tribal people have benefited vastly less than most non-tribal population groups from modern health-care provisions and services—both preventive and curative. While this is partly related to a relative remoteness of tribal habitations with limited accessibility to modern health-care facilities, a relative neglect (arising from lack of political will) of tribal people, at large, by the state cannot be downplayed. Added to such basic tribal disadvantages are their own lingering perceptions and prejudices relating to health and modes of treatment, and also their specific diets and food habits thought to be

---

[22] Note that such relative worsening of maternal mortality among the tribal population in the recent past might have contributed to the lately observed (as discussed in Chapter 2) larger shifts of the sex-ratio towards masculinity.

conducive to greater nutritive deficiencies.[23] However, as noted earlier, several commonly held notions, assumptions, and presumptions regarding several aspects of demographic behaviour of Indian tribes abound in the relevant literature, continuing to remain unestablished and untested 'half-truths'. Thus, the need to place tribal demography on firmer ground is imperative for a sound and effective understanding of tribal problems and their remedies.

Gender Differential in Mortality and Gender Discrimination

Given an increasingly dominant perspective that survival chances constitute one major aspect of human (and even material) well-being (see Sen 1998), the gender differential in mortality is obviously an important issue, as it reflects the relative well-being of male and female populations. As already mentioned, the sex-ratio of a (closed) population serves as an overall index of gender differential in mortality, which is broadly shaped by two sets of factors—biological (that is, female deaths due to maternity and childbirth or the biological advantages of females in survival), and sociocultural (that is, gender discrimination in intra-household distribution of food and health care). An adequate understanding of these mechanisms in a given society calls for looking beyond the overall sex ratio in the population. For example, the age-specific sex-ratios could help locate the most vulnerable ages in which one sex has a relative mortality disadvantage, and this could provide a clue as to whether this gender differential is primarily due to biological reasons or familial discrimination factors. Similarly, it is also useful to know whether gender-specific social bias works through discrimination in distribution of food and nutrition or largely by discrimination in health care and related needs. Many such issues have been engaging researchers working on the (non-tribal) mainstream population for a fairly long time now—especially in South Asian countries and since the early 1980s (for recent review of the literature, see Kishor 1995; Harriss 1999; DeRose et al. 2000). The core facts from this (relatively) large body of literature could be summarized thus: a) the low (and indeed falling) female–male ratio in India is chiefly due to pervasive (and worsening) relative mortality disadvantage of female infants and young children, which is basically

[23] For various studies relating to these issues, see Basu 1994b and Chaudhuri 1986.

a manifestation of familial discrimination and neglect of 'daughters' (Das Gupta 1987; Croll 2000); b) while there is some evidence of anti-female distribution of food and nutrients, this is not as robust a cause as it was commonly thought to be; 3) rather, gender discrimination in spheres of health care and medical attention is found more pronounced and instrumental; and 4) this anti-female discriminatory social order seems to be fundamentally rooted in a broad sociocultural mooring of unequal gender relations, patriarchy, and/or 'son preference', which is most stark in the north and northwestern regions, and least in the southern states of India.

Although tribal gender relations have been drawing the attention of anthropologists for a long time, systematic investigations into its demographic implications in, for example, sex differential in mortality and other indices of well-being like recent researches on such issues for the mainstream population, are remarkably rare. For example, sex differentials in mortality and nutritional status (particularly among infants and children), widely used as an index of gender discrimination, have rarely been studied in appropriate detail for Indian tribal populations. Among the local-level studies (as reported in Table 4.1), there are relatively few that have touched upon the issue of gender differential in mortality. Some of those studies are not free of methodological difficulties but even putting aside the issue of methodological soundness, they provide a rather mixed picture on gender bias in tribal mortality. For example, a distinct female advantage in survival chances has been reported for some individual tribes in particular locations.[24] In contrast, an anti-female bias in nutritional status and mortality (especially among infants and children) has been indicated in some tribe-and-region-specific studies.[25] Interestingly, however, the sex ratio (number of females per 1000 males), which is generally taken to be indicative (albeit indirectly) of sex differential in mortality and gender discrimination, is almost always found more balanced (like state-level aggregate data) among tribal vis-à-vis non-tribal populations (see Table 4.1).[26] This, as noted earlier, confirms,

[24] See Nag 1954; Verma 1977; Sinha 1990; Sinha 1993; Basu and Kshatriya 1989; and Basu 1994a.

[25] See Sharma and Khan 1990; Ray and Roth 1984; Harriss et al. 1990; Nag 1954; Sain 1994; Chetlapalli et al. 1991; Bagchi 1994; and Basu 1994a.

[26] There seem to be a few exceptions (Kerala and Goa) where the tribal female–male ratio, though not really low in comparison with other regions,

though indirectly, the relatively egalitarian nature of tribal gender relations (and hence less gender bias in mortality). Furthermore, indirect support to the hypothesis of less gender bias in mortality in tribal population has also been provided by statistical analyses of district-level census data for 1981 and 1991 (Murthi *et al.* 1995; Drèze and Murthi 2000; and Kishor 1993). As the regression results clearly show, the higher the proportion of the ST population in a district, the lower the anti-female bias in child survival. Consistent with this is also district-level analyses of census data for most Indian regions showing a relatively high ST juvenile female–male ratio (especially vis-à-vis the SC group), which serves as more direct evidence of gender discrimination than the overall sex ratio does (Agnihotri 1996; 1999).

However, given the enormous tribal diversity, it is not perfectly clear whether all Indian tribes share this trait of gender equity in mortality. In fact, the tribal female–male ratio in the majority of studies (see Table 4.1) is lower than that found in societies such as Western and many African countries, Sri Lanka, and Kerala in India, known for gender equality and female autonomy. While this could be an indication of a certain degree of assimilation within a broad anti-female mainstream Hindu structure, there could be other influences as well, say, migration patterns of tribes at a sub-national level. On this issue light could only be thrown by a detailed and disaggregated analysis of age–sex patterns of mortality for tribals and the non-tribal group, but such studies are indeed rare. For example, one study of tribal areas of Pakistan shows a lower death rate for females (15.6) than for males (17.5) (Ashraf 1962:95–9). In another study of four tribal groups in eastern India, the death rate was found, though relatively high, lower (except one tribe) for females during 1964–8 (Upadhaya n.d.). Some indirect estimates of gender differential in the overall mortality level (based on Model Life Tables) at the all-India level for the 1961–71 and 1971–81 decades show a distinct female (relative) advantage among the tribal population, as against the reverse finding for the non-tribal population (Sinha 1984, 1990).

Unsurprisingly, the extent of estimated female advantage in the tribal death rate is not uniform across time and region in India. For

---

appears noticeably lower than that of the (non-tribal) general population. The question of why there is a relative female 'disadvantage' among the tribal people vis-à-vis the general population in states with a relatively balanced overall sex-ratio, is of much interest and certainly deserves systematic research.

example, indirect (all-India) estimates with the 1991 census report a negligible gender differential in tribal infant/child mortality up to the second year, but tribal girls between the third and fifth years appear to experience an increasing relative mortality disadvantage with age (vis-à-vis their male counterparts) (Rajan and Mohanachandran 2001:4506–08). In contrast, such female disadvantage begins even at the infancy among the aggregate SC community. In a few states (some of which have above average tribal concentrations, e.g. Bihar, Orissa, Gujarat, and Nagaland) female (relative) disadvantage in estimated survival probability begins to surface, like the SC population, even before the completion of the first year of life for the ST population. Since social/familial discrimination against gender is generally reflected in sex-differentials in mortality, especially in childhood years,[27] this finding is suggestive of tribal people adapting themselves increasingly to an anti-female (mainstream) sociocultural mould characterized by a strong 'son preference'.

The limited evidence that exists on intra-family distribution of food and age–sex composition of nutritional status among the tribal vis-à-vis non-tribal households gives a somewhat varied picture across time and space. For example, a study based on a nutritional survey of children (under five years) in two villages in West Bengal during the early 1980s finds almost the same degree of anti-female bias between tribal and non-tribal communities (Sen and Sengupta 1983).[28] On the other hand, a study based on anthropological field surveys on intra-household food distribution among select tribal and non-tribal groups of West Bengal concludes that the traditional Hindu system of male dominance and the associated anti-female familial bias is relatively absent among tribal people (Basu et al. 1986). There are a few other micro-level field studies on nutritional intake/anthropometric status of children and adults of specific tribal groups elsewhere in India. Although these studies are not always methodologically sound, they are, on the whole,

[27] See also Agnihotri 1999; Gangadharan and Maitra 2000.

[28] Since tribal people in these surveyed villages are (proportionately) a very small minority, the absence of any difference between them in terms of degree of anti-female discrimination could be a reflection of almost complete tribal emulation of the mainstream sociocultural milieu and practices. Indeed, a similar survey (sponsored again by the World Development Economics Research) in a tribal-dominated village (where tribal people are the majority at 86 per cent) in Midnapore district of south Bengal in 1987–8 showed less gender bias in the nutritional status of children (Pal 1999:1167).

not suggestive of a definitive female discrimination among tribes, albeit with a few exceptions.[29]

According to one explanation, less anti-female bias among tribal societies derives chiefly from the tribal women's higher economic worth, resulting from their greater participation in the labour force. This postulated link arises because empirical studies of Rosenzweig and Schultz (1982) and Kishor (1993) have established an overall inverse association between female labour force participation and female disadvantage in child survival. However, the precise mechanism underlying this relationship remains unclear. While there can conceivably be several distinct possibilities, there is little evidence to distinguish between these alternative hypotheses (for a useful discussion on this, see Murthi et al. 1995:754). However, analyses of the 1981 district-level census data find a significant negative association between female disadvantage in child survival and the proportion of tribal population even after controlling for the female labour force participation rate (Murthi et al. 1995; Kishor 1993), a finding which suggests that tribal societies do have some features (other than just a greater 'economic worth' of women) that contribute to enhancing relative female survival chances. They are most likely to pertain to the sociocultural sphere. Relatively balanced gender relations and less patriarchal kinship systems generally characterize tribal societies vis-à-vis non-tribal mainstream people, and these could well be related to a greater 'cultural worth' of tribal female children. For example, a survey among children aged 1–5 years of SC farm labourer households in a village of West Bengal found a greater nutritional deficiency among girls in a situation where adult female wage labour participation was found no less than their male counterparts (Chaudhury 1984).[30] This

---

[29] See Pande and Devi 1991; Shaheen et al. 1992; Rao et al. 1994; Shukla and Reddy 1997; Pingle 1990; Rao et al. 1992, 1993. When nutritional levels are found higher among females (Rao et al. 1993; Rao 1992), we take this as an absence of anti-female discrimination, rather than existence of anti-male bias. This is because females have well-known biological advantages in food intake, health, and survival, which means a higher nutritional value to females out of the same quantity of food to both sexes.

[30] The author attributes the finding of lower nutritional levels of girls to their lower (perceived) economic value vis-à-vis that of male children. This differential originates from the greater engagement of boys in 'economically gainful activities' (as cowherds or attached labourers), many of which are unsuitable for girls, as well as from the parents' much greater dependence on sons (than on daughters) as a security for old age.

finding for the SC community, thus, supports the view that intrinsic sociocultural norms and values, rather than women's productive worth alone, are more important in shaping women's status, gender relations, and/or relative female survival chances in a community.

Interestingly, the phenomenon of high female labour force participation itself has sometimes been hypothesized as an important source of female disadvantage in child survival and nutritional achievements in tribal societies (Harriss et al. 1990). As the argument runs, the higher female wage work participation, when combined with relatively little (culturally shaped) female autonomy over household decisions (say, in food and health expenditure), fails to bring nutritional gain for children. Rather, it often jeopardizes the interests of children as it eats into the mothers' capacity for child care, especially during the seasons of peak female activity. The adverse consequence of this, as the evidence from two tribal groups near Warangal of Andhra Pradesh suggest, is disproportionately borne by female children, particularly those in infancy. Unfortunately, this otherwise very illuminating paper does not adequately probe into the crucial question of why female children and infants appear to suffer disproportionately (compared to male counterparts) from the brunt of the predicament of tribal women, namely, constrained freedom in household decisions as well as an abridged capacity for child care. In any case, the question at issue is inescapably linked as much with the nature of gender relations as well as the value and status of women in tribal societies as with its continuing trend over time.

As mentioned earlier, cultural traits often exert an independent influence in shaping female status in a society. For example, a recent study in the Himalayas shows that a greater female-workforce participation and a higher female-literacy rate among the Garhwali women (as compared to those for the whole of Uttar Pradesh) could not make much difference to women's position (in terms of well-being and autonomy in household decisions), whereas tribal females in the same mountainous region, facing the same harsh physical and ecological circumstances, appear to enjoy a much bigger 'say' in household affairs (Rana 1996). An Indian Council of Medical Research-sponsored study on the Gonds of Mandla district (Madhya Pradesh) in the late 1980s, a tribal group which has long been in relatively closer contact with non-tribal mainstream sociocultural patterns, found tribal women dispossessed of the autonomy to take household decisions. This resulted in a male-bias in household expenditure patterns, despite the contribution of women to household earnings being no less than that of their male counterparts (Mawar *et al*. 1993). Such evidence indicates the sway of mainstream (Hindu) sociocultural patterns in constricting female autonomy and women's status in tribal societies, although tribal household poverty and low material circumstances meant that women could not be withdrawn from the productive labour force. This stage of tribal transformation resembles what is often seen among scheduled caste communities—that poverty and material circumstances make female work participation almost a necessity, albeit within a socio-cultural orbit of restricted autonomy and status of women.

This, however, is not to deny the possible favourable influence on gender relations of greater female work participation in tribal societies. In fact, these two influences, both economic and cultural, are often so closely linked with each other that it is almost impossible to separate them. For instance, the differences between social groups in the work participation rate of women outside the household are often a manifestation of differential sociocultural taboos or sanctions. Although some tribal women do not, like non-tribal (Hindu) counterparts, have the right to perform religious duties, '[h]er loss in position is compensated by granting her sufficient freedom in her movement and action', because 'a woman is considered an economic asset and considerable value is placed on a hard-working, industrious and dutiful wife' (Choudhury 1978:19).[31] In many regions, tribal women not only participate more in paid/gainful work but also have a higher earning capacity than non-tribal women, sometimes even higher than that for males. For example, the average daily wage earning for tribal men and women were respectively Rs 4.22 and 4.26 while the respective figures for the SC people were 4.20 and 3.23 (Government of India 1986).

To summarize: despite difficulties and limitations relating to data quality and methodology, these limited number of micro-level studies, on balance, do suggest less gender bias in (infant/child) mortality and familial resource allocation (that is, food and health care) in tribal societies in comparison with non-tribal counterparts (SC in particular).

---

[31] Some researchers, especially in the context of several African societies, have made a case for the need to draw a distinction between gender equality and female autonomy (Afonja 1990). The basic argument is that 'the autonomy of women can...be infused with inequality between men and women' (ibid:209), and that 'development is intensifying the subordination of women to men' (ibid:209).

But there are indications, especially in the recent past, of an ongoing erosion of this traditional tribal feature of gender-equity. As already noted the substantial falls in the overall female–male ratio in the tribal population over the last several decades are pointers, though indirectly, to this trend. We present in Appendix Table A4.1 some evidence from a few recent large-scale surveys (NSS and NFHS-2) on sex-differentials in morbidity and medical attention separately for ST, SC, and others. The proportion of females reporting ailments, medical treatment, hospitalization, or medical expenditure per treatment appears less than that for males—across almost all the three social groups. It is, however, impossible to be sure whether this is a reflection of female biological advantages in morbidity (and mortality) or less medical attention to females. But the extent of gender-differential on these counts seems to be somewhat less in the tribal group than among non-tribal people, especially SC groups. For instance, the average expenditure per hospitalized case over twelve months in private hospitals for SC males is nearly four times larger than that for their female counterparts, but the corresponding male–female gap in medical expenditure is much less for ST and other groups. Interestingly, it is only in the Charitable Trust that average expenditure per hospitalization case of females appears to exceed that of males both among the ST and SC groups.

In Appendix Table A4.2, the anthropometric indices calculated from nutritional information of children aged below 3 years by sex for ST, SC, and others as collected by NFHS-2 for 1998–9 are presented. They do not show a markedly different gender pattern of under-nutrition among aggregate tribal children. While some degree of female disadvantage in nutrition seems discernible among non-tribal children, the data do not suggest its clear absence among their tribal counterparts. The state-level data seem to suggest that a regional pattern of sex-differential in nutritional achievement often imposes itself upon tribal and non-tribal groups alike across a state. There are, of course, cases like Maharashtra and Karnataka where tribal children show a marked female advantage in terms of weight-for-age measure of under-nutrition amidst a sharp disadvantage found for their non-tribal female counterparts. The opposite situation, though it exists, seems rarer (Bihar).

Appendix Table A4.3 presents the proportion of children (aged below 3 years), who received treatment after having had fever or diarrhoea, by sex and social group. The aggregate picture that emerges is that the sex-differential in medical attention among the ST group does not appear much different from the pattern found among non-tribal people. Despite state-level variations, the overall picture one detects from this Table is that of a broad regional pattern of discrimination (which is obviously one of the non-tribal mainstream population) in food and curative health care pervading across tribal communities too. This seems consistent also with recent NSS information (for 1995–96) as discussed above (see Table A4.1), which does not suggest remarkable differences between these social groups in terms of the sex-composition of either the number of reported ailments' hospitalization cases, expenditure per ailment, or distribution of hospitalized cases. It, therefore, seems reasonable to conclude that India's tribal population on the whole presently do not show a sharply different pattern from the mainstream (anti-female) type of gender differentials in nutritional achievements, morbidity, and medical attention.

Indeed, an emerging trend in 'son preference' among certain tribal groups has already been noticeable (Dubey and Bardhan 1978:102). This is reaffirmed by such findings as an increasing frequency of dowry marriages in tribal communities, for whom the traditional custom has always been bride-price (Narasimhan 1999:70). According to the NFHS-2 data, for India the degree of 'son preference' (gauged in terms of the percentage of respondents wanting 'more sons than daughters' or 'at least one son') seems no less among the ST population (or indeed rather slightly greater than the forward caste groups) than non-tribal groups.[32] This tribal trend towards greater gender imbalances is, if real, certainly undesirable and unfortunate too. Noticing the lately emerging deterioration in women's status in tribal societies, some social scientists and activists have sought to identify the major factors (Agarwal 1990; Fernandes and Menon 1987; Roy Burman 1987). First, this trend seems (at least partly) to be related to the declining economic worth of women along with a shrinking scope for females' participation in productive activities, a trend that results from multiple forces. For example, increasing restrictions on forest-based traditional livelihood patterns, in which tribal women have traditionally had a very prominent place, appear to have curtailed the economic role of women in such tribal household economies (Fernandes and Menon 1987). The increasing abolition of common property resources and large-scale displacement of tribal habitation

[32] The figures (in per cent) are respectively as follows: ST: 38 and 91.5; SC: 37.9 and 87.3; Others: 30.0 and 78.2 (IIPS 2000:120).

Table A4.1 Differentials in nutrition and medical attention: A comparison between ST, SC, and others, rural India, 1995–6

	Scheduled Tribes (ST)			Scheduled Castes (SC)			Others (Non-ST/SC)		
	M	F	(M/F)	M	F	(M/F)	M	F	(M/F)
Number of persons reporting ailment during last 15 days per 1000	42	43	(0.98)	52	55	(0.95)	56	60	(0.93)
Per 1000 distribution of treatments (not treated as in-patient of hospital) during last 15 days	77	72	(1.07)	226	215	(1.05)	697	712	(0.98)
Number of persons reporting medical treatment of ailing patients during last 15 days per 1000	801	766	(1.05)	837	827	(1.01)	842	818	(1.03)
Number of persons hospitalized during the last 365 days per 1000	9	8	(1.12)	13	11	(1.18)	15	11	(1.36)
Average total medical expenditure per ailment (not treated as hospital in-patient) during last 15 days (Rs)	70	66	(1.06)	130	104	(1.25)	142	133	(1.07)

Per 1000 distribution of hospitalization cases during last 365 days (any hospital)	65	61	(1.07)	211	193	(1.09)	723	745	(0.97)

Average expenditure per hospitalized case during last 365 days (Rs):

a) Public hospital	1,368	1,105	(1.24)	2,023	1,471	(1.38)	2,846	2,189	(1.30)
b) PHC	1,117	675	(1.65)	624	490	(1.27)	824	781	(1.06)
c) Public dispensary	2,341	1,618	(1.45)	2,900	1,084	(2.68)	1,647	2,423	(0.68)
d) Private hospital	2,872	2,496	(1.15)	11,119	3461	(3.21)	3,982	3,325	(1.20)
e) Any hospital	1,821	1,400	(1.30)	5,405	2,022	(2.67)	3,481	2,726	(1.28)
f) Nursing home	4,213	2,220	(1.89)	4,777	2,857	(1.67)	4,313	4,215	(1.02)
g) Charitable trust	1,266	3,574	(0.35)	1,157	1,539	(0.75)	7,253	2,602	(2.79)
h) Others	2,926	1,263	(2.32)	3,644	4,981	(0.73)	4,532	1,292	(3.51)

Source: NSS, Morbidity and Treatment of Ailments 52nd Round (July 1995–June 1996), November 1998.
Figures in parentheses are respective male–female ratios.

Table A4.2 Percentage of children under age 3 years classified as undernourished on three anthropometric indices of nutritional status, by tribes/caste group and sex, India and major states, 1998–9

		Weight-for-age Percentage below –3 SD			Height-for-age Percentage below –3 SD			Weight-for-height Percentage below –3 SD		
		Male	Female	Ratio (M/F)	Male	Female	Ratio (M/F)	Male	Female	Ratio (M/F)
India*	SC	20.3	22.5	0.90	26.8	28.8	0.93	3.1	2.9	1.07
	ST	26.4	27.7	0.95	27.9	29.3	0.95	4.1	5.4	0.76
	Others	12.5	14.7	0.85	17.2	19.9	0.86	2.1	1.6	1.31
Andhra Pradesh	SC	13.8	14.1	0.98	18.3	18.8	0.97	0.9	1.2	0.75
	ST	7.1	7.4	0.96	7.1	18.5	0.38	0	0	–
	Others	2.3	7.4	0.31	11.3	8.9	1.27	1.5	0	–
Bihar	SC	29.0	27.3	1.06	37.8	34.2	1.11	5.2	6.0	0.87
	ST	34.4	38.6	0.89	39.7	33.3	1.19	7.8	7.0	1.11
	Others	20.4	16.8	1.21	27.7	22.9	1.21	6.1	3.8	1.61
Gujarat	SC	17.5	18.1	0.97	26.3	31.3	0.84	2.3	3.4	0.68
	ST	24.2	24.0	1.01	26.3	31.7	0.83	2.8	4.4	0.64
	Others	8.3	11.3	0.73	12.9	19.8	0.65	1.8	1.1	1.64
Haryana	SC	10.4	14.4	0.72	31.1	27.9	1.11	0.0	1.0	0.00
	ST	–	0.0	–	–	0.0	–	–	0.0	–
	Others	9.5	6.5	1.46	20.6	19.4	1.06	1.5	0.5	3.00
Karnataka	SC	21.0	25.0	0.84	14.3	21.9	0.65	8.5	5.0	1.70
	ST	31.3	25.8	1.21	28.1	16.1	1.75	0.0	3.2	0.00
	Others	12.6	19.0	0.66	14.9	19.7	0.76	3.7	4.7	0.79

State	Category									
Madhya Pradesh	SC	30.9	28.8	1.07	32.1	32.3	0.99	3.7	5.6	0.66
	ST	27.8	35.4	0.79	30.8	36.7	0.84	4.6	4.9	0.94
	Others	13.4	16.2	0.83	16.3	21.1	0.77	3.5	3.2	1.09
Maharashtra	SC	14.2	16.5	0.86	14.0	17.4	0.80	1.7	0.0	–
	ST	39.8	31.9	1.25	25.6	13.0	1.97	9.3	6.5	1.43
	Others	14.8	16.8	0.88	12.3	16.1	0.76	1.5	1.8	0.83
Orissa	SC	27.0	21.7	1.24	25.7	19.6	1.31	5.3	0.7	7.57
	ST	27.0	26.1	1.03	20.6	19.0	1.08	5.8	5.6	1.04
	Others	11.4	13.0	0.88	7.6	12.2	0.62	3.8	1.4	2.71
Punjab	SC	10.9	12.6	0.87	23.8	28.1	0.85	0.7	2.2	0.32
	ST	–	0.0	–	–	0.0	–	–	0.0	–
	Others	4.8	6.0	0.80	6.4	14.8	0.43	0.0	0.0	–
Rajasthan	SC	32.6	39.5	0.83	20.9	32.5	0.64	1.5	2.4	0.63
	ST	38.3	38.9	0.98	28.6	26.7	1.07	3.4	6.7	0.51
	Others	25.2	22.7	1.11	18.5	15.4	1.20	1.9	0.8	2.38
Sikkim	SC	6.3	0.0	–	12.5	14.3	0.87	0.0	0.0	–
	ST	4.1	2.4	1.71	4.1	11.9	0.34	2.0	–	–
	Others	4.9	6.9	0.71	11.3	8.6	1.31	–	1.7	–
Tamil Nadu	SC	15.4	13.3	1.16	21.5	12.7	1.69	4.0	2.7	1.48
	ST	0.0	40.0	0.00	0.0	100.0	0.00	0.0	0.0	–
	Others	14.3	0.0	–	0.0	0.0	–	0.0	0.0	–
Uttar Pradesh	SC	21.9	26.4	0.83	32.3	40.7	0.79	3.1	2.6	1.19
	ST	29.0	36.4	0.80	43.8	36.4	1.20	3.2	0.0	–
	Others	14.8	20.8	0.71	24.1	29.4	0.82	1.5	1.4	1.07

(Contd.)

Table A4.2 (contd.)

		Weight-for-age Percentage below –3 SD			Height-for-age Percentage below –3 SD			Weight-for-height Percentage below –3 SD		
		Male	Female	Ratio (M/F)	Male	Female	Ratio (M/F)	Male	Female	Ratio (M/F)
West Bengal	SC	17.9	23.5	0.76	17.3	25.8	0.67	3.2	1.5	2.13
	ST	22.0	24.1	0.91	14.0	37.9	0.37	0.0	3.6	0.00
	Others	10.8	17.6	0.61	13.8	23.7	0.58	1.1	1.4	0.79

Note: *represents 14 states

Source : IIPS (2000).

Weight-for-age:
For calculating percentage below -3SD, Percentage of HW8 <(-300) is calculated
For calculating percentage below -2SD, Percentage of HW8 <(-200) is calculated
Height-for-age:
For calculating percentage below -3SD, Percentage of HW5 <(-300) is calculated
For calculating percentage below -2SD, Percentage of HW5 <(-200) is calculated
Weight-for-height:
For calculating percentage below -3SD, Percentage of HW11 <(-300) is calculated
For calculating percentage below -2SD, Percentage of HW11 <(-200) is calculated

Table A4.3 Percentage of children (below 3 years) who received treatment among those having experienced diarrhoea and fever in two weeks preceding the survey, by scheduled tribe/caste group, India and major states, 1998–9

States	Per cent of children (below 3 years) who received Treatment for Diarrhoea						Per cent of children (below 3 years) who received Treatment for Fever					
	SC		ST		OTHERS		SC		ST		OTHERS	
	Male	Female	Male	Female	Male	Female	Male	Female	Male	Female	Male	Female
Andhra Pradesh	73.91	70.00	80.00	75.00	69.57	65.38	63.64	60.00	33.33	50.00	77.78	80.77
Bihar	58.33	41.54	16.67	18.75	42.50	61.90	62.20	51.28	60.00	31.82	63.93	52.46
Haryana	88.24	95.00	–	–	100.00	87.10	85.71	77.78	71.43	76.19	79.41	86.21
Gujarat	68.18	60.71	72.00	71.43	70.00	59.46	92.59	95.45	–	–	90.91	86.67
Karnataka	81.25	70.00	50.00	25.00	70.37	56.67	85.00	71.43	60.00	50.00	87.10	70.97
Sikkim	28.57	80.00	24.00	38.89	27.78	22.22	81.58	84.38	88.24	78.13	85.25	86.79
Madhya Pradesh	67.35	51.06	50.00	44.59	68.52	57.14	57.35	62.79	48.10	61.67	62.07	66.67
Maharashtra	96.67	84.38	85.71	67.86	74.81	75.68	41.51	41.46	37.50	16.67	80.39	55.88
Punjab	76.47	–	–	100.00	100.00	73.33	90.63	88.00	–	100.00	100.00	92.31
Tamil Nadu	62.50	75.00	–	0.00	–	–	77.36	58.97	75.68	48.72	72.88	68.89
West Bengal	33.33	41.67	71.43	100.00	63.89	51.61	0.00	28.57	31.25	31.25	62.50	31.58
Uttar Pradesh	63.83	61.86	57.89	62.50	60.08	67.00	70.00	89.47	0.00	50.00	–	–
Rajasthan	53.85	67.39	64.58	52.38	60.48	47.27	71.26	60.24	66.67	60.00	68.45	61.76
Orissa	51.79	44.23	34.48	10.26	60.78	47.06	30.00	34.62	58.82	75.00	50.48	44.83
India*	63.78	61.52	52.67	45.08	65.37	61.48	66.61	62.03	58.19	51.78	72.69	66.71

Note: *represents 14 states

away from their traditional natural setting have unleashed forces which are generally unfavourable to women. For example, the right (and hence, an implicit ownership) to common property resources has traditionally been gender-equitable, and have often been based on collective organizations and institutions. But major state initiatives undertaken for tribal development (for example, distribution of land, transforming shifting cultivation into settled agriculture, and compensation for displaced tribals) are mostly found on the mainstream notion of a male-centric patriarchal household, thereby pushing tribal females (and communal and collective institutions) into relative jeopardy (see Agarwal 1990).

On the other hand, settled tribal agriculturist communities have been gradually internalizing many conservative Hindu sociocultural norms and values, within which women's work outside home is seen as lowly (Roy Burman 1987). Indeed, an increasing volume of anthropological research attributes the contemporary evidence on gender discrimination and female disadvantage in tribal communities to growing assimilation and integration with the mainstream (non-tribal) culture, social practices, and values (Bleie 1987; Thamizoli 1997). Besides, there has also been a general bias of new (and labour-saving) agricultural technology against female farm employment opportunities. Some researches, especially in the Himalayan context, suggest that recent trends of commercialization and technological changes with inherent male-biases in labour absorption, seem to have brought in a male-dominated ideology, which has, thereby, disrupted the age-old sociocultural values favourable to female freedom and autonomy (Singh 1997). However, it has been argued that agricultural diversification and technological change, as such, do not necessarily lead to deterioration in relative economic worth and social standing in tribal communities, especially until the emergence of rapid growth of industries (Dubey and Bardhan n.d.).

Thus, while India's tribal women (on the whole used until not so long ago) to enjoy a distinctly better status, freedom, autonomy, and less discrimination as compared to their mainstream Hindu counterparts, they have been finding themselves increasingly alike those in the mainstream anti-female sociocultural regime. Tribal women with a social status worse than their non-tribal mainstream counterparts are often identifiable, especially in regions where tribal assimilation with Hindu culture had started quite early (for example, Rajasthan)

(Sharma and Sharma 1993).[33] This said, there is much scope as well as need for further systematic investigations into the nature and trend of intra-household gender bias in tribal households and their sociocultural underpinnings (female autonomy). Like the increasing number of studies on these issues for the mainstream population, there should be more such studies[34] on the role of tribal sociocultural ramifications (for example, female autonomy and kinship patterns) in shaping their demographic behaviour and outcomes.

Discussion and Concluding Remarks

It would be useful to consolidate the major revelations from our foregoing review of major aspects of contemporary India's tribal demographic behaviour and their implications. Some emergent points about tribal fertility—namely, that tribal fertility, like fertility of the general population, is diverse across regions and tribes, varies in lower to higher levels than non-tribal fertility, and that it has been declining over time—do not sound startling as such. But underneath this apparently diverse picture,[35] there is an aggregate baseline pattern, namely, that overall tribal fertility is (and has been) no higher and indeed even lower than their otherwise most comparable social group of SC people. This is certainly remarkable, particularly in the light of the fact that ST and SC groups are overall on a similar economic footing in terms of levels of material living and of poverty (as shown in Chapter 2). Indeed, this relatively lower tribal fertility in the contemporary period is not new, and is, as was shown in the preceding chapter, traceable to the historical past. There are recent instances of tribal groups maintaining relatively low fertility by use of traditional contraceptive herbs/medicines and abortion (Mutharayappa 1994). But traditional sociocultural features (for example, relatively high female age at marriage, prolonged breastfeeding/longer birth-interval, and

[33] Indeed, some authors appear unsure as to whether a high degree of patriarchy and female subjugation, as sometimes observed among some de-notified and nomadic tribes, is their traditional sociocultural trait or an outcome of their long-standing interactions with the mainstream (Hindu) society and culture (Bokil 2002).

[34] Harbison et al. 1989; Maharatna 2000b.

[35] In fact, the observed variations in fertility rates among diverse individual tribal groups have often prevented researchers from looking at the all-India aggregate differences between social groups (Nag 1973).

greater female autonomy and gender equity), that were historically favourable to maintaining comparatively low tribal fertility, are, of late, losing ground—of course, in varying pace across regions and tribes. And this process seems to have made the fertility of tribes in specific regions even surpass the level of non-tribal counterparts (Das and Shah 1991; Verma 1977 in Table 4.1) in contemporary periods. While this can be viewed as a 'pre-transition rise of fertility', especially among late-modernizing tribes, it could also take the form of a slower pace of fertility decline among many tribal groups that have remained relatively more isolated from mainstream development efforts and family-planning programmes.

As a sequel to the long-standing influences of Hindu traditions, it became prestigious for many tribal people to adopt the early marriage practice as early as the 1930s through the 1960s (Roy Burman 1987:53; Sachchidananda 1964:46), and this has continued till recently (Mann 1985), and perhaps even today in specific locations. Indeed, by the early 1950s, the Hindu influence on tribal marriage patterns and practices was lamented about: 'The tribals invariably married late, and it is only due to the unhealthy influence of the Hindu castes, that early marriages and customs of bride price entered tribal life' (Mehta 1953:240). Ironically, the early age female marriage among tribal communities is often reckoned as an important factor for their comparatively high fertility in several regions of contemporary India (Nag 1973). In several regions, this tribal process presumably has neutralized (at least partly) the fertility-reducing effect of family-planning programmes, resulting in a slower pace of fertility decline, while the non-tribal people, being ahead of tribals in the modernization process, have already started delaying female marriages. For example, a relatively high fertility level has been observed among the tribes of Dangs district (Rajasthan) where the majority is composed of practising Hindus (see Das and Shah 1991 in Table 4.1).[36] To this, must be

---

[36] In fact some tribes, at least in particular locations, who had come into contact with mainstream Hindu society and culture relatively early (Bhils and their sub-groups/clans in Rajasthan) are currently showing 'a change in attitude towards child marriage and a growing preference for post-puberty marriage' (Shashi 1995:41; see also Rizvi 1987:103–5). Such trends have sometimes (not always) been viewed as 'retribalization' in the sense that tribals, after failing to get absorbed in the Hindu social structure, return to their traditional customs and cultural norms (Thakur and Thakur 1994:19–22). There are,

added the implications of differential success and/or reach of family planning programmes between tribal and non-tribal areas (Naidu 1979; Benjamin et al. 1988).

Like tribal fertility, some familiar points have also emerged about tribal mortality. The conclusions, namely, that the mortality level varies across tribes and regions, and that tribal mortality, along with mainstream mortality, has declined over time may appear (relatively) unsurprising, but they do involve and open up many interesting and important issues. Strikingly enough, the (aggregate) baseline pattern of contemporary mortality differential (especially in infancy and childhood years) is one of tribal levels being no higher, and indeed even lower, than their closest non-tribal population group (SC). Following our analysis in the last chapter, this contemporary tribal (relative) mortality advantage could well be a lingering echo of the historical past when some aspects of tribal life and environment inherently had some relative advantages from standpoints of health and mortality. For example, a careful survey of about 1,500 individuals of a primitive tribe, Maria Gonds, in five tribal villages of Gadchiroli district (Maharashtra) in the 1980s, has found them 'better off' in terms of food, nutrient intake, and anthropometry than their counterparts in the general population of the state (Rao et al. 1992). While, as the authors (Rao et al. 1992:65) conclude, '[t]he tribal population inhibiting isolated regions with little exploitation by outside people and with sufficient employment potential is found to be nutritionally better', an almost opposite scenario could also be found for specific tribes in other regions (Rao et al. 1993).

Recent trends no longer point to a continuation of tribal mortality advantage, often suggesting the reversal.[37] There seems to have been consistent and steady erosion of (traditional) tribal mortality advantage along with development and integration of the economy over the last several decades. Both large-scale survey data (in Table 4.3) and micro-level studies for some specific tribes and regions (Choudhury 1988; Verma 1977; Kumar 1986 in Table 4.1) show an extremely high tribal

---

however, instances in specific locations where tribal people appear to have never changed their traditional practice of relatively delayed female marriages (Hemam and Reddy 1998).

[37] It is notable that this alleged mortality (and/or health) advantage of tribal people, especially in the past, is nowadays branded as a 'myth' (Singh 1987).

mortality level (usually proxied by IMR or childhood mortality). It is an important question whether and how far such evidence reflects their enhanced contact and sociocultural assimilation with the mainstream population or their relative vulnerability in terms of nutrition and accessibility to modern health provisions. The current evidence of high maternal and child mortality in tribal communities (Bhat 2002) seems largely attributable to much less accessibility to modern medical facilities (Rajaratnam *et al.* 1997).

Unlike the mainstream population in many Indian regions (Das Gupta 1987; Kishor 1995), a consistent (relative) absence of female disadvantage in mortality among Indian tribes is in consonance with a legacy of more balanced and equitable gender relations in tribal society and culture. But there appears some distinct indications of a reversal of such historic gender equity among tribes, both in terms of mortality and other indicators of well-being.[38] As was shown in Chapter 1, like the total population, the female–male ratio in the tribal population has been declining over the past several decades, and by a relatively large magnitude over the last two decades. This invites apprehension about whether the sex differential of tribal mortality has been conforming increasingly to the anti-female mainstream pattern. And our review of contemporary evidence broadly testifies to the hypothesis of emerging gender biases among tribal communities in terms of sex-differentials in mortality and in other related indicators of well-being (nutrition and health care). The lower caste (SC) people, who generally came within the mainstream society earlier, do show stark anti-female patterns already.[39] In fact, anthropological literature often attributes the ongoing tilt of tribal gender relations in an anti-female direction

[38] Ironically, over the recent past there has been a perhaps growing concern in official circles for promotion of gender equity and female status in India's general population. The recent World Bank reports and special emphasis on gender-equity issues by various research-funding agencies like UNDP are testimony to such growing global concern. In fact, researchers and administrators have recommended various policy measures (educational savings accounts for girls and provision of mid-day free meals at schools and other motivational programmes) for mitigating the effects of son preference and anti-female biases (Arnold *et al.* 1996, and Mutharayappa *et al.* 1997).

[39] Noting vastly more balanced juvenile sex-ratios for tribals than for the low caste (SC) population, Agnihotri (1996:3375–6) writes, '[t]his may have something to do with the pattern of "assimilation" of these two groups in the mainstream of the society—tribals have been relatively isolated from this "mainstream" even where their population percentage is moderate.'

to increasing influences from neighbouring (mainstream) caste Hindus and their patriarchal norms and values (Thamizoli 1997; Chauhan 1996). Given very little gender biases in traditional tribal societies, its contemporary anti-female trend is indeed an unfortunate story. In this context, preservation and wide publicity of these aspects of gender equality and female autonomy of traditional tribal culture should be an immediate policy recommendation.[40]

This said, our foregoing analyses have also shown that contemporary trends and patterns of tribal demographic outcomes constitute an important, though complex, area of academic research with useful insights and policy implications. There is a lot yet to be unearthed on tribal demographic behaviour, its transition and wider implications; its obvious corollary is the need for further detailed, rigorous, and systematic demographic studies of Indian tribes, most desirably in a comparative perspective. In the following chapter, we will focus on broad demographic trends of the aggregate tribal population (in comparison with non-tribal counterparts) in one historically prominent tribal belt in eastern India, namely Jharkhand, in the post-Independence period.

[40] One line of argument suggests that the status of women (and gender relations) among primitive tribes, while usually being high and relatively balanced, are hardly comparable (intrinsically) with those belonging to modern (western) societies. Because, as one author writes, 'the lives of primitive women is due to their being members of societies with a simple technology and economy, rather than to their being women' (Evans-Pritchard 1965:44). However, this line of thought cannot undermine our argument that the (relatively) high status of women and balanced gender relations that have traditionally characterized India's tribal people, are chiefly related to their broad sociocultural milieu, irrespective of their state of economy and technology. First, India's aggregate ST population, though, as we have shown earlier, almost at the same material level of living as their SC counterparts, appear to be distinctively different particularly in respect of gender relations and related criteria. Moreover, India's broad regional variations in female autonomy and status of women seems on balance more attributable to sociocultural (rather than economic and technological) variations [Sen 1998]. Relatedly, the evidence on tribes suggests that the recent (tribal) sociocultural tendency to conforming to the broad mainstream pattern of gender biases, are the outcomes more of increasing acculturation and integration than anything else (for example, economic and technological progress).

5

Trends of Tribal Demography in Jharkhand in the Post-Independence Period*

Introduction

The past (historical) patterns of tribal demographic behaviour as well as their contemporary metamorphosis and trends have been analysed in the preceding two chapters. What has emerged as an aggregate baseline pattern is the low fertility and mortality level of tribes in comparison with those of non-tribal counterparts (e.g. SC) in the historical past, echoed in the contemporary period. Given this broad baseline framework, it should be illuminating to focus on tribal demographic trends in a specific region over the post-Independence period. In this chapter, we undertake a demographic analysis of the tribal population in Jharkhand, which was lately made a separate state in 2000 by carving out much of the south of the erstwhile state of Bihar.

There are several reasons why a detailed and systematic study of the tribal demography of Jharkhand in a comparative perspective should be particularly useful and instructive. First, as is well-known, the tribal people in this region have acquired prominence for various reasons other than demographic factors alone. The location is historically the homeland of a few major tribes (for example, Santhals) with a long-established heritage in economic and cultural spheres. Along with the long-standing processes of 'invasion', oppression, and

* This chapter draws on Maharatna and Chikte (2003).

exploitation by non-tribal people in this region rich in natural resources, the area has remained the site of recurrent major tribal revolts, unrest, and protest movements since the early colonial period. Second, as was noted earlier (in chapter 1), the tribal population growth rate in a large part of the eastern region (including Jharkhand), unlike other states in India, have been much slower than that of the non-tribal population during this period. While a slow long-term growth of tribes in this region is apparently consistent with the baseline demographic pattern of India's tribal population, namely, relatively low birth rate and death rates, especially in the earlier period of rudimentary modern health care system, this is hardly relevant to contemporary times. There must have been other factors at work, such as tribal migration and displacement, and in this chapter we will examine plausible hypotheses relating to the slower population growth of the tribes in this region. As will be clearer, demographic trends and processes for the tribal population in Jharkhand are crucial for understanding this region's development problems and possible remedies.

Long-Term Growth of Tribal Population and Changes in Broad Socioeconomic Indicators in Jharkhand: A Comparative Perspective, 1951–91

Table 5.1 presents information on long-term changes in population, literacy, female–male ratio for the total population, including ST and SC groups during four decades, starting from 1951 for Jharkhand, Bihar and India, as a whole. As can be seen, Jharkhand has always been a region of tribal concentration. While tribal people had constituted around 36 per cent of the total population of the region in the early 1950s, their share had declined noticeably to around 27 per cent by the beginning of the 1990s. And this has been accompanied by rises in the share of the SC population during this period. Furthermore, these patterns of differential change in the relative population share between ST and SC groups in Jharkhand are somewhat the same for the entire state of Bihar, both before and after the separation of Jharkhand. Strikingly, a declining tribal share observed in these eastern regions contrasts sharply with steady rises at all-India level (and in many other states).

The differential changes in the share of population of these two broad social groups appear quite consistent with their respective rates of population growth. Indeed, the decline (the rise) in the relative share of the total population for ST and SC groups matches well with

Table 5.1 Long-term trends in broad demographic and related indicators, Jharkhand, 1951–91

State	Year	Total Popn.	% ST to Total Population	% SC to Total Population	Long-term growth rate** (1951–91)			Literacy rate by Social Group			% of Urban to total population*	Sex Ratio (f/m)		
					All	SC	ST	All	SC	ST		All	SC	ST
Jharkhand	1951	9,697,254	35.38	8.41	–	–	–	17.87*	5.77**	6.78*	11.49*	961	951	1009
	1991	21,843,911	27.66	11.85	2.03	2.89	1.42	41.39	18.45	27.52	21.25	922	922	975
Bihar@	1951	30,528,693	2.03	13.90	–	–	–	18.57	4.67	5.75	7.40	998	1030	996
	1991	64,530,554	0.89	15.47	1.87	2.14	-0.18	29.73	14.25	22.00	10.40	907	911	924
Bihar(erstwhile)	1951	40,225,947	10.07	12.57	–	–	–	18.40	4.88	6.72	8.42	989	1017	1007
	1991	86,374,465	7.66	14.55	1.91	2.28	1.23	38.48	15.11	26.55	13.14	911	914	970
India	1951	356,879,394	5.29	–	–	–	–	24.02	7.47	6.23	17.97	947	957	988
	1991	838,583,988	8.08	16.48	2.14	2.54*	2.70*	52.21	30.06	29.60	25.73	927	922	972

Note: **Long-term annual exponential growth rate, 1951–91 = (ln 1991 popn.- ln 1951 popn.)/40*100

Sex Ratio = Females per 1000 Males

*Figures refer to 1961–91; See note 1 to Table 5.2

@Bihar, exclusive of Jharkhand

Source: Census of India, relevant volumes, various years.

their lowest (highest) growth rate of population over the entire post-Independence period. While rates of population growth in the region comprising today's Bihar have been lowest across all social groups (vis-à-vis those in Jharkhand and erstwhile Bihar), the tribal population seems to have experienced even a decline in their absolute number. Thus, it is clear that the long-term population increase as per census counts has been the slowest for the tribal population in the entire region, with the SC population having experienced the highest growth rate. Note too that this relatively slow population growth of the ST population seems to have been a regional feature, as this does not tally with the (highest) growth rate of the ST population at the all-India level (see Table 5.1).

It is noteworthy that increases in literacy level, although from extremely low levels, have been much larger among the ST population, both in Jharkhand and Bihar, notwithstanding high levels of remaining illiteracy. This, however, is somewhat in contrast with almost uniform levels and increases in literacy between ST and SC groups at the all-India level over the period. Notable too is Jharkhand's faster pace of urbanization than in areas of present-day Bihar over these four decades. The slowest growth of the ST population in the Jharkhand region appears even more bizarre in the face of its much faster urban and industrial (including mining and manufacturing) growth. For example, one recent study of district-level indices of social development[1] shows that most of the areas belonging to Jharkhand (except Santhal Parganas and Palamu) fall in the category of 'most developed' in the ranking of districts of undivided Bihar (Pathak and Pandey 1994). Indeed, the NSS 48th Round Survey in the early 1990s reports that the area owned per household among ST group (1.11 ha) is many-fold larger than for SC people (0.15 ha) in erstwhile Bihar. According to a recent human development survey (in 1994) by NCAER, the proportion of the tribal population in absolute poverty in this state, though it is nearly 50 per cent, is less than that of the SC population (by about 10 per cent point) (Chakrabarty and Ghosh 2000).

The sex-ratio in the population has (almost unidirectionally) become unfavourable to females over these years across all social groups and regions, but has always remained more balanced among the ST population than for other social groups. While the relatively high tribal

[1] This is constructed by aggregating several indicators like the proportion of single females in the age group of 15–19 years, the level of literacy, urbanization, provisions of drinking water, electricity, and hospitals, in 1981.

sex-ratio is indicative of their comparatively more balanced gender relations and less anti-female discrimination vis-à-vis non-tribal communities, large declines in the sex-ratio across all social groups (tribal and non-tribal), being largest within the geographical area of Bihar, are notable.

However, among the broad demographic and development indicators (as presented in Table 5.1), it is singularly in the matter of population growth that the tribal people of Jharkhand (and of course of Bihar too) appear to have fared worse than the SC and general population groups. This relative slowness of tribal population growth (vis-à-vis SC and general groups) has been broadly true across almost all districts in the decades between 1951 and 1991 (see Table 5.2). Since tribal population constitutes a substantial chunk of Jharkhand's total population, the former's slow population increase must have left some shadow on the region's total population increase. [Note that rates of overall population growth in Jharkhand (and erstwhile Bihar till recently) have been somewhat lower than the all-India figures.] Since a slow growth of tribal population appears pervasive across all regions of Jharkhand over the entire post-Independence period (see Table 5.2), this is very unlikely to be an artefact of biases in census enumeration. While one may wonder if its clue lies in conversion of tribals into the SC category or other non-tribal categories in this region, this hypothesis does not have ready empirical support, and is indeed inconsistent with long-standing tribal movements for identity here and even elsewhere in India. Moreover, unlike southern and western regions, there are often distinguishable differences between the surnames of tribes and castes in the eastern region, making infiltration from one category to another more difficult in the latter.

Thus, the record of slow growth of the tribal population in Jharkhand is, of course, an important question that deserves attention and systematic investigation. We must note at the outset that a relatively slow growth of the enumerated tribal population seems to have been a characteristic of much of the eastern region comprising Bihar, Orissa, and West Bengal. This is clearly borne out for the entire post-Independence period by information presented in Table 5.3 (except perhaps West Bengal in 1961–71 and 1981–91). [Even in the 1951–61 decade, when most Indian states registered much larger increases of the enumerated tribal population, following the induction of many tribes in the schedule with its modification of 1956, Bihar interestingly witnessed a nearly stagnant size of the tribal population.] It is indeed

Table 5.2 Annual exponential growth rates of population in Jharkhand by social group and by decade

District	Social Group	1951–61	1961–71	1971–81	1981–91	1951–91
Santhal Pargana	ALL	1.42	1.75	1.54	2.11	1.7
	SC	3.37	1.24	3.08	1.50	2.3
	ST	–0.14	1.21	1.70	0.67	0.86
Hazaribaug	ALL	2.12	2.42	2.63	2.55	2.43
	SC	3.32	1.93	5.64	2.63	3.38
	ST	0.15	2.00	2.44	2.10	1.67
Ranchi	ALL	1.47	2.00	1.62	1.75	1.71
	SC	3.10	2.59	2.25	2.12	2.52
	ST	1.57	1.41	1.33	1.16	1.37
Palamu	ALL	1.86	2.36	2.43	2.46	2.28
	SC	3.38	2.17	2.23	2.51	2.57
	ST	2.84	2.28	2.02	2.32	2.37
Singhbhum	ALL	1.87	1.73	1.60	1.73	1.73
	SC	2.02	3.67	4.43	1.96	3.02
	ST	3.07	1.48	1.15	1.36	1.76
Dhanbad	ALL	2.46	2.15	3.66	2.35	2.66
	SC	5.93	0.73	3.96	2.28	3.22
	ST	1.14	1.93	2.14	1.56	1.69
Jharkhand	ALL	1.80	2.04	2.13	2.15	2.03
	SC	3.67	1.83	3.75	2.30	2.89
	ST	1.38	1.49	1.54	1.26	1.42

Notes: 1) Jharkhand was created primarily out of the erstwhile Santhal Pargana and Chota Nagpur regions. The Jharkhand region historically used to include the following six districts: Santhal Parganas, Hazaribaug, Ranchi, Singhbhum, Dhanbad, and Palamu. This geographical definition has remained unchanged till 1971. In 1974, Giridih district was created out of Hazaribaug. In 1991, Ranchi was divided into Gumla and Lohardaga; Singhbhum was split into Purbi Singhbhum and Paschimi Singhbhum; Sahibganj, Godda, Dumka and Deoghar districts were created by splitting the erstwhile district of Santhal Pargana. Thus, in the 1991 census, Jharkhand had 13 districts. Jharkhand however, was further divided in 2001 to comprise of 18 districts. In our study (for the sake of convenience of exposition), we have used the undivided districts of Jharkhand. We have presented relevant information (rates and ratios) for six larger districts, out of which these new districts were created.

2) Annual Exponential Growth Rate = $(\ln P_{t+10} - \ln P_t)/10 * 100$

Source: Census reports.

Table 5.3   Exponential average annual rate of growth of population, tribal and total, eastern Indian states and all-India, 1951–91

	Bihar (erstwhile)		Orissa		West Bengal		Eastern India		India	
	ST	Total	ST	Total	ST	Total	ST	Total	ST	Total
1951–61	0.38	2.0	3.5	1.9	5.7	3.3	2.5	2.4	4.6	2.0
1961–71	1.6	1.9	1.8	2.2	2.1	2.4	1.7	2.4	2.2	2.2
1971–81	1.7	2.2	1.5	1.8	1.7	2.1	1.7	2.4	2.7	2.2
1981–91	1.3	2.1	1.7	1.8	2.2	2.2	1.7	2.1	2.3	2.1
1991–2001	1.7	2.4	1.3	1.5	1.4	1.6	1.6	2.0	2.2	2.0

Source: Sinha (1994, 1990); Govt. of India (2004).

notable that this phenomenon of relatively slow growth of the tribal population in the eastern region has not drawn much serious academic attention, which is quite curious in the light of a fairly high growth of the tribal population at the all-India level.[2] There can be little doubt that this phenomenon of slow population growth had wider significance from the standpoint of both tribal and non-tribal populations in the region.

Broadly speaking, data errors aside, there are two possible hypotheses (not necessarily mutually exclusive) in explaining this relatively slow growth of tribal population in Jharkhand. One relates to a slow rate of natural increase, which, in turn, may be related either to relatively low birth or high death rates or both. The second hypothesis relates to a process whereby tribal people experience a comparatively large net out-migration from the Jharkhand region. In fact, the existing literature on the demography of Bihar (and to some extent of Jharkhand), while scattered and limited with casually formulated indications in support of either of the two[3], seems to offer no single conclusive explanation for the slow growth of tribal population in this

[2] There exist a few studies, which while noting a slow tribal growth in the eastern states, hardly go beyond merely hinting at some possible reasons, namely net out-migration, low rates of natural increase presumably due to a high mortality rate, or a greater dent in sterilization programmes in tribal areas with higher levels of material deprivations, and hence with a greater attractiveness of cash incentives, and/or because of the relative ease, with which innocent (and less articulate) tribal people could be brought into sterilization camps) (see Sinha and Thatte 1994; Chand 1994; Bose 1988).

[3] See Sinha and Thatte 1994; Sinha and Sinha 1994; Bandyopadhyay 1999; Ekka 2000; Sharma 1994; Chand 1994.

region. In the following sections of this chapter, we review and attempt to stylize the available evidence pertaining to these hypotheses. It emerges that substantial outflows of tribal population from this region seem to have been relatively important for holding tribal population growth down in the earlier decades, while the explanation in more recent periods increasingly rests on slower (relative) improvement (or at times even worsening) of tribal mortality and health.

Differentials in Fertility and Mortality and Natural Rate of Growth

As population growth is basically a net outcome of interactions between three major components, namely fertility, mortality, and migration, let us begin our analysis by examining the trend in the natural rates of population growth. As mentioned earlier, a systematic analysis of levels and trends of fertility and mortality indicators (let alone for tribes) in the Jharkhand region is seriously constrained by a remarkable lack of demographic (especially civil registration) information. Erstwhile Bihar (of which Jharkhand has been a region) is well-known for low levels of civil registration coverage, especially until the 1980s.[4] Even though there are a few available time series of estimated birth and death rates for erstwhile Bihar (Pathak and Pandey 1994, Table 2:146), such series are almost non-existent separately for Jharkhand or for its ST and SC social groups. Consequently, there is hardly any systematic study on the natural rates of growth of the tribal population in this region. Although relatively low birth and high death rates among the tribes of Bihar (and Jharkhand region) have sometimes been held responsible for their low population growth (Chand 1994:408–09), these statements often appear poorly substantiated speculations or even 'over-generalizations' of local-level information on specific tribal groups.

On the other hand, some indirect estimates based on census age distribution data have portrayed erstwhile Bihar's tribal demographic regime as being one marked by relatively high birth and death rates, with a relatively slow rate of natural increase (after adjusting for migration) (Sinha and Thatte 1994:403). The validity of such indirect

---

[4] The registration coverage and quality has also been very low in West Bengal. Indeed, it has often been necessary till the 1980s to exclude Bihar and West Bengal from the Tables providing state level registration-data-based demographic rates (Bhat *et al.* 1984: 34; RG 1999).

estimates depends crucially upon the degree of appropriateness of the assumptions, both relating to the quality of data and the model used. Indeed, this often remains uncertain and unknown, leaving the results largely arbitrary. First, even a small variation in the parameter value used (say C15) can produce, depending upon the choice of model stable population, quite a substantial change in the estimated birth and death rates. Relatedly, since the selection of model tables in specific circumstances is substantially subject to the researcher's own judgment and assumptions (implicit or explicit), the indirect estimates need to be interpreted cautiously. Relatively large migration flows, which have, for a long time, been a characteristic feature of undivided Bihar, especially among the tribals of the Jharkhand region, compounds the difficulty of applying indirect techniques that are frequently contingent upon the broadly closed (national) population.

Before discussing the pattern of changes in tribal demographic parameters in Jharkhand, it would be useful to begin with a background of broad demographic changes in erstwhile Bihar. In Table 5.4, we present estimated birth, death, and natural rates of growth of the total population of erstwhile Bihar (in which Jharkhand constituted about a quarter of population). As can be seen, although there has been a secular decline both in estimated birth and death rates, Bihar's figures have always remained higher than corresponding national averages. The estimated natural rates of population growth in Bihar appear always to have been higher than the census-enumerated decadal growth rates. This discrepancy reflects several possibilities, including underestimation of natural rates and/or of net in-migration. As we will see, the latter is unlikely and indeed inconsistent with the evidence of net-out migration from Bihar, especially in the post-Independence period.

It is noteworthy that the rate of growth of the enumerated population in the present state of Bihar (that is, exclusive of Jharkhand) in the 1990s has been one of the highest, surpassing the all-India figure by as much as seven points. Since birth, death, and natural growth rates in Table 5.4 refer to erstwhile Bihar (and only up to 1997), they can hardly be a guide to explaining the recent (1991–2001 decade) spurt in population of truncated Bihar's population growth. Notably, the overall population growth in Jharkhand, though higher than the all-India rate, is far less than that of (present-day) Bihar. The removal of the Jharkhand region from erstwhile Bihar must have made a major contribution to this recently recorded jump in population growth in newly divided Bihar, since the entire slow-growing tribal population then fell outside its jurisdiction.

Table 5.4 Birth, death, and natural population growth rates, Bihar and India, 1951–2001

	(erstwhile) Bihar CBR Per 1000	CDR Per 1000	Natural Growth Rate (Enumerated Decadal Growth Rate) Per 1000	India CBR Per 1000	CDR Per 1000	Natural Growth Rate (Enumerated Decadal Growth Rate) Per 1000
1951–60	43.4	26.1	17.3 (19.8)	41.7	22.8	18.9 (21.5)
1961–70	41.9	23.3	18.6 (21.3)	41.2	19.0	22.2 (24.8)
1971–80	41.4	19.3	22.1 (24.1)	37.1	15.0	22.1 (24.7)
1981–90	36.9	13.3	23.6 (23.5)	32.5	11.4	21.1 (23.9)
1991–97[$]	31.9	10.3	21.6 (27.1)[#] (28.4)[@] (23.2)[^]	28.4	9.3	19.1 (21.3)

Notes: [#] erstwhile Bihar (inclusive of Jharkhand); [@]present Bihar (i.e. exclusive of Jharkhand); [^] Jharkhand; [$]Rates of growth of enumerated population refer to 1991–2001.

Source: Sinha (1994); Sinha and Gotpagar (1994); RG (1999); Dept. of Family Welfare (1997); Jain (1967).

Table 5.5 presents three indicators of fertility for tribal and non-tribal groups in Jharkhand, Bihar, and India in the contemporary period. The information on measures of reproductive performance separately for ST and SC groups for Jharkhand are remarkably scanty. For example, our indirect estimates of CBR based on the census proportion of the population below 15 years during the early decades after Independence, indicate that fertility levels of the ST population, while found somewhat lower, was not vastly different from corresponding non-tribal levels. A special survey by the Registrar General's office in 1984 reported period fertility levels (i.e. TFR) for ST being, though lower than SC level, higher than that of the non-ST/SC group. That the completed fertility of the older cohort of tribal women (i.e. the average number of children ever born to women aged 40–49 years) was the lowest testifys to a rise in tribal fertility from its past lower level, indicating a 'pre-transition fertility rise'.

The NFHS data for the 1990s confirms the onset of fertility decline across the broad social spectrum in these regions (including Jharkhand),

Table 5.5 Fertility levels of ST, SC and others, Jharkhand, Bihar and India, 1961–1999

	CBR			TFR			Average no. of children ever born to women 40–49 years		
	ST	SC	Total	ST	SC	Total	ST	SC	Total
Jharkhand									
1961–71	42.0	43.3	55.0						
1971–81	38.0	40.7	39.9						
1981			33.7			3.9			4.7*
1991			33.7			3.8			4.7*
1996–99 [NFHS-2]			23.7	2.3	2.9	2.8			
Bihar (erstwhile)									
1951–61			44.0			6.2			
1961–71	42.2	42.4	41.9			6.3			
1971–81	38.2	40.5	40.5						
1971 [rural]				5.2*	4.2*	4.6*			
1972 [rural]						5.2			
1981			36.9			5.7	4.6	4.7	4.8
1984 [rural]				6.4	7.0	5.9#	3.8	4.1	4.2
1985						5.4			
1991			36.2			5.3			
1994 (NCAER) [rural]	38	41	37.0	5.1	5.7	5.3			
1990–93 [NFHS-1]				3.4	4.0	4.1#	4.8	5.5	5.3#
1996						4.5			
1997									
1996–99 [NFHS-2]				2.5	3.9	3.1#	4.6	5.4	4.8#
India									
1950–60			41.7						
1971			36.9			5.4			
1979 [rural]	32.1	33.8	33.8#	4.1	4.7	4.7#			
1981			33.9			4.9			
1984 [rural]			33.9	5.3	5.4	4.8#			
1991			29.5			4.3			
1990–93 [NFHS-1]				3.6	3.9	3.3#	4.8	5.4	4.8#
1994 [NCAER] [rural]	35.0	35.0	32.0	4.4	4.7	4.3			
1996–99 [NFHS-2]				3.1	3.2	2.7#	4.7	4.9	4.2#

*TMFR; #non-ST/SC

(*Contd.*)

Source: IIPS, NFHS-2, Jharkhand; IIPS, NFHS-2, Bihar; Registrar General
(RG) 1980; 1984a,b; 1999; 1997; Satia and Jejeebhoy (1991); Pathak and
Pandey 1994:Table 9; Chakrabarty and Ghosh (2000); and authors' own
calculations of CBRs for 1961–71 and 1971–81 decades for Jharkhand and
Bihar on the basis of district-level C(15) ratios and the regression coefficients
estimated by Parasuraman and Rajan (1990:132); fertility measures for ST,
SC and all for 1971 and 1981 for erstwhile Bihar are the authors' own
calculations based on data on the number of births over a year and children
ever born by age of currently married women given in respective Fertility
Tables of censuses.

but the social differentials in fertility have continued, albeit with
narrowing gaps over time. For instance, the second NFHS results
report the ST fertility to be lower, although by only about half a child,
as compared to non-tribal groups during the late 1990s. Since there
should be virtually no difference in tribal fertility between erstwhile
Bihar and Jharkhand (which was the home of almost entire tribal
population of Bihar, see Table 5.1), Table 5.5 suggests Jharkhand's
somewhat lower tribal fertility (or birth rate) as compared to non-
tribal groups, especially SC. This is in conformity with our finding
that tribal fertility in the Indian subcontinent has generally been lower,
until perhaps very recently, than that of non-tribal groups, especially
SC. While the somewhat lower tribal fertility in Jharkhand does not
appear surprising within this broader tribal perspective, it is difficult,
without looking into differential patterns of mortality and migration,
to be certain whether this could be a major explanation for a record of
the slowest growth of the tribal population in Jharkhand.

Table 5.6 presents results of large-scale surveys on mortality
differentials between ST, SC, and total population groups in Jharkhand,
Bihar (erstwhile), and India. The evidence on overall mortality levels
of ST and SC separately is rather scanty. Even this limited evidence is
often based on a relatively small number of sample cases (as in NFHS),
leaving the possibility of large sampling errors. However, a cross-
sectional (rather than time series) comparison between social groups
can be reasonably valid. The problem of small samples, is of course,
less serious with NSS or SRS data. In any case, notwithstanding
possible limitations of data on such mortality indicators as IMR and
under-five mortality, the tribal people of erstwhile Bihar (and hence of
Jharkhand), do not appear, interestingly, more vulnerable than their
SC counterparts. Indeed a lower tribal mortality level (both overall
and in infancy and childhood years) than that of the SC group emerges

Table 5.6 Mortality levels of ST, SC, and others, Jharkhand, Bihar, and all-India, 1971–99

	CDR			IMR			Under-five mortality		
	ST	SC	Total	ST	SC	Total	ST	SC	Total
Jharkhand									
1981						68.0			93
1991						89.0			136
1990–93									
1996–99						54.3			78.3
Bihar (erstwhile)									
1951–60			26.1						
1971						145.0			
1981			13.9						
1984 [rural]	17.4	17.7	14.2#	77.6	98.7	94.0@			
1991			9.8			98.3#	97.2	120.4	94.0#
1992			10.9			75.0@			
1993			10.6						
NFHS-1 (1987–1991)	9.0	(1990–92)	11.5	97.2	120.4	94.0#	135.0	171.0	132.3#
1994		11.0	10.0						
1995			10.5						
1997			10.0						
NFHS-2 (1988–98)		(1996–98)	11.3	81.9	86.3	61.2#	116.6	133.8	89.3#
India									
1951–60			22.8			139.0			

Year/Source						
1961						
1971		14.9				
1979 [rural]	113			129.0		223^
1981	159	136				
1984 [rural]	15.0	17.0	12.5			
1991		12.9#	103.2	115.0@	286^	152.0
1992		9.8		111.0#		
1993		10.1		77.0@		94.0
		9.3	131.7			
NFHS-1 (1987–1991)		9.7				
1994 [NCAER] [rural] (1990–92)	9.0	13.0		61.8#	126.0	
		11.0				
NFHS-2 (1988–98) (1996–98)	9.0	9.7	84.2	83.0	119.3	82.6#

@ Indirect estimates provided by the Registrar General's District Level Estimates of Fertility and Child Mortality, Occasional Paper No. 1 of 1997;
^ number of child deaths per 10,000 population.

Source: RG (1999; 1980; 1997); Jain (1967); Chakrabarty and Ghosh (2000).

from Table 5.6 as a fairly consistent pattern till recently (around the mid-1990s). In fact, the Registrar General's special survey on infant and child mortality differentials in 1984 found IMR much lower among the tribal population than that of even non-ST/SC groups in erstwhile Bihar. Note too that the NCAER survey in 1994 has reported the lowest overall death rate among the tribal population at the all-India level. Of course, there might be some influences of differential response biases and sampling errors on these mortality estimates by the social group. This said, it should be stressed that the tribals' relative superiority in mortality is not really new or surprising in the light of the recent researches (Maharatna 2000). For example, the tribals' (relative) advantage in infant and childhood mortality (vis-à-vis non-tribal population groups, especially SC) has been found fairly common across space and time in the Indian subcontinent (Maharatna 1998, 2000, and literature cited therein).[5] The results reported in Table 5.6, in conformity with the baseline pattern of differentials, do not support the hypothesis of higher tribal mortality as the key to their slower population growth vis-à-vis SC in Jharkhand until the recent past. Even if a lower natural population growth was to be a major reason

[5] The plausible reasons for this include some healthy aspects of traditional tribal practices relating to infant-feeding and child rearing (that is, prolonged breastfeeding, longer spacing between children, better timing and nature of food supplementation, relative absence of familial gender discrimination in distribution of food and other basic necessities). Besides, there are other healthy dimensions of their lifestyle and habitation (that is, less crowding, greater intimacy with natural environment). Even recent researches on some major tribes in Jharkhand show that their traditional food habits and diets (including usage of roots, tubers, vegetables, fruits, etc.) have sufficient nutritive value, but, due to their ignorance of this value, are not consumed in adequate quantities (Sinha 2003). The existing Indian literature and evidence on these aspects are extremely limited and scattered, and further research on these issues is much needed. However, as was pointed out earlier, global literature on health and survival of (traditional) tribal people suggests their relative health/ mortality advantage because of greater adaptability to the natural environment, but that they generally lose this type of adaptation (hence health/survival advantage) in course of acculturation (Wirsing 1985). For example, as we would see shortly, such traditional tribal advantages in health and mortality in Jharkhand (and even in the whole of India) seem to be vanishing rather fast in more recent times. This is largely because of the growing (relative) tribal disadvantage (vis-à-vis non-tribals) in accessibility to modern health provisions and care (for evidence of tribal disadvantages in health and infrastructure, see Chakrabarty 1998; Singh 2001).

for slower tribal population growth (vis-à-vis SC) in the Jharkhand region, it should have been via lower birth rate, as the tribal population seem to have had relative mortality advantage till recently.[6] But, as discussed above, the birth rate of tribal people in Jharkhand (and hence in erstwhile Bihar) has not been low enough to be able to fully (or even perhaps mostly) account for a persistently slower population growth (vis-à-vis SC group), especially in more recent decades.

It is notable that the NFHS-1 results for the early 1990s indicate increases in infant- and child-mortality levels, particularly among the ST and SC groups of erstwhile Bihar, from the 1984 levels. Indeed, current mortality indices (as revealed by NFHS-2 data) in Bihar and Jharkhand, particularly in infancy and childhood years, appear remarkably high among all social groups as compared to the respective levels at all-India levels. This reflects a greater material vulnerability of people (including tribes) of these regions. More importantly, tribal people currently appear most deprived in terms of access to modern health facilities, including those relating to maternity and safe child delivery. For example, according to indirect estimates based on NCAER 1994 survey information, the 'maternal mortality ratio' of tribal women turns up to be higher than that of SC people and indeed the highest at the all-India level (Bhat 2002, Table 3). There are strong indications that the extent of relative mortality advantage of tribes in the region vis-à-vis that of SC people (that is, the gap in IMR or child mortality between ST and SC) has faded over the last several decades (see Table 5.6). This is a fairly common trend across the whole of India as shown in the preceding chapter. Note that NFHS-2 data has recently shown a negligible difference in IMR (and indeed reversal of the gap in the case of under-five mortality) between these two groups at an all-India level. This can well be taken to imply an accentuation of (relative) vulnerability of tribal people, in terms of provisions and accessibility of health facilities generally (see Maharatna 2000 for discussion on various Indian regions).

Thus while the latest NFHS data (and other micro-level studies) do suggest an emergence of relative tribal mortality disadvantage, which could contribute significantly to their slower population growth over the recent past, there is a remarkable dearth of direct and reliable

[6] For instance, the estimated tribal death rate being lower by two persons per 1000 population vis-à-vis SC (according to the 1984 special survey by the Registrar General's office) is offset by an estimated lower tribal birth rate (see Tables 5.5 and 5.6).

evidence on natural rates of growth by the social group. A limited number of indirect demographic estimates for this region often tend to posit a lower natural growth of the tribal population as the major explanation for persistently slow tribal population growth (Thatte and Sinha 2003; Sinha and Thatte 1994). For example, a recent study on indirect estimates of birth and death rates show a noticeable drop in the natural rate of growth of the tribal population in Jharkhand in 1981–91 from the earlier decade, chiefly because of an increase in the estimated death rate (Thatte and Sinha 2003, Table 9). While this seems consistent with the scenario, as discussed above, of increases in tribal (relative) mortality disadvantage as reported by large-scale surveys of 1990s, this is not full explanation for slow tribal growth in the earlier decades. [As an illustration, the natural rate of tribal growth, according to this study, rose in 1971–81 by about 2.5 per 1000 than in the earlier decade, while there was a negligible difference in the actual rate of tribal growth between these decades (ibid Table 2)].

For example, the indirect estimates are often vitiated by considerable migration streams for which adequate adjustments seem almost impossible because of paucity of direct migration information. Indeed migration streams (both ways), particularly of tribal people, have remained for long (till perhaps recently) a prominent regional characteristic of Jharkhand (and of erstwhile Bihar). We now turn to an examination of the role of tribal migration in accounting for the relatively low increases in the enumerated population in these regions, especially in the earlier decades.

The Role of Tribal Migration

Today's Jharkhand region, which was originally carved out from the erstwhile Chotanagpur and Santhal Parganas plateau, has witnessed substantial migration flows over a fairly long historical period. As the region is rich in mineral resources, mining had developed in districts like Dhanbad, Kodarma, and Giridih in the middle of the nineteenth century. Relatedly, Jharkhand (particularly the Chotanagpur region) had experienced considerable infrastructural developments quite early, which led to some far-reaching demographic changes in the region. For example, the Jharkhand region had started acting as an attracting force for many people outside the region. Table 5.7, which we reproduce from Weiner (1978), gives a clear indication of a steady rising inflow of people into this region.

As can be seen, there has been a sustained influx of people into the Jharkhand region, starting from the last decade of the nineteenth century. Indeed, the percentage share of migrants from north Bihar alone rose from about 10 per cent in 1881 to nearly 40 per cent in 1951 in Manbhum (a large part of which became merged with present-day Dhanbad) (Bandopadhyay 1999:21). Again, Ranchi had received more than 60 per cent of in-migrants from north Bihar alone in 1881, which, however, subsequently declined over the following decades (Bandopadhyay 1999:21). People had migrated into the Jharkhand region from such far-flung places as Punjab, Bombay, and Rajputana Agency too, with an increase in its percentage share from 5 per cent to16 per cent between 1881 and 1951 (Bandopadhyay 1999:22). During 1931–41 there was a slump in the coal industry in the wake of the Great Depression of the 1930s, but the Second World War had stimulated the mining industry, fuelling an 'incessant' immigration into this region (Bandopadhyay 1999). All this clearly shows that there has been a continuous and considerable non-tribal inflow into the Jharkhand region over a fairly long period before Independence. As Tables 5.7 and 5.8 show, this long-term rising trend in the absolute number of in-migrants into Jharkhand has continued in the post-Independence period too, although without much increase in its proportionate share in the total population. However, it is noteworthy that an overwhelming share in this immigration flow has continued to be constituted by migrants from north Bihar and four adjoining states. Dhanbad district alone, a seat of mining, accounted for more than one-third of the total in-migrants of Jharkhand, according to the 1981 census information. While such substantial in-migration flows into Jharkhand could have inflated the population growth of the non-tribal population in the region, they, as such, cannot explain the persistently slow growth of the tribal population.

Table 5.7   In-migration into Santhal Parganas
and Chotanagpur, 1891–1971

Year	Immigration
1891	96,000
1901	1,79,000
1911	2,93,000
1921	3,07,000
1931	3,07,000
1941	NA
1951	4,80,000
1961	10,73,920
1971	14,29,805

Source: Weiner 1978

Table 5.8   In-migration into Jharkhand, 1981

Total no. of Immigrants	Immigrants coming from			
	North Bihar	Adjacent States*	Other States	Other Asian Countries outside India
16,281,03 (100)	90,95,25 (55.9)	57,52,98 (35.3)	10,02,40 (6.2)	4,30,40 (2.6)

*Includes Madhya Pradesh, Orissa, Uttar Pradesh, and West Bengal.

Source: Calculated from Census of India 1981, Series-4, Bihar, Part vA&B, Migration Tables, D-1.

To assess the role of migration in shaping the population growth of a region or of a social group in a region, we need to know about the magnitudes of both influx and exodus of people. More specifically, the key question for our present purpose of explaining slow tribal population growth in Jharkhand relates to the nature and magnitude of tribal migration. Beginning from the nineteenth century, the tribals of Jharkhand have migrated chiefly to parts of Bengal and to the tea gardens of Assam. The tribal out-migration in 1891 was found to be of the order of 3,33,000 in 1891. This continuously increased to 947,000 in 1921 (Weiner 1978:161). Historically, especially since the late-nineteenth century, Bihar stands out as the largest sender of emigrants (see Report for Bihar, Census of India 1951, chapter 1:56–57). There are strong indications that the majority of these Bihari emigrants are tribals from the Jharkhand region (that is, erstwhile Chotanagpur and Santhal Parganas).[7]

The newly introduced process of industrialization in the latter half of the nineteenth century in this region deprived local tribals of the natural resources on which they were substantially dependent. They were thus compelled, due to increasing pressure of unemployment and poverty, to migrate for livelihood to Assam and other neighbouring states (Bandopadhyay 1999). Alienation of tribals from their homelands as well as from their traditional land rights, along with a mounting influx of non-tribal in-migrants into Jharkhand's tribal areas, are often held responsible for the large-scale tribal exodus that has

[7] To illustrate: the total immigrants into Assam in 1921 from Chotanagpur alone numbered 318; only 139 were from Bihar (exclusive of Chotanagpur)—the former constituted nearly 60 per cent of total immigrants into Assam (see Report for Assam, Census of India 1921).

been taking place from this region over a long historical span. Combined with such push factors for tribal emigration were some pull forces like 'preference' of employers, particularly of tea planters of Assam and Bengal, for tribal migrant workers from the Jharkhand region, as because of their diligence and easy acclimatization in tea gardens.[8] Indeed the large volume of out-migration, resulting in an adverse balance of migration (that is, net outflow), is held responsible for a low population growth in the tribal districts of erstwhile Bihar, and hence of Jharkhand (census reports; Sharma 1994).[9] The balance of immigration into, and emigration from, Bihar has been chronically negative over a long period of time since the late-nineteenth century. This adverse balance of migration largely accounts for the slow growth of the population, particularly in the Chotanagpur Natural Division (see Report for Bihar, Census of 1951, chapter 1:57).[10]

In the post-Independence period, industrialization and urbanization processes in Jharkhand continued and became even more intense, thereby maintaining and perhaps accentuating the historical push forces for tribal emigration from the region. Ironically, there is no reason and evidence to explain why the historical pattern of tribal (relative) vulnerability and the compulsive need for out-migration along with

[8] For example, the 1921 census report for Assam writes that '[e]nquiries show a general opinion that the so-called "jungly" coolies of the Central Provinces and Chota Nagpur (Mundas, Santals, Gonds, etc.) are the best men for the climate and the work of tea gardens' (Census of India 1921, vol. 3, part 1, Report, chapter 3:38).

[9] It should be noted that much of the tribal emigration is presumably of a 'seasonal character coinciding unfortunately with the time of census-taking' (Report for Bihar, Census of India 1961, vol. IV, part 1-A(i):323). As the census report explains, '[t]he tide of seasonal migration is generally at its height in February when the census enumeration is taken, and it is certain that if the census were held later, say in June, the number of emigrants from Bihar to other states would be much smaller, and the enumerated population would be correspondingly larger' (ibid:323).

[10] To illustrate the (possible) influence of out-migration on the recorded rate of population growth: while the number of emigrants from Bihar declined to 350 per 10,000 natural population in 1931 from 470 in 1921, there has been a rise in the annual rate of growth of the tribal population to 0.90 during this decade from −1.45 per cent in 1911–21. Although it is difficult to be absolutely sure whether this surge in population growth was directly attributable to the decline in the volume of emigration, a considerable influence of emigration on Bihar's population growth seems beyond reasonable doubt.

industrial and mining development in the region should have ceased to be relevant after Independence. Rather, the post-Independence development process has continued to be accompanied by acute (relative) tribal deprivation and distress, and has been accentuated by their relative vulnerability and related forced movements in this region. For example, with various development projects launched in Jharkhand, some 30 lakh people were displaced during 1951–95, with 90 per cent of them being tribals (Ekka 2000). However, the historical pull forces for tribal emigration to tea gardens and factories in neighbouring states have waned over time, especially after Independence.

While all this indicates tribal out-migration from Jharkhand as a plausible contributory factor for their slower population increase, especially before and even for some time after Independence, the age–sex composition of emigrants could also have some bearing in shaping the rate of population growth. For example, a proportionately large number of young and reproductive-age emigrants should have had a dampening effect on tribal fertility too. According to some rough estimate, had there been no out-migration of tribes, the tribal population of Chotanagpur and Santhal Parganas would have been about 6 million rather than 4.5 in 1971 (Weiner 1978:162). While it seems that migration patterns and magnitudes could well have had much to do with differential patterns of population growth between tribal and non-tribal peoples of Jharkhand, the empirical basis for this refers mostly to the pre-Independence period. Indeed there is a distinct lack of systematic studies on migration (especially out-migration) flows of people of Jharkhand in the post-Independence period.

As noted above, the tribal exodus from the Jharkhand region to Assam and West Bengal predominantly, was prominent mostly in the pre-Independence period. The areas of Chotanagpur and Santhal Parganas has been known for long as the sending areas of a large (tribal) net out-migration prior to the 1930s (Corbridge 1988). The study on inter-state migration by Weiner (1978) does not give much concrete evidence to substantiate the process of tribal out-migration after 1931. Though inferences about the dampening effects of contemporary tribal exodus from Chotanagpur and Santhal Pargana on their population growth have sometimes been made, they seem to be more logically derived than empirically established. This relative dearth of empirical research on more contemporary tribal migration flows from Jharkhand seems to have something to do with fewer details in the presentation of recent census data on migration than earlier.

For example, as the 1961 census report for Bihar lamentingly notes in the chapter on migration, '[i]t would have been interesting to allocate the emigrants from Bihar to other states by the districts of their origin, but unfortunately such statistics have not been tabulated for 1961 or any of the previous censuses in recent time. The last census for which such data are available is 1921' (Census of India 1961, vol. IV, part 1-A(i), chapter V:324). This district-level break-up of emigrants is even more necessary for our present analysis of the tribal demography of Jharkhand.

On the other hand, a few recent studies (Ekka 2000; Ranjan 2002) have focused more on the 'displacement of tribals', rather than emigration as such, as many new development projects in the region have displaced a large number of tribal people from their homeland. However, what is rarely clear from these studies is where these tribals go after being displaced. If the 'displaced' tribals remain within the region, this should not (directly) affect the overall tribal rate of population increase. Whether displaced tribals go out of the state (inter-state migration) or are resettled elsewhere within the region (intra-state movement), often remains an open question. Detailed and reliable accounts of the demographic consequences of such displacements, which could help us understand the broad demographic changes in the tribal population, are almost unavailable. In many cases, even the source for the stated magnitudes of 'tribal displacement' is not made very clear (Ranjan 2002). As has been suggested in some studies, however, at some point of time, the permanent tribal out-migration was somewhat arrested partly because of saturation of the receiving areas, and partly due to the resistance of local people against such outflows (Chand 1994). However, this argument is not well substantiated in terms of concrete data and information; contemporary literature on the tribal out-migration from Jharkhand is often devoid of a reasonable degree of empirical rigour.

In our attempt to explain the lower growth rate of tribal population in terms of exodus and movement, we encountered several difficulties in using census information. For instance, since district-level information on out-migration (let alone for tribes) is not provided in recent census reports, the direct quantification of out-migrants from Jharkhand could not be made. To illustrate, let us take the example of erstwhile Bihar. While one can estimate the total number of enumerated out-migrants on the basis of birthplace data to various states, it seems difficult to know for sure how many of them were from Jharkhand or how many of them were tribals. This is chiefly because of the absence of a district-level (and caste-wise) break-up of these out-migrants from the whole of Bihar. This problem becomes even more pressing while dealing with Jharkhand as a newly separated state from Bihar.

Although it is difficult to know directly (from census information) about Jharkhand's share in total out-migrants, there might be some scope for arriving at fairly reasonable inferences indirectly or even on the basis of fragmentary (and micro-level) evidence. Since most of (erstwhile) south Bihar constitutes Jharkhand, one could have made reasonably valid estimates of tribal out-migration on the basis of direct or indirect evidence on the contribution of south Bihar's share in the total of out-migrants from the state. [However, our search, so far, did not succeed in getting such information.] Therefore, owing to a lack of such indication, we cannot make any concrete estimate of tribal out-migration from Jharkhand during the post-Independence period.

Still, one could perhaps, on the basis of migration data of erstwhile Bihar, form a reasonable judgement about the extent of tribal out-migration from Jharkhand. Table 5.9 provides census information on total migration flows in (erstwhile) Bihar during 1961–91. As can be seen, migration flows and mobility of population have been a prominent feature of this region's demography. Since Independence, Bihar has remained a 'sending region' on a net basis but it is worth noting that there has been a steady decline in the proportion of net out-migrants since the early 1950s through the 1970s. It is of interest that despite such substantial net out-migration from (erstwhile) Bihar over the entire post-Independence period, its overall rate of population growth has been hardly below the national average (except in the 1961–71 decade, which witnessed severe drought and famine conditions in the state). But the remarkably slow rate of growth that characterized the tribal population of the state during all post-Independence decades (Table 5.2) seems to support the hypothesis that a substantial (if not overwhelming) chunk of the total (net) exodus from erstwhile Bihar was constituted by tribal people of Jharkhand. For example, a declining trend in the proportion of net (total) out-migration between 1951 and 1981 has a consistent correspondence with a steadily rising trend in the tribal population growth during this period, while it has dropped with a spurt in net out-migration during the 1981–91 decade. The meagre rises in the growth rate of the tribal population in relation to the magnitudes of a decline in net (proportionate) emigration during 1951–91 suggests that tribal outflow alone is not sufficient to account

Table 5.9   Volume of migration, (erstwhile) Bihar, 1961–91

Year	In-migrants	Out-migrants (% males)	Net Migrants (2)–(3)	Share of net migrants total to natural population (%)
1951[@]	11001 (51.0)	1516100 (69.2)	–1505099	–25.99
1961	1097041 (43.5)	2042685 (63.8)	–945644	–19.95
1971	1176408 (38.1)	2201399 (61.6)	–1024991	–17.87
1981	1330920 (33.9)	2536882 (56.6)	–1205962	–16.96
1991[*]	1236209 (25.7)	3147295 (53.3)	–1911086	–21.64

Note: [@]Emigrants are exclusive of Muslim exodus and immigrants are reduced by Muslim exodus. Total natural population = census enumerated population + out-migrants - in-migrants.

Source: Ram and Singh, (1994), *Compiled from Census of India, State Profile, 1991.

for the extent of tribal sluggishness in the growth of population, especially in recent decades. In fact, it has often been remarked by census reports that the regional pattern of emigration from erstwhile Bihar had started changing before Independence: the volume of emigration from Chotanagpur and South Bihar (areas of tribal concentration) started declining since 1931, 'but emigration from North Bihar Plain to other states has increased' (Census of India 1961, vol. IV-Bihar, part1-A(i), chapter V:326). Therefore, in accounting for the slow growth of the tribal population in Jharkhand, the phenomenon of tribal emigration flows from the region to other states was no longer as important or dominant over the post-Independence period as it had historically been since the late nineteenth century. Thus, it seems to be a reasonable conclusion that accentuation of tribal vulnerability and their mortality disadvantage is becoming a increasingly dominant contributory factor for their slow population growth over more recent decades. The worsening vulnerability of the tribal population in this region is contributed by shrinking avenues of economic emigration to other states that they had historically resorted to, coupled with displacements, dislocations, and disruptions of their livelihood patterns, apart from their increasing relative deprivation in health care and education.

This said, tribal out-migration has not ceased to be relevant for explaining their present slow population growth rate. Note that the extent of out-migration from erstwhile Bihar has generally been (proportionately) higher among males than females, which suggests a relative dominance of economic (male-selective) migration for taking advantage of outside employment opportunities, with the family staying back home. But notably, the sex-composition of out-migrants has been getting increasingly balanced over past several decades. This trend, together with recent rises in the overall number of out-migrants from the region, could be interpreted as indicative of an increasing trend of family migration. Note that such an increasing trend of family migration (as implied by our analysis) may well be consistent with an ongoing process of development-associated displacements (presumably, mostly of tribal households of the Jharkhand region). Even if one assumes that the proportionate share in out-migration of all social groups is somewhat uniform, the sheer figures of overall net out-migration from erstwhile Bihar do point to the concrete role that migration phenomenon plays in shaping current population growth, especially among tribes of Jharkhand. As already noted the tribes of Jharkhand has a long history of migrating. Earlier, the tribal out-migration, largely in response to pull forces of economic opportunities in tea gardens and factories, was largely an adult and young peoples' movement (with some male bias). But after large-scale tribal displacements accelerated over the post-Independence period, their out-migration increasingly became a forced family migration to places, which, unlike earlier times, were not typically growing and dynamic.[11] This, however, is still in need of further systematic substantiation.

Concluding Remarks

Since Jharkhand has historically been the homeland of almost the entire tribal population of erstwhile Bihar, analysing the tribal demography in Bihar is tantamount to doing it for Jharkhand. Strikingly, Jharkhand, as a whole, fares no worse, or is relatively better off, than Bihar in terms of broad socio-economic indicators, although the absolute levels are far from adequate. But Jharkhand's tribal population has experienced a persistently slower population growth than that of the non-tribal counterparts. This contrasts sharply with the pattern of a higher growth of tribal population (both in relative and absolute terms)

[11] For example, as one author writes, '[t]he movement [of tribes] in the post-Independence period has been to Sundarbans in West Bengal and Andaman and Nicobar Islands, especially by tribals from the Jharkhand region' (Xaxa 2003).

in most other states (particularly outside eastern India) and, of course, at the aggregate (all-India) level. Notwithstanding the dearth of reliable demographic data for this region (let alone for tribals), the foregoing scrutiny of available information does not clearly support the hypothesis of a slower natural rate of tribal growth during the earlier decades after Independence. Although tribal fertility, in line with our baseline pattern for Indian tribes, has been found generally lower, the tribal mortality indicators overall—again in conformity with the baseline (aggregate) differential—have not been any higher than that of SC people until rather recently. It is not easy, especially with limited and incomplete civil registration data, to be able to ascertain the relative contribution of (lower) fertility levels (until recently) to a slower population growth of tribal people in Jharkhand, taking account of their differential mortality levels. For example, more recent available information generally points to relatively high mortality rates prevailing among tribal infants, children, and perhaps among other ages too.

On the other hand, a substantial tribal outflow to other states over a long period is a major factor for slower tribal population growth in Jharkhand until recent past. Over the last several decades, with the drying up of the demand for tribal migrant labour outside Jharkhand, accentuation of tribal displacements, and hence disruptions in livelihood patterns, aggravation of tribals' (relative) inaccessibility to modern amenities, health and education, seems to be experiencing relatively large (and perhaps indeed growing) mortality disadvantage. This is manifested clearly in slower declines (or even sometimes rises) in mortality levels of the tribal population in Jharkhand over the recent past. This, together with current declines in their fertility levels, is most likely to have contributed to a slowing down of natural growth of the tribal population in more recent periods. While such slowing down of tribal natural increase can, perhaps, explain a large part of their slower growth rates in the current decades, tribal out-migration, of a circular and seasonal nature as well as of a forced distress kind, seems to have some contribution too, though possibly by less quantum than before. Estimating exact magnitudes of such net tribal out-migration as well as the trend and impact of natural growth rates is, of course, hampered by a dearth of reliable information, but this is perhaps not impossible, especially if new relevant information is generated, both by individual researchers and large-scale survey agencies. Further detailed research is necessary for formulating an appropriate development strategy for both the tribes and the region as a whole.

That people facing acute adverse circumstances in their own areas move out of their homeland undoubtedly represents an unhappy state of affairs, and must be arrested. This said, migrations and movements of families are something in which tribals have had long experience. This feature of tribal communities has throughout history provided them with a safety-valve against relentless occurrence of exigencies, and has helped them develop their time-tested resilience. As will be illustrated (in the following chapter) with the field-based case study of seasonally migrant Santhals in West Bengal, while migration and movements are generally prone to causing disruptions, particularly from the standpoint of a firmly stationed household equilibrium, they have the potential of making migrant households move forward—at least on some counts.

Table A5.1   Trends in female–male ratio by social group, Jharkhand, 1951–91

District	Social Group	1951	1961	1971	1981	1991
Santhal Pargana	SC	982	1006	959	964	930
	ST	1008	1001	1001	982	973
	ALL	980	980	959	957	935
Hazaribaug	SC	1058	1058	1053	1010	951
	ST	943	979	1008	975	943
	ALL	975	992	979	967	935
Ranchi	SC	983	976	974	959	936
	ST	987	1025	1013	1014	983
	ALL	984	987	973	963	945
Palamu	SC	985	1001	979	974	935
	ST	1088	1007	976	983	957
	ALL	977	984	963	957	930
Singhbhum	SC	601	922	951	953	954
	ST	1054	1050	1018	1006	992
	ALL	970	960	942	942	937
Dhanbad	SC	831	810	797	830	825
	ST	1004	919	967	942	933
	ALL	821	795	792	814	826
All-Jharkhand	SC	951	973	960	956	922
	ST	1009	1017	1007	996	975
	ALL	961	960	945	940	922

Note: See Note 1 to Table 5.2.

6

On the 'Brighter Side' of Tribal Mobility
A Case Study of Santhals in
Rural West Bengal

Even a sketchy reading of tribal history would suggest that the indigenous and so-called tribal people of India have, by dint of their perseverance, resilience, and deep-rooted sociocultural and organizational strengths, withstood, and indeed often overcome, persistent odds and adversities meted out to them in the course of history.[1] Indeed, our foregoing analyses of tribal demographic behaviour and responses have been bearing out this broad historical message of the tribals' inherent vigour and strength, especially in the sociocultural sphere. While Indian tribes, when studied from a demographic angle, appear to have been historically less vulnerable than their non-tribal counterparts (as shown in Chapter 3), the relative position of tribals as illustrated by contemporary demographic trends (analysed in Chapters 4 and 5), has been slipping back rather fast. This certainly

---

[1] Of course, the intensity of adversities and oppositions faced by tribes in India's history was milder than the outright genocide or seclusion of tribal people elsewhere (for example, America and Australia). Unlike most other parts of the world, the rising civilization in the Indian subcontinent neither eliminated nor absorbed these primitive inhabitants of the land, allowing materially less advanced tribal communities to continue with their own sociocultural distinctiveness and isolation from the mainstream (Fürer-Haimendorf 1985:1). This said, as mentioned in Chapter 1, some Indian tribes have been heading towards extinction too.

reflects a widening gap in the distribution of benefits of contemporary material advancements and progress.[2]

Historically, tribals, when faced with an onslaught of adversities, seem to have resorted more readily to migration and mobility as a survival response than their non-tribal counterparts would do under a similar predicament. As illustrated by the study of the tribal demography of Jharkhand in the last chapter, tribal people, largely because of greater compulsive circumstances (for example, threatened livelihood security), often backed by a relative proneness consistent with their sociocultural moorings, are more migratory and mobile than their non-tribal counterparts (for evidence in other Indian regions see, for example, Fürer-Haimendorf 1945:43–4; Joshi 1997). Although a high degree of mobility and migration by tribals is often viewed as a sign of distress and disruption, it could conceivably have the potential to initiate advancement and dynamism. In fact, the present chapter, based on primary evidence in rural West Bengal, shows how tribal seasonal migration and mobility could catalyse an advancement, for example, in the sphere of demographic transition, indeed much ahead of their less mobile counterparts.

Seasonal Migration and Demographic Behaviour: Issues and Hypotheses

As already noted, despite the long-standing process of assimilation and acculturation, contemporary tribal people, overall, are still socioculturally distinct from the mainstream.[3] It is also clear that tribes, as a whole, typically stand last, and are, essentially, even behind (non-

---

[2] Recent reviews of evidence and literature generally testify to a virtual absence of a perceptible impact of various tribal development policies and programmes on their relative socio-economic position. Indeed, some scholars have recently expressed serious doubt on the efficacy of government policies and programmes for tribal welfare, and thereby, on the extent of political will, to eliminate their persisting social and economic backwardness (for example, Mohanty 2003).

[3] For example, one micro-level anthropological study in 1959, while noting a considerable intermingling in the economic sphere between the Santhals and the Hindu mainstream society in rural areas of Birbhum district (which is one of the locations in our present study) had commented that '[Santhals] have not been absorbed in the vertical hierarchical order of the Hindu caste organization', and '[t]he Santhals still adhere to their traditional culture at least in the major cultural traits' (Mukherjee 1960: 305; italics added).

tribal) lower caste (i.e. SC) people in the march towards modernization. Consequently, tribals could be hypothesized not only to be the last in showing a fertility transition, but could well be expected to experience (as noted previously in Chapters 1 and 4) a relatively pronounced pressure for a 'pre-transition fertility rise' before it begins to decline. Such a pre-transition fertility rise, though it is relevant to the non-tribal population too, should occur later among tribals, as they are behind non-tribals in processes of modernization and Sanskritization. Also, owing to their relative isolation and backwardness, they remained less encompassed by the national family planning programme.[4] While, as indicated earlier, a relatively late female marriage practice characterizes traditional tribal communities, its possible decline, along with their ongoing emulation of the traditional Hindu norm of early female marriage could also contribute, in some places, to a chronologically later occurrence of a 'pre-transition rise' in tribal fertility. As will be elucidated, we have found indications of such a pre-transition rise of fertility, resulting in a slower pace of fertility transition among the Santhals in one location of our study, where they inhabit as a small and somewhat segregated ethnic minority group.

This said, the Santhals of another location, where they live in exclusive tribal villages, and migrate seasonally to neighbourhood districts for farm employment, appear ahead in terms of fertility regulation and transition. The tribal proneness (possibly backed by the liberalism and flexibility in their sociocultural features and organization) to migration and mobility, could sometimes enable them to overcome their original (relative) backwardness, especially vis-à-vis the SC group.[5] Indeed, there is considerable recent evidence of an

[4] We will show some evidence later on a meagre performance on the family planning programme arena among the Santhals in a specific cluster of villages, within which they are a small minority. There is similar evidence elsewhere, reporting very limited use and knowledge of contraceptive methods among the tribes (for example, Ram 1999).

[5] Although tribes generally (and globally) have a nomadic inclination, all Indian tribes are not necessarily typically nomadic or highly mobile. Nor is it true that SC people do not migrate at all. While there are many tribal groups who are sedentary and settled agriculturists, some migrate seasonally as a survival strategy in the face of adverse circumstances (for example, drought-proneness, hilly areas with little prospect of cultivation) in home areas (for example, Breman 1985; and Jayaraman 1979). Some recent evidence shows that migration decisions (even of the seasonal type) seems to depend not only

increasing trend of tribal migration, especially of a circular nature by adult males, females, and other family members (Racine 1997; Breman 1985, 1996; Rogaly 1998; Rogaly *et al.* 2001). Such (rural–rural) seasonal migration by families has a long history dating back to pre-colonial and colonial periods, particularly in the tribal-concentrated regions like central India (Bates and Carter 1992). What emerges however, from the very limited literature on the impact and implications of the currently growing seasonal migration is of a mixed nature. On the one hand, this is often portrayed as a survival strategy of a very vulnerable group, who are not able to extricate themselves from acute poverty at home (for example, Breman 1985, 1996). In this perspective, the seasonal migration, hardly seen as a route to upward mobility, has serious negative consequences, especially in matters like labour relations, children's schooling and health care, living conditions, and women's safety from sexual abuse (for example, Rao and Rana 1997 and literature cited; Rogaly 1998). As Breman (1985), on the basis of his intensive study of Surat district of Gujarat remarks: 'seasonal migration is a matter of survival or, at best consolidation, and hardly ever results in a accumulation or re-investment in the home area' (p. 216).

On the other hand, seasonal migration, though often resorted to as a survival strategy, seems to enable migrant households in several Indian locations to consolidate (if not accumulate) their economic position, and this could well be seen as a potential route to some amelioration of their vulnerability at home. In fact, the seasonal migrants in several

---

on economic circumstances in sending areas, but is often selective of social groups with specific features—social, cultural, and political (for example, Kalam 1997; Mahadev and Racine 1997; and Rogaly 1998 and literature cited). For instance, as Breman (1996) has argued on the basis of evidence in parts of Gujarat, some people are almost forced to migrate (seasonally) not because of inadequate employment opportunities in their local areas, but due to denial of local employment to them. This said, tribal people (overall) are known to possess a greater proneness (and/or readiness) to circular mobility than non-tribals, given broadly the same circumstances faced at home areas by both. For example, in a survey of three villages in Dohad block in Panchmahals district of Gujarat in 1971–2, the majority of tribal households were found migrating seasonally (mostly with the family, except one or two members) to urban areas for employment and income during agricultural slack seasons (Govt. of Gujarat 1974). This testifies to the tribal people's remarkable capability (unhindered by taboos and norms) of responding to such economic opportunities by seasonal mobility.

instances have been able to save some amount of cash, both because of austerity and hard work at distant places (Weber 1924 quoted in Breman 1985; Epstein 1973:207–11), and a higher wage rate earned in receiving areas (for example, Krishnaiah 1997). Many recent studies show that seasonal migration (mostly by tribal households from semi-arid/backward settings) bring some economic and social changes, especially among migrant household that are not forced into it by a debt-bondage trap or by extreme destitution associated with dearth of livelihood opportunities at local areas.[6] Our present study reaffirms such a dynamic aspect of seasonal migration with a particular reference to its impact on fertility behaviour and transition among the migrant Santhals in a particular location in West Bengal.

There is evidence in rural West Bengal, though scattered and limited, that incomes earned through seasonal migration and the migrant households' efforts towards economic upliftment at home areas have been beneficial (for example, Rogaly 1998; Rogaly et al. 2001). The seasonal migration for agricultural work, especially by tribals of the border regions of Bihar and West Bengal and from elsewhere in West Bengal to the southern central regions, is not new. Formerly, it was sporadic and of a short duration, but since the increase in agricultural productivity and cropping intensity in West Bengal in the 1980s due to the spread of HYV technology, seasonal migrants find longer duration employment for transplanting and harvesting (Rogaly 1999:361 and references cited). These tribal seasonal migrant households generally return home with a lump sum of cash, and are even able to accumulate savings, although on a rather small scale (Rogaly 1996; Chaudhuri 1998; see also Krishnaiah 1997 for similar evidence for Andhra Pradesh). A recent socio-economic survey among migrant households in a backward village of Bankura district of West Bengal portrays seasonal migration by agricultural workers as 'a blessing for them' (Chaudhuri 1998:335). Thus, it would be reasonable to hypothesize that seasonal migration facilitates fertility transition among migrants directly by raising incomes and aspirations, and indirectly by

---

[6] See for example, Krishnaiah 1997, Haberfeld et al. 1999; Hema Kumari 1993; Rogaly 1998; Rogaly et al. 2001; Chaudhuri 1998; Gupta and Prajapati 1998; Rani and Shylendra 2001; Mosse et al. 2002 among others. Several ethnic communities in Sahel (who are akin to many Indian tribes) are also often reported to resort to seasonal migration 'as part of a range of strategies designed, not just to cope with livelihood failure, but to optimize livelihood security' (Hampshire 2002; italics added).

empowering and liberating migrant women.[7] It also augments social interactions and diffusion of newer ideas and information about fertility choice and regulation.[8]

Moreover, frequent pregnancy and childbirth must incur extra inconvenience to families who undertake recurrent (seasonal) movements. Therefore, fertility control would be welcomed more by couples who have a high degree of circular mobility for work and income.[9] Indeed, a recent study undertaken in parts of West Bengal finds that 'the fewer the number of dependants (those unable to carry out manual work), the greater the likelihood of migration' (Rogaly 1999:363). Although this correlation, by itself, is not sufficient proof of greater deliberate fertility regulation among the migrating households, this adds plausibility to the hypothesis of their greater readiness to accept family planning. In fact, systematic Indian studies on fertility effects of seasonal migration are very rare. One fairly comprehensive empirical study on the effects of migration in Ludhiana district of Punjab, based on surveys during 1977, strongly indicates that the rural–rural migration (mostly when both husband and wife migrate) is significantly associated with a lower fertility level (Oberai and Singh 1983, Table 5:371–3). The study concludes that 'the act of migration itself causes a decline in fertility' (ibid:415).[10] However, it is undeniable that seasonal migration is likely to entail some adverse outcomes at familial and social planes (for example, sexual abuse of

[7] There is substantial literature suggesting a distinct link between greater female autonomy/women's status and lower fertility in South Asia (Dyson and Moore 1983; Koenig and Foo 1992 for a useful review; Dharmalingam and Morgan 1996; Morgan and Niraula 1995; Malhotra et al. 1995; and Basu 1992 among others). On liberating and empowering effects on women of seasonal migration, see for example, Rogaly 1998; Teerink 1995. For example, Teerink (1995) states that migrant tribal women are 'more free from social control than when they stay at their in-laws in the home village'.

[8] See Bongaarts and Watkins (1996) on the role of 'social interactions' in fertility transition in contemporary developing countries.

[9] Difficulties may include the relative captivity and occasional immobility of pregnant (and sometimes lactating) adult females, the difficulty of travelling with infants and very young children, child rearing being often hampering a mother's opportunities for working and earning cash as a seasonal migrant labourer.

[10] See also Goldstein (1978) for some evidence and plausible explanations that relate migration causally to a low-fertility level in the context of Thai studies during the 1960s.

women and forced school dropouts, especially among girls). It is almost impossible to incorporate such costs adequately in estimating net gain from seasonal migration from the standpoint of an individual household. But what seems to emerge from the foregoing discussion is that migrant households on balance would be more likely to achieve a lower fertility by greater use of contraception, as compared to their non-migrant counterparts, other things being the same. Our present comparative study of migrant and non-migrant households in two locations of West Bengal provides evidence and indications concordant with this hypothesis.[11] Indeed as our study shows, the rural–rural seasonal migration undertaken by Santhali people of one particular location seems to have played a substantial positive role in accelerating the fertility transition in their local area.

A detailed study of tribal fertility is potentially useful, as it can bring out important insights, both into existing theoretical perspectives on fertility behaviour and its transition into policy matters. There is a newly emerged 'minority demography' which, however, focuses, often exclusively, on various ethnic, religious, or racial minority groups (for example, Bittles and Roberts 1992; Coleman 1982). But our present study takes a somewhat broader and comparative approach, namely one of comparing fertility and family planning patterns between: (a) the Santhals and their most comparable group, namely, SC people within a same location; and (b) the Santhals of two contrasting rural locations. Such comparisons, hopefully, would capture the implications for fertility (and its transition) of regional as well as intra-regional differences between social groups.

Background Description of Study Areas and Data Collection

The primary data that we analyse below comes from our household demographic survey among the Santhals and SC households in select villages of two districts of West Bengal, namely Birbhum and

---

[11] Note that our hypothesized fertility-reducing effect of seasonal migration is not exactly of the type which is chiefly due to forced spousal separation frequently analysed in the relevant global literature (for example, Menken 1979; Massey and Mullan 1984, and De Walle 1975). Unlike in many African and Latin American regions, the seasonal migration that we analyse in the present context of rural West Bengal, is predominantly of the type which does not entail forced spousal separation.

Bankura.[12] The survey was conducted in several rounds between October 1996 and October 1998. Santhals constitute one of the largest tribes of India and are mostly concentrated in eastern India (West Bengal, Bihar, Orissa, and Tripura). The Santhals are one of the largest among 38 scheduled tribes of West Bengal, presently constituting about 55 per cent of the total tribal population of the state. They live in a variety of eco-environments—some in relatively isolated hilly tracts, some in mining-industrial pockets, and relatively few in agricultural plain land (Fürer-Haimendorf 1985:109). They have a deep-rooted cultural tradition and heritage, which has co-existed with, and has, in many places, been influenced by, a contrasting but dominant Hindu culture and social structure.[13]

Two Locations of West Bengal: Nanoor (Birbhum) and Khatra (Bankura)

The selection of the two locations of West Bengal was greatly influenced by our purpose to explore implications (for fertility behaviour and its change) of regional differences in geophysical environment, sociocultural milieu, and also in the level and pattern of development, especially in respect of infrastructures in social sector. Bankura, situated in the western part of the state, lies in a sub-humid zone with undulating terrain, high surface water runoff and soil erosion, and a few relatively adverse climatic and geophysical conditions. This is related to its remoteness from the Bay of Bengal, its lateritic soil and undulating topography, and an absence of streams (Kar 1997). On the other hand, Birbhum district, situated in the central-east of the state, is relatively diverse in terms of topography and other geo-physical features. Table 6.1a presents broad background information on the two districts. While

[12] Apart from the villages of these two districts, we also collected information from an exclusive Santhal hamlet of another relatively backward district Purulia. However, partly because the Purulia village does not fit in well with either of the two types of locations (especially in terms of migration pattern) that we have chosen for a contrast, and partly because the sample size in Purulia village is rather small, we refrain from including this information in the following detailed comparative analysis between the two types of location. However, the information from the Purulia hamlet has been included in the logit regression analysis of all data put together (in section 4 below) that seeks to estimate predictive powers of several explanatory variables.

[13] In fact, the Santhals entered the limelight of modern history for a resistance movement (known as the Santhal Rebellion of 1855) against oppression and exploitation by Hindu landlords and usurers which had began much earlier.

Bankura district is larger in terms of land and population size than Birbhum, its population density is much smaller (particularly as compared to whole state). Although the difference between these two districts in terms of proportion of land brought so far under cultivation is not remarkably large, the proportion of irrigated area is substantially higher in Birbhum. This certainly reflects Birbhum's edge in terms of agricultural production and productivity over Bankura. Indeed, on most of the indicators of physical/social infrastructure development, Birbhum appears somewhat ahead of Bankura (see Table 6.1a), with a striking exception of a lower, albeit marginally, incidence of overall rural poverty in the latter.

Table 6.1a   Background information on two districts of Birbhum and Bankura, West Bengal, 1991–2001

	Birbhum	Bankura	West Bengal
General (1991)			
Area (sq. km.)	4,545.0	6,882.0	88,752
Total Population	25,556,64	28,050,65	680,779,65
Land/Man Ratio			
(sq. km. per 10,000)	17.8	24.5	13.0
% of cultivable area	74.1	56.9	63.1
% of irrigated to net cultivated			
area	55.3	50.8	35.0
% of ST population to total	7.0	10.33	5.6
% of SC population to total	31.0	31.36	23.6
% of Santhals to tribal			
population (1981)	90.0	83.0	62.1[*]
Decadal growth rate of population			
1991–2001 (%)	17.9	13.8	17.8
% of population in poverty			
1993–94, (Rural)	40.9	37.0	41.0
Physical/Social Infrastructure			
% of inhabited villages having			
(1991)			
a) Any educational facility	81.0	76.89	75.80
b) Any medical facility	28.81	25.75	27.26
c) Any source of drinking water	99.28	98.74	98.19
d) Electricity connection	79.08	39.94	43.56
% of villages connected by *pucca*			
(metalled/surfaced) road	17.43	21.12	24.77
Estimated per cent of villages not			
connected with pucca road			
(2000–2001)	65.5	58.3	–

(*Contd.*)

Table 6.1a (*contd.*)

	Birbhum	Bankura	West Bengal
Estimated coverage (per cent of habitations) of safe drinking water, 2000	69.6	48.6	–
Composite Index 2000–2001@	52.1	58.7	59.6
Literacy/Education			
% literate (1991) #			
ST	14.8	32.4	27.8
SC	27.7	22.0	42.2
Total	48.56	52.04	57.7
Santhals (1981)	8.0	18.0	22.9*
Female literacy			
1991	37.2	36.6	46.6
2001	52.2	49.8	60.2
Health and Family Welfare Performance			
% of children getting complete immunization 1998–99	34.9	67.3	–
Per cent of eligible couples effectively protected, 2000	44.6	43.7	35.4
% of girls marrying below 18 years	59.30	50.00	–
% of currently married women age 15–44 years using any modern method of contraception	56.70	54.40	–
Number of conventional contraceptive users per 1000 eligible couples, 1998–99	5.6	4.62	4.8
% of primary school children faced with some health problem (Rural) 1996 (Special Check-up)	77.4%	93%	101%
Number of health centres per 10,000	.25	.28	.16
Number of sub-centres per 10,000	1.3	1.6	1.01
Number of beds in hospitals and health centres per 10,000	7.3	9.4	8.8
Demographic Indicators			
CBR (TFR)			
1981	35.12 (4.40)	32.37 (4.10)	34.67 (4.30)

(Contd.)

1991	31.34 (3.81)	28.27 (3.46)	29.01 (3.61)
2001	26.10 (3.0)	22.20 (2.60)	22.5 (2.60)
IMR (under 5 mortality)			
1981	103 (141)	83 (89)	95 (124)
1991	87 (117)	63 (85)	62 (94)
Female–Male Ratio 1991			
Total population	0.946	0.951	0.917
ST	0.976	0.972	0.964
SC	0.943	0.960	0.931

Notes: [#]Literacy rate refers to population aged 7 years and above; [@] composite index for each district is arrived at by standardizing and aggregating of several socioeconomic and demographic indicators, the ranking being higher, the higher is the value of the composite index.

Source: 1991 Census Reports; Govt. of India (1994a, 2001); Govt. of West Bengal (not dated); RG (1997); Guilmoto and Rajan (2002).

What stands out in Bankura is its distinctly lower growth rate of population. While its estimated birth rate appears lower, this does not seem attributable to a larger prevalence of contraception and family planning. In any case, the birth rate differential is much less than commensurate with the differential in population growth rate. Again, there is virtually little indication (based on infant/child mortality) in favour of the hypothesis of relatively high mortality as a major explanation for the slower growth of population in the district. In this context, a relatively larger outflow (including perhaps seasonal migration) from Bankura could well be a significant contributory factor. As a rough illustration, the proportion of persons born in Bankura but enumerated in other districts within the state, according to 1991 census (at 7.4 per cent), is larger by almost 2 per cent point than the corresponding figure for Birbhum.

This said, the lower infant/child mortality estimates in Bankura are notable and are consistent with its overall record of better health and family welfare infrastructure (for example, number of health and sub-centres) and performance (for example, per cent children immunized) (Table 6.1a). This could, at least partly, be related to the fact that Bankura is one out of only two districts of the state (other than Calcutta city), which happens to have a medical college hospital.[14] While

---

[14] The existence of a medical college hospital could make a difference, in terms of health provisions and performance within the district, because several

Bardhaman is the only other district town (outside Calcutta city) that has a medical college hospital, its population size (both within the district and in terms of its service coverage) is more than double the size of Bankura's. It is also of interest that there is higher tribal literacy in Bankura, which may be indicative of a relatively high level of aspirations in the exclusive tribal locations, in which, as we would show later, material levels seem to have been improved by seasonal migrations for work and incomes. In any case, these district-level aggregate statistics cannot reveal wide intra-district variations, especially in facilities and infrastructure, between tribal and non-tribal locations.

In fact, the Santhals of Bankura are generally concentrated in semi-arid, rocky, and hilly tracts, and the villages that we have surveyed belong to the administrative block called Khatra Block II (Khatra hereafter), which falls within a chronically drought-prone region of the district.[15] On the other hand, the survey villages of Birbhum district belong mostly to the administrative block named Nanoor, which extends over the south-eastern part of the district. These villages of Nanoor fall within a large rolling upland topography between the two rivers, the Mayurakshi and the Ajoy. The soil in the region is mainly brown and alluvial, and crops like wheat, paddy, peas, and sugarcane are grown here.

Table 6.1b presents census-based background information on these two sub-regions (blocks) of respective districts, from each of which a cluster of villages/hamlets was chosen for a detailed survey. The Nanoor block (of Birbhum district) is bigger, both in terms of area and population than Khatra block (of Bankura). Although proportionate shares of tribal and SC populations are not vastly different between the two districts, Khatra block has a comparatively large tribal concentration. The Santhals are numerically a major tribe, both in the regions, and, of course, within the state (Table 6.1a).[16]

---

state health sector grants and projects are implemented by various departments of medical college (for example, the Department of Community Health and Medicine, and Public Health). This generally makes for relatively higher health expenditure and better health-related provisions in the district concerned.

[15] Each district is divided into several administrative 'blocks' with clearly defined jurisdictions.

[16] In a recent round of surveys, the National Sample Survey Organization of Ministry of Planning has considered only Santhals as a 'major' tribe of West Bengal, and the other relatively smaller tribes of the state are Oraon, Bhumij, and Munda (see Govt. of India 1994a).

Table 6.1b   Background information on two blocks of Nanoor and Khatra, West Bengal, 1991–2001

	Nanoor Block	Khatra Block	West Bengal
General			
Area (sq. km.)	309.2	215.6	88,752
Total Population	1,68,364	62,216	680,779,65
% of cultivable area	72.9	33.3	–
% of irrigated area	76.2	7.7	–
% of ST population to total	2.0	31.0	5.6
% of SC population to total	32.9	25.4	23.6
Literacy/Education			
% literate# (1991)			
ST	10.3	34.0	27.8
SC	24.2	30.3	42.2
Total	–	–	57.7
Number of primary schools			
per 1000 population, 1991	0.81	1.22	–
Physical and Social Infrastructure			
% of rural population served by,			
Education facilities	92.4	88.0	–
Medical facilities	59.3	10.5	–
Approach by *pucca* road	0.98	20.1	–
Power supply	99.6	17.0	–
Demographic Indicators			
Female–Male ratio 1991			
Total population	0.957	0.941	0.917
ST	1.014	0.952	0.964
SC	0.962	0.927	0.931

Note: # Literacy rate refers to population aged 7 years and above.
Source: 1991 Census Reports; Govt. of India (1994a, 2001).

It is also clear that Khatra block is agriculturally backward and vulnerable to drought, as large parts of the area are uncultivable (only a third of the total land has, so far, been brought under cultivation as against three-fourth in Nanoor). Moreover, an extremely low level of irrigation facilities in Khatra (only one-tenth of land is irrigated as compared to three-fourth in Nanoor) keeps its agriculture almost exclusively dependent on monsoon rainfall. In terms of most other infrastructures too, especially medical facilities and power supply,

Khatra appears far more deprived than Nanoor block (except perhaps in road connections) (see Table 6.1b).

Strikingly, the literacy rate among the tribal population in Khatra, though quite low in absolute terms, is much higher than that of Nanoor. This is consistent with, as noted above, the overall tribal literacy rate in Bankura being more than twice as large as that of Birbhum (Table 6.1a). Note that tribal literacy in Khatra is about 4 per cent point larger than that of the SC group, and it is about 10 per cent point larger at the entire district level (see Table 6.1b). (While 18 per cent of Santhals of Bankura were recorded as literate in 1981, this is very likely to have surpassed the 1991 figure of 22 per cent for SC.) Thus, unlike Nanoor (and Birbhum district, on the whole, as well as the state of West Bengal), the tribal population of Khatra (even perhaps of the whole Bankura district) do not stand behind (or are indeed somewhat ahead of) the SC group in basic education and implied levels of awareness and aspirations. Also noteworthy (and somewhat related) is the fact that the metalled road coverage in Khatra block, though quite inadequate, is better than Nanoor's miserable level (see Tables 6.1a, and 6.1b).

The selection of specific villages and hamlets from within these two contrasting administrative blocks of two districts was influenced, in large part, by our prior familiarity with them. Consequently, our survey may well be branded as a micro-demographic one, as the villages were chosen neither strictly randomly, nor did they cover very large areas. For the detailed demographic survey, we selected three adjoining villages from Nanoor block, namely Thupsara, Bamunia, and Jahanabad (to be collectively called Thupsara henceforth). Similarly, a cluster of three exclusive Santhali hamlets (which we will call Chitrihutu after the name of one of the hamlets surveyed) was selected from Khatra block (see Map). Because of the interviewers' prior familiarity with the villages, we could save some resources (for example, time and travel). We covered almost all households belonging to Santhal and SC communities in these villages and hamlets, except, of course, those in which no one was available and/or willing to respond at the time our visits.

The villages/hamlets chosen are all relatively remote in the sense that the villagers do not have easy access to motorable road/highway connections to commute to the nearest big town/city. This ensures the minimum possible level of mediating influences from close proximity or regular interactions with urban areas, especially on the villagers'

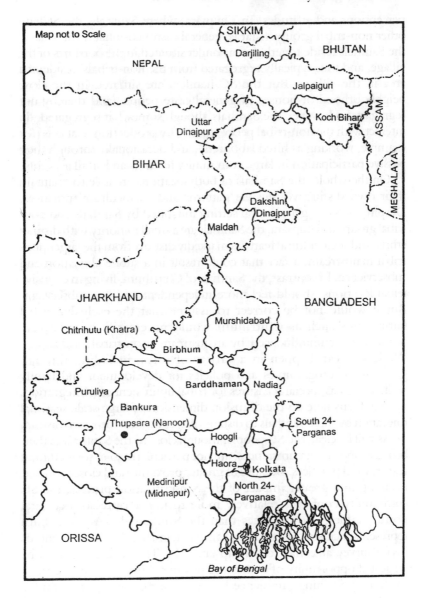

Map of West Bengal with Thupsara and Chitrihutu

Note: The marked locations of Thupsara and Chitrihutu are approximate, not exact on the map.

perceptions and attitudes. In Thupsara, where Santhals, the SC and other non-tribal groups (that is, general caste) co-inhabit the village, the Santhals reside together in a hamlet situated in the outskirts of the village, and thus typically segregated from the non-tribals' residential area in the village. But the SC hamlets are situated in the close neighbourhood of houses of general caste people, and thereby not segregated. However, the Santhals, though somewhat segregated, do interact with the non-tribal people mostly by production relations (for example, working as hired labourers), and occasionally through their passive participation in large community festivals and similar events.

On the whole, the Santhals of both locations are able to maintain their own distinctive lifestyle patterns and sociocultural practices. Despite the same geophysical setting inhabited by Santhals and non-tribal groups in Thupsara, the Santhals are a small minority with distinct ethnic and sociocultural features markedly distinct from the larger non-tribal mainstream, a fact that could result in a subtle alienation and subservience. In contrast, the Santhals of Chitrihutu, living in exclusive tribal locations, should feel more independent and less subservient. But it would not be correct to assume that the exclusive tribal habitations such as Chitrihutu would necessarily be relatively untouched or uninfluenced by mainstream (non-tribal) influences. While this can happen in a variety of ways, including through government programmes and policies for development and family welfare such as special measures for tribal upliftment and integration, we will focus here on the diffusion dimension of large-scale seasonal migration by these Santhals to distant villages beyond their own district.

As will be clear, the SC people, though close to the Santhals in their broad economic circumstances, are not particularly so in sociocultural features and practices. Because of greater proximity and closer contact, resulting in a greater impact of the Sanskritization process, the SC community conforms relatively more to upper caste sociocultural norms, values, and practices than the Santhals do. As Chitrihutu represents a cluster of exclusive Santhali hamlets, the SC households in our survey, all come from Thupsara alone. This would hopefully be an added opportunity of examining possible differential implications for family planning prevalence between Santhals living in exclusive tribal areas and Santhals co-inhabiting as a minority in non-tribal villages.

As noted earlier, Thupsara represents a fairly developed region, especially in terms of the spread of HYV technology, particularly since the 1980s. Although a considerable proportion of arable land is under canal irrigation (for example, Mayurakshi Canal project), it is quite inadequate in the years of scanty monsoon rain, and farmers thus depend substantially on private tube-wells and pump-sets. At least half of the arable land of Thupsara is cultivated twice or in some cases even more in a single year. Although paddy is the main crop here, vegetables are also grown over the year. Agriculture is the main occupation of most villagers, with very limited non-agricultural activities performed by a few, who occasionally also participate in farm activities. In any case, farm labour is required almost all round the year, which is a major reason why labourers cannot migrate seasonally to other places for better earnings.

In contrast, Chitrihutu is agriculturally backward. The soil is harsh, rocky, and infertile. Indeed this entire block (of which only 7.5 per cent land is irrigated, as shown in Table 6.1b), is one of the seven officially declared 'drought-prone' regions of Bankura district, and it is included under Government of India's Drought Prone Area Programme (DPAP). As monsoon rainfall is almost the only source of irrigation in the region, it is only during the *kharif* season (i.e. July–October) that paddy can be cultivated from traditional varieties of seeds. But reasonable levels of productivity and returns are achievable only in the years of adequate and well-timed monsoon rain.[17] Understandably, the ownership of land is hardly a guarantee or a significant index of the level farm output or material level of living in this area. And the Santhals of Chitrihutu obviously do not find it worthwhile to invest on modern inputs (for example, HYV seeds, pesticides, and fertilizers), because of the high risk of crop failure. Threats of famine and drought occur with considerable frequency in this region; therefore most people are in search of employment for a large part of the year. There are some possible sources of local employment and wage income including spells in public works in surrounding areas (for example, road construction, or even pond digging, or canal) and/or some handicraft activities or other occasional paid work, all of which are sporadic, irregular, and uncertain. Under

[17] The topographical zone to which Bankura and Purulia belong is with laterite soil, and receives about eighty per cent of the total annual rainfall during the four monsoon months of June to September. The monsoon in these regions is generally erratic with prolonged breaks between July and October, and 'these abnormalities affect agricultural productivity of this zone' (Reserve Bank of India 1984:48).

these circumstances, the seasonal migration in response to a demand from agriculturally developed districts is understandably one of the few options open for economic betterment and in some cases, even for the livelihood of these Santhali inhabitants.

Although there is a narrow metalled road passing nearby these hamlets, the number of buses plying here is rather few. The major motorway (on which buses ply more frequently) is about 5/6 km away from this location, and the primary health centre (PHC) is about 8 km away. Historically, many Santhali families have been migrating seasonally to parts of neighbouring districts (for example, Burdwan and Hoogly) (see migration flows in the Map) during the kharif harvesting season (September–October). As noted earlier, due to an enhanced labour demand over the recent past, they now migrate in larger numbers during other seasons of the year as well (for example, sowing of boro crops in February/March). It is important to note that, unlike age–sex selective migration in other regions across the globe, they generally migrate with family (adult males, females, other employable members, and very young children, if any), although one or two elderly persons stay back at home to look after the homestead and school-going children. During the kharif season (June–August) they stay in their home villages for three to four months to cultivate their own land.

Our questionnaire was designed with a focus on questions relating to reproductive behaviour and preferences, and family planning practices. It has two parts: the first part consists of questions relating to basic information on all family members, their status, demographic, educational and occupational, together with questions on economic and other circumstances of the household (for example, land and other assets owned, number of rooms, source of drinking water etc). Answers in this part are collected from the head of the household. The questions in the second part, for which the respondents are the ever-married women, relate to marital and birth history, fertility preference, contraceptive practices, views on ideal family size and family planning, etc., and also questions relevant to evaluating the extent of female autonomy.

The survey was performed by field investigators after undergoing several sessions of training and briefing, and they were already familiar with the respective localities. The most formidable problem, one fairly common in demographic surveys across developing countries, relates to inaccuracies in reported age. Almost none of the household members have an exact record of the date of birth, and most of the reported ages are based on guesses and memory. The standard methods of ascertaining age under such circumstances such as cross-examining, referring to some landmark events (for example drought, flood), imputing one's age on the basis of birth intervals with brothers/sisters or other members, were tried. Notwithstanding these efforts, age data possibly have some inaccuracies, and caution is warranted while interpreting results, especially those with a bearing on age information.

Apart from recall lapses, inarticulation and shyness among women respondents, especially about their views and preferences regarding reproductive behaviour, contraception, and ideal family size, has been a problem faced by the interviewers. Consequently, the fieldworkers had to draw on their reserves of patience and perseverance. Many Santhali women were not available for interviews until the evenings, as they were out at work during the day. Notwithstanding such hurdles, appropriate care was taken to obtain accurate responses.

Broad Socio-Economic and Other Differentials

Table 6.2 presents information on broad socio-economic differences between the two clusters of villages. The Santhals are (as expected) far less numerous than the SC people in Thupsara,[18] but both groups seem to be on a similar economic footing and circumstances. In ownership of land and other assets, occupation, and migration propensity, both Santhal and SC communities appear fairly close to each other. Barring a few minor anomalies such as more SC households without land but possessing a radio, these two groups in Thupsara appear on the same level of material well-being.[19] Thus, the demographic and related differentials that may emerge between these two social groups in Thupsara can hardly be attributed to economic and material differences *per se*. For example, it is in terms of the incidence of ever school participation among males aged six years,

[18] While all SC households surveyed by us belong to one village, namely Thupsara, the Santhal households from two adjoining villages have been included in the survey. This means that the Santhals of a single village constitute an even smaller proportion of the total than what appears from Table 6.2.

[19] Although this economic similarity between Santhals and SC people in Thupsara is unlike the all-West Bengal scenario of greater economic vulnerability of aggregate tribal people (vis-à-vis SC), this broadly coincides with the all-India picture of similar economic and material levels between SC and ST groups.

and above that the SC group of Thupsara appears ahead of the ST (i.e. the Santhals), a fact which corroborates with the state-level differential in literacy rates (Table 6.1a and 6.2). Since a child's school participation essentially rests on parental decisions, the differential in school participation between two social groups in the same location, despite similar material circumstances, should have something to do with differing parental perceptions, awareness, and motivation relating to the schooling of children.[20] Thus, despite being economically no richer than the Santhals, the SC people of Thupsara could be considered to be ahead in awareness, exposure to newer ideas, and aspirations. Being closer and more proximate to upper caste mainstream people and society as well as being politically mobilized because of their much larger number, might have been important factors for this relative advantage of SC people, as compared to Santhals in Thupsara.[21] But, such relative backwardness (relating to aspirations and dynamism), as is seen among the Santhals vis-à-vis the SC group of Thupsara, is not inevitable or predestined for tribes as is illustrated by much greater school participation among the Santhals of Chitrihutu, who reside in exclusive tribal areas.

[20] For evidence on the question of why poor parents are generally not very keen to send children to schools and related issues, see for example, PROBE Team (1999); also Maharatna (1997). Discriminatory treatment, and an insensitive delivery/teaching of students, from backward and lower rungs of society, particularly of a small minority of Santhali students as in Thupsara, could well have dampened parental motivation for children's school education. A recent survey of a sample of schools in West Bengal by the Pratichi Trust (India) did find some evidence of a distinct discriminatory attitude against students of a lower caste and tribal households by teachers, the majority of whom belong to general/higher castes (Rana et al. 2002).

[21] In fact, the relative isolation of tribals from general caste mainstream society is considered a major reason for which tribes have lagged behind SC people in reaping benefits from various state privileges and protectionist measures for SC, ST, and other backward communities. To quote from a recent paper on the relative disadvantage of ST vis-à-vis SC in benefiting from the policy of reservations and protections: 'The scheduled castes have... had a greater exposure to the larger society as compared to the scheduled tribes. This is to say that opportunities made available to the larger societies or the higher castes in the form of knowledge, information, technology, employment, etc. were also in sight for the scheduled castes, even though they were denied access to it. Such advantages were absent for the scheduled tribes. Tribes, thus, suffered the disadvantage of isolation in this regard' (Xaxa 2001:2768).

Table 6.2   Background information on Santhals and SC groups,
two locations, West Bengal, 1996–8

	Thupsara Santhals	SC	Chitrihutu Santhals
Number of households	97	151	101
Population	492	669	533
Sex ratio (F/M)	104	98	89
Average land owned per household (acres)	0.20	0.22	2.52
Average land leased in per household (acres)	0.47	0.57	0
Per cent of pure wage labourer households[*]	37	35	0
Per cent of households owning no land	69	54	0
Per cent of households who cultivate leased-in land	42	43	0
Per cent of households owning land of size (acres):			
>0–<0.5	14	29	3.4
>3	0	0.6	10.0
Average number of rooms per household	1.70	2.26	2.27
Per cent of households without any asset (e.g. bicycle, watch, radio, etc.)	66	60	10
Per cent of households possessing:			
Bicycle(s)	27	20	69
Watch/clock	8	19	57
Radio	10	26	37
Per cent of people aged 6 years and above who have ever been to school:			
Males	23	41	75
Females	4	12	51
Per cent of households migrating seasonally for work	0	0	68

[*]Include households, which neither own any land nor lease in any land for cultivation.
Source: Survey data.

Indeed, there are a few notable contrasts in socio-economic and related indicators between the Santhals of Thupsara and Chitrihutu.[22] First, while more than half the households in Thupsara (both for Santhali and SC communities) do not own any land, no household in Chitrihutu is totally landless. Note too a much larger average size of land holding in Chitrihutu as compared to the corresponding figure for Thupsara. While about 35 per cent of households are wage labourers in Thupsara, there is none in this category in Chitrihutu. A similar differential pattern is observed in the incidence of tenancy/share cropping: while about 42 per cent households reportedly have leased land for cultivation in Thupsara, the corresponding figure for Chitrihutu is nil (see Table 6.2).

Although Santhali households of Chitrihutu are in greater possession of land than their counterparts in Thupsara, this by itself could not guarantee a better economic standard of the former. This is reflected clearly in a large proportion of Santhali households of this region who migrate seasonally well beyond their own district for farm employment (particularly in harvesting and transplanting). Slightly more than two-third of Santhali households of Chitrihutu reportedly migrate seasonally to other districts every year, while none from Thupsara does so (see Table 6.2). Adult Santhali males, females, and working children from semi-arid tracts of Bankura have been migrating as farm labourers in agriculturally advanced regions (for example, Burdwan and Hooghly) for a fairly long time. As noted earlier, this migration flow and duration have increased over the recent past (Rogaly 1999:359–69).[23] The wage

[22] A very low recorded sex ratio (F/M) for Chitrihutu is rather disturbing. While further exploration into this issue is called for, its explanation, if it is real, is very likely to have something to do with the nature of migration to other areas.

[23] According to the estimate of a Bankura correspondent of a leading Bengali daily, over a span of only two weeks as many as 70,000 labourers boarded special buses from Bankura town to reach villages of Burdwan and Hoogly districts for transplanting work on farms (see Rogaly 1999:361). The most common reason expressed by some big farmers of Bardhaman, who hire in migrant Santhals during harvesting and transplanting seasons, is the Santhals' greater diligence and honesty as compared to local labourers, who are more prone to shirking, and are more difficult to supervise (partly because of political mobilization). Moreover, the employers' tendency to pay a lower wage rate (than perhaps the statutory minimum) to migrant Santhals cannot but be real, often by exploiting the relatively weak bargaining power of the migrants as well as their muted political voice in areas far away from home, compared to local labourers. Some of these issues are dealt with in Rogaly (1999).

rate in receiving areas is often higher than what they can get in their own backward region. Most adult Santhals migrate with families including young children, and stay in the makeshift accommodation provided by their employers in receiving villages.[24]

Interestingly, while seasonal migration is a response to adverse economic circumstances at home, the Santhals of Chitrihutu are better off so far as the possession of items like bicycles, watches, and radios is concerned (Table 6.2). This relative superiority seems consistent with, as noted previously, a greater educational participation and perhaps aspirations as well.[25] While more than 60 per cent of the households in Thupsara do not possess any consumer durables, the corresponding figure for Chitrihutu is only 16 (see Table 6.2). A better material level of the Santhals of Chitrihutu (as reflected in their somewhat greater possession of assets) seems largely attributable, consistent with a few other studies (discussed in earlier sections), to accumulation of savings from their seasonal migrations. The direct

---

[24] A single spouse is sometimes seen to migrate with other village neighbours, generally under familial compulsions such as the need for the spouse's presence at the local village to look after the elderly, the sick, or school-going children of the family. This type of seasonal migration by family members together, excluding elderly or school-going children, especially from relatively vulnerable tribal areas, is often resorted to in other states as well (see for example, Joshi 1997; Government of Gujarat 1974). As reported by Joshi (1997), seasonal migration, mostly for rail/road construction work, from villages of Jhabua district in Madhya Pradesh is not selective of age, sex or marital status. The question of why Santhals of Thupsara do not migrate seasonally is of interest. First, the presence of a small Santhal hamlet in a non-tribal village like Thupsara is presumably a result of past permanent move and settlement (perhaps as attached labourer households)—of course, at the behest of powerful and wealthy landlords and farmers. This past permanent move implies that those tribal households had a negligible stake in their original homeland. Second, as noted earlier, the landless Santhali labourers in Thupsara are normally employed throughout the year because of multiple cropping, sometimes even under an informal debt-bondage or similar other commitments. Conversely, because of ownership of land (as an important asset, though mostly unproductive and infertile), the Santhals of Chitrihutu can never think of making a permanent move out elsewhere, and therefore, resort to seasonal migration for incomes and employment.

[25] Though seemingly incompatible, the familial seasonal migration does not interfere with children's school participation because, as previously indicated, school-going children (especially male and not very young) are often left behind at home under someone's (for example, the elderly or older female child) care.

(albeit limited) economic benefits of seasonal migration as well as some indirect effects (for example, escalation of aspirations and exposure to newer ideas, information, and commodities, as well as women's autonomy) should have a distinct bearing on fertility behaviour and its transition in Chitrihutu, an issue to which we will return presently.

Table 6.3 presents distribution of the working-age population among major occupation categories by sex for the two locations. As can be seen, there is a distinct difference between Santhal and SC people in women's work-participation patterns: while an overwhelming majority of Santhali women report agricultural work as their prime occupation, about three quarter of SC women of Thupsara do not participate in any directly productive activity at all. In Chitrihutu, females participate in farm activities to a greater extent than their male counterparts do; this seems consistent with a male-bias in educational participation, as the per cent of 'students' in the Santhali male population (aged 15–55 years) in Chitrihutu is nearly four times as large as that of females (see Table 6.3). However, this greater masculinity in educational participation should not be viewed as an outcome of an anti-female attitude of discrimination or the low social status of females in tribal communities. As discussed earlier (in Chapter 2), the burden of domestic chores (including caring of children and the elderly) culturally falls disproportionately more on young girls in tribal households, who, owing to the absence of adult supervision at home, often forgo chances of continuing with school education.[26]

Table 6.3   Percentage distribution of population aged 15–55 years by prime occupation and sex, two locations, 1996–7

Location	Agricultural Production		Household Work		Non-agricultural Activities		Student		Other	
	M	F	M	F	M	F	M	F	M	F
Thupsara										
Santhals	95	79	0	11	4	0	1	0	0	0
SC	92	22	0	73	4	5	4	0	0	0
Chitrihutu										
Santhals	63	77	2	10	5	0	15	4	8	0

The category 'other' includes mainly regular jobs in the service sector (e.g. guard, clerk, police, govt. service).
Source: Survey data.

[26] See Srivastava (1998:607–09) on these issues and also the literature cited therein.

The issue of sex-bias in educational enrolment aside, the proportion of students in the adult population is relatively much larger in Chitrihutu. Ignoring possible (though rather limited) influences of differential age-reporting biases, this reaffirms (albeit indirectly) their higher levels of aspiration and awareness than those of not only their Santhali counterparts but of SC people too in Thupsara.[27] Unlike the SC community, the Santhali females in both locations are almost as much involved in productive activities as their male counterparts, a fact, which as has been emphasized already, is typical of tribal communities across India, and is conducive to more balanced gender relations. It is of interest to see how far this holds true among Santhali, as compared to SC women in our study areas. Our questionnaire includes several relevant questions for woman respondents to assess their relative autonomy both in making decisions on the day-to-day running of households and also in freedom of movement.[28] The odds ratios (not shown here), which have been calculated on the basis of the respective ratios for SC women as the reference category (that is, used as the numerator), reflect the extent to which Santhali women (both of Thupsara and Chitrihutu) appear to have autonomy and freedom. It is found that Santhali women in both locations, on the whole, do appear, expectedly, more able to exercise autonomy than their SC counterparts can do, except on a few matters (for example, whether the wife should work outside home), for which a joint decision is more common. Similarly, with few exceptions (for example, in health centre and market), the SC women appear to enjoy less freedom of movement as compared to their Santhali counterparts.

The smaller degree of autonomy of SC women as compared to their Santhali counterparts is in broad consonance with the differential marriage patterns and practices (see Table 6.4). For instance, the mean age at marriage (irrespective of the present age of women) appears relatively higher among Santhali women of Thupsara than their SC counterparts. The marriage age, particularly of females in South Asian

[27] There might be some influence on this high school participation of 'ashram' (free and residential) schools for tribal children that had been set up in tribal areas under government schemes for tribal development.
[28] The questions on female autonomy that were asked by us are the same as those employed in recent researches on these issues (for example, Morgan and Niraula 1995; Dharmalingam and Morgan 1996). It is found that women with greater autonomy are more likely to have lower fertility, and they are also more likely to use contraception than women with less autonomy.

Table 6.4   Age at marriage, marriage patterns/practices and nuptiality differentials, Thupsara and Chitrihutu, 1996–8

	Thupsara				Chitrihutu	
	Santhals	N	SC	N	Santhals	N
Median age at first marriage by current age of women:						
All ages	18.0	101	16.5	166	16.0	168
> 35 years	18.0	38	16.1	52	16.0	53
< 20 years	15.5	7	15.5	20	16.0	23
Per cent of married women by age:						
15–20	30	27	60	30	54	24
20–24	86	14	90	17	83	29
Per cent distribution of ever-married women by distance from their parental home:						
Same village	26	101	18	166	7	170
Within 4 km	35	101	24	166	18	170
Mean distance (km)	11.3	101	9.2	166	19.7	170
Per cent distribution of ever-married women by marriage type and payment:						
Marriage Type:						
Love marriage	24	101	6	166	10	170
Negotiated marriage	76	101	94	166	90	170
Marriage Payment:						
Bride Price	95	101	3	166	100	170
Dowry	0	101	66	166	0	170
No payment	5	101	31	166	0	170

Source: Survey data.

societies, is shaped mostly by sociocultural norms and values, which may, however, change over time. That the mean marriage age of the Santhali females of Chitrihutu is not much different from that of SC women of Thupsara is indicative of a greater influence on them (vis-à-vis Santhals of Thupsara) of the traditional Hindu cultural norm of early marriage. Note too that the proportion of love marriages among Santhal women of Chitrihutu, like the SC females of Thupsara, is extremely small, while it is about one quarter among the Santhals of

Thupsara.[29] However, Santhals of neither location practise dowry, unlike the SC community. As early female marriage, incidence of dowry, and arranged marriage are generally found in a society in which women's status and autonomy is relatively low, an overall higher female status and autonomy (compared to SC females) appears to be a general cultural trait of the Santhal tribe. Therefore, it would be of interest to see if this greater autonomy among Santhali females does translate, in congruence with relevant literature, into lower fertility. With the foregoing discussion as a background, we now turn to the fertility differentials and plausible explanations for them.

Fertility Differentials and Explanations: The Role of Seasonal Migration

Fertility differentials that we analyse here are based chiefly on our survey information on the number of children ever born and the number of live births to all ever-married women over the last twelve months. It should be noted at the outset that because of the small sample size (especially from the standpoint of a standard large-scale demographic survey) special care and caution is required for calculating and interpreting the fertility measures.[30] In fact, we do not go for

[29] In a recent study of female *bidi* (indigenous cigarettes) workers in a Tamil Nadu village, an enhanced incidence of love marriage along with a tendency for earlier marriage have been observed and explained largely in terms of their increased economic independence and personal autonomy (Dharmalingam 1994). But this tendency of more independent females to choose partners and marry earlier than the less autonomous (and more dependent) cohorts could do, should be distinguished clearly from the decline in the age of female marriage among tribal communities due to their wider emulation of the Hindu norm of early marriage.

[30] Large-scale surveys like NFHS or Rapid Household Surveys are of relatively little use for estimating detailed demographic rates for minority social groups like ST, as the number of cases, selected on random proportional principle, often turn out to be extremely small, say, for a particular district. For example, in the recently held Rapid Household Survey (RHS) during 1998–99 the number of ST women selected within the entire state of West Bengal were only 50 among whom none was aged above 25 years. Likewise, the numbers for ST and SC in NFHS are also often embarrassingly small and are hardly amenable to calculation of many demographic rates like average age at marriage or TFR. Indeed, our sample size, especially for the ST population, though not selected randomly from the entire district, is much larger than the total number of sample cases selected by these large-scale surveys.

calculating TFR partly because of possible influences of age-misreporting on age-specific fertility rates (on which TFR is based), and largely due to small sections of the population exposed to the risk of pregnancy. In Table 6.5, we present two measures of fertility: the mean number of children ever born to ever-married women aged 40–49 years, and the general fertility rate (GFR) expressed as the number of births in a year per 1000 women aged 14–49 years. These two measures give cohort and current measures of fertility, but a judgement about differential patterns of fertility trends cannot be made merely on this basis. While fertility estimates presented in Table 6.5 may be subjected to doubt on the ground of an inadequate number of respondents, our detailed scrutiny of individual cases attempts to avoid serious distortion in the conclusions based on average figures. As can be seen, there is considerable fertility differential both between Santhal and SC women in the same location (Thupsara), and also between the Santhal fertility of two locations (that is, between Thupsara and Chitrihutu). In Thupsara, Santhal women appear to have higher fertility than the SC group not only at current period but also for the cohort of women who had begun their reproductive career in the 1960s.[31] A larger average number of children per woman aged 40–49 in the Santhali community of Thupsara than that of their SC counterparts is indeed suggestive of a 'pre-transition fertility rise' that the former might have experienced, while the latter group (i.e. SC) has perhaps already begun a fertility reduction. This finding could well be seen as a reaffirmation of the proposition that Santhals get modernized later than the SC people. This inference seems consistent with the conclusions of preceding chapters, namely that tribal fertility has historically been lower than that for the SC communities, and that the gap seems to have narrowed in the recent past. Note too that in terms of GFR (which captures the reproductive performance for more recent periods), the indicated fertility levels appear noticeably lower among SC women than that of their Santhali counterparts in Thupsara.

Interestingly, Santhali women of Chitrihutu have the lowest fertility among the groups, and this low fertility is observed even for the older cohort of women who have reached the end of their reproductive span, with the mean number of children ever born being 3.6 to women aged 40–49 years. The GFR among the Santhali women of Chitrihutu

[31] It should be noted that this corroborates well with the timing of the 'pre-transition' fertility rise in the tribal population at an aggregate all-state level.

Table 6.5 Fertility differentials between Santhals and SC group, two locations, 1996–8

Fertility Measure	Thupsara			Chitrihutu
	Santhals	SC	% diff	Santhals
Average number of children ever born to women aged 40–49	6.3	5.0	26	3.7
(N)	(27)	(35)	–	(31)
GFR#	146	112	30	79
(N)	(101)	(166)	–	(155)

#Based on number of births in last 12 months to ever-married women aged 14–49 years.
Source: Survey data.

is remarkably low too (indeed close to the levels found for the lowest fertility regions of India like Kerala).[32] Notwithstanding the well-known difficulties and limitations arising out of the small sample size and GFR as a measure of fertility,[33] it appears that the Santhals of Chitrihutu have, on an average, a lower fertility level as compared to that of the Santhals and SC communities of Thupsara.

There could be several reasons for the observed fertility differentials between the two contrasting locations of our study. Let us begin with possible influences of nuptiality differentials, if any. As noted earlier, the average age at marriage is generally higher among the Santhali women vis-à-vis their SC counterparts. However, a higher mean age

[32] The GFR for state of Kerala in 1991 was 89, with the TFR being 3.3, and thus the GFR of 79 found for rural Santhals of Chitrihutu in 1996 should be very close to Kerala's in 1997 with a TFR of 1.8.

[33] Since GFR is not neutral to age-distribution of females within the reproductive span, one should be careful about comparing GFRs between two groups, if they have different age-distributions of women. Note that the proportion of younger women (say below 30 years) to the total of ever-married women aged 14–49 is lower among Santhals of Chitrihutu (27 per cent), as compared to the Santhali (33 per cent) and SC (41 per cent) groups in Thupsara. This is consistent with a lower GFR among Chitrihutu's women, as fecundity (or age-specific natural fertility) is (biologically) higher among younger adults than among older adult women. But the actual outcome in non-natural fertility population groups would ultimately depend on several other factors, such as possible differentials in the degree and pattern of contraception and deliberate fertility control, apart from the influence of differential age-pattern of childbearing.

of marriage among Santhali women aged above 35 years than of those below 20 years in Thupsara is suggestive of their recent tendency to go in for early marriages. But proper caution is required because of the very small sample size in the younger age group, as well as because of the possible (downward) bias due to truncation of those currently below 20 years but never married and/or would marry later, although such cases would be relatively negligible. In any case, the proportion of marriages at 15 years or less is much smaller among Santhali women than among SC counterparts in Thupsara, and the proportion of early marriage is found larger among the women currently aged 20 years or below (44 per cent) than among older cohort (35 years +) (16 per cent). No similar decline is suggested by the mean age of marriage data for the Santhali women of Chitrihutu (see Table 6.4).[34] Also, there is a suggestion of a slight decline in the average marriage age among SC women of Thupsara in the recent past. Putting aside the issue of a small sample size for a moment, these differentials could be interpreted to imply several things. First, as indicated earlier, a relatively low marriage age among the Santhali females of Chitrihutu (as compared to Santhali counterparts of Thupsara) could be a reflection of an earlier (and/or greater) influence on them of Hindu sociocultural practices. This, despite the former's habitation within exclusive tribal areas, is not surprising in the light of their high degree of circular mobility and greater exposure to (non-tribal) mainstream society and culture than the non-migrating Santhals of non-tribal areas could have.

Since circular mobility entails travel, temporary settlement away from home, and possibly social interactions (at various levels), this might help migrant Santhals of Chitrihutu acquire an effective exposure to newer ideas/attitudes, and lifestyles of the upper caste rural population, perhaps offsetting the effects of geophysical isolation and exclusiveness. Conversely, tribal habitation in proximity with SC and upper caste groups within the boundaries of a single village, as the non-migrating Santhals of Thupsara, may not ensure percolation of mainstream influences on tribal perceptions, attitudes, and aspirations. An indicated recent decline in the average marriage age of Santhali women in Thupsara could be a reflection of a delayed adaptation of the traditional Hindu norm of early marriage. As suggested by the

[34] Rapid Household Survey 1998–9 district-level data broadly confirm the trends suggested by our survey data. For example, the mean age at female marriage in Birbhum is 15.3 and 15.2 years respectively for ST and SC groups, while the corresponding figures for Bankura are 15.7 and 15.4 years.

foregoing, the Santhals of Thupsara have lagged in being 'Sanskritized' and modernized as compared to their counterparts of Chitrihutu, who, despite being located in an exclusive tribal region, seem to be in greater touch, through regular spatial mobility, with the world beyond their own village.

In any case, the observed differentials in mean age at marriage (and in overall nuptiality) do not provide an adequate explanation of fertility differentials as reported in Table 6.5. For example, although SC women of Thupsara appear to marry relatively early, they evince a lower fertility than that of Santhals. However, an indicated decline in the marriage age of the Santhali females in Thupsara over the recent past, if real, might have some contribution to a currently observed high fertility.

Indeed, the differentials in other proximate (biological) determinants of fertility, such as duration of breastfeeding and postnatal abstinence, do not seem to constitute a major explanation of the observed fertility differentials either. For example, while Santhali women of Chitrihutu show the lowest fertility, they appear to breastfeed children for a shorter duration (21 months) as compared to both Santhali and SC women of Thupsara (28.2 and 39 months respectively). Secondly, the SC women of Thupsara show a longer average duration of postnatal abstinence (3.2 months) than that for the Santhali women of both locations (about a month each). In any case, the role of biological determinants and nuptiality in fertility behaviour becomes negligible once the populations concerned practise modern contraception.[35] Therefore we turn now to examining the role of fertility regulation and family planning in explaining the observed fertility differentials.

Table 6.6 presents information on the extent and pattern of use of, and unmet need for, family planning. While 60 per cent of the SC women of Thupsara got sterilized, the corresponding figure for the Santhal women was only 12. However, Santhals of Chitrihutu, though sterilized to a less extent (24 per cent of the respondents) than their SC counterparts of Thupsara, show a much wider acceptance for

---

[35] The relevant information does not point to any significant differentials in the pattern and incidence of abortion (spontaneous and induced), miscarriages, primary and secondary sterility between these groups. For example, the proportion of miscarriages and spontaneous abortion cases to the total number of births appears fairly the same at around 2.5 per cent across all three groups under our study. Nor does the extent of childlessness or sterility appear to differ as much as to be an explanation for observed fertility differences.

non-terminal methods of contraception. As much as 34 per cent of eligible women of Chitrihutu appear to be using non-terminal contraceptives, while the corresponding figures for Santhali and SC women of Thupsara are only around 10 per cent. The Santhals of Thupsara are seemingly least influenced by modern ideas relating to advantages of fertility regulation and family planning, as testified also by their largest ideal number of children as well as unmet need for family planning (see Table 6.6). In contrast, the Santhals of Chitrihutu appear to be 'mature' users of modern methods of fertility regulation, with their lowest levels of fertility as well as the unmet need for family planning.[36] This lagging behind of the Santhals of Thupsara, both behind their co-resident SC community and the Santhals of Chitrihutu in terms of family planning acceptance (including sterilization) can hardly be construed as a reflection of a low demand for fertility regulation. The mean ideal number of children for Santhals of Thupsara, though it is higher than that of SC group by about one birth,[37] is far below the natural limit (and perhaps far below their current fertility level too), pointing to their felt need for fertility regulation. This is, indeed, reflected in their fairly large unmet need for family planning. Secondly, they did express an overwhelming preference for a 'small' family size too.

Related to this is the fact that, despite a very high rate of sterilization among SC women of Thupsara, the fertility level is much higher than that of the Santhals of Chitrihutu. The clue possibly lies in the supposition that many SC women must have undergone sterilization only after the number of children born has already crossed the respective 'ideal'. As many as 83 per cent of SC women who got sterilized, are recorded to have already had excess births (over the ideal number). In contrast, the use of non-terminal methods more effectively enables

[36] Although the unmet need for family planning is lowest among the Santhals of Chitrihutu, it is still fairly large. This could, perhaps, be a reflection of a growing motivation to have a smaller family (as also evidenced by their smallest ideal number of children).

[37] The relatively larger mean ideal number of children among the Santhals of Thupsara may partly be a result of *ex post facto* rationalization of achieved fertility. Since the correlation coefficient between the ideal and actual numbers of children among women for whom the latter number exceeded the former is, though positive but far from perfect ($r = 0.38$), the expressed mean ideal number of children probably entailed pre-transitional perceptions relatively favourable to a large family.

couples to end up with the desired number of children, and hence with a smaller unmet need. All this is consistent with the SC women's higher level of unmet need than that of the Santhals of Chitrihutu (Table 6.6), who, by relying more on the non-terminal methods could (presumably) achieve both lower levels of fertility and unmet need, despite a high incidence of sterilization among the former. This, in turn, brings us to the question of what makes the Santhals of Chitrihutu the best performers in terms of voluntary fertility regulation through modern contraception.

Table 6.6 Family planning practices, fertility preferences, and unmet need for family planning (FP), Thupsara and Chitrihutu, 1996–8

	Thupsara				Chitrihutu	
	Santhals	(N)	SC	(N)	Santhals	(N)
Per cent of women respondents sterilized	12	(101)	60	(166)	24	(170)
Per cent eligible women using non-terminal method*	10	(88)	8	(86)	34	(106)
Per cent of women preferring 'small' family size	95	(101)	100	(166)	98	(170)
Mean Ideal Number of Children	3.6	(101)	2.8	(166)	2.5	(170)
Unmet need for FP**	35	(89)	25	(147)	22	(68)

* Includes women who are currently married but are neither sterilized nor pregnant.
** Per cent of currently married women (not having reached menopause) whose numbers of children ever born have either exceeded or are equal to their respective ideal numbers, but who are not using any contraceptive method.

Source: Survey data.

As already noted, the Santhals of Chitrihutu represent a situation where a high degree of mobility, particularly seasonal migration for farm employment, could be seen as a route to better level of living and related augmentation of aspirations. Starting off with similarly high levels of poverty in the two broad regions around the early 1970s, the proportionate reduction in rural poverty by the end of 1980s (when agricultural growth in the state was peaking) has been twice as large in Bankura district than that experienced by Birbhum.[38] While this by

---

[38] District-level poverty estimates for 1972–3, 1987, and 1993–4 were collected through personal communication with Jean Drèze and are originally from Jain and Tendulkar 1988, and Drèze and Srinivasan 1996. The pace of poverty reduction thereafter slowed down in rural Bankura, while Birbhum,

itself is not enough proof of the role played by growing seasonal out-migration in Bankura's poverty alleviation, a substantial involvement of the seasonal migrants from areas like Chitrihutu in the rapid agricultural growth in the progressive regions of the state is doubtless. Indeed, one of the very few contemporary researchers, who have analysed seasonal migration streams and their significance in the context of West Bengal's agricultural growth, describes it 'as potentially progressive as that described by Lenin in 19th century Russia' (Rogaly 1999:375).

While direct economic gains from seasonal migration help escalate migrants' aspirations (relating to, for example, children's education and 'quality'), the periodic mobility and movements of the family create, as noted before, disincentives against frequent (unplanned) childbearing. Indeed, apart from such direct effects of seasonal migration, there should emerge, as discussed previously, some indirect (and related) effects, which have some bearing on the fertility behaviour. Similar to the way tribes in the past reportedly learnt the methods of settled cultivation from non-tribal people, the Santhali (seasonal) migrants gained an added scope for exposure to newer ideas, attitudes, and perceptions about the ideal family size, and fertility regulation. On the potential of migration as a channel for ideational change and diffusion, the following quote, though made in the context of rural–urban migration, is illuminating:

> These return migrants not only have lower fertility themselves but also spread these norms in the rural areas. They usually return with new ideas, attitudes and values acquired during their stay in the cities and the people at their native place often seek their advice and listen to them with respect (Bhatia and Sabagh 1980).

Although rural–urban migration does differ on several counts from (rural–rural) seasonal migration being analysed here, the differential in its agency role in the diffusion process between them is not of kind, but chiefly of degree. For example, it is the mobility and seasonal migration of the Santhals of Chitrihutu that paves the way for them

---

during those years had experienced a substantial poverty decline in rural areas, placing the latter only marginally worse than the former district in terms of incidence of poverty in 1993–94 (as seen in Table 6.1a). An overall slowdown in poverty reduction in rural areas of the state in the 1990s has been noted, and often been related (at least partly) to a slowdown of overall agricultural growth in the state (see Chapter 1 in Rogaly *et al.* 1999).

to keep in touch with more articulate non-tribal people of various distant places. This should help them acquire a greater degree of exposure to modern ideas, lifestyles, and aspirations, which could be instrumental in preparing them for implementing a small family norm (perhaps as a part of escalated aspirations). Thus seasonal migration, as is undertaken by the Santhals of Chitrihutu, could indeed be viewed as an important channel for enhanced social interactions, to which recent researches have assigned a significant role in facilitating fertility transition (for example, Bongaarts and Watkins 1996). This is in contrast with the non-migrating Santhals of Thupsara, who, despite their inhabitation, albeit as a subdued minority, with general caste (non-tribal) sections in the same village, seem to have less social interactions favourable to the spread of the small family norm and effective information on its methods. The role of migration (circular) mechanisms in demographic changes in home areas could be even greater, as people who migrate are often found more innovative, dynamic, and open to ideas, as compared to those who do not.[39] This, however, does not apply to people, who have virtually no other option but to undertake migration for their livelihood (as probably is the case with some groups in other Indian locations, see for example, Breman 1985, 1996). But the seasonal migration by the Santhals of Chitrihutu does not match with the scenario of acute desperation in local areas; it seems more in the nature of a response to opportunities. Therefore, what emerges is a possible range of mechanisms by which mobility and seasonal migration could play an agency role in diffusion of ideas relating to fertility control, these being undeniably easier to intuitively visualize than empirically quantify in accordance with their relative strengths. All said, it is difficult to ignore some broader regional influences beyond those of seasonal migration on the fertility behaviour of the Santhals of Chitrihutu.

[39] To illustrate: a recent comparative study in Tamil Nadu finds a lower fertility along with a higher contraceptive prevalence among the rural migrants than those of non-migrating people (Sivakumar 2001). Although this differential might have been influenced by selectivity of rural migrants by socio-economic background (for example, intensity of deprivation), the possible dynamic effects of migration on fertility transition cannot be ignored. A recent survey of literature on seasonal migration by women workers (not necessarily tribal) in various Indian locations has found a delaying of female marriage, and a lower fertility among the migrant women, both of which have been labelled as 'positive' consequences of migration (Hema Kumari and Tataji 1998).

As noted before, the infant and child mortality estimates have historically been lower in Bankura than in Birbhum district, presumably because of the wider reach and better quality of health and child immunization services in the former. While a positive association between infant/child mortality and fertility is quite common across time and space, the exact causal mechanisms behind this are not fully clear as yet. At any rate, the magnitude of (proportionate) differential in fertility is not commensurate with differentials in infant/child mortality between Bankura and both of Birbhum and West Bengal. This indicates the substantial role that factors other than child/infant mortality play. Coming down to more local level information, the Khatra block had a smaller medical infrastructure than the Nanoor block.

Furthermore, Bankura's district-level achievements in family welfare programmes (for example, couple protection rate, per cent using modern methods of contraception) have not been any better than Birbhum and West Bengal as a whole (see Table 6.1a).[40] Unfortunately, the block-level information on the functioning of family welfare programme could not be gathered. However, what has emerged from our conversations with the staff of the primary health centres catering to the study villages in both locations is suggestive of relatively better organization, enthusiasm, and motivation, among the staff responsible for implementing the family welfare programme in Khatra than in Nanoor. This relative superiority of Khatra is partly related to special efforts and programmes for the development of tribal villages, and perhaps partly because the Santhals of Chitrihutu are more strongly motivated and concerned about fertility control. As an illustration of the migrant Santhals' strong motivation for fertility control, as we were told by the Medical Officer of Hirbandh Primary Health Centre, most of them carry a stock of contraceptive pills and/or condoms with them to their destinations. Remembering the child's next date of immunization, even when the parents are away from home is, as we were told, also not rare.

[40] For example, the per cent of couples protected from undesired pregnancy was almost the same (48.1 and 49.1 respectively) in Bankura and Birbhum, and among those, 40.5 and 41.9 per cent couples were sterilized up to March 1995 (West Bengal 1995). As noted before, there is hardly any indication that Bankura district, as a whole, has achieved any particularly commendable position vis-à-vis Birbhum in terms of functioning and achievements of the family welfare programme.

We now attempt to estimate, by applying the binary logit regression technique to our household-level data, the predictive significance of several possible factors that can influence contraceptive use among eligible women. The variables and their definitions are presented in Table 6.7. It is of interest to see how far the contraceptive prevalence among the eligible women is predicted by various plausible influences, such as caste affiliation (SC or ST), landownership, education level, women's age and occupation, migration behaviour, and finally, the independent location effects. The binary logit model has been estimated for all households combined (Table 6.8) as well as separately for SC and Santhal households (Table 6.9).

Table 6.7 Description of variables and their mean values

Variable	Description of the Variable	Mean
Using con	Dummy: 1 if woman respondent is using any contraception, 0 otherwise (predicted)	
Age	Age of the respondent woman (in years)	31.27
Caste	Dummy: 1 if woman respondent belongs to ST, 0 if belongs to SC	0.65
Land	Size of land owned by the household of the respondent (in acres)	3.51
Migration Dummy:	1 when respondent's household migrates seasonally, 0 otherwise	0.24
Education Dummy:	1 if the respondent has ever been to school, 0 otherwise	0.14
Occupation	Dummy: 1 if respondent's prime occupation is not household work, 0 otherwise	0.57
Dist1	Dummy: 1 if the location belongs to Birbhum district, 0 otherwise	0.55
Dist2	Dummy: 1 if the location belongs to Purulia district, 0 otherwise	0.18

The location belonging to Bankura district is treated as the reference category for the other regional dummies, for example, Dist 1 and Dist 2.
Source: Field Survey (see text for details).

The likelihood of contraceptive use turns out to have, quite expectedly, a highly significant positive association with the age of women, with the additional (and standard) feature of diminishing marginal effects of the latter, as the coefficient on the squared age variable is negative and highly significant. The positive effect of the rising age of women on their likelihood of contraceptive use has always been highly significant in all cases, all groups together as well as for separate estimates for SC and Santhals (see Tables 6.8 and 6.9). And this relation is too obvious to deserve elaboration. In all the households combined, a larger land size appears to be associated with lower probability of contraceptive use, a finding, which is not very surprising so long as land size is not a good proxy for household income (as is largely the case for the Santhals of Chitrihutu). Conversely, a good number of landless households belonging to the SC community of Thupsara fall in the category of sterilized couples (see Table 6.1b and 6.6).

Table 6.8   Binary logit regression estimates on current contraceptive use and their marginal effects, three locations, West Bengal, 1996–8

		Dependent variable: Usingcon
Variable	Coefficient	Marginal Effects
Constant	−3.0632*	−0.5268*
	(−1.894)	(−1.896)
Age	0.4053***	0.0691***
	(4.374)	(4.266)
Age^2	−0.0052***	−0.0009***
	(−3.962)	(−3.881)
Caste	−1.6167***	−0.2781***
	(−3.538)	(−3.589)
Land	−0.1115***	−0.0192***
	(−3.095)	(−3.052)
Migration	−0.1008*	−0.1735*
	(−1.710)	(−1.691)
Education	1.6212***	0.2788***
	(3.621)	(3.421)
Occupation	−0.5569*	−0.0957*
	(−1.655)	(−1.653)
Dist 1	−4.6486***	−0.7996***
	(−6.246)	(−5.882)
Dist 2	−5.324	−0.9158***
	(5.729)***	(−6.772)
No. of observations	479	479
Log Likelihood Function	−200.85	−
Pseudo-R^2	0.45	−

*significant at 10 per cent level; **at 5 per cent level; and ***at 1 per cent level.
Source: Field Survey.

Table 6.9   Binary logit regression of current contraceptive use, ST and SC, three locations, West Bengal, 1996–8

Dependent variable: Using con

Variable	Scheduled Caste		Santhals	
	Coefficients	Marginal Effects	Coefficients	Marginal Effects
Constant	−11.6757***	−2.6442*	−7.6841***	−1.3837***
	(−3.915)	(−1.832)	(−3.884)	(−4.097)
Age	0.6577***	0.1490*	0.2499***	0.0450**
	(3.682)	(1.802)	(2.300)	(2.328)
Age^2	−0.0089***	−0.0020*	−0.0028**	−0.0005
	(−3.438)	(−1.770)	(−1.908)	(−1.925)
Land	−0.1024	−0.0232	−0.0412	−0.0074
	(−0.691)	(−0.655)	(−1.323)	(−1.326)
Migration	11.9348	2.7029	1.8892***	0.3402***
	(0.088)	(0.085)	(5.044)	(5.173)
Education	−0.1310	−0.0297	4.2266***	0.7611***
	(−0.168)	(−0.167)	(7.464)	(6.982)
Occupation	−0.8764**	−0.1984	0.6865	0.1236
	(−2.094)	(−1.458)	(1.585)	(1.607)
Log Likelihood Function	−94.9467	–	−126.3155	–
Pseudo-R^2	0.35	–	0.33	–
Sample size	168	168	311	311

*Significant at 10 per cent level; **at 5 per cent level; and ***at 1 per cent level.
Source: Field Survey.

The school attendance of women appears, quite expectedly in accordance with recent literature on fertility determinants, to enhance the likelihood of contraceptive use. This relationship derives largely from the fact that the extent of school attendance is relatively larger among both the SC community of Thupasara and Santhals of Chitrihutu, who are far ahead in terms of sterilization/contraception as compared to the least literate group, namely the Santhals of Thupsara. It is interesting that the coefficient on education turns out to be insignificant in the separate estimation involving the SC community, while it is significantly positive for Santhals (Table 6.9). This seems consistent with the point mentioned earlier, namely that the SC community in Thupsara has undergone large-scale sterilization in the wake of mass mobilization activities and pro-poor participatory politics of ruling Left parties, and a related escalation of aspirations. In fact, these effects appear to have overwhelmed the effects of a steady, though not very rapid spread of female education, female empowerment and related mechanisms, which are often accorded importance in contemporary literature on this issue.

The finding that household work is the prime occupation of women is associated with a greater likelihood of contraceptive use, though only marginally significant (at 10 per cent level), is of interest. This estimated relationship, with a woman's major work hours spent on domestic chores, should imply her limited role in productive activities, restricting her economic value and autonomy, which is often thought favourable to fertility control and contraception. On the other hand, this hypothesis loses relevance in a situation where a decision for sterilization is imposed on the housewife by her husband, or the head of the family, or at best taken by mutual consensus. Indeed, the finding has been largely shaped by a large number of SC women who do not work much outside home but are sterilized, and conversely by a large majority of Santhali women of Thupsara who take part in productive work but do not use any contraceptive method. This is reaffirmed by a more significant negative coefficient on occupation when housework is assigned zero in a separate regression for SC, and by a positive coefficient among the Santhali women with slightly lower than borderline significance level (Table 6.9). In any case, all this seems to reaffirm that female work-participation and associated female autonomy alone is not sufficient to ensure a lower fertility or greater contraception. For this to happen, the supplementary influences, such as female education, scope for diffusion of ideas, and wider accessibility of control methods seem necessary. Likewise, the expected positive causality between migration propensity and probability of contraceptive use has not been confirmed largely because of the presence of a large number of sterilized SC women of Thupsara, who do not migrate at all. A negative relationship, though only at the borderline significance level, between migration and contraceptive use has partly been contributed by the presence of the Santhali women of Purulia hamlet from where relatively few households migrated seasonally.

However, a positive link of seasonal migration with contraceptive use strongly reaffirmed in a highly significant negative coefficient of contraceptive use on both the regional dummies (Dist1 and Dist2), with Chitrihutu being treated as the reference category. Indeed, the coefficient on the migration variable is significantly positive in a separate estimation for Santhals, but not for the SC community (see Table 6.9). All this, in conformity with our earlier conclusion, shows that seasonal migration has a significant predictive power for contraceptive use. Indeed a large part of the explanation for why the Santhals of Chitrihutu have had comparatively lower fertility, lower mortality, and a higher education level seems to lie in their long-standing tradition of seasonal migration and its gradual and accumulated diffusion (and related) effects.

Discussion and Concluding Remarks

This chapter has analysed evidence of differential patterns of fertility behaviour and control among a single tribe, the Santhals, between two contrasting locations in West Bengal. In one location, they are a small ethnic minority and hence relatively subservient amidst non-tribal mainstream society, and they appear to stand even behind their closest non-tribal counterparts (SC) in terms of fertility regulation (mostly female sterilization), and related levels of awareness and aspirations. In the other location, where they live more independently in exclusive tribal areas, with a tradition of migrating out seasonally to dynamic agricultural pockets for employment and income, they appear to be far advanced on those counts. The relative disadvantage of the Santhals' minority existence in the non-tribal location lies, not in the economic sphere as such, but in relative seclusion from newer ideas, information, and aspirations, which are more infused in the SC community by greater contact and interactions with higher caste society and political mobilization activities.[41] But this tribal disadvantage of 'isolation' is offset by diffusion and similar dynamic effects of seasonal

[41] The difficulty of communicating with relatively introvert Santhals was mentioned to us by local political cadres and family planning personnel alike. As a consequence, there could be greater ideational barriers to acceptance of family planning, such as misconceptions and fear about control methods. However, the reason why mass mobilization activities of dominant political parties did not encompass Santhali and SC people equally is perhaps related to the tiny size of the former (only about 2 per cent of the total; see Table 6.1b), which presumably make them seen unimportant from the standpoint of electoral politics. This is, of course, one of the several outstanding sources of special disadvantages suffered globally by minority communities, even in otherwise vibrant and apparently well-functioning democratic polities (Bhengra *et al.* 1998).

migration (via, for example, enhanced social interactions and empowerment), as illustrated by much better performance in demographic transition (that is, lower levels of fertility and child mortality) among the Santhals in exclusive tribal areas. A related implication of this comparative finding seems to be that greater work participation and autonomy of females that characterize Santhals generally as a tribe does not translate automatically into fertility transition, unless newer ideas, information, and aspirations give them directions.

Migration, even when beneficial in forms of enhanced income or survival or livelihood, is hardly ever viewed as costless. Since the cost of migration is often considerably psychological, hypothetical, and beyond pecuniary measurements, the dominant verdict on the impact of 'seasonal migration' continues to be of 'on the one hand, on the other hand' type (for example, Joshi, no date; Rogaly et al. 2001; Rani and Shylendra 2001). Against this uncertainty, the present study has succeeded in highlighting its brighter side with a special reference to its role in fertility transition, thereby taking (albeit indirectly) an issue with any generalized conclusion that portrays seasonal migration essentially as a 'survival' response to crisis situation.

This said, it is difficult to hide the tentativeness of the conclusion drawn from the less than fully comprehensive nature of the evidence examined. Indeed, the complexity of factors and forces involved in disentangling a relative (and independent) impact of seasonal migration on the demographic behaviour, the net of mediating influences—regional, social, and developmental—is probably formidable. For example, possible influences of differentials in broader regional features (for example, lower infant/child mortality in Bankura or differentials in performance, quality of health and family planning machinery between these two locations and relatedly, differential communication network) on fertility behaviour and control seem pertinent considerations. Still, all this seems likely to be, at best, supplementary forces to the broader fundamental changes initiated by direct and indirect effects of seasonal migration. The detailed role that seasonal migration is hypothesized to have played in fertility transition in Chitrihutu, is indeed broader than just the (involuntary) fertility suppressing-effect that sex-selective migration (with attendant forced spousal separation) is often reported to produce globally. Certainly, the present study calls for further and more focused research on unravelling the degrees and exact mechanisms by which seasonal mobility facilitates diffusion of ideational changes and similar dynamic forces in sending areas.

Despite potential difficulties of generalizing on such local level evidence, all possible and practical encouragement to mobility and seasonal migration, particularly from backward pockets, does emerge as a policy prescription from the present study. Those include expansion of the transport and communications network and greater flexibility of school enrolment norms and school calendar as well as support for women, children and elderly, who generally stay back home. These suggested measures should, by no means, be construed to constitute an alternative, either to the broader (long-term) programmes of balanced regional development or to the development of the reproductive health infrastructure and family welfare programmes.

7

Conclusion

There can be no denying that the literature on Indian tribes, developed mostly by anthropologists over a fairly long period, is already quite voluminous. But the necessity for further research on them, especially from diverse angles, is equally indisputable. Even after the substantial accumulation of tribal literature, one is often haunted by confusion and 'so what' type questions, that are certainly far away from any clear 'conclusion'. This is not entirely surprising in view of the growing complexities involved in the dynamics of India's economy, society, politics, and culture. But this has been partly because the Indian anthropological discourse on tribes has developed its own direction, orientation, and predilections that have prevented it from under-standing the 'tribes' from diverse angles. For example, while some aspects of tribal demographic behaviour are investigated by micro-level anthropological research, these findings generally appear peripheral to the central concerns of anthropology, and are rarely in accord with notions and methods developed by the scientific discipline of 'demography'. There are distinct traditions of so-called 'anthropological demography' and 'minority demography' in the global forum, but such relatively new (inter-disciplinary) approaches have hardly made their presence felt as yet in the Indian literature on tribes. The present monograph with its focus on general (and hence common) patterns of tribal demographic phenomena at an aggregate level has posed a departure from typical anthropological approach.

A demographic study by nature and, of course, by its potential is essentially multidisciplinary. Understanding and explaining demographic processes and phenomena often need to go beyond demographic tools and measurements, and must encompass other domains of human life, like economics, sociology, anthropology, sociology, and even biology. Indeed, the major motivation of this book has been to examine, from the standpoint of overall experiences of Indian tribes, the robustness of the currently prominent postulate that assigns a key role to 'culture' in shaping demographic behaviour and outcomes in a population. More specifically, it seeks to examine whether distinctive tribal features—sociocultural, lifestyle-related, and others—and their trends, as mostly chronicled by anthropologists, are reflected, in conformity with relationships postulated in the light of experiences of the general population, in tribal demographic behaviour and trends. Thus, while an air of uncertainty over the distinction between tribes and castes has always remained prominent in the existing literature, our present attempt at unfolding general demographic patterns of tribes and their broad sociocultural underpinnings (vis-à-vis non-tribal counterparts) is a good opportunity to sharpen the notion of 'tribes'.

The book set out by examining tribal demographic phenomena and their changes in a comparative perspective over a long historical time frame beginning roughly from the start of census operations around the 1870s. Despite possible inaccuracies, census information can be quite useful, particularly for aggregative and comparative insights (as discussed in Chapter 1). For example, the pattern of growth of the aggregate tribal population has been historically not very different from that of the general population, except for specific periods of epidemics and famines, which have had a possibly differential mortality impact. In relatively favourable periods in history, the tribal population seem to have experienced even larger growth than the general population (for example, 1881–91, 1901–11).

In the post-Independence period, the recorded rate of growth of the aggregate tribal population (after preparing official ST and SC lists) has almost always been higher than that of the general population. This was partly related to a widening recognition of newer tribes, coupled with a tendency for infiltration into the tribal enumeration category, especially in some regions (that is, southern and western states) in the early decades after Independence. But the 'pre-transition rises' of fertility, particularly among the lately modernized groups almost certainly played a part. However, the growth of the tribal population, like the general population, did slow down—albeit moderately—in the 1981–91 decade, possibly heralding the onset of demographic transition. Moreover, the regional distribution of the tribal population has remained broadly unaltered over a long period, with central India having the highest tribal concentration, followed by eastern, western, and southern states (in that order). However, a declining trend in the share of eastern states (Orissa and Bihar in particular) in the country's aggregate tribal population over the post-Independence period is indeed striking. This is almost certainly related to the slower growth of tribal population in these states, which, in turn, reflects their relative vulnerability, deprivation, and movements, particularly over the recent decades. This said, the working of so-called 'homeostatic' mechanisms, keeping long-term growth low or balanced with non-human resources can hardly be denied, as illustrated by findings on tribal demographic behaviour (for example, fertility, mortality), both past and contemporary, particularly in our detailed study of Jharkhand's tribal demography (in Chapter 5).

For instance, tribal populations have always had a greater balance in sex ratio than found among non-tribal groups. Given that the sex ratio is a fairly good (overall) index of gender inequities and discrimination in a society, the more balanced sex ratio in the tribal population is indicative of more balanced gender relations and less discrimination as compared to non-tribal groups. This is substantially congruous with anecdotal, ethnographical, and anthropological evidence that has piled up over more than a century. No less importantly, the relatively balanced gender relations in the tribal population are largely an intrinsic sociocultural feature, rather than necessarily an outcome of greater labour force participation and higher 'economic worth' of tribal women. It seems more of a gender-balanced sociocultural structure and values of a community that is supportive of and consistent with greater gender equality in the division of labour, than the other way round.

First, despite regional and local-level diversities, the ST and SC groups at aggregate (all-India) level do not appear very differently stationed, and have a similar socio-economic footing in terms of such hardcore indicators as income, consumption, asset possessions, poverty, occupation, although they have vastly different sex ratios. While this is not to deny the somewhat famine-like situation of acute poverty, mass hunger/under-nutrition gripping specific tribal pockets (for example, Kalahandi region in Orissa), such a local-level scenario is attributable, more to a specific complexity of regional circumstances than to general forces influencing the overall tribal population at the country-level. For example, the aggregate tribal population appear to own more land per household than the SC counterparts do on the whole; or the former are, according to large-scale sample survey results not considerably more inflicted by 'income-poverty'. However, on the matter of two key provisions, namely health and education, tribals, overall, do appear most deprived, and even distinctly worse than the aggregate SC population.

Considering the overall level of household poverty, the need for female-participation in the labour force and income-earning activities should not, thus, differ greatly between ST and SC communities. Therefore, the higher degree of work participation of tribal females, often thought instrumental for their higher status, does not result essentially from their special economic circumstances; it cannot be ignored that a tribal cultural ideology and values is supportive of a more equal gender division of labour. Conversely, 'economic determinism' of such cultural features as gender relations is not adequate for explaining the much lower degree of labour-force participation of SC females than their tribal counterparts, when both share a very similar economic footing (for example, incidence of poverty, asset ownership, unemployment), and sometimes even the same geophysical setting.

A substantial body of evidence in the Indian subcontinent suggests that the expansion of basic education (especially of females) plays an important role in the betterment of gender relations generally, and in improving the status and autonomy of women in particular. But strikingly, recent researches show that the (intrinsic) sociocultural setting of stark patriarchy (as observed in much of northern India) restricts (or even impedes) such agency effects of expanding female education. The intrinsic nature of sociocultural elements involved in gender relations is also attested to the fact that relatively high female status and autonomy has almost always been reported in tribal communities, even with extremely low levels of female education or even before notions of any formal education entered their mindsets. It is not far-fetched to postulate that a clue to the origin of south India's sociocultural background of greater gender equality and female autonomy lies in the (comparatively) lingering dominance and infusion of 'tribal' society and culture in the history of the region (since the pre-Dravidian era). Ironically, while questions of how fast and how best Indian tribes could be brought within the 'mainstream' has always been a major concern, a large chunk of the 'mainstream' (of north and northwestern states) could well benefit from lessons available on gender relations in tribal society.

This said, the functional value of school education in empowering and enlightening women, who play a significant agency role in shaping demographic outcomes and changes, cannot be undermined. For example, if we continue to go by the sex ratio as a rough index of gender relations, its long-term trend does point to a temporal erosion of the traditional tribal feature of balanced gender relations, an erosion that has occurred rather rapidly over recent decades. As we have seen in the context of the historical past, the high female–male ratio in the tribal population was corroborated by several sociocultural features, broadly akin to higher gender equity, female status, and autonomy. For instance, tribal females' nuptial features in the past—namely, marrying relatively late and only after 'maturity' and mostly on a self-chosen (consent) basis, freedom to divorce and remarry, the comparatively large proportion of celibates—are reasonable pointers to the relatively high status and autonomy that tribal women had enjoyed historically. This, as well as the implied absence of 'son preference', in turn, seems to have had its reflection, in line with the fertility differential between sociocultural settings with different degrees of patriarchy and female autonomy, in a comparatively low tribal fertility in the historical past. This could be achieved because of sociocultural practices like a longer duration of breastfeeding and child spacing, postpartum taboos, and the use of traditional indigenous abortion and contraceptive methods. As recent researches suggest, a large chunk of historical populations across the globe had evolved various institutional and cultural mechanisms to keep a long-term check on childbearing,[1] but their basis and efficacy seem to have called for reasonable level of female autonomy and equity in gender relations. Similarly, because of several traditional sociocultural features, lifestyle patterns and practices (for example, prolonged breastfeeding and relatively long child-spacing together with greater intimacy and adaptability with the natural environment), India's overall tribal mortality, particularly in infancy and childhood years, seems to have been historically lower than that of their non-tribal counterparts. While this may sound startling, especially in relation to the current commonplace situation being almost the opposite, it evokes little surprise when placed along with similar findings for tribes in parts of sub-Saharan Africa and even elsewhere in the world (Wirsing 1985). Indeed, such traditional features of tribal demographic behaviour have continued as an aggregate baseline in contemporary times too,

[1] See for example, Cleland 2001; Wilson and Airey 1999; Davis 1986.

although, owing to the mounting complexities of tribal existence as well as the substantial accumulation of evidence over time, the picture appears more complicated and varied. For example, availability of modern medicines/treatment for secondary sterility and sexually transmitted diseases, together with negative effects on traditional practices such as reduction of breastfeeding duration, indigenous contraceptive methods, and sexual abstinence might have often led to (pre-transition) rises in tribal fertility. Moreover, features of tribal societies, akin in some respects to European marriage patterns, has been replaced, in varying pace across tribes and regions, by mainstream Hindu practices, like early marriage via parental negotiations with dowry as a prerequisite. Such lowering of the female marriage age has, in many cases (especially where modern family planning programmes are not effective), pushed up tribal fertility or impeded its transition in the recent past. On the other hand, there are locations where tribal people have experienced an even larger fertility decline compared to their counterparts, as they could be more easily brought under mass sterilization programmes by cash incentives, informal coercion, or sometimes even because of their greater affinity and acceptability of fertility control.

Regarding mortality, the past (relative) superiority of the aggregate tribal population, particularly in infancy and childhood years, though it has continued at an aggregate level till recently, has been eroded or reversed in the recent past. This reflects chiefly a growing relative deprivation and vulnerability in livelihood and well-being, including modern health care facilities. In fact, in some regions such as Bihar, Orissa, and Madhya Pradesh, the tribal population have experienced some (occasional) increases in mortality levels in the recent past. Although the overall trend of contemporary mortality levels (that is, infant and child mortality, maternal and adult male death rates) for the aggregate tribal population is, like those of non-tribal groups, one of decline, the pace and magnitude of which are clearly lower for tribals. This would seem ironical if tribes used to experience, as India's overall tribal population arguably did, a relative superiority in mortality (vis-à-vis non-tribal groups) in the historical past, when modern medical science was rudimentary, and adaptability to the natural environment, lifestyle, and other related factors were comparatively important in shaping mortality. The gradual erosion and even reversal in more recent periods, of tribal mortality advantages clearly mean that tribals have been lagging behind non-tribal population groups in experiencing contemporary mortality improvements. This, in fact, reaffirms the recent accentuation of their relative deprivation in nutrition and health-care facilities, which is very possibly linked to their growing relative disadvantage of insecurity of livelihood caused by encroachment, exploitation, and displacement.

This said, tribal people, historically, have been showing remarkable resilience to withstand and overcome various adversities. For example, tribals, when faced with distress and disruptions due to external factors, have often resorted to mobility and migration relatively readily. While mobility and migration have frequently been a sheer survival response, it is hard to deny a relative flexibility and liberalism of the tribal sociocultural structure and organization that facilitates this process. For instance, our case study of the Santhals in parts of West Bengal has illustrated the great potential that tribal people have—via various dynamic and diffusion effects of seasonal migration and mobility of families—to improve their material and social standing, and in making substantial advancement in demographic transition. As a corollary, balanced gender relations and greater female autonomy, as is generally observed among tribal communities, would not automatically be conducive towards a fertility transition unless newer ideas, attitudes, and information regarding fertility control and methods are percolated among them.

In this context, no less worrying than the growing relative deprivation and vulnerability among the aggregate tribal population, is the contemporary reversal of traditional gender equities among them. The declining female–male ratio, especially over the last few decades in the tribal population, is a broad indication of the shift of gender relations against females. There is mounting evidence of growing relative disadvantages that tribal females have been facing along with contemporary processes of economic expansion and integration by, for example, the breakdown of the traditional forest-based tribal economy and environment, of shifting cultivation, as well as growing displacement and forced migration. Apart from anti-female biases that change production organization and patterns affecting tribal economy and resource bases, direct evidence of female discrimination at the household level (that is, sex-differential in mortality, nutritional status, medical attention) seems to be surfacing in tribal communities—of course, in varying pace across locations. This is a manifestation of the trend among tribal people to enter the mainstream (Hindu) sociocultural fold. While such an acculturation process and its anti-female implications for tribal gender relations have drawn the attention of researchers earlier, our present demographic study reaffirms these trends in terms of a more systematic and focused evaluation of available statistical evidence at a more general, aggregative level. Indeed, it is increasingly evident that the gender discrimination and biases of the general population have been intensified because of the growing (felt) compulsion of family size limitation without compromising on an intense 'son preference'. There are growing indications that even the traditional south Indian setting of a lesser degree of patriarchy and greater gender equalities is currently being eroded by the overpowering influence of anti-female social biases and practices. Ironically, it is the long-standing gender equity in tribal and indigenous communities of India that could perhaps come to the rescue of the mainstream society and culture marked by stark gender biases, intense 'son preference', even their growing pervasiveness.

Bibliography

Afonja, S. (1990), 'Changing Pattern of Gender Stratification in West Africa', in Tinker (ed.), *Women and World Development* (New York: Oxford University Press).

Agarwal, B. (1994), *A Field of One's Own: Gender and Land Rights in South Asia* (Cambridge: Cambridge University Press).

———— (1990), 'Tribal Matriliny in Transition: Changing Gender, Production, and Property Relations in North-East India', World Employment Programme Research Working Paper, WEP 10/WP 50, International Labour Office, Geneva.

———— (1985), 'Work Participation of Rural Women in Third World', *Economic and Political Weekly*, 20(51–2): A155–A164.

Agarwal, B.C. (1977), 'Interaction Between Tribes and non-Tribes', in S.C. Dube (ed.), *Tribal Heritage of India*, vol. 1 (New Delhi: Vikas Publishing House).

Agarwal, H.N. (1967), 'Reproductive Life of Onge Women', *Vanyajati*, July: 139–49.

Agarwala, S.N. (1972), *India's Population Problem* (Bombay: Tata McGraw-Hill).

———— (1966), 'Raising the Marriage Age for Women: A Means to Lower the Birth Rate', *Economic and Political Weekly*, No. 1: 797–98.

Agnihotri, S. (2003), 'Survival of the Girl Child: Tunnelling Out the Chakravyuha', *Economic and Political Weekly*, 38(41): 4351–61.

———— (2000), *Sex Ratio Patterns in the Indian Population: A Fresh Exploration* (New Delhi: Sage Publications).

———— (1999), 'Inferring Gender Bias From Mortality Data: A Discussion Note', *Journal of Development Studies*, 35(4): 175–200.

———— (1996), 'Juvenile Sex Ratios in India: A Disaggregated Analysis', *Economic and Political Weekly*, 31(52).

———— (1995), 'Missing Females: A Disaggregative Analysis', *Economic and Political Weekly*, 30(19): 2074–84.

Anthony, T.V. (1992), 'The Family Planning Programme: Lessons from Tamil Nadu's Experience', Paper presented at the Symposium on India's Development in the 1990s (New Delhi: Centre for Policy Research).

Arnold, F., M.K. Choe and T.K. Roy (1996), 'Son Preferences, the Family Building Process, and Child Mortality In India', East-West Centre Working Papers Population Series No. 85.

Ashraf, K. (1962), *Tribal People of West Pakistan: A Demographic Study of Selected Population* (Peshawar: Peshawar University).

Bailey, F.G. (1961), '"Tribe" and "Caste" in India', *Contributions to Indian Sociology*, vol. 5.

Bagchi, T. (1994), *Profile of Some Indian Tribes* (Calcutta: Punthi Pustak).

Bajkhaif, Mohammed Omes and K. Mahadevan (1993), *Infant Mortality of Indian Muslims: Determinants and Implications* (Delhi: B.R. Publications).

Bandyopadhyay, M.(1999), 'Demographic Consequences of Non-Tribal Incursion in Chotanagpur Region during Colonial Period (1850–1950)', *Social Change* 29: 3 and 4.

Banerjee, D. (1973), 'Health Behaviour of Rural Populations', *Economic and Political Weekly*, December 22.

Banerjee, Sumanta (1979), *Family Planning Communication: A Critique of the Indian Programme* (New Delhi: Radiant Publishers).

Bang, A., M.H. Reddy, and M.D. Deshmukh (2002), 'Child Mortality in Maharashtra', *Economic and Political Weekly*, 37(49), December 7.

Bardhan, P. (1874), 'On Life and Death Questions', *Economic and Political Weekly*, Special Number.

Basu, A.M. and S. Amin (2000), 'Conditioning Factors for Fertility Decline in Bengal: History, Language Identity, and Openness to Innovations', *Population and Development Review*, 26(4).

Basu, A.M. (2002), 'Why Does Education Lead to Lower Fertility? A Critical Review of Some of the Possibilities', *World Development*, 30(10): 1779–90.

————— (1999), 'Fertility Decline and Increasing Gender Imbalance in India, Including a Possible South Indian Turnaround', *Development and Change*, 30: 237–63.

————— (1992), *Culture, the Status of Women and Demographic Behaviour* (Oxford: Clarendon Press).

————— (1991), 'Demand and Its Socio Cultural Context', in Satia, J.K., and S.J. Jejeebhoy (eds), *The Demographic Challenge: A Study of Four Large Indian States* (Bombay: Oxford University Press).

————— (1990), 'Anthropological Approach to Tribal Health', in Bose, A., T. Nongbri, and N. Kumar (eds), *Tribal Demography and Development in Northeast India*.

————— (1989a), 'Culture, the Status of Women in North & South India', in Singh, S.N., M.K. Premi, P.S. Bhatia (eds), *Population Transition in India*, 2 volume (Delhi: B.R. Publishing Corporation).

————— (1989b), 'Is Discrimination in Food Really Necessary for Explaining Sex Differentials in Childhood Mortality?', *Population Studies*, 43(2).

————— (1986), 'Birth Control by Assetless Workers in Kerala: The Possibility of Poverty-Induced Fertility Transition', *Development and Change*, 17(2).

Basu, A.M. (1978), 'Kota Women of Nilgiri Hills', in *Tribal Women in India* (Calcutta: Indian Anthropological Society).

Basu, A., S.K. Roy, B. Mukherjee, P. Bharati, R. Gupta, and P. Mazumdar (1986), 'Sex Bias in Intra-household Food Distribution: Roles of Ethnicity and Socio-economic Charactersitics', *Current Anthropology*, 27(5): 536–39.

Basu, M.P. (1967), 'A Demographic Profile of Irula', *Bulletin of Anthropological Survey of India*, 16, 267–89.

Basu, S.K. (ed.) (1994), *Tribal Health in India* (Delhi: Manak Publications Private Limited).

————— (1994a), 'The State-of-the-Art-Tribal Health in India', in Basu (1994b).

————— (1994b), *Tribal Health in India* (Delhi: Manak Publications Private Limited).

————— and G. Kshatriya (1997), 'Fertility and Mortality Trends in the Kharia Tribals of Orissa', *Social Change*, 27(1/2).

————— and G. Kshatriya (1989), 'Fertility and Mortality Trends in Tribal Populations of Bastar District, Madhya Pradesh', *Biology and Society*, 6: 100–12.

Bates, C. (1988), 'Congress and Tribals', in Sheppardson, M.and C. Simmons (eds) (1988).

Bates, C. and M. Carter (1992), 'Tribal Migration in India and Beyond', in Prakash, G. (ed.) (1992), *The World of Rural Labourer in Colonial India* (New Delhi: Oxford University Press).

Benjamin, A., B. Cowarn, H.N. Grewal, and K.K. Wadhera (1988), 'Fertility and Contraception Patterns in Tribal Areas of Madhya Pradesh', *Health and Population*, 11(4): 171–83.

Bennette, L. (1992), 'Women Poverty and Productivity in India', EDI Seminar Paper No. 43, The World Bank.

Bentley, G.R., T. Goldberg, and G. Jasienska (1993), 'The Fertility of Agricultural and Non-Agricultural Traditional Societies', *Population Studies*, 47(13).

Berhman, S.J., L. Corsa, and R. Freedman (eds) (1969), *Fertility and Family Planning: A World View* (University of Michigan).

Berreman, G.D. (1993), 'Sanskritization as Female Oppression in India', in: Miller B.D. (ed.) (1993).

————— (1977), 'Demography, Domestic Economy and Change in Western Himalayas', *Eastern Anthropologist*, 30(2): 157–92.

Béteille, André (1998), 'The Idea of Indigenous People', *Current Anthropology*, 39(2): 187–93.

————— (1992), *Society and Politics in India: Essays in a Comparative Perspective* (New Delhi: Oxford University Press).

————— (1986), 'The Concept of Tribe with Special Reference to India', *European Journal of Sociology*, 27: 297–318.

Béteille, André (1974), *Six Essays in Comparative Sociology* (New Delhi: Oxford University Press).

Bhagat, R.B. and S. Unisa (1991), 'Religion, Caste/Tribe and Marriage of Females in India: A Study based on Recent Census Data', *Journal of Family Welfare*, 37(1).

Bhagwan, S. (1997), 'Bada Madia: A Population Crisis', *Tribal Research Bulletin*, 19(1).

Bhat, C., L.N. Kadekar, and K.C. Rao (eds) (1993), *Sociology of Development and Change* (New Delhi: Orient Longman).

Bhat, P.N. Mari, S. Preston, and T. Dyson (1984), *Vital Rates in India 1961–81* (Washington DC: National Academy Press).

Bhat, P.N. Mari (2002a), 'Maternal Mortality in India: An Update', *Studies in Family Planning*, 33(3): 227–36.

———— (2002b), 'Returning a Favour: Changing Relationship between Female Education and Family Size in India', *World Development*, 30(10): 1791–1803.

———— and S. Halli (1999), 'Demography of Brideprice and Dowry: Causes and Consequences of the Indian Marriage Squeeze', *Population Studies*, 53(2): 129–48.

———— (1998a), 'Demographic Estimates for Post-Independence India: A New Integration', *Demography India*, 27(1).

———— (1998b), 'Emerging Regional Differences in Fertility in India: Causes and Correlations', in Martine *et al.* (eds) (1998).

———— (1989), 'Mortality and Fertility in India, 1881–1980', in Dyson, T. (ed.) (1989), *India: Historical Demography* (London: Curzon Press), pp. 73–118.

Bhatia, J.C. and G. Sabagh (1980), 'Migration and Fertility in India', *Demography India*, 9(1&2).

Bhattacharjee, P.J. and G.N. Shastri (1976), *Population in India: A Study of Inter-State Variations* (New Delhi: Vikas Publishing House).

Bhengra, C.R., C.R. Bijoy, and S. Liithui (1998), *The Adivasis of India* (London: Minority Rights Group International).

Birdsall, N. and S.W. Sinding (2001), 'How and Why Population Matters: New Findings, New Issues', in Birdsall, N., A.C. Kelley, and S.W. Sinding (eds), *Population Matters* (Oxford: Oxford University Press).

Bittles, A.H. and D.F. Roberts (1992), *Minority Populations: Genetics, Demography and Health* (London: Macmillan).

Bleie, T. (1987), 'Gender Relations Among Oraons in Bangladesh', *Economic and Political Weekly*.

Bloch, F., V. Rao, and S. Dasai (2004), 'Marriage celebrations as conspicuous consumptions: Signalling social status in rural India', *Journal of Human Resources*, 39(3).

Boban, Jose K. (1998), *Tribal Ethnomedicine: Continuity and Change* (New Delhi: APH Publishing Corporation).

Bokil, M. (2002), 'De-notified and Nomadic Tribes. A Perspective', *Economic and Political Weekly*, 12 January.

Bongaarts, J. and S.C. Watkins (1996), 'Social Interactions and Contemporary Fertility Transition', *Population and Development Review*, 22(4): 639–82.

Bose, Ashish (1988), *From Popualtion to People*, vol. 2 (New Delhi: B.R.Publishing Corporation), Chapter 14.

———— (ed.) (1967), *Patterns of Population Change in India 1951–61* (Bombay: Allied Publishers).

———— (1960), *India's Basic Demographic Statistics* (New Delhi: B.R. Publishing Corporation).

————, U.P. Sinha, and R.P. Tyagi (eds) (1990), 'Demography of Tribal Development' (New Delhi: B.R. Publishing Corporation).

————, T. Nongbri, and N. Kumar (eds) (1990), *Tribal Demography and Development in Northeast India* (New Delhi: B.R. Publishing Corporation).

Bose, N.K. (1975), *The Structure of Hindu Society*, Translated from Bengali by André Beteille (New York: Orient Longman).

———— (1941), 'The Hindu Method of Tribal Absorption', *Science and Culture*, VII: 188–94.

Boserup, E. (1970), *Women's Role in Economic Development* (London: George Allen and Unwin).

Bredie, J.W.B. and G.K. Beeharry (1998), 'School Enrolment Decline in Sub-Saharan Africa: Beyond the Supply Constraint', World Bank Discussion Paper No. 395.

Breman, Jan (1996), *Footloose Labour: Working in India's Informal Economy* (Cambridge: Cambridge University Press).

———— (1985), *Of Peasants, Migrants, and Paupers: Rural Labour Circulation and Capitalist Production in West India* (New Delhi: Oxford University Press.

Bulatao, A. Rodolf and Casterline B. John (2001), *Global Fertility Transition, Population and Development Review*, A Supplement to volume 27, 2001 (New York: Population Council).

Cain, Mead (1982), 'Perspectives on Family and Fertility in Developing Countries', *Population Studies*, 38(2).

Caldwell, John (2001), 'Globalization of Fertility Behaviour', in Bulatao and Casterline (eds) (2001).

———— (1999), 'The Bangladesh Fertility Decline: An Interpretation', *Population and Development Review*, 25(1).

———— (1980), 'Mass Education as a Determinant of the Timing of Fertility Decline', *Population and Development Review*, 6(3): 225–55.

———— (1978), 'A Theory of Fertility: From High Plateau to Destabilization', *Population and Development Review*, 4(4).

———— and B.J. Caldwell (2003), 'Pre-transitional Population Control and Equilibrium', *Population Studies*, 57(2): 198–215.

————, P.H. Reddy and Pat Caldwell (1988), *The Causes of Demographic Change* (Madison: University of Wisconsin Press).

Carr-Saunders, A.M. (1922), *The Population Problem* (Oxford: Clarendon Press).

Cassen, I.R.M. (1978), *India: Population, Economy, Society* (London: Macmillan Press Ltd).

Central Statistical Organization (1998), *Selected Socio-economic Statistics*, Department of Statistics and Programme Implementation, Ministry of Planning and Programme Implementation, India, 1998.

CSO (1991), *Estimates of State Domestic Product and Gross Fixed Capital Formation* (New Delhi: Govt. of India Press).

Chakrabarti, A. and N. Banerjea (2000), 'Primary Education in Himachal Pradesh: A Case Study of Kinnaur District', *Journal of Educational Planning and Administration*, 14(4).

Chakrabarty, G. (1998), 'Scheduled Castes and Tribes in Rural India: Their Income, Education, and Health Status', *Margin*, 30(4).

————— and P.K. Ghosh (2000), *Human Development Profile of Scheduled Castes and Scheduled Tribes in Rural India: A Benchmark Survey*, Report No. 4 (New Delhi: National Council of Applied Economic Research).

Chakravorty, B. and C.R. Malakar (1969), 'Demographic Data: An Imperative Need for the Welfare of the Tribal Population in India—A Pilot Study of the Totos in Totopara, West Bengal', in Govt. of West Bengal, Bureau of Applied Economics and Statistics (ed.) (1969), *Demographic Problems of Eastern India*, Calcutta.

Chand, S.K (1994), 'Tribal Population and Development in Bihar', in Sinha and Sinha (1994).

Chatterjee, B. (1998), 'Poverty in West Bengal: What we have Learnt', *Economic and Political Weekly*, 33(47&48): 3003–18.

Chatterjee, P., P.K. Bose, and R. Samaddar (1998), 'Discipline and Development', in Chatterjee, P. (1998) (ed.), *The Present History of West Bengal: Essays in Political Criticism* (New Delhi: Oxford University Press).

Chandrasekhar, S. (1972), *Infant Mortality, Population Growth and Family Planning in India* (Chapel Hill: University of North Carolina Press).

Chaudhuri, A. (1998), 'Seasonal Migration—A Technique for Self-Preservation by the Rural Poor: A Case Study in West Bengal', *Demography India*, 27(2).

Chaudhuri, Buddhadeb (ed.) (1992), *Tribal Trnasformation in India*, Volume III (New Delhi: Inter-India Publications).

————— (1985), *Tribal Health: Socio-Cultural Dimensions* (New Delhi: Inter-India Publications).

Chauhan, A. (1996), 'The Status of Tribal Women in India', in *Trends in Social Science Research*, 3(2).

Chauhan, B.R. (1978), 'Tribalization', in Vyas *et al.*

————— (1967), *A Rajasthan Village*, Udaipur, MLV Tribal Research Institute (Govt. of Rajasthan).

Chetlapalli *et al.* (1991), 'Estimates of Fertility and Mortality in Kutia Kondhs of Phulbani District, Orissa', *Journal of Human Ecology*, 2(1): 177–20.

Choudhury, K. (2001), 'State Policy Towards Educational Development of STs in India: The Human Rights Perspective', *Journal of Educational Planning and Administration*, 15(1).

Choudhury, M. (1984), 'Sex Bias in Child Nutrition', *Social Change*, 13(3), 50–2.

Choudhury, N.C. (1978), 'Womenhood in Tribal India', in *Tribal Women in India* (Calcutta: Indian Anthropological Society).

Choudhury, R.P. (1988), 'Child Mortality Determinants among Two Tribes of Rajmahal Hill (Bihar)', *Indian Journal of Physical Anthropology and Human Genetics* 14(1&2), 71–83.

Cleland, John (2001), 'The Effects of Improved Survival on Fertility: A Reassessment', in Bulatao and Casterline, *Global Fertility Transition, Population and Development Review*.

————, James F. Philips, Sajeda Amin, and G.M. Kamal (1994), *The Determinants of Reproductive Change in Bangladesh: Success in a Challenging Environment* (Washington DC: The World Bank).

———— and C. Wilson (1987), 'Demand Theories of Fertility Transition: Iconoclastic View', *Population Studies*, 41, 5–30.

Coale, Ansley (1969), 'The Decline of Fertility in Europe from the French Revolution to World War II', in Berhman *et al.* (1969).

———— (1965), 'Factors Associated with the Development of Low Fertility: An Historic Summary', United Nations World Population Conference 1965, Belgrade.

———— and Paul Demeny (1983), *Regional Model Life Tables and Stable Populations*, second edition (New York: Academic Press).

———— and S.C. Watkins (eds) (1986), 'The Decline of Fertility in Europe Since Eighteenth Century as a Chapter in Demographic History', in Coale, Ansley and S.C. Watkins (eds), *The Decline of Fertility in Europe* (Princeton: Princeton University Press).

———— and Roy Treadway (1986), 'A Summary of the Changing Distribution of Overall Fertility, Marital Fertility, and Proportion Married in the Provinces of Europe', in Coale and Watkins (1986).

———— and Susan C. Watkins (eds) (1986), *The Decline of Fertility in Europe* (Princeton: Princeton University Press).

Coale, A. and J. Banister (1994), 'Five Decades of Missing Females in China', *Demography*, 31(3): 459–79.

Coale, A.J. (1986), 'The Decline of Fertility in Europe since the Eighteenth Century as a Chapter in Human Demographic History', in A.J. Coale and S.C. Watkins (eds) (1986), *Decline of Fertility in Europe* (Princeton: Princeton Univesity Press).

Coleman, D.A. (ed.) (1982), *Demography of Immigrants and Minority Groups in the United Kingdom* (London: Academic Press).

Colson, E. (1953), *The Makah Indians* (Manchester: Manchester University Press).

Corbridge, S. (1988), 'The Ideology of Tribal Economy and Society: Politics in Jharkhand , 1950–1980', *Modern Asian Studies* (22), Part 1: 1–42.

Croll, E. (2000), *Endangered Daughters: Discrimination and Development in Asia* (London: Routledge).

Currey, B. (1978), 'The Famine Syndrome: Its Definition for Preparedness and Prevention in Bangladesh', *Ecology of Food and Nutrition*, 7(2).

Das, A.K. and S.K. Banerjee (1964), 'Certain Aspects of Population Growth amongst the Tribals of West Bengal', *Bulletin of the Tribal Research Institute*, 3: 1–14.

Das, N.C. (1979), 'Fertility Study of a Juang Village', *Eastern Anthropologist*, 32(3): 185–91.

Das, N.P. and U. Shah (1991), 'Contraceptive Prevalence and Maternal and Child Health Status among Tribals', in Pati and L. Jagatdeb (eds), *Tribal Demography in India* (New Delhi: Ashish Publishing House).

Das, V. (ed.) (2003), *The Oxford India Companion: Social and Social Anthropology* (New Delhi: Oxford University Press).

Das Gupta, M. (2001), 'Synthesizing Diverse Interpretations of Reproductive Change in India', in Sather and Phillips (2001).

————— (1999), 'Liberté, Egalité, Fraternité: Exploring the Role of Governance in Fertility Decline', *Journal of Development Studies*, 35(5).

————— (1995), 'Fertility Decline in Punjab, India: Parallels with Historical Europe', *Population Studies*, 49(3): 481–500.

————— (1990), 'Death Clustering, Mother's Education and Determinants of Child Mortality in Rural Punjab, India', *Population Studies*, 44: 489–505.

————— (1987), 'Selective Discrimination against Female Children in Rural Punjab', *Population and Development Review*, 13.

————— and P.N. Mari Bhatt (1995), 'Intensified Gender Bias in India: A Consequence of Fertility Decline', Working Paper No. 95.02, Harvard Center for Population and Development Studies, Cambridge, MA (forthcoming in *Population Studies*).

Das Gupta, A., R.K. Som, M. Mazumdar, and S.N. Mitra (1955), *Couple Fertility*, in National Sample Survey No. 7, Calcutta: Dept. of Economic Affairs, Ministry of Finance, Govt. of India.

Dasgupta, Partha (1993), *An Inquiry into Well-Being and Destitution* (Oxford: Clarendon Press).

————— (1930), *An Inquiry into Well-being and Destitution* (Oxford: Clarendon Press).

Davis, K. (1986), 'Low Fertility in Evolutionary Perspective', *Population and Development Review*, 12, Supplement.

————— (1951), *The Population and India and Pakistan* (Princeton: Princeton University Press).

De, D.C. (1970), 'A Demographic Study of Onges of Little Andaman', *Bulletin of Anthropological Survey of India*, 19(2), 111–26

De Haan, A. (1999), 'Livelihoods and Poverty: The Role of Migration—A Critical Review of the Migration Literature', *Journal of Development Studies*, 36(2).

DeRose, L., M. Das, and S.R. Millman (2000), 'Does Female Disadvantage Mean Lower Access to Food?', *Population and Development Review*, 26(3).

De Walle, F.V. (1975), 'Migration and Fertility in Ticino', *Population Studies*, 29(3).

Deaton and Drèze (2002), 'Poverty and Inequality in India: A Re-Examination', *Economic and Political Weekly*, Sep. 7, p. 3729.

Deka, A. (1989), 'Reproductive Performance and Selection among the Jaintias of Village Sa-Phai', in *Genetical Demography of Indian Population*, Anthropological Survey of India.

Department of Family Welfare (1996), Ministry of Health and Family Welfare, Government of India, *Family Welfare Programme in India*, Year Book1993–94, New Delhi.

Desai, S. (1994), *India: Gender Inequalities and Demographic Behaviour* (New York: Population Council).

Dey, S.K. (1969), 'Fertility in the Hill Districts of Assam', *Social Welfare*, 8–10.

Dharmalingam, A. and S.P. Morgan (1996), 'Women's Work, Autonomy, and Birth Control: Evidence from Two South Indian Villages', *Population Studies*, 50: 187–201.

Dharmalingam, A. (1994), 'Economics of Marriage Change in South Indian Village', *Development and Change*, 25: 569–90.

Dornan, S.S. (1975), *Pygmies & Bushmen of the Kalahari* (Cape Town: C. Struik [PTY] Ltd).

Drèze, Jean and M. Murthi (2001), 'Fertility, Education, and Development: Evidence from India', *Population and Development Review*, 27.

————— (2000), 'Fertility, Education and Development: Further Evidence from India', The Development Economics Discussion Paper Series, No. 20, STICERD, London School of Economics.

Drèze, Jean and A. Sen (1989), *Hunger and Public Action* (Oxford: Clarendon Press).

Drèze, Jean and P.V. Srinivasan (1996), 'Poverty in India: Regional Estimate1987–88', Development Economics Research Programme, STICERD, Discussion Paper No. 70, London School of Economics.

Drèze, Jean and G. Kingdon (2001), 'School Participation in Rural India', *Review of Development Economics*, February.

Drèze, Jean and Amartya Sen (2002), *India: Development and Participation* (New Delhi: Oxford University Press).

————— (eds) (1997), *Indian Development: Selected Regional Perspectives* (New Delhi: Oxford University Press).

————— (1995), *India: Economic Development and Social Opportunity* (New Delhi: Oxford University Press).

Drèze, Jean, P. Lanjouw, and N. Sharma (1998), 'Economic Development in Palanpur, 1957–93', in P. Lanjouw, and Stern (eds) (1998), *Economic Development of Palanpur over Five Decades* (Oxford: Clarendon Press).

Driver, E.D. (1963), *Differential Fertility in Central India* (Princeton: Princeton University Press).

Dube, S.C. (ed.) (1977a), *Tribal Heritage of India, Vol 1: Ethnicity, Identity and Interaction* (New Delhi: Vikas Publishing House).

————— (1977b), 'Introduction', in Dube (1977a).

Dubey, D.C. and A. Bardhan (1978), 'Development, Status of Women and Fertility: Case Study of a Tribal Group', *Demography India*, 7(1&2): 91–103.

————— (eds), 'Development, Status of Women and Fertility: Case Study of a Tribal Group (mimeo) Indian Institute of Political Science, Bombay.

Dyson, Tim (2001), 'Birth Rate Trends in India, Sri Lanka, Bangladesh and Pakistan: A Long, Comparative View', in J. Philips and Z. Sathar (eds), *Fertility Transition in South Asia* (Oxford: Clarendon Press).

————— (1991), 'On the Demography of South Asian Famines', Parts I and II, *Population Studies*, 45: 1 and 2.

————— (ed) (1989), *India's Historical Demography* (London: Curzon Press).

————— (1977), 'The Demography of the Hazda—in Historical Perspective', in *African Historical Demography*, Proceedings of a Seminar held in Centre of African Studies, University of Edinburgh.

————— and G. Somawat, 'An Assessment of Fertility Trends in India', in Srinivasan and Mukerji (1983).

————— and Mick Moore (1983), 'On Kinship Structure, Female Autonomy and Demographic Behaviour in India', *Population and Development Review*, 9.

————— and Mike Murphy (1986), 'Rising Fertility in Developing Countries', in Woods and Rees (1986).

————— (1985), 'The Onset of Fertility Transition', *Population and Development Review*, 11.

Egero, Bertil, and Mikael Hammarskjold (eds) (1994), *Understanding Reproductive Change: Kenya, Tamil Nadu, Punjab and Costa Rica* (Sweden: Lund University Press).

Ekka, Philip (2000), 'Jharkhand Tribals: Are They Really a Minority?', *Economic and Political Weekly*, December 30.

Elwin, Verrier (1943), 'Conception, Pregnancy and Birth among the Tribesmen of the Maikal Hills', *Journal of Royal Asiatic Society of Bengal*, 9(4).

————— (1939), *The Baiga* (London: John Murray).

Ember, C.R. (1983), 'The Relative Decline in Women's Contribution to Agriculture with Intensification', *American Anthropologist*, 85: 285–304.

Enthoven, R.E. (1920), *Tribes and Castes of Bombay* (Bombay: Govt. Press).

Epstein, T.S. (1973), *South India: Yesterday, Today and Tomorrow* (London).

Evans-Princhard, E.E. (1965), *The Position of Women in Primitive Societies and other Essays in Social Anthropology* (London: Faber and Faber Ltd).

Fahim, H. (ed) (1982), *Indigenous Anthropology of Non-Western Countries* (Durham, NC: Carolina Academic Press).

Fernandes, W. and G. Menon (1987), *Tribal Women and Forest Economy: Deforestation , Exploitation and Status Change* (New Delhi: Indian Social Institute).

Frisch, Rose (1997), 'Body Fat, Menarche, and Fertility', in *Encyclopedia of Human Biology*, second edition, vol. 2 (New York: Academic Press).

Fuchs, S. (1973), *The Aboriginal Tribes of India* (New Delhi: Macmillan).

Fürer-Haimendorf, Christopher (1989), 'The Struggle For Survival', in Singh (1989).

———— (1985), *Tribal Populations and Cultures of the Indian Subcontinent* (Leiden-Koln: E.J. Brill).

———— (1982), *Tribes of India: The Struggle for Survival* (New Delhi: Oxford University Press).

———— (1979), *The Gonds of Andhra Pradesh: Tradition and Change in an Indian Tribe* (London: George Allen and Unwin).

———— (1945), *Tribal Hyderabad*, Hyderabad Govt., HEH the Nizam.

———— (1943), *The Chenchus: Jungle Folk of the Deccan* (London: Macmillan).

Gaikwad, J.S. (1986), 'A Demographic Profile of Tribals in Maharashtra State', *Tribal Research Bulletin*, 9(1).

Garg, B.M (1960), 'Status of Women in Tribal Communities in India', *Indian Journal of Social Work*, 21(2).

Garenne, M.L. and Rose Frisch (1994), 'Natural Fertility', *Study Designs and Statistics for Infertility Research*, 5(2): 259–81.

Gandotra, M.M. (1989), 'Fertility, Mortality and Contraceptive Prevalence in Tribal Population', in S.N. Singh, M.K. Premi. P.S. Bhatia, A. Bose (eds), *Population Transition in India*, vol. 2 (Delhi: B.R. Publishing Corporation).

Gangadharan, L. and P. Maitra (2000), 'Does Child Mortality Reflect Gender Bias: Evidence from Pakistan', *Indian Economic Review*, 35(2): 113–31.

Gangadharan, V. (1999), *Fertility Behaviour in Tribal World* (New Delhi: Reliance Publishing House).

Gazdar, H. and S. Sengupta (1999), 'Agricultural Growth and Recent Trends in Well-Being in Rural West Bengal', in Rogaly *et al.* (eds) (1999).

Ghosh , A.K. (1976), 'The Kota of the Nilgiri Hills: A Demographic Study', *Journal of Biosocial Science*, 8: 17–26.

Ghurye, G.S. (1959), *The Scheduled Castes* (Bombay: Popular Book Depot).

———— (1943), *The Aborigins—'So called' and their Future* (Poona: Gokhale Institute of Politics and Economics).

Goldstein, S. (1978), 'Migration and Fertility in Thailand, 1960–70', *Canadian Studies in Population*, vol. 5: 167–80.

Government of Gujarat (1974), Final Report on the Survey of Seasonal

Migration of Labour in Panchmahal District, 1971–72, *Quarterly Bulletin of Economics and Statistics*, 14(2), April–June.

Government of India (2001), National Commission on Population, *District-wise Social Economic Demographic Indicators* (New Delhi: Yojana Bhavan).

———— (2000), Ministry of Human Resource Development, *Selected Educational Statistics*, 1998–99, Delhi.

———— (1998), *National Commission For Scheduled Castes and Scheduled Tribes*, Fourth Report, 1996–97 and 1997–98.

———— (1997a), NSSO, *Econimic Activities and School Attendance by Children of India*, NSS 50th Round (1993–94), Report No. 412.

———— (1997b), *Family Welfare Programme in India Year Book 1995–96*, Ministry of Health and Family Welfare, New Delhi.

———— (1995), NSSO, Ministry of Planning, *Sarvekshana*, vol. 19(2), Issue 65, New Delhi.

———— (1995), Ministry of Human Resource Development, *Educational Development of Scheduled Castes and Scheduled Tribes*.

———— (1994a), Ministry of Planning, Dept of Statistics, *Sarvekshana*, 17(4), April–June 1994, Issue No. 59.

———— (1994b), Ministry of Planning, Dept of Statistics, *Sarvekshana*, 18(1), July–Sept, 1994, Issue No. 60.

Government of India (1989), NSSO, 42nd Round (July 1986–June 1987), Report No. 365, *Participation in Education*, New Delhi, Table 18, P.A.II. 79–80.

———— (1989), NSSO, 42nd Round (July 1986–June 1987), Report No. 365, *Participation in Education*, New Delhi, Table 21.2, 16, P.A.II. 73–74, 92.

———— (1989), NSSO, Ministry of Statistics and Programme Implementation; 42 Round, *Morbidity and Utilisation of Medical Services*, Report No. 364 (New Delhi).

———— (1986), *Statistical Profile of Women Labour*, second edition. Labour Bureau, Ministry of Labour.

———— (1985), Ministry of Education, *Statewise Information on Education of Scheduled Castes and Scheduled Tribes*, New Delhi.

———— (1977), *Commissioner of Scheduled Castes and Scheduled Tribes, Report 1975–76 and 1976–1977 (Part I)*, Ministry of Home Affairs.

———— (1968a), *Census of India 1961*, vol. 12, Orissa, Part I-B, Report on Vital Statistics and Fertility Survey (New Delhi: Office of the Registrar General).

———— (1968b), *Census of India 1961*, vol. 11, Andhra Pradesh, Part I-F Report on Vital Statistics and Fertility Survey (New Delhi: Office of the Registrar General).

———— (1966a), *Census of India 1961*, vol. 3, Assam, Part I-B, Report on Vital Statistics (New Delhi: Office of the P :gistrar General).

———— (1966b), *Census of India 1961*, vol. 5, Gujarat, Part I-B, Report on Vital Statistics (New Delhi: Office of the Registrar General).

Government of India (1961), Report of the Scheduled Castes and Scheduled Tribes Commission, vol. I, 1960–61, p. 7.

————— (1947), *Statistical Handbook No. 1 (Revised)*, The Population of India According to Communities, second edition (New Delhi: Manager of Govt. Press.

————— (1933), *Census of India 1931,* vol. 1, India, Part 1, Report (Delhi: Manager of Publications).

Government of West Bengal (no date), *Health on the March West Bengal 2000–01*, State Bureau of Health Intelligence.

Government of West Bengal (1995), *Family Welfare Statistics at a Glance*, Department of Health and Family Welfare.

Goyal, R.P. (1964), 'Birth Rate can be Reduced a Third by Late Marriage', *Yojana,* August 30.

Griffiths, P., Z. Mathews, and A. Hinde (2000), Understanding the Sex Ratio in India: A Simulation Approach', *Demography*, 37(4): 477–88.

Grigson, W.V. (1938), *The Maria Gonds of Bastar* (London: Oxford University Press).

Guha, R. (1999), *Savaging the Civilized: Verrier Elwin, his Tribals and India*, (New Delhi: Oxford University Press).

Guha, S. (1999), *Environment and Ethnicity in India 1200–1991* (Cambridge: Cambridge University Press).

Guilmoto, C. and S.I. Rajan (2002), 'District Level Estimates of Fertility from India's 2001 Census', *Economic and Political Weekly*, February, 16, 2002.

————— (2001), 'Spatial Patterns of Fertility Transition in Indian Districts', *Population and Development Review*.

————— (2000), 'Spatial Patterns of Fertility Transition in Indian Districts', *Population and Development Review*, 27(4): 713–38.

Gupta, A. (2001), 'Left Front Rule in West Bengal: Domination without Hegemony', *Economic and Political Weekly*, 36(45), 10 November.

Gupta S. (2003), *On the Allocation of Public Goods to Villages in India* (mimeographed), London School of Economics.

Gupta, S.K. (1985), *The Scheduled Castes in Modern Indian Politics: Their Emergence as a Political Power* (New Delhi: Munshiram Manoharlal Publishers).

Gupta, S.P. and B. Prajapati (1998), 'Migration of Agricultural Labourers in Chattisgarh Region of Madhya Pradesh: A Micro Level Study', *Indian Journal of Labour Economics*, 41(4).

Haberfeld, Y., R.K. Menaria, B.B. Sahoo, and R.N. Vyas (1999), 'Seasonal Migration of Rural Labour in India', *Population Research and Policy Review*, 18: 473–89.

Hampshire, K. (2002), 'Fulani on the Move: Seasonal Economic Migration in the Sahel as a Social Process', *Journal of Development Studies*, 38(5): 15–36.

Handwerker, W. (1983), 'The First Demographic Transition: An Analysis of

Subsistence Choices and Reproductive Consequences', *American Anthropologist*, 85.

Harbison, S.F. T.M.K. Kharleque, and W. Robinson (1989), 'Female Autonomy and Fertility Among the Garo of North Central Bangladesh', *American Anthropologist*, 91(4).

Harriss, B. (1999), 'The Intrafamily Distribution of Hunger in South Asia', in Drèze, J., A. Sen, and A. Hussain (eds) (1999), *The Political Economy of Hunger: Selected Essays* (Oxford Clarendon Press).

Harriss, J. (1993), 'What is Happening in Rural West Bengal? Agrarian Reform, Growth and Distribution', *Economic and Political Weekly*, June 12.

Harriss, B. S. Gillespie, and J. Pryer (1990), 'Poverty and Malnutrition at Extremes of South Asian Food Systems', *Economic and Political Weekly*, December 22: 2783–99.

Hajnal, J. (1965), 'Europian Marriage Pattern in Prospective', in Glass, D.V., D.E.C. Eversly (eds), *Population in History* (Chicago: Aldine Publishing Company).

Helm, J. (ed) (1968), 'Essays on the Problem of India', Seattle: American Ethnological Society.

Hema Kumari, T.A. (1993), 'Migration of Female Tobacco Graders: A Quest for Survival and Development', in Bhat *et al.* (eds) (1993).

Hema Kumari, T.A. and U. Tataji (1998), 'Seasonal Migration of Women Workers: Process, Patterns and Consequences', *Indian Journal of Social Work*, 59(3).

Hemam, S. and Reddy, B.M. (1998), 'Demographic Implications of Socioeconomic Transition among the Tribal Populations of Manipur, India', *Human Biology*, 70(3).

Henin, R.A. (1969), 'The Patterns and Causes of Fertility Differentials in the Sudan', *Population Studies*, 23(2):171–98.

_____ (1968), 'Fertility Differentials in the Sudan', *Population Studies*, 22(1): 147–64.

Heward, C., and S. Bunwaree (eds) (1999), *Gender Education and Development Beyond Access to Improvement* (London: Zed Books Limited).

Hill, Allan G. (1985), 'The Recent Demographic Surveys in Mali and their Main Findings', in his edited volume, *Population, Health and Nutrition in the Sahel: Issues in the Welfare of Selected West African Communities* (London: KPI).

Hockings, P. (1999), *Kindreds of the Earth: Badaga Household Structure and Demography* (New Delhi: Sage Publications).

Howell, Nancy (1979), *Demography of the Dobe Kung* (New York: Academic Press).

_____ (1976), 'The Population of the Dobe Area Kung', in Lee and DeVore (1976).

Inden, R. (1990), *Imagining India* (Oxford: Blackwell Publishers).

International Institute for Population Science (1995), India, National Family Health Survey 1992–93, Bombay.

International Institute for Population Science (2000), India, National Family Health Survey 1998–99, Bombay.

Jabbi, M.K. and C. Rajyalakshmi (1997), 'Education of SC and ST Students of Bihar', *Social Change,* 27(1/2).

Jagannadhan, V. (1973), *Family Planning in India—Policy and Administration* (New Delhi: Indian Institute of Public Administration).

Jain, D. and N. Banerjee (eds) (1985), *Tyranny of the Household* (Delhi: Shakti Books).

Jain, L.R., Sundaram and S.D. Tendulakar (1988), 'Dimensions of Rural Poverty: An Inter-regional Profile', *Economic and Political Weekly,* 23 (45–7) 2395–408.

Jain, S.P. (1967), 'State Growth Rates and their Components', in Bose (1967), *Patterns of Population Change in India 1951–61* (Bombay: Allied Publishers).

Jay, E.J. (1968), 'The Anthropologists and Tribal Welfare', in Vidyarthi (1968).

Jayachandran, U. (2001), 'Understanding School Attendance and Children's Work Participation in India', *Journal of Educational Planning and Administration,* 15(1).

Jayaraman, T.K. (1979), 'Seasonal Migration of Tribal Labour: An Irrigation Project in Gujarat', *Economic and Political Weekly,* October 13.

Jeffery, R. and A. Basu (eds) (1996), *Girl's Schooling, Women's Autonomy and Fertility Change in South Asia* (New Delhi: Sage Publications).

Jejeebhoy J.S., and A.Z. Sathar (2001), 'Women's Autonomy in India and Pakistan: The Influence of Religion and Region, *Population and Development Review,* 27(4): 687–712 (December 2001).

Jejeebhoy, Shireen J. (2000), 'Women's Autonomy in Rural India: Its Dimensions, Determinants and the Influence of the Context', in Harriet B. Presser and Gita Sen (eds), *Women's Empowerment and Demographic Process: Moving Beyond Cairo* (New York: Oxford University).

Jolly, K.G. (1990), 'Family Planning Programme in Tribal Areas', in Bose *et al.* (1990).

Jose, A.V. (ed.) (1989), *Limited Options: Women Workers in Rural India,* ILO (Delhi).

Joshi, Y.G. (1997), *Tribal Migration* (Jaipur: Rawat Publications).

Kalam, M.A. (1997), 'Moorings and Mobility in an Indian Context: An Anthropological Perspective', in Racine (1997).

Kamal Nahid (1999), 'Population Trajectories of East and West Bengal during Twentieth Century (Ph.D., work in Progress), London School of Economics.

Kapoor, A.K. and G. Kshatriya (2000), 'Fertility and Mortality Differantials among Selected Tribal Population Groups of North-Western and Eastern India', *Journal of Biosocial Science,* 32(2).

Kar, Samir, Kumar (1997), *Poverty Alleviation amongst ST and SC Population in the District of Bankura: An Economic Evaluation* (unpublished) Ph.D. dissertation (Burdwan University, West Bengal).

Karkal, M. (1968), 'Age at Marriage', *The Journal of Family Welfare*, 14(3).

Kelkar, G. and D. Nathan (1991), *Gender and Tribe: Women, Land and Forests in Jharkhand* (New Delhi: Kali For Women).

Kishor, Sunita (1995), 'Gender Differentials in Child Mortality: A Review of the Evidence', in Das Gupta, M. *et al.* (eds), *Women's Health in India: Risk and Vulnerability* (New Delhi: Oxford University Press).

————— (1994), 'Fertility Decline in Tamil Nadu, India', in Egero and Hammarskjold (1994).

————— (1993), '"May God Give Sons to All": Gender Differentials in Child Mortality', *American Sociological Review*, 58(2).

Klasen, S. (1996), 'Nutrition, Health and Mortality in Sub-Saharan Africa: Is there a Gender Bias?', *Journal of Development Studies*, 32(6): 913–32.

————— (1994), 'Missing Women Reconsidered', *World Development*, 22(7): 1061–71.

Koenig, M.A. and G.H.C. Foo (1992), 'Patriarchy, Women's Status, and Reproductive Behaviour in Rural North India', *Demography India*, 21(2): 145–66.

Konner, Melvin (1976), 'Maternal Care, Infant Behaviour and Development among the Kung', in Lee and DeVore (1976).

Kosambi, D.D. (1956), *An Introduction to the Study of Indian History* (Bombay: Popular Book).

Krishnaiah, M. (1997), 'Rural Migrant Labour System in Semi-Arid Areas: A Study in Two Villages in Andhra Pradesh', *The Indian Journal of Labour Economics*, 40(1).

Krishnaji, N. (2000), 'Trends in Sex Ratio: A Review in Tribute to Ashok Mitra', *Economic and Political Weekly*, April 1, 1161–65.

————— (1992), *Pauperising Agriculture: Studies in Agrarian Change and Demographic Structure* (Bombay: Oxford University Press for Sameeksha Trust).

————— (1983), 'Poverty and Fertility: A Review of Theory and Evidence', *Economic and Political Weekly*, Annual Number, May.

Krzwicki, L. (1934), *Primitive Society and Its Vital Statistics*, London.

Kulkarni, S. (2002), 'Tribal Communities in Maharashtra', in Samuel J. (ed.) (2002).

————— (1991), 'Distortion of Census Data on Scheduled Tribes', *Economic and Political Weekly*, February 2.

Kumar, Alok (1986), *Tribal Culture and Economy* (Delhi: Inter-India Publications).

Kumar, K., P.N. Bhattacharjee, and A. Maitra (1967), 'Some Demographic Aspects of Munda in Ranchi District, Bihar', *Bulletin of Anthropological Survey of India*, 16(1&2): 71–74.

Kumar, A.K. Shiva (2003), 'Marked Difference: Community in Elementary Education', *The Times of India* (Pune Edition), January 8.

Kynch, J. and A. Sen (1983), 'Indian Women: Well-Being and Survival', *Cambridge Journal of Economics*, 7.

Lee, Richard B. and Irven DeVore (eds) (1976), *Kalahari Hunter-Gatherers: Studies of the Kung San and their Neighbours* (Cambridge, MA: Harvard University Press).

Lieten, G.K. (2000), 'Children, Work and Education-II: Field Work in two U.P. Villages', *Economic and Political Weekly*, 35(25)17 June: 2171–8.

Lorimer, Frank (1954), *Culture and Human Fertility* (Paris: UNESCO).

McDonald, P. (2000), 'Gender Equity in Theories of Fertility Transition', *Population and Development Review*, 26(3): 427–42.

Madan, T.N. (1982), 'Anthropology as the Mutual Interpretation of Cultures: Indian Perspective', in Fahim (1982).

Mahadev, P.D. and J.R. Racine (1997), 'To Migrate or to Stay?', in Racine (1997).

Mahapatra, U.D. (1970), 'Study of Fertility in a Tribe of Northeast India (Khasi)', *Journal Social Research*, 13(1): 74–82.

Maharatna, Arup, and Rasika Chilte (2003), 'The Demography of Tribal Population in Jharkhand 1951–91' (forthcoming), *EPh*.

Maharatna, Arup (2002a), 'India's Family Planning Programme: An Unpleasant Essay', *Economic and Political Weekly*, 37(10), 9 March.

———— (2002b), On Seasonal Migration and Family Planning Acceptance: A Tale of Paper Presented at the Interregional Seminar on Reproductive Health, Unmet Needs, and Poverty: Issues of Access and Quality of Services organized by the Committee for International Co-operation in National Research in Demography (CICRED) and the University of Chulalongkorn at Bangkok during 25–30 November 2002.

———— (2000a), 'Fertility, Mortality and Gender Bias among Tribal Population: An Indian Perspective', *Social Science and Medicine*, 50: 1333–51.

———— (2000b), 'Tribal Fertility in India: Socio-Cultural Influences on Demographic Behaviour', *Economic and Political Weekly*, 35 (34), 19 August.

———— (2000c), 'India's Tribal Population: A Demographic Perspective' (mimeo), Indian Institute of Advanced Study, Shimla.

———— (1998), 'On Tribal Fertility in Late Nineteenth and Early Twentieth Century in India', Working Paper Series No. 98.01, Harvard Centre for Population and Development Studies, Harvard University.

———— (1998a), 'Fertility, Mortality and Gender Bias among Tribal Population: An Indian Perspective', Working Paper No. 98.08, Harvard Centre for Population and Development Studies, Harvard University.

———— (1998b), 'Tribal Fertility, Family Planning and Seasonal Migration: A Case Study of Santhals of West Bengal', Paper presented at the Workshop on Migration and Sustainable Livelihoods, held at University of Sussex, June 5, 6, 1998.

———— (1997), 'Children's Work Activities, Surplus Labour, and Fertility: A Case Study of Peasant Households in Birbhum, West Bengal', *Economic and Political Weekly*, 32(7).

Maharatna, Arup (1996), *The Demography of Famines: An Indian Historical Perspective* (New Delhi: Oxford University Press).

Majumdar, D.N. (1950), *Affairs of a Tribe* (Lucknow: Universal Publishers).

———— (1947), *The Matrix of Indian Culture*, Nagpur University.

Majumdar, M. and S. Subramanian (2001), 'Capability Failure and Group Disparities: Some Evidence from India for the 1980s', *Journal of Development Studies*, 37(5).

Malakar, C.R. (1972), 'Female Age at Marriage and Birth Rate in India', *Social Biology*, 19:297–301.

Malhotra, A. Vanneman, and S. Kishor (1995), 'Fertility, Dimensions of Patriarchy, and Development in India', *Population and Development Review*, 21(2): 281–306.

Malhotra (1994), 'Genetico-environmental Disorders and their Impact on Mortality and Morbidity Profile among Tribal Population', in Basu, S. (1994), *Tribal Health in India*, 269–71.

Malhotra, R. (1997), 'Incidence of Poverty in India: Towards a Consensus on Estimating the Poor', *Indian Journal of Labour Economics*, 40(1).

Mamoria, C.B. (1958), *Tribal Demography in India* (Allahabad: Kitab Mahal).

Mandelbaum, D.G. (1974), *Human Fertility in India: Social Components and Policy Perspectives* (New Delhi: Oxford University Press).

———— (1970), *Society in India*, 2 vols (Berkley: University of California Press).

Mandelbaum, D. (1954), 'Fertility of Early Years of Marriage in India', in K.M. Kapadia (ed.), *Professore Ghurye Felicitation Volume* (Bombay: Popular Book Depot).

Mann, K. (1985), 'Bhil Women: Changing World View and Development', *Human Science*, 34: 57–66.

Martine, G., M. Das Gupta, and L. Chen (eds) (1998), *Reproductive Change in India and Brazil* (New Delhi: Oxford University Press).

Massey, D.S. and B. Mullan (1984), 'A Demonstration of the Effect of Seasonal Migration on Fertility', *Demography*, 21(4):501–18.

Mawar, N. *et al.* (1993), 'Understanding Employment Income in Relation to Status of Tribal Women: A Case Study of Gonds in Madhya Pradesh', *Social Change*, 23(4).

McAlpin, M.B. (1983), *Subject to Famine: Food Crises and Economic Change in Western India, 1860–1920* (Princeton: Princeton University Press).

Mehta, B.H. (1953), 'Historical Background of Tribal Population', *Indian Journal of Social Work*, 14(3):236–306.

Menken, J. (1979), 'Seasonal Migration and Seasonal Variation in Fecundability: Effects on Birth Rates and Birth Intervals', *Demography*, 16(1).

Merewether, F.H.S. (1898), *A Tour Through the Famine Districts* (London: A.D. Inns and Co).

Messey, D. and B. Mullan (1984), 'A Decomposition of the Effect of Seasonal Migration of Fertility', *Demography*, 21(4).

Meenakshi, J.V. R. Ray, and S. Gupta (2000), 'Estimates of Poverty for SC, ST and Female Headed Households', *Economic and Political Weekly*, July 29.

Miller Beatrice D. (ed.) (1993), *Sex and Gender Hierarchies* (Cambridge: Cambridge University Press).

———— (1981), *The Endangered Sex: Neglect of Female Children in Rural North India* (Cornell: Cornell University Press).

———— (1969), 'Revitalization Movements: Theory and Practice', in Pradhan *et al*. (1969) Anthropology and Archaeology: Essays in Commemoration of Verrier Elwin 1902–64 (Bombay: Oxford University Press).

Miri, M. (ed) (1993), *Continuity and Change in Tribal Society* (Shimla: Indian Institute of Advanced Study).

Misra, P.K. (1977), 'Patterns of Inter-Tribal Relations', in Dube (1977).

Mishra, V., J.A. Palmore, and S.K. Sinha (1994), 'Indirect Estimates of Fertility and Mortality at the District Level, 1981', Occasional Paper No. 4 of 1994, Office of the Registrar General, India.

Misra, V.N. (2000), 'Role of Female Labour Force Participation in Rural Poverty and Non-Farm Employment: Indian Experience', *Indian Journal of Labour Economics*, 43(2).

Mohana, T.S. (1997), 'Tribal Education: A Case Study of Indravelli Mandal in Andhra Pradesh', *Social Change*, 27(1&2).

Mohanty, B.B. (2003), 'Policy for Tribal Development in India: Protective Discrimination or Discrimination Protected?' (mimeo), presented at All India conference at Maharana Pratap University, Udaipur, December 2003.

———— (2002), 'Preferential State Policies and Educational Progress of Scheduled Tribes', presented at the National Seminar on Educational Progress of the Scheduled Castes and Scheduled Tribes since Independence: A State Level Scenario held at Ambedkar Institute of Social and Economic Change, Mumbai during May 14–15, 2002.

———— (2001), 'Land Distribution among Scheduled Castes and Tribes', *Economic and Political Weekly*, 36(40): 3857–68.

Morgan, P.S., and B.B. Niraula (1995), 'Gender Inequality and Fertility in Two Nepali Villages', *Population and Development Review*, 21(3): 541–62.

Mosse, D., S. Gupta, M. Mehta, V. Shah, J. Rees, and the KRIBP Project team (2002), 'Brokered Livelihoods: Debt, Labour Migration and Development in Tribal Western India', *Journal of Development Studies*, 38(5): 59–88.

Mudgal, S., V.J. Rajput, M. Chandsoria, and K.K. Kaul (1979), 'Tribals of Madhya Pradesh: Knowledge, Attitude and Practice, Survey of Infant Feeding Practices', *Indian Paediatrics*, 16(7): 617–22.

Mukherjee, B. (1960), 'Santhals in Relation to Hindu Caste', *Man in India*, 40(4): 300–05.

Murthi, N., A. Guio and J. Drèze (1995), 'Mortality, Fertility, and Gender Bias in India: A District-Level Analysis', *Population and Development Review*, 21: 199–210.

Mutharayappa, R. (2000), *Tribal Fertility Mortality and Healthcare Practices* (New Delhi: Mithal Publications).

———— (1998), 'Fertility and Family Planning among Jenu Kuruba and Kadu Kuruba Tribes of Karnataka', *Man in India*, 78(1–2): 119–126.

———— (1994), 'Factors Affecting Fertility Among Tribals', *Man and Development*, 16(4): 63–79.

————, M.K. Choe, Fred Arnold, and T.K. Roy (1997), 'Is Son Preference Slowing Down India's Transition to Low Fertility?', *NFHS Bulletin No. 4*, International Institute For Population Sciences (Mumbai).

Nag, Moni (1984), 'Fertility Differential in Kerala and West Bengal: Equity–Fertility Hypothesis as Explanation', *Economic and Political Weekly*, 21(1): 33–34.

———— (1980), 'How Modernization can also Increase Fertility', *Current Anthropology*, 21(5): 571–80.

———— (1976), 'Differential Fertility Patterns in India', in G.R. Gupta (ed), *Contemporary India: Some Sociological Perspectives* (New Delhi: Vikas Publishing House Ltd).

———— (1973), 'Tribal–Non-Tribal Fertility Differential in India', *Demography India*, 2(1).

———— (1968), 'The concept of Tribe in the contemporary socio-political context of India' in Helm (1968).

———— (1962), *Factors Affecting Human Fertility in Non-industrial Societies: A Cross-Cultural Study* (Yale University Publications in Anthropology), no. 66.

———— (1954), 'A Demographic Study of the Kanikkar of Travancore', *Bulletin of the Deptt. of Anthropology*, vol. 3, no. 2.

Nag, N.G. (1990), 'Some Demographic Characteristics of Scheduled Tribes with Special Reference to Gujarat, Madhya Pradesh, Rajasthan and Maharashtra', in A. Bose et al. (eds), *Tribal Demography and Development in Northeast India* (New Delhi: B.R. Publishing Corporation).

———— (1984), 'Some Demographic Characteristics of Scheduled Tribes— With Special Reference to Gujarat, Madhya Pradesh, Maharashtra and Rajasthan', paper presented at the Symposium on Tribal Demography and Development organized by Indian Association for the Study of Population (IASP), Bhopal, October 10–12, 1984.

Nagarajan, R. (2000), 'Verification of Authenticity of Reported Cases of Sterilization and IUD Insertion under Target and Target-free Approaches: A Field Investigation in Rural Maharashtra', paper presented at the Millennium Conference on Population, Development and Environment Nexus organized by IASP at Delhi during February 14–16, 2000.

———— (1997), 'Lower Fertility T.N's Success', *The Hindu*, October 1997.

Naidu, N.Y. (1979), 'Family Planning by Tribals', *Eastern Anthropologist*, 32(3).

Naidu, T.S. (1998), 'The Shompen Aboriginal Population and Problems of Survival in Great Nicobar Island', *Journal of Family Welfare*, 44(2): 59–66.

Naik, T.B. (1956), *The Bhils: A Study* (Delhi: Bharatiya Adimjati Sevak Sangh).

Narayana, D. (2001), *Macroeconomic Adjustment Policies, Health Sector Reform and Access to Health Care in India* (Thiruvanthapurm: Centre for Development Studies).

Natarajan, D. (1971), *Changes in Sex Ratio, Census Centenary Monograph No. 6, Census of India 1971*, Registrar General's Office, New Delhi.

Narasimhan, S. (1999), *Empowering Women: An Alternative Strategy for Rural India* (New Delhi: Sage Publications).

Nathan, Dev (ed) (1997), *From Tribe to Caste* (Shimla: Indian Institute of Advanced Study).

National Council of Educational Research and Training (1999), *Sixth All India Educational Survey: Main Report*, New Delhi.

Nigam, S. (1990), 'Disciplining and Policing the Criminals by Birth, Part I: The Making of a Colonial Stereotype—The Criminal Tribe and Castes of North India', *Indian Economic and Social History Review*, 27(2).

NCAER (1994), Human Development Indicators Survey 1994, New Delhi.

Oberai, A.S. and H.K.M. Singh (1983), *Causes and Consequences of Internal Migration: A Study in Indian Punjab* (New Delhi: Oxford University Press).

Odaga, A. and W. Heneveld (1995), *Girls and Schools in Sub-Saharan Africa: From Analysis to Action*, World Bank Technical Paper No. 298.

Padhi, S. and S. Mishra (2000), *Premature Mortality, Health Status and Public Health Care Facilities in Orissa: A Study in Accessibility and Utilization*, Nabakrushna Choudhury Centre for Development Studies, Bhubaneshwar.

Padhi, S. (2001), 'Infant and Child Mortality in Orissa: An Analysis with NFHS Data', *Economic and Political Weekly*, 36(34), August 25.

Padmanabham, P.B.S. (1985), 'Demography of Naika—A Study of Rural–Urban Differences and Change', in Chaudhuri (1985).

Pakrasi, Kanti and Samita Manna (1989), 'Socio-Economic Factors Influencing Breast- Feeding and Weaning of Infants by Tribal Mothers in West Bengal', *Indian Journal of Physical Anthropology and Human Genetics*, 15(1/2).

Pal, S. (1999), 'An Analysis of Childhood Malnutrition in Rural India: Rule of Gender, Income and other Household Characteristics', *World Development*, 27 (2): 1151–71.

Palmore, James (1978), 'Regression Estimates of Changes in Fertility 1955–60 to 1965–75 for most major nations and territories', Honolulu: Papers of East-West Population Institute, No. 58.

Pande, Vijaya and Rohini Devi (1991), Nutrient intake of Selected Tribal Population in Kinwat Area, *Tribal Research Bulletin*, 12(2).

Pandey, G.D. (1994), 'Demographic Characteristics of Tribal and Non-Tribal Females: A Comparative Study', *Man in India*, 74(1): 39–47.

————— (1989), 'A Study of Couple Fertility in a Tribal Population of Madhya Pradesh', in S.N. Singh, M.K. Premi, P.S. Bhatia, and A. Bose (eds), *Population Transition in India*, vol. 2 (New Delhi: B.R. Publishing Corporation).

Pandey, G.D. and R.S. Tiwary (1993), 'Demographic Characteristics in a Tribal Block of Madhya Pradesh', *Social Change*, 23(2&3): 124–31.

Pandey, P.L., D.C. Jain, G.D. Pandey, R. Chouley, and R.S. Tiwari (2000), 'Some Aspects of Social Factors Affecting Fertility Behaviour of Gond Woman', *Man in India*, 80(3&4).

Parasuraman, S. and S.I. Rajan (1990), 'On the Estimation of Vital Rates among the Scheduled Tribes in Western India', in A. Bose, U.P. Sinha and R.P. Tyagi (eds), *Demography of Tribal Development* (New Delhi: B.R. Publishing Corporation).

Parthasarthy, G. (1996), 'Trends in Wages and Employment of Agricultural Labourer', *Indian Journal of Agricultural Economics*, vol. 51 (1, 2), Jan–June, 145–67.

Pathak, K.B., U.P. Sinha, and A. Pandey (eds) (1994), *Dynamics of Population and Family Welfare 1993* (New Delhi: Himalaya Publishing House), 282–304.

Pathak, K.B. and A. Pandey, 'Social Development and Dynamics of Population in Bihar: An Appraisal', in Sinha and Sinha (1994).

Pathy, Jaganath (1992), 'The Idea of Tribe and the Indian Scene', in Chaudhuri (1992).

Pati, R.N. (1991), 'Sociocultural Dimensions of Birth Spacing among Tribals of Orissa: An Overview', in R.N. Pati and L. Jagtdeb (eds), *Tribal Demography in India* (New Delhi: Ashish Publishing House).

Pati, R.N. and L. Jagatdeb (eds) (1991), *Tribal Demography in India* (New Delhi: Ashish Publishing House).

Pfeffer, G. and D.K Behera (eds) (1997), *Contemporary Society: Tribal Studies*, vol. 2 (among 6 vols) (Delhi: Concept Publishing Company).

Pingle Urmila, 'Central Indian Tribal Societies Under State of Modernization, Strategies to Face the Challenge', in Ashish Bose, U.P. Sinha, and R.P. Tyagi, *Demography of Tribal Development* (1990), 163.

Pradhan, M.C., R.D. Singh, P.K. Misra, and D.B. Sastry (eds) (1969), *Anthropology and Archaeology: Essays in Commemoration of Verrier Elwin 1902–64* (Oxford University Press).

Premi, M.K. (1982), *Demographic Situation in India*, Papers of the East-West Population Institute, No. 80.

Preston, Samuel (1978), *The Effects of Infant and Child Mortality on Fertility* (New York: Academic Press).

PROBE Team (1999), *Public Report on Basic Education in India* (New Delhi: Oxford University Press).

Puri, D. (1992), 'Breastfeeding among Tribals: An Aid to Fertility Control', *Journal of Family Welfare*, 38(2): 55–60.

Quilici, F. (1972), *Primitive Societies* (London: Collins Publishers).

Racine, Jean-Luc (1997), *Peasant Moorings: Village Studies and Mobility Rationales in South India* (New Delhi: Sage Publications and French Institute).

Radhakrishna, M. (2000), 'Colonial Construction of a "Criminal Tribe":
Yerukulas of Madras Presidency', *Economic and Political Weekly*, July 15.
————— (1989a), 'The Criminal Tribes Act in Madras Presidency:
Implications for Itinerant Communities', *Indian Economic and Social History
Review*, 26(3).
————— (1989b), 'From Tribal Community to Working Class Consciousness:
Case of Yerukula Women', *Economic and Political Weekly*, April 29.
Rahman, L. and V. Rao (2004), 'The Determinants of Gender Equity in
India. Examining Dyson and Moor's Thesis with New Data', *Populations
and Development Review*, 30(2).
Rajan, S.I. and P. Mohanachandran (2001), 'Infant and Child Mortality
Estimates for Scheduled Castes and Scheduled Tribes', *Economic and Political
Weekly*, December 1.
————— (1998), 'Infant and Child Mortality Estimates, Part I', *Economic
and Political Weekly*, May 9.
Rajan, S.I., S. Sudha, and P. Mohanchandran (2000), 'Fertility Decline and
Worsening Gender Bias in India: Is Kerala No Longer an Exception?',
Development and Change, 31: 1085–92.
Rajaratnam, A., J. Rajaratnam, and T. Kamalaloss (1997), 'Maternal and Child
Health Practices and Nutritional Status of Malto Tribals in Bihar', *Man in
India*, 77(1).
Rakshit, H. (1972), 'The Dorla and Dhurwa of Bastar: A Demographic
Profile', *Journal of Indian Anthroplogical Society*, 7: 115–28.
Ram Bachan Ram and Birendra Prasad Singh (1994), 'Levels, Trends and
Reasons of Migration in Bihar', in Sinha and Sinha (1994).
Ram, U. (1999), 'Availability and Use of Oral Pills and Condoms in the Tribal
Areas of Thane District of Maharashtra' (mimeo), Gokhale Institute of
Politics and Economics, Pune.
Ramesh, B.M., S.C. Gulati, and Robert D. Retherford (1996), *Contraceptive
Use in India 1992–93*, National Family Health Survey, Subject Reports,
No. 2, Mamba and Honolulu.
Rana K., A. Rafique, and A. Sengupta (2002), *The Delivery of Primary
Education: A Study in West Bengal* (New Delhi: The Little Magazine Books).
Rana, R.S. (1996), 'Garhwali Women: Limits of Change', *Economic and
Political Weekly*, 31(19): 1125–26.
Randall, Sara (1996), 'Whose Reality? Local Perceptions of Fertility Versus
Demographic Analysis', *Population Studies*, 50(2): 221–34.
Rani, U. and H.S. Shylendra (2001), 'Seasonal Migration and Rural–Urban
Interface in Semi-Arid Tropics of Gujarat :Study of a Tribal Village', *Journal
of Rural Development*, 20(2): 187–217.
Ranjan, A. (2002), 'Bihar Adivasis—from Development to Exploitation', in
Struggles for Survival, Samuel J. (ed.) (2002).
Rao, D. Hanumantha (1992), 'Nutritional Status of Maria Gonds—A Primitive
Tribe of Maharashtra', *Indian Journal of Dietics*, 29: 61–66.

Rao, D. Hanumantha, G.N.V. Brahman, K.M. Rao, C.G. Reddy, and N.P. Rao (1993), 'Assesment of Nutritional Status of Jenu Kurubas—A Primitive Tribe of Karnataka', *Indian Journal of Nutrition and Dietics*, 30(66): 66–71.

Rao, D. Hanumantha, K. Mallikarjuna Rao, G. Radhaiah, and N. Pralhad Rao (1994), 'Nutritional Status of Tribal Preschool Children in 3 Ecological Zones of Madhya Pradesh', *Indian Pediatrics*, vol. 31, no. 6, 1994.

Rao, N.R., J.R. Rele, and J.A. Palmore (1987), 'Regression Estimates of Fertility for India 1971 and 1981', Occasional Paper no. 3 of 1987 (New Delhi: Office of the Registrar General and Census Commissioner of India).

Rao, Nitya and Kumar Rana (1997), 'Women's Labour and Migration', *Economic and Political Weekly*, 32(50).

Rao, V. (1997), 'Wife Beating in Rural South India: A Qualitative and Econometric Analysis', *Social Science and Medicine*, 44(8): 1169–80.

Rao, N.B. and S. Kulkarni (1999), 'Disparities in School Facilities in India: The Case of Scheduled Caste and Scheduled Tribe Children', *Journal of Educational Planning and Administration*, 13(2): 175–85.

Rao, V. (1993), 'Dowry Inflation in Rural India: A Statistical Investigations' Population studies 47(2): 283–293

Ray, A.K. and E. Roth (1991), 'Indian Tribal Fertility Patterns from Orissa', *Man in India*, 71(1): 235–39.

——— (1984), 'Demography of the Juang Tribal Population of Orissa', *American Journal of Physical Anthropology*, 65: 387–93.

———, and B. Mohanty (1984a), 'Marital Fertility Parameters of the Koya Dora of Orissa', *Journal of Human Biology*, 13: 255–63.

———, and B. Mohanty (1984b), 'Intermediate Fertility Variables for an Indian Tribal Population', *South Asian Anthroplogy*, 5: 1–6.

Ray, N. (1972), 'Introductory Address', in Singh, K.S. (ed.) (1972), *Tribal Situation in India* (Simla: Indian Institute of Advanced Study).

Ray, R. (2000), 'Poverty, Household Size, and Child Welfare', *Economic and Political Weekly*, September 2.

Ray, Sharat Chandra (1912), *The Mundas and their Country* (Calcutta: The Kuntaline Press).

Raza, Moonis and Aijazuddin Ahmad (1990), *An Atlas of Tribal India* (New Delhi: Concept Publishing Company).

Registrar General (2001), Census of India, 2001, Series 1, India, Provisional Population Totals, Paper 1 of 2001.

———, India (1999), *Compendium of India's Fertility and Mortality Indicators: 1971–1997*, New Delhi.

——— (1998), Census of India 1991, *State Profile 1991, India*, Table 12.

———, India (1997), *District Level Estimates of Fertility and Child Mortality for 1991 and Their Interrelations With Other Variables*, Occasional Paper No. 1 of 1997, New Delhi.

Registrar General (1994a), Census of India 1991, Primary Census Abstract Part II-B(i), vol. I (New Delhi: Government of India).

————— (1994b), Census of India 1991, Primary Census Abstract Part II-B(i), vol. II (New Delhi: Government of India).

————— (1993), Census of India 1991, Series-1, Paper-1 of 1993, *Union Census Abstract for Scheduled Castes and Scheduled Tribes*.

————— (1992), Census of India 1991, Series-1, Paper-2 of 1992, *Final Population Totals: Brief Analysis of Primary Census Abstract*.

————— (1991), Census of India 1991, *State Profile*, 1991.

————— (1989a), *Fertility Differentials in India, 1984*, Vital Statistics Division, New Delhi.

————— (1989b), *Mortality Differentials in India, 1984*, Vital Statistics Division, New Delhi.

————— (1988), Census of India 1981, *Female Age at Marriage*, Occasional Paper No. of 1988.

————— (1982), *Levels Trends and Differentials in Fertility 1979*, Vital Statistics Division, New Delhi.

————— (1981), *India: Survey on Child and Infant Mortality 1979*, New Delhi

—————, Census of India 1981, *Fertility Tables* (separate vols for each state), New Delhi.

————— (1980), *Survey on Infant and Child Mortality, 1979: A Preliminary Report'*, New Delhi.

————— (1977), Census of India 1971, *Female Age at Marriage*, Paper 4 of 1977, New Delhi.

————— (1976a), Census of India 1971, Series-1, India, Part II-C (ii), *Social and Cultural Tables*, New Delhi.

————— (1976b), *Fertility Differentials in India: 1972*, New Delhi.

————— (1975), Census of India 1971, Paper 1 of 1975, *Scheduled Caste and Scheduled Tribes*, New Delhi.

————— (1966a), Census of India, vol. 1, India, Part V-A (I), Special Tables for Scheduled Castes, New Delhi.

————— (1966b), Census of India, vol. 1, India, Part V-A (II), Special Tables for Scheduled Tribes, New Delhi.

————— (1966c), Census of India, vol. 1, India, Part II-A (II), Union Primary Census Abstract, New Delhi.

Rele, J.R. (1987), 'Fertility Levels and Trends in India, 1951–81', *Population and Development Review*, 13(4).

————— (1967), *Fertility Analysis through Extension of Stable Population Concepts*, Population Monograph Series no. 2 (Berkley: University of California Press).

Reserve Bank of India (1984), *Report of the Committee on Agricultural Productivity in Eastern India*, Bombay.

Rizvi, S.H.M. (1987), *Mina: The Ruling Tribe of Rajasthan* (New Delhi:B.R. Publishing Corporation).

Rodge, V.R., V.N. Patnam, and J.R. Rodge (2001), 'Activity and Time Spending Patterns of Tribal Girls of Nanded', *Tribal Research Bulletin*, 24(1).

Rogaly, Ben, D. Coppard, A. Rafique, K. Rana, A. Sengupta, and J. Biswas (2002), 'Seasonal Migration and Welfare/Illfare in Eastern India: A Social Analysis, *Journal of Development Studies*, 38(5), 2002.

Rogaly, Ben, J. Biswas, D. Coppard, A. Rafique, K. Rana, and A. Sengupta (2001), 'Seasonal Migration, Social Change and Migrants' Rights: Lessons from West Bengal', *Economic and Political Weekly*, December 8.

Rogaly, Ben, Harriss-White, B., and Bose, S. (eds) (1999), *Sonar Bangla? Agricultural Growth and Agrarian Change in West Bengal and Bangladesh* (New Delhi: Sage Publications).

Rogaly, Ben (1999), 'Dangerous Liaisons? Seasonal Migration and Agrarian Change in WestBengal', in Rogaly *et al*. (1999).

───── (1998), 'Workers on the Move: Seasonal Migration and Changing Social Relations in Rural India', *Gender and Development*, 6(1).

───── (1996), 'Agricultural Growth and the Structure of "Casual" Labour Hiring in Rural West Bengal', *Journal of Peasant Studies*, 23(4).

Rose, P., and M. Tembon (1999), 'Girls and Schooling in Ethiopia', in Heward and S. Bunwaree (1999) (eds), *Gender, Education and Development* (London: Zed Books).

Rosenzweig, Mark, and T.P. Schultz (1982), 'Market Opportunuties, Genetic Endowments, and Intra-family Resource Distribution: Child Survival in Rural India', *American Economic Review*, 72: 803–15.

Roth, E. and A. Ray (1985), 'Demographic Patterns of Sedentary and Nomadic Juang of Orissa', *Human Biology*, 57: 319–25.

Roy Burman (1993), 'Tribal Population: Interface of Historical Ecology and Political Economy', in Miri (1993).

───── (1992), 'Transformation of Tribes and Analogous Social Formations', in Chaudhuri (1990), vol. 3.

───── (1987), 'Development and Tribal Women of India', *Mainstream*, 19&20, November 25.

───── (1983), 'Transformation of Tribes and Analogous Social Formations', *Economic and Political Weekly*, 18(27): 1172–74.

───── (1972), 'Tribal Demography: A Preliminary Appraisal', in: Singh (1972).

Roy, Sarat Chandra (1915), *The Oraons of Chotanagpur: Their History, Economic Life, and Social Organization* (Ranchi: The Brahmo Mission Press).

Säävälä, M. (1999), 'Understanding the Prevalence of Female Sterilization in Rural South India', *Studies in Family Planning*, 30(4).

Sachchidananda (1964), *Culture Change in Tribal Bihar: Munda and Orao* (Calcutta: Bookland Pvt. Ltd).

Saggar, M., and I. Pan (1994), 'SCS and STS in Eastern India: Inequality and Poverty Estimates', *Economic and Political Weekly*, 5 March.

Saha, Anamitra, and Swaminathan (1994), 'Agricultural Growth in West Bengal in 1980s: A Disaggregation by Districts and Crops', *Economic and Political Weekly*, March 26.

Saha, S.S. (1993), *Genetic Demography Anthropometry of Muria Tribe* (New Delhi: Mittal Publications).

Sain, Ruby (1994), 'Nutritional Status of Tribal Children in Birbhum District', *Economic and Political Weekly*, June 18: 1513.

Samuel, J. (ed.) (2002), *Struggles for Survival*, National Centre for Advocacy Studies, Pune.

Sanday, P.R. (1973), 'Toward a Theory of Status of Women', *American Anthropologist*, 75: 1682–1700.

Sarkar, J.M. (1989), 'Some Demographic Traits of Bhils and Garasia: A Comparative Study', in *Genetical Demography of Indian Population* (Calcutta: Anthropological Survey of India).

Sathar, Z.A., and James F. Phillips (eds) (2001), *Fertility Transition in South Asia* (Oxford: Oxford University Press).

Satia, J.K. and S. Jejeebhoy (1991), *The Demographic Challenge: A Study of Four Large Indian States* (Bombay: Oxford University Press).

Saxena, D.N. (1990), 'Family Building, Fertility and Family Welfare among Two Tribal Communities of Uttar Pradesh', in Bose *et al.* (1990).

Saxena, R.P. (1964), *Tribal Economy in Central India*, Firma K.L. Mukhapadhyyay, Calcutta.

Sen, A.K. (1998), 'Mortality as an Indicator of Economic Success or Failure', *Economic Journal*, 1–25.

Sen, Amartya (1999), *Development as Freedom* (Delhi: Oxford University Press).

————— (1994), 'Population: Delusion and Reality', *New York Review of Books*, September 22.

————— (1989), 'Women's Survival as a Development Problem', *Bulletin of the American Academy of Arts and Sciences*, November.

————— (1985), *Women, Technology and Development*', ILO Report.

————— and S. Sengupta (1983), 'Malnutrition of Children in West Bengal', *Economic and Political Weekly*, Annual Number (19–21).

Sen, D.K. (1956), 'Some Notes on the Fertility of Jaunsari Women', *The Eastern Anthropologist*, 10(1).

Sen, G. and C. Sen (1985), Women's Domestic Work and Economic Activity', *Economic and Political Weekly*, 20(17), April 27.

Sengupta, P. and J. Guha (2002), 'Enrolment, Dropout and Grade Completion of Girl Children in West Bengal', *Economic and Political Weekly*, 27 April.

Sengupta, S. and H. Gazdar (1999), 'Agricultural Growth and Recent Trends in Well-being in Rural West Bengal', in Rogaly *et al.* (1999).

————— (1997), 'Agrarian Politics and Rural Development in West Bengal', in Drèze and Sen (1997).

Shaban, A. (2002), 'Growth and Disparities of Incomes Across Indian States', *Man & Development*, September.

Shah, V.P., and T. Patel (1985), *Social Context of Tribal Education* (Delhi: Concept Publishing House).

Shaheen, Maneka Vijaya Pande, and Dr D.S. Mahurkar (1992), 'Nutritional Status of Children in Ashram School', *Tribal Research Bulletin*, 14(1).

Shariff, A. (1999), *India: Human Development Report* (New Delhi: Oxford University Press).

Sharma, A.N. (1994), 'Nature and Extent of Migration in Bihar', in Sinha, U.P. and R.K. Sinha (eds) (1994), *Population and Development in Bihar* (New Delhi: B.R. Publishing Corporation).

Sharma, K. (1978), 'Fertility and Mortality in Khonds: A Tribal Community of Orissa', *Man in India*, 58(1): 77–88.

Sharma, K.K.N., and A.S. Khan (1990), 'Fertility and Mortality Trends of the Khairwar Tribal Women of Madhya Pradesh', *Man in India*, 70(4): 447–53.

Sharma V. and A. Sharma (1993), 'The Status of Women, Fertility and Family Planning among Tribals of South Rajasthan', *Journal of Family Welfare*, 39(4): 20–25.

Shashi, S.S. (ed.) (1995), *Tribal Culture, Customs and Affinities: A Cross-Regional Anthology* (Delhi: Anmol Publications Pvt. Ltd).

Shaheen, Maneka, V. Pande, and D.S. Mahurkar (1992), 'Nutritional Status of Children in Asham School', *Tribal Research Bulletin*, 14(1).

Sheppardson, M., and C. Simmons (eds) (1988), *The Indian National Congress and the Political Economy of India 1885–1985* (Avebury: Aldershot).

Shiva, V. (1988), *Staying Alive: Women, Ecology and Survival in India* (New Delhi: Kali for Women).

Shukla, Sanjay, and N.S. Reddy (1997), 'Diet and Nutritional Status of Muria of Bastar (M.P.), *Vanyajati*, July.

Singh, A.K., M. Jayaswal, and A. Hans (1993), 'Understanding the Health of Tribals', *Social Change*, 23 (2&3).

————— (1987), 'The Myth of Healthy Tribal', *Social Change*, 17: 3–23.

Singh, G. (2001), 'Scheduled Tribes in India: Poverty and Social Opportunity', *Margin*, 34(1): 71–91.

Singh, G.S. (1997), 'Work Participation and Social Status of Women: A Case Study of Kullu Valley', *Man and Development*, December.

Singh, K.S. (1997), 'Tribe into Caste: A Colonial Paradigm (?)', in Nathan (1997).

————— (1989), *Our Tribal Heritage*, Ranchi: The National Tribal Festival 1989 held by the Regional Development Commissioner, Ranchi and Anthropological Survey of India.

————— (ed.) (1972), *Tribal Situation in India* (Shimla: Indian Institute of Advanced Study).

Singh, R. (1963), 'Reproductive Life of Birhor Woman', *Bulletin of the Tribal Research Institute*, 5(3).

Singh, S.N., M.K. Premi, P.S. Bhatia, and A. Bose (1989) (eds), *Population Transition in India* (Delhi: B.R. Publishing Corporation), 2 vols.

Sinha, R.R. and J.K. Sinha (1994a), 'Population Structure and Development Pattern of Tribals in Bihar', in Sinha and Sinha (eds), *Population and Development in Bihar* (New Delhi: B.R. Publishing House).

Sinha, S. (2003), *Health Status in the Major Tribes of Oraons and Mundas of Ranchi, Jharkhand*, presented at the National Seminar on Population and Development in Jharkhand', Ranchi, March 2–3, 2003, organized by IIPS.

———— (1957), 'Tribal Cultures of Peninsular India as a Dimension of Little Transition in the Study of Indian Civilization: A Preliminary Statement', *Man in India*, 37(2): 93–118.

Sinha, U.P. (1994), 'Demographic Situation of the Tribal Population in India', in Pathak *et al.* (1994)

———— (1993), 'The Demographic Situation of Tribal Population in India', in Miri (1993).

———— (1990), 'The Demographic Profile of Tribal Population in India', in Bose *et al.* (1990).

———— (1986), *Ethno-Demographic Study of Tribal Population in India* (mimeo), International Institute for Population Sciences, Bombay.

———— (1984), 'Sex Composition and Differential Mortality Among Tribals of India', *Indian Journal of Social Work*, XLIV (4):387–92.

———— (1979), 'Growth and Distribution of Tribal Population in India, 1961–71', in Srinivasan and Mukerji (1979).

———— and K.B.Gotpagar (1994), 'Mortality in Bihar', in Sinha and Sinha (1994).

———— and R.K. Sinha (eds) (1994), *Population and Development in Bihar* (New Delhi: B.R. Publishing Corporation).

———— and S.M. Thatte (1994), 'Tribal Population in Bihar: A Demographic Profile', in Sinha and Sinha (1994).

Sivakumar, M.N. (2001a), 'Selectivity in Rural-Urban Migration: Evidence from Tamil Nadu', *Man and Development,* March.

———— (2001b), 'Timing of Marriage and Spacing of First Birth: A Time Series Analysis Study', *Man in India*, 81(3/4).

S. Karia, S.A. (1997), 'Shades of Wildness: Tribe, Caste, and Gender in Western India', *The Journal of Asian Studies,* 56(3): 726–745.

Soonawala, Rustom P. (1993), 'Family Planning: The Indian Experience', in Senanayake, P. and R.L. Kleinman (eds) (1993), *Family Planning: Meeting Challenges: Promoting Choices* (New York: The Parthenon Publishing Group).

Sopher, D.E. (1980), *An Explanation of India* (London: Longman).

Sreedevi, K., and P. Rajyalakshmi (1998), 'Anthropometry, Diet and Morbidity of Tribal Pre-School Children in Kurnool', *Indian Journal of Social Work,* 59(2).

Srinivas, M.N. (1977), 'The Changing Position of Indian Women', *Man*, 12: 221–38.

———— (1966), *Social Change in Modern India* (Bombay: Allied Publishers).

Srinivasan, K. (1998), 'Population Policies and Programmes Since Independence', *Demography India*, 27(1).

_____ (1995), Lessons from Goa, Kerala and Tamil Nadu: The Three Successful Fertility Transition States in India', *Demography India*, 24(2): 163–94.

_____ (1995), *Regulating Reproduction in India's Population: Efforts, Results, and Recommendations* (New Delhi: Sage Publications).

Srinivasan, K., and S. Mukerji (eds) (1983), *Dynamics of Population and Family Welfare* (Bombay: Himalaya Publishing House).

_____ (eds) (1979), *Dynamics of Population and Family Welfare in India* (Bombay: Popular Prakashan).

_____ (eds) (1979), *Dynamics of Population and Family Welfare* (Bombay: Himalaya Publishing).

Srinivasan, P. (2002), 'Poverty and Agricultural Research', in Parikh, K. and R. Radhakrishna (eds), *India Development Report* (New Delhi: Oxford University Press).

Srivastava, G. (1997), 'Reasons for Discontinuance of Primary Education among Tribals of Assam', *Social Change*, 27(1/2).

Srivastava, R. (1998), 'Migration and the Labour Market in India', *Indian Journal of Labour Economics*, 41(4).

Ssennyonga, J.W. (1993), 'Pastoral Demography in the Context of Human Ecology: A Case Study of the Samburee of Kenya', in C.M. Cottam and S.V. Rao (eds) (1993), *Women, Aid and Development* (Delhi: Indicator Publishing House).

Subbarayan, V. (not dated) *Forgotten Sons of India* (place, publisher not given)

Sundaram, K. (2001), 'Employment and Poverty in 1990s: Further Results from NSS 55th Round Employment, Unemployment Survey, 1999–2000', *Economic and Political Weekly*, August 11.

Suryanarayana, M.H. (2001), 'Scheduled Castes, Their Disadvantages and Deprivation: A Rural All-India Profile', *Artha Vijnana*, XLIII (1/2).

_____ (2000), 'How Real is the Secular Decline in Rural Poverty?', *Economic and Political Weekly*, June 17.

Svedberg, P. (1996), 'Gender Biases in Sub-Saharan Africa: Reply and Further Evidence, *Journal of Development Studies*, 32(6): 933–43.

_____ (1990), 'Undernutrition in Sub-Saharan Africa: Is there a Gender Bias?', *Journal of Development Studies*, 26(3): 469–86.

Swaminathan and V.K. Ramachandran (1999), 'New Data in Calorie Intakes', *Frontline*, 16(5).

Szreter, Simon (1996), *Fertility, Class and Gender in Britain, 1860–1940* (Cambridge: Cambridge University Press).

Teerink, R. (1995), 'Migration and its Impact on Kandeshi Women in the Sugar Cane Harvest', in Schenk-Sandbergen, L. (ed) (1995), *Women and Seasonal Labour Migration* (New Delhi: Sage Publications).

Tendulkar, S., K. Sundaram, and L.R. Jain (1993), *Poverty in India, 1970–71 to 1988–89*, ILO ARTEP, New Delhi.

Thakur, D. and D.N. Thakur (eds) (1994), *Tribal Life in India*, Vol. b (New Delhi: Deep and Deep Publications).

Thamizoli, P. (1997), 'Gender Inequality, Tribal and Caste Women, Past and Present: A Case Study of the Nilgiries, Tamil Nadu', *Man in India*, 77(1).

Thangaraj, M. (1995), *Demographic and Occupational Characteristics of the Scheduled Castes and Scheduled Tribes in India*, Working Paper 134, Madras: Madras Institute of Development Studies.

Thatte, S.M. and U.P. Sinha (2003), 'Growth and Distribution of Tribal Population in Jharkhand, 1961–1991', paper presented at National Seminar on Population and Development in Jharkhand, organized by IIPS, held at Ranchi, March 2–3, 2003.

Thurston, E. (1901), *Castes and Tribes of Southern India*, Madras Govt. Press, vol. 1.

Tinker, I. (ed.) (1990), *Women and World Development* (New York: Oxford University Press).

Tripathi, R.S. (1992), 'Fertility Behaviour Among the Kols of Manipur Block, Uttar Pradesh', in P.D. Tiwari and R.S. Tripathy (eds) (1992), *Dimensions of Scheduled Tribes Development of India: Problems and Prospects* (New Delhi: Uppal Publishing House).

United Nations (1983), *Manuel X: Indirect Techniques for Demographic Estimation*, Dept. of International Economic and Social Affairs, Population Studies no. 81 New York.

———— (1967), *Manual IV: Methods of Estimating Basic Demographic Measures from Incomplete Data*, Dept. of Economic and Social Affairs, Population Studies no. 42, New York.

Unnithan-Kumar, M. (1997), *Identity, Gender and Poverty: New Perspectives on Caste and Tribe in Rajasthan* (Providence and Oxford: Berghahn Books).

———— (1991), 'Gender and "Tribal" Identity in Western India', *Economic and Political Weekly*, Review of Women Studies, April 27.

Verma, K.K. (1977), *Culture, Ecology and Population: An Anthropo-Demographic Study* (New Delhi: National Publishers).

Verma, N.M.P. (2000), 'Educational Deprivation of Women and Dalits in South Asia', *Indian Journal of Human Rights*, 4(1&2).

Vidyarthi, L.P. (1978), *Rise of Anthropology in India: A Social Science Orientation, Volume 1, Tribal Dimensions* (Delhi: Concept Publishing Company).

———— (ed.) (1968), *Applied Anthropology in India* (Allahabad: Kitab Mahal).

Vijaya Pande, and Rohini Devi (1991), 'Nutrient Intake of Selected Tribal Population in Kinwat Area', *Tribal Research Bulletin*, 12(2).

Visaria, P. (1996), 'Structure of Indian Workforce 1961–1994', *Indian Journal of Labour Economics*, 39(4).

Visaria, Pravin, M. (1968), 'The Sex Ratio of the Population of India' (mimeographed), Department of Economics, University of Bombay.

Volchok, B.Y. (1964), 'The Interaction of Caste and Tribal Communities in Central India', *Journal of Social Research*, 7(1/2).

Vlassoff, Carol (1991), 'Progress and Stagnation: Changes in Fertility and Women's Position in an Indian Village', *Population Studies*, 46: 195–212.

Vyas, N.N., R.S. Mann, and N.D. Chaudhary (eds) (1978), *Rajasthan Bhils*, Udaipur: Manikyalal Verma Tribal Research and Training Institute.

Walker, T.S., and J.G. Ryan (1988), *Against the Odds: Village and Semi-Arid Tropics* (mimeo), ICRISAT, Hyderabad.

Weiner, M. (1978), *Sons of Soil, Migration and Ethnic Conflict in India* (New Delhi: Oxford University Press).

West Bengal, Deptartment of Health and Family Welfare (1995), *Family Welfare Statistics: At a Glance*.

Westoff, C.F. (1992), 'Age at Marriage, Age at First Birth and Fertility in Africa', *World Bank Technical Paper*, No. 169, Washington D.C.

White, C.M.N. (1959), *A Preliminary Survey of Luvale Rural Economy*, The Rhodes-Livingstone Papers Series No. 29 (Manchester: Manchester University Press).

Wiercinski, M. (1996), 'Some Problems in the Demography of the Tribal Population in India', *Mankind Quarterly*, 36(3/4): 261–69.

Wilson, C., and P. Airey (1999), 'How can a Homeostatic Perspective enhance Demographic Transition thereby?', *Population Studies*, 53: 117–28.

Wirsing, R.L. (1985), 'The Health of Traditional Societies and Effects on Acculturation', Current Anthropology, 26(3): 303–22.

Woods, Robert, and Philips Rees (eds) (1986), *Population Structures and Models, Developments in Spatial Demography* (London: Allen & Unwin).

World Bank (1995), *World Development Report 1995* (Oxford University Press).

Xaxa, V. (2003), 'Tribes in India', in V. Das (ed.) (2003).

——— (2001), 'Protective Discrimination: Why Scheduled Tribes Lag Behind Scheduled Castes', *Economic and Political Weekly*, July 21.

Yorke, M. (1979), 'Kinship, Marriage and Ideology among the Raj Gonds: A Tribal System in the Context of South India', *Contribution to Indian Sociology*, 13(1).

Index